CROSSINGS

BEFORE YOU START TO READ THIS BOOK, take this moment to think about making a donation to punctum books, an independent non-profit press,

@ https://punctumbooks.com/support/

If you're reading the e-book, you can click on the image below to go directly to our donations site. Any amount, no matter the size, is appreciated and will help us to keep our ship of fools afloat. Contributions from dedicated readers will also help us to keep our commons open and to cultivate new work that can't find a welcoming port elsewhere. Our adventure is not possible without your support.

Vive la Open Access.

Fig. 1. Detail from Hieronymus Bosch, *Ship of Fools* (1490–1500)

First published in 2025 by punctum books, Earth, Milky Way.
https://punctumbooks.com

ISBN-13: 978-1-68571-280-8 (print)
ISBN-13: 978-1-68571-281-5 (ePDF)

DOI: 10.53288/0417.1.00

LCCN: 2025939388
Library of Congress Cataloging Data is available from the Library of Congress

Editing: SAJ and Eileen A. Fradenburg Joy
Book design: Hatim Eujayl
Cover design: Vincent W.J. van Gerven Oei
Cover image: "Bhaager Maa," Barisha Club Durga Puja, Kolkata, 2021. Artists: Rintu Das and Pallab Bhowmick, with sculptors Debayan Pramanik, Pratap Majumdar, and Sumit Biswas. Photo © Arindam Halder

p. punctumbooks

spontaneous acts of scholarly combustion

HIC SVNT MONSTRA

CROSSINGS

Migrant Knowledges, Migrant Forms

Edited by Natalya Din-Kariuki,
Subha Mukherji,
and Rowan Williams

p.

Contents

Acknowledgments

We thank our huge team of contributors for their patience and for their faith in the project as it made its stop-start way through the pandemic and through shifting landscapes of migration. We are thankful to our commissioning editors Vincent W.J. van Gerven Oei and Eileen A. Fradenburg Joy at punctum books for trusting us with the imaginative freedom we wanted to shape this volume, and for their advice and support. We are thankful to SAJ for their meticulous copyediting on behalf of the press. We would also like to register our enormous gratitude to Dunstan Roberts for coming on board as copyeditor and proceeding to become much more than that — guiding us with his eagle eyes and unerring critical instincts, and saving us from errors and imprecisions as we prepared our manuscript for submission. Warm thanks to Jen Pollard for stepping in at the last moment to help us with images. We acknowledge a Career Support Grant awarded by the University of Cambridge and a research grant from the University of Warwick which have helped us cover image costs and copyediting. The book is indirectly a product of an event, Migrant Knowledge, Early Modern and Beyond, co-organized by us and held in Cambridge in late 2019 under the auspices of a European Research Council Consolidator Grant project, Crossroads of Knowledge in Early Modern England, led by Subha Mukherji; we have a far-reaching debt to the ERC that goes beyond the dates of the project (FP7/2007–2013/ERC grant agreement no. 617849). There are many others who have indirectly helped this book take shape — too many to mention — through their imaginative engagement at various points of time. It has been a truly collective effort. Any oversights or imperfections that remain are our own.

N.D.K., S.M., and R.W.

I.

Introduction

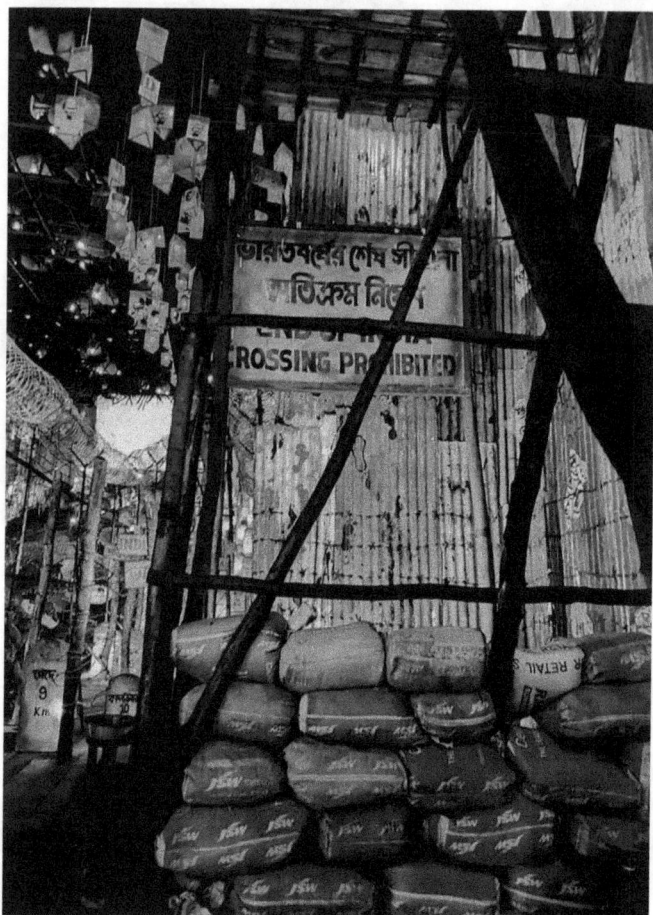

Fig. 1.1. Background to the migrant Durga idol in *Bhaager Maa* ("Mother, divided," or "Mother of Partition"), installation by Rintu Das and Pallab Bhowmick, Barisha Club, October 2021. Source: Rintu Das.

1

Crossings: Life and Art[1]

Subha Mukherji

A border between two nations, marked by barbed wire, photos of missing people, and a cautionary signpost proclaiming,
"End of India. Crossing Prohibited": who would have thought
this image (fig. 1.1) could be from the religious festival of Durga
Puja in Kolkata? Durga Puja — "the worship of Durga" — is one
of the biggest Hindu festivals of India, an annual event most
widely and exuberantly celebrated in and around Kolkata. The
civic space turns into a giant party, with pandals or pavilions
at every street corner, housing idol-clusters of increasingly aesthetic, and arguably secular, interest. The conventional setting
has been majestic, and arranged like a proscenium stage, with
the deities on a raised platform at a suitable remove from awe-
struck mortal spectators.

1   Yota Batsaki's intellectual companionship and input at various stages of my
    writing of this essay have gone beyond the call of her duty or my claim. In
    both gratitude and pleasure, I am happy to remain her debtor. I am thank-
    ful, too, to Daniel Dombey whose intellectual engagement during the
    fraught years over which the realities of migration and my thinking about
    it developed felt like a gift and a grace.

Fig. 1.2. Bhaager Maa ("Mother, divided," or "Mother of Partition"), migrant Durga. Source: Rintu Das.

Durga is traditionally represented as a triumphant mother Goddess vanquishing evil (in the form of a demon), riding a tiger, visiting the earth — her parental home — every autumn with her divine children in tow, each embodying a particular talent and power. But the image in figures 1.2 and 1.3 was part of the scenography of the Barisha Club pavilion in October 2021, which signaled a radical iconographic departure. Here, the el-

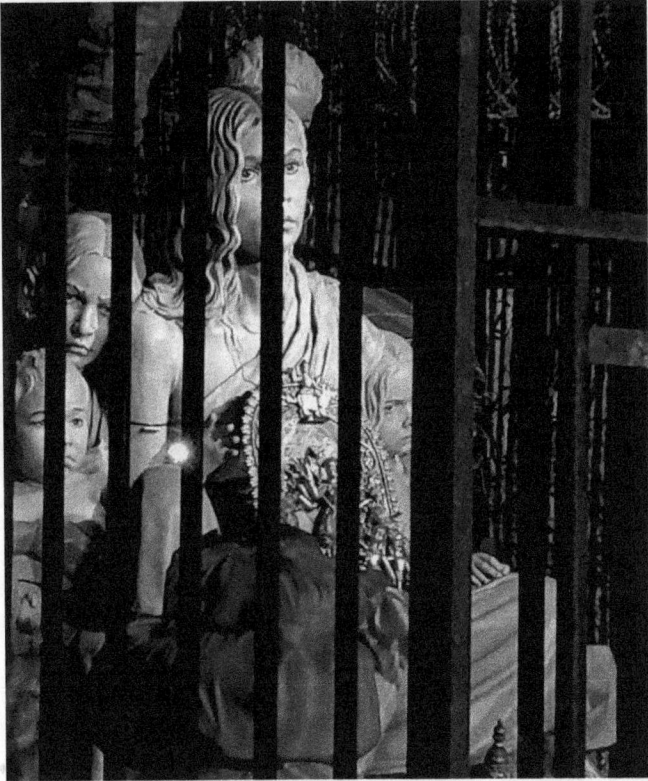

Fig. 1.3. Bhaager Maa ("Mother, divided," or "Mother of Partition"),
migrant Durga. Source: Rintu Das.

evated dais is a barbed cage in the limbo of a detention center at
the checkpoint between India and Bangladesh.[2]

This Durga (made by artist Rintu Das with sculptors Debayan Pramanik, Pratap Majumdar, and Sumit Biswas) is an
uprooted, disoriented refugee, sitting terrified with her four
children, clutching on to their "poor luggage," in a no-man's

---

2   The cover image of this book is of the same installation, from another
    angle.

land—a border now freshly charged with hatred, fear, and peril.[3] The Goddess has a disarmingly human face. It is a face caught in the headlights sinisterly focused on the "prohibited" crossing-point, but is also in the shadow—the near shadow of newly minted edicts, and the longer shadow of the Bengal partition.[4] Curiously, she holds a precious and symbolic possession on her lap: a little brass statue of the Dhakeshwari Durga, the adopted Durga of Dhaka who was smuggled out of Bangladesh during the Partition of Bengal and rehomed lovingly in Kumortuli (the potters' quarters) in Kolkata, on the verge of being dislocated again. In a proleptic telescoping of roles, Das's own clayey Durga, originating in Kumortuli, is at once a devotee of Dhakeshwari who clings to her idol as she sits in a stateless interspace, and a reincarnation—a Goddess who crossed over once and never thought she would have to cross back, or that she would be reduced to a portable relic.

This new aesthetic of the Puja comes out of the heart of specific contextual knowledges, speaks to them, and often carries uncertainties and intimations which were, at the point of creation, unquantifiable, undocumentable, and, for many, unspeakable. It also suggests the inaccessibility of certain knowledges in the state of migrancy: the unknowability of the other, and the obscurity of what awaits across the border. In the very act of putting the spotlight on the difficulties of territorial crossings, it crosses representational boundaries with simultaneous vulnerability and defiance. The formal watershed in this tradition came around 2020, in the wake of two new laws implemented by the Indian Government. December 2019 saw the passing of the Citizenship Amendment Act (CAA), and its twin proposal, the National Register of Citizens (NRC). Packaged as positive legis-

---

3   Anthony Munday et al., *Sir Thomas More* (Bloomsbury Arden Shakespeare, 2013), scene 6, l. 86.

4   For a more detailed discussion of the politics and aesthetics of this Puja installation, see Subha Mukherji, "Footfalls Echo in the Memory: Displaced Durgas and Migrant Forms," *Humanities Underground*, October 2021, https://humanitiesunderground.org/2022/02/22/footfalls-echo-in-the-memory-displaced-durgas-and-migrant-forms/.

lation, the CAA amended the Citizenship Act of 1955 to accept "illegal" migrants who came to India after India's independence, up until 2014, fleeing from religious persecution in their home states in neighboring Bangladesh, Pakistan, and Afghanistan, but conspicuously excluded Muslims — the largest majority in those countries — alongside other Indic-origin religious minorities like the Rohingyas. The NRC — which originally (as of 1951) applied only in Assam, a state largely shaped by migration — was suddenly reactivated and updated in 2019, designed in tandem with the CAA to identify "citizens" and exclude "illegal" immigrants from all of India on the basis of documents going back to 1971. While primarily targeted at Muslims who have lived in India for years, including those born in the country, this count also included many Hindus whose ancestry went back to Pakistan or Afghanistan or Bangladesh. Amidst the proliferation of obscurantist Acts and Bills, the precise targets of these new rules were not distinguishable to all, and still are not. Anyone who has had to leave one of these neighboring countries for India, and any member of a long-settled religious minority in India, was susceptible to the consequent miasma of despair. There are many families still frantically looking for documents they will never find. Memories of the bloody Partition of Bengal in 1947 into Hindu-majority West Bengal (part of India) and Muslim-majority East Pakistan (which was to become independent Bangladesh in 1971) have been stirred all over again by these exclusionary laws drafted to deny people dignity and identity.

The blue-grey screen visible on the far-left corner in the background of the refugee Durga installation plays a video showing a muddy patch quivering with footprints hastily left by stealthy feet, big and small, as they fall at night. The footage is uncannily similar to the BBC's YouTube video report of October 12, 2021, which shows Afghan refugees leaving foot-marks on the rough ground while frantically fleeing the Taliban across the Iran-Turkey border, as Turkey tightened controls. The muddy feet in Durga's back-screen — pattering to a soundtrack of howling guard dogs and panicked human cacophony — are counter-pointed with exquisite prints of the Goddess's feet in the long

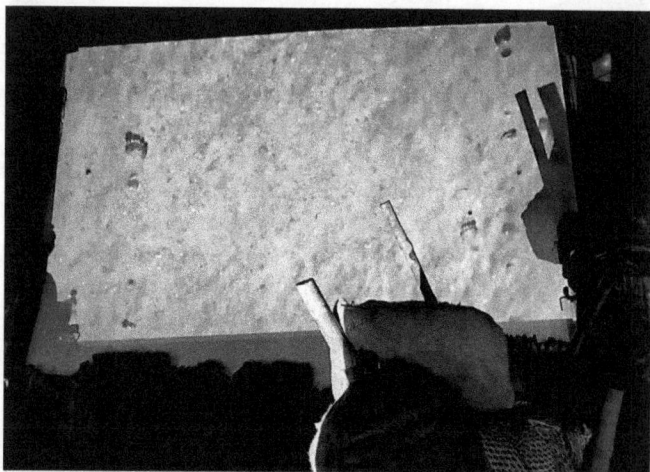

Fig. 1.4. Bhaager Maa ("Mother, divided" or "Mother of Partition"),
migrant Durga. Source: Rintu Das.

foreground, dyed crimson in the traditionally auspicious foot-
paint called *aalta,* leading up to what might have been the altar
(figs. 1.4 and 1.5).

Das had been playing with the idea for a long time, and had a
team of three clay artists working on it since long before the BBC
footage was aired. The fortuitous co-appearance of the idol and
the news clip in the same week signals a terrible convergence:
The barbed wire and walls rising around the world, the governments excluding people — whether citizens or aliens — and the
fascist demagogues whipping up majoritarian hatred, are distinct in particulars but identical in essence. Artistic representations of a whole new kind are registering this and speaking
across borders, inducing a dialogue as only tribes of artworks
can do. And as the anthropologist Alfred Gell intuited, artworks
do have a way of forming tribes.[5] Just such an ecology is sur-

5   Alfred Gell, *Art and Agency: An Anthropological Theory* (Oxford Univer-
    sity Press, 1998).

Fig. 1.5. Bhaager Maa ("Mother, divided," or "Mother of Partition"), migrant Durga. Source: Rintu Das.

facing spontaneously not only across Kolkata,[6] but as part of a wider emergent phenomenon of "migrant forms": forms that respond to the imaginative and ethical demands of the unknowable reality of mass displacement in a way that governments, institutions, and public discourse have calamitously failed to do.

As the crisis of statelessness has revealed itself to be global, continuous, and continually evolving, such moves as the CAA have exposed the fantasy that citizenship is a guarantee of refuge or a repository of rights.[7] The legacy of this postwar Eurocentric

---

6   To mention just one example, witness Bhabatosh Sutar and Pradip Das's work *Chol Chitra* at Naktala Udayan Sangha's *Puja* in 2021, which framed the pandal with an ominously empty train stuck on a border with bags and baggage spilling out, and signposts marking the distance to various cities-turned-checkpoints in Bangladesh. The work alludes to both Khushwant Singh's novel *Train to Pakistan* (1956) and Atin Bandyopadhyay's tetralogy *Nilkontho Pakhir Khonje* (1960) to relate the plight of newly displaced people to the Partition of India as well as the Bengal Partition. See figs. 11.3 and 11.4 in Supriya Chaudhuri's essay in this volume for telling images.

7   See Gerald Daniel Cohen, *In War's Wake: Europe's Displaced Persons in the Postwar Order* (Oxford University Press, 2011), esp. chap. 4, "Displaced

humanism still haunts discourses of displacement.[8] Decentering
it brings a clarity now urgent. In a world as radically vulnerable
to deracination as ours, citizenship itself is a precarious and ma-
nipulable thing—both for refugees and for those who thought
they belonged but are lost in the maze of newly forged bureaucratic categories. Like citizenship, humanitarianism has also
ceased to be unambiguously a part, and a mark, of a benign history. As Stephen Hopgood predicted in 2013, the moral project
of human rights was always already about to face its "endtime"
unless the West loosened its ownership of it and forged solidarity with local activisms across the world.[9] Creative responses are
making us think again, and think hard, about the meaning of
belonging and its complexities. The role of the arts to step in
and step up to the tasks of creating imaginative communities,
recalibrating our understanding of human rights, and forging
possible forms of life that law and politics are failing to deliver,
has never been more critical. But their work is transnational
and plural, and we must find interpretive structures for grasping their "understood relations."[10]

Imaginative engagements do not only bring into view the in-
terconnection of the local with the global, but cross-temporal
continuities too. From the women who flee from their Egyptian suitors and seek asylum in the Peloponnese in Aeschylus's
The Suppliants, to those who explore the loss of home amidst
war crimes in Euripides's *The Trojan Women,* Greek tragedy is
eloquently aware of the affective precarities of refuge.[11] William

Persons in the 'Human Rights' Revolution," 79–99.

8   On writing about exile and "modernist cosmopolitanism," see Lyndsey
    Stonebridge's introduction to her illuminating and impassioned book,
    Placeless People: Writing, Rights, and Refugees (Oxford University Press,
    2018), 8–9.

9   Stephen Hopgood, *The Endtimes of Human Rights* (Cornell University
    Press, 2013).

10 William Shakespeare, *Macbeth,* ed. A.R. Braunmuller (Cambridge Univer-
    sity Press, 2017), 3.4.124.

11 On how Greek tragedy offers "preshocks of the suffering of migrants from
    Afghanistan, Syria, East Africa, and other places in trouble," but also for
    a sensitive reading of contemporary poetry and lyric exploring migrant

Shakespeare's Othello, honored and needed as a serving general, thought he belonged to the multicultural fabric of early modern Venice, until crossing the race bar on the sexual axis plunges him into the disorienting discovery that he has always been a vagrant in Venice: "an extravagant and wheeling stranger / Of here and everywhere."[12] Even in Shakespeare's less deceptively diverse England, wanderers from outside (the etymological meaning of "extravagant") were perceived to be threats. A draft proclamation from 1601 cited "these hard times of dearth" amongst its reasons for urging the deportation of "Negroes and Blackamoors."[13] This was really the work of Caspar van Senden, a merchant from Lübeck, and Thomas Sherley, a minor courtier, seeking to forcibly transport African prisoners of war from England to Spain and Portugal in a money-making plan which came to nothing, but nonetheless suggests a certain xenophobic mindset they were playing to. After all, a 1596 letter written on Queen Elizabeth's behalf to the Lord Mayor had complained in a similar vein of the importation of "to manie" "Blackmoores" who were bleeding resources away from her "natural subjects."[14] The surge of dislocation, forced relocation, and economic migration are at a statistically unprecedented high in our times. But it is not an anomaly — just the end wanting to forget its beginning. It is the particulars, and the scale (which Edward Said identified as the differentia of the late twentieth century as an "age of the refugee"), that are distinct to specific historical junctures and discrete calamities.[15] Migration has challenged humans, and hu-

---

tragedy, see John Kerrigan, "Lampedusa: Migrant Tragedy," *Cambridge Journal of Postcolonial Literary Inquiry* 8, no. 2 (2021): 138.

12 William Shakespeare, *Othello,* ed. Norman Sanders (Cambridge University Press, 2018), 1.1.136–37.

13 "Licensing Casper van Senden to Deport Negroes [draft]," in *Tudor Royal Proclamations,* vol. 3: *The Later Tudors, 1588–1603,* ed. Paul L. Hughes and James F. Larkin (Yale University Press, 1969), 221–22.

14 Queen Elizabeth to the Lord Mayor et al., July 11, 1596, referred to in John Roche Dasent, ed., *Acts of the Privy Council of England: New Series, 1542–1631,* vol. 26: *1596–1597* (Mackie, 1902), 16–17.

15 Edward Said, "Reflections on Exile," in *Reflections on Exile and Other Literary and Cultural Essays* (Granta, 2012), 174. Said wrote this essay in the

manitarianism, for a very long time. The phrase "poor luggage," which the Barisha Club installation immediately brought to my mind, is from the extraordinary speech with which Sir Thomas More addresses — and disarms — a xenophobic London mob of 1517, rioting against European immigrants, in *The Boke of Sir Thomas More*, a collaborative play from the turn of the sixteenth century (c. 1592–1601), in a scene almost certainly written by Shakespeare:

> Grant them removed, and grant that this your noise
> Hath chid down all the majesty of England.
> Imagine that you see the wretched strangers,
> Their babies at their backs, with their poor luggage,
> Plodding to th' ports and coasts for transportation,
> And that you sit as kings in your desires,
> Authority quite silenced by your brawl,
> And you in ruff of your opinions clothed:
> What had you got? I'll tell you:
> [...]
> You'll put down strangers,
> Kill them, cut their throats, possess their houses
> And lead the majesty of law in lyam
> To slip him like a hound. Alas, Alas! Say now the King,
> [...]
> Should so much come too short of your great trespass
> As but to banish you: whither would you go?
> What country, by the nature of your error,
> Should give you harbour? Go you to France or Flanders,
> To any German province, Spain or Portugal,
> Nay, anywhere that not adheres to England:
> Why, you must needs be strangers. Would you be pleased
> To find a nation of such barbarous temper
> That, breaking out in hideous violence,
> Would not afford you an abode on earth,

---

wake of the 1983 massacre of (mostly) Palestinian refugees in Sabra and Shatila in Beirut.

Whet their detested knives against your throats,
Spurn you like dogs, and like as if that God
Owed not nor made not you, nor that the elements
Were not all appropriate to your comforts
But chartered unto them? What would you think
To be thus used? This is the strangers' case,
And this your mountainish inhumanity.[16]

The past is gut-wrenchingly present. More's haunting portrayal of "wretched strangers" is more vivid than ever in our historical moment. The figure of the stranger arriving at shores unknown with their frayed luggage and terrified children is increasingly familiar, and one that crosses over from life to art — or forms of representation which have taken on the function of art in a more visible and urgent way than before. In a new age of censorship under ethno-nationalist governments, photojournalism has emerged as one of these forms — unstoppably mobile itself, and wordlessly getting around the censorship that the verbal arts are immediately vulnerable to.[17] Along with other crises, it has crystallized lived moments of forced passage into indelible depiction. In India, a context close to me, a draconian lockdown was imposed at four hours' notice on March 24, 2020, straight after an orgy of super-spreader election rallies by Prime Minister Narendra Modi and Home Minister Amit Shah, and the disastrous launch of the Hindu pilgrimage-festival of Kumbh Mela which the government not only refused to cancel but ad-

---

16   Munday et al., *Sir Thomas More*, 6.83–156. This speech appears in the addition by Hand D, which has been credibly ascribed to Shakespeare. See Alfred W. Pollard et al., *Shakespeare's Hand in the Play of Sir Thomas More*, ed. W.W. Greg (Cambridge University Press, 1923).

17   The late Danish Siddiqui, chronicler of iniquity and disaster, put out photos of mass cremations in Delhi in 2021 that silently exposed the government's false statistics about COVID-19 deaths. See, for example, Danish Siddiqui, "Mass Cremations Begin as India's Capital Faces Deluge of COVID-19 Deaths," *Reuters*, April 22, 2021, https://www.reuters.com/news/picture/mass-cremations-begin-as-indias-capital-idUSKBN2CA049.

Fig. 1.6. Migrant laborers queuing at the border between Gujarat and Madhya Pradesh to return home. Photo by Indian Express Archive / Bhupendra Rana.

vertised on March 21 as being "safe" to attend.[18] Overnight, this lockdown turned millions of laborers into uprooted refugees, trudging miles with their "poor luggage" and their babies to cross borders between states to get home to their villages, some dropping dead from heat or exhaustion or hunger.

Images such as Bhupendra Rana's (fig. 1.6), broadcast country-wide in the media, crossed the understood limits of representation to burn into the nation's collective psyche and change our visual imaginary forever. Indeed, Durga herself had migrated as the world locked, unlocked, disinfected, and reinfected itself, and as the double plague of populist authoritarianism and its criminal negligence of COVID-19 ravaged India. For Das and his team's idol of 2021 was a sequel to his Durga as a migrant-mother the previous autumn (2020), in collaboration with ceramicist Pallab Bhowmick, which had distilled the despair of

---

18 Hannah Ellis-Petersen, Aakash Hassan, and Manoj Chaurasia, "Kumbh Mela: How a Superspreader Festival Seeded Covid Across India," *The Guardian,* May 29, 2021, https://www.theguardian.com/world/2021/may/30/kumbh-mela-how-a-superspreader-festival-seeded-covid-across-india.

Fig. 1.7. Mural of migrant laborers, Behala Art Festival, Kolkata, by
Sanatan Dinda. Photo by Panchali Banerjee.

a whole new class of internally displaced people created by the
government-imposed three-week curfew: "[T]hose images that
yet / Fresh images beget."[19] The Behala Art Fest, which started
in Kolkata in 2020, featured spontaneous murals on the theme
in 2021, around the time the migrant Durgas appeared with
the same makeshift luggages and bewildered babies (fig. 1.7). A
repository of images began to form, which captured this new,
avoidable precarity produced by the combined forces of nationalist myth and pandemic hypocrisy.

The 2020 reimagining of Durga as Annapurna (the Goddess of grains or bounty), herself a displaced mother but one
who gives out "traan" (sacks of aid), had stunned and shocked
viewers, defying any culturally endorsed response that this art
form might normally invite, not to speak of conventional aesthetic criteria (fig. 1.8). Some alleged that it was a rehash of *Dar-*

---

19 From Yeats's poem "Byzantium." Cf. W.B. Yeats, *Selected Poetry* (Penguin,
    1991), 174.

Fig. 1.8. "Maarir deshe, traaner beshe / Annapurna bhyalay bheshe" ("In the land of plague, in the form of aid / Comes Annapurna adrift on a raft"): Displaced Durga by Rintu Das with Debayan Pramanik, Pratap Majumdar, and Sumit Biswas, October 2020. Photo by Subha Mukherji.

pamoyee, one of Bikash Bhattacharya's famous *Durga* series of oil paintings (1989), where a coarsely clad laborer with a child in her arms, standing in a muddy field against a rivulet, turns around to look out of the painting at the viewer with piercing eyes, with a third eye on her forehead uncovering the divine in ordinary womanhood. But to charge the work with derivativeness is to miss the point about adaptation and intertextuality. It is also to ignore the fact that Bhattacharya's paintings — notwithstanding their democratizing of exalted figures — reside in elite galleries and sell at museum prices, while Barisha Club's Durga inhabited the different world of popular, proletarian art in easily accessible public places, claimed a new symbolism and forged a distinct semiotic from the margins. Das and Bhowmick are not the natural inheritors of artists such as Bhattacharya. Others — including myself — found the assemblage too busy, and the genres too uneasily mixed. But the ongoing negotiation between the festive, sensuous plenitude of the show and the desolate destitution inscribed in its heart conveyed a sense of *seeking* form. What overwhelmed me at first proved moving as a sense of process became palpable: the rawness of a mimetic mode emerging out of the heart of an experience from which it had not gained enough distance to settle into aesthetic selection, assured shape, or defined affect. Others yet have questioned this new aesthetics of idol-making, which flies in the face of a long iconography that has been "sacred," metamorphic, and increasingly polished. Is this art at all? David Freedberg, writing about the power of images in 1989, was struck by how well we have "to turn the troubling image into something we can safely call art."[20] In our age of displacement, artistic agency is manifesting itself in the reverse process, in crossing the fence that keeps "art" safe.

An unlikely partner of the migrant Durga is "Little Amal," the giant puppet of a Syrian girl aged nine who fled home because of war and walked through Europe, crossing many borders, looking for her mother, and a home (fig. 1.9). She arrived in London in October 2021. The Good Chance Theatre (featured in our book) arranged her big walk.

Instead of moving into a gallery, Amal came to the South Bank, where the grown-ups saw her sad face and sang to welcome her. But when the children reached out and touched her — as they can't touch a statue in a museum — she turned her face, her eyes grew bright, and she seemed to smile, as artworks in museums don't. The children were full of wonder at a figure so like them and yet so other. She has an amazing story to

---

20 David Freedberg, *The Power of Images: Studies in the History and Theory of Response* (University of Chicago Press, 1989), 425.

Fig. 1.9. Little Amal on the Southbank, London, 2021. Photo by Faraj Alnasser.

tell, with no ending yet. Everywhere she goes, her story changes and grows — like her journey. It started in Arabic but now it is braided like her hair: in many tongues and many colors, in words and songs and drums, in the rustle of the leaves and the whistle of the winds. In so many things too: straw, and wire, and woodchips, and paper, and cables. Her parts fray when the weather is rough. Amal travels light, for she has no things. But if you picked up her story, how much would it weigh? London made her a little home. She went on to Lviv afterwards, and then New York.

Amal's crossings — from Aleppo through Gaziantep to New York — were risky but full of hope, and her arrivals, while none of them permanent, have ended up joyful, as life has met art under the open skies. But what of the desperate passages across the wine-dark sea? Among the most powerful images of our time are not only walls and luggage, but boats, ships, and beaches. These have a long imaginative history: associations of childhood, play, holidays, maritime adventures, and odysseys. T.S. Eliot's coastal lines in "Marina," going back to Shakespeare's *Pericles,* haunt us with their moving distillation of the wonder and grace of restoration, whether at home or abroad, on sea or land, or in the heart:

> What seas what shores what grey rocks and what islands
> What water lapping the bow
> And scent of pine and the woodthrush singing through the fog
> What images return.[21]

In Shakespeare's last plays, the sea does not just take away but gives back — like the cycles of nature, it is tragicomic in its curative movements. That very sea, and lines such as Eliot's, have acquired entirely different associations in recent years, as water has overwhelmed fragile bows of inflatable dinghies, and the imagined scent of hospitable foreign pines has been usurped by the dark salt of an indifferent ocean — with a little help, of course, from unscrupulous human agents capitalizing on the deepening migration crisis, as well as other, more insidious, and ostensibly benevolent agents. The genre of the marine plot has turned. The figure of the lost child on a human shore has transited from being an image of hope and faith, to one of incurable pain, unfathomable loss, and irredeemable separation. In 2015, Nilüfer Demir's searing photo of two-year-old Alan Kurdi, washed ashore in Bodrum where the plastic boat from Damascus in which his family was fleeing war capsized, etched itself on the conscience of Europe. And yet, the same year, EU nations continued to oppose search-and-rescue operations to reduce the EU's "pull-factor" — ostensibly in a drive to check

---

21 T.S. Eliot, *Collected Poems, 1909–1962* (Faber and Faber, 1974), 115.

Fig. 1.10. Exhausted Rohingya refugee touches the shore in Bangladesh after the long crossing of the Bay of Bengal from Myanmar. Photo by Reuters / Danish Siddiqui.

trafficking but problematically entangled with a dehumanizing rhetoric, such as David Cameron's description of immigrants as "swarms" (continued most recently by Suella Braverman as she warned of "an invasion on the southern coasts").[22] Refugees in boat after rescue boat have been "snubbed at sea," to borrow the cosmopolitan refugee-poet W.H. Auden's words, as they waited off the shore of Italy in worsening conditions while the far-right interior minister Matteo Salvini refused to allow them to embark — a tradition now kept in health by Georgia Meloni.[23]

---

22 Braverman infamously used this phrase in her Commons statement on October, 31, 2022. See, among many other online reports and recordings, *The Independent*, "Suella Braverman Calls 'Broken' Immigration System an 'Invasion on South Coast," *YouTube*, October 31, 2022, https://www.youtube.com/watch?v=hG-E8GwWjYc.

23 W.H. Auden, *The Age of Anxiety: A Baroque Eclogue* (Faber and Faber, 1949), 115. Auden was haunted by the plight of refugees, not least those unlike him, with less choice and fewer rights in their placelessness. See his extraordinary, despair-filled poem, "Refugee Blues," about Jewish refugees

As thirty-two desperate asylum seekers including a pregnant woman and three children drowned while crossing over from the French coast to Britain for refuge in November 2021, the then Home Secretary of the UK, Priti Patel, advocated a policy of "push-back": pushing small boats back into the sea, exposing them actively to danger, rather than offering desperate people safe routes as an alternative to human smuggling. Patel's response was only a sequel to the anxious debate in August 2020 over rendering the English Channel "unviable" for crossing, with the UK's then minister for immigration declaring his resolve to "make" it unsafe. The logic of this comeback focused the moral vacuity of the discourse of risk. Meanwhile, look at how artists have responded to such crossings. Danish Siddiqui's shot of an exhausted Rohingya refugee reaching and touching the shore of Bangladesh after crossing the Myanmar–Bangladesh border by boat (2017) distills the affective realities underlying the risk taken by those who have no choice (fig. 1.10). It captures the desolation, disbelief and hope of innumerable crossings of this age and the desperate longing for solidity across liquid graves. As Said wrote, "The pathos of exile is in the lack of contact with the solidity and the satisfaction of earth."[24]

As people have been trying to cross borders for some sort of solidity, and governments and institutions have been anxiously resisting, repelling, or negotiating these attempts, creative engagements — whether through images or words, music or movement, dancing or cooking — are traversing in the opposite direction, in a chiasmic relation to the crossings of life. Even as Israel orders foreign visitors to the West Bank to declare to the defense ministry if they fall in love with a Palestinian (while dual nationals, volunteers, and academics struggle to find a way to continue with their lives), love and food and graffiti on the separation wall continue to spill over and find knowing forms. Yotam Ottolenghi and Sami Tamimi's book *Jerusalem* (2012),

---

from Nazi Germany in the 1930s: W.H. Auden, *Selected Poems*, ed. Edward Mendelson (Faber and Faber, 1979), 83–84.

24 Said, "Exile," 179.

charting a love story across prohibited political and sexual boundaries through the art of food, was a vanguard that now demands sequels. In Pingla, a little village in Bengal inhabited entirely by Muslims, everyone shares the same surname: *chitra-kar,* meaning "image-maker"; their artisanal identity trumps their religious one. They have, for generations, had only one occupation: making scroll paintings on mythical, historical, and, increasingly, contemporary subjects. One of their most abiding themes is Hindu mythology. This crossover has happened for a long time with an ease and a pleasure that come out of the cultural braid that is India. But it has become a political act of defiance since the country took a turn towards a *Hindutva* that separates out the strands and reduces the richness of the immemorial mix.[25] The irrepressible continuity of the artistic practice of Pingla is a minor miracle — perhaps slipping under the radar because of its "marginal" location — against the backdrop of the ideological project of communalizing art. The Vishva Hindu Parishad (VHP)'s calculated attack on the famous painter M.F. Husain's lyrical, stylized drawing of *Saraswati* (1976), the Goddess of learning and the arts, some twenty years later, to denounce a Muslim artist's depiction of a Hindu Goddess naked — as if the Hindu pantheon is a stranger to nudity — at a delicate political moment, was a dispiriting case in point. It resulted in a spate of ultra-right Hindu-nationalist vandalism across Indian states, including the burning of sixteen of Husain's works in an Ahmedabad gallery. Art's crossings do not always succeed, their risk can misfire, and they can be vulnerable to retrospective distortion. But they do interrogate the responsibilities of response, and have the power to change the public discourse about migration. Migrant forms effect a generic turn and a reversal of agencies between life and art, between experience and expression, between physical action and events in the

---

25 *Hindutva,* literally "Hindu-ness," is a term to denote a strident Hinduism as cultural identity, originating in an ideology (usually traced back to V.D. Savarkar) formulated to connect Indian nationalism and culture with the religion of Hinduism.

mind and the cultural psyche. They cross various invisible and prohibited borders — formal, political, and social. They do not cross to cross back. This book takes its place in this emergent ecology, both speaking to it and participating in it.

Our Place in the Field

As a work of critical mediation, this volume enters the field of migration studies, which has been developing rapidly in recent times in response to the world we inhabit and the increasing precarity of habitation within it. Emma Cox, Sam Durrant, David Farrier, Lyndsey Stonebridge, and Agnes Woolley's compendial and visionary *Refugee Imaginaries* radically re-maps refugee experience, placing it at the core rather than the margins of modernity.[26] With this volume, we share an interdisciplinary approach, an engagement with "narrative as a knowledge base,"[27] and a commitment to foregrounding the work the humanities can do in imagining and rehumanizing forced migration. With Lyndsey Stonebridge's committed, passionate, and moving *Writing and Righting* (2021), it hopes to take on, in a small way, the challenge of registering and understanding inequity and trying to effect change.[28] Her earlier book, *Placeless People* (2018), has been inspirational in blending law, moral philosophy, politics, and literature in its exploration of the writing of displacement after the Second World War. But while she traces a line from European Jewish emigration to Palestinian refugee experience, our book widens the remit to find place for many other refugee groups and experiences, as well as migrations that are cognate in some ways but distinct in others. Clair Wills's exploration of what V.S. Naipaul calls "the human story" of strangeness in postwar Britain, *Lovers and Strangers* (2017), has been a model for how to combine a revelatory range of sources (including "new urban

26 Emma Cox et al., eds., *Refugee Imaginaries: Research Across the Humanities* (Edinburgh University Press, 2020).

27 Ibid., 4.

28 Lyndsey Stonebridge, *Writing and Righting: Literature in the Age of Human Rights* (Oxford University Press, 2021).

art forms") as historical evidence, and how to unpack the entangled histories of white and non-white immigration.[29] *Travelling While Black* (2020), a powerful collection of essays written by Nanjala Nyabola as an advocate for refugees as well as a person on the move, probes the tensions between mobility and belonging in eye-opening ways; there are synergies with our book but our foci are specific.[30] Sam Durrant and Catherine Lord's *Essays in Migratory Aesthetics* (2007) has shown the way by addressing the impact of human movement on aesthetic practice: a preoccupation that we take forward and develop at a different stage in the history of cultural aesthetics.[31] Josephine McDonagh's capacious exploration of the shaping of nineteenth-century British fiction by mass emigration in her *Literature in a Time of Migration* (2021), and her intuition of an analogy between the crossing of print genres and the dynamics of borders, are methodologically contiguous to our interest in the entwinement of migration, knowledge, and form, though our range and remit — both formal and temporal — are distinct.[32] The vanguard volume edited by Elena Fiddian-Qasmiyeh, Gil Loescher, Katy Long, and Nando Sigona, *The Oxford Handbook of Refugee and Forced Migration Studies* (2014), is nothing short of foundational, being arguably the first comprehensive survey of the still-emergent field of refugee studies. The subsequent expansion of the field meets those pioneering editors' invitation and challenge to new researchers to build "a sense of common purpose."[33] Thanks to

29 Clair Wills, *Lovers and Strangers: An Immigrant History of Post-War Britain* (Allen Lane, 2017), xxii. "Human story" is a phrase from V.S. Naipaul, *The Enigma of Arrival: A Novel* (Penguin, 1987), 109.

30 Nanjala Nyabola, *Travelling While Black: Essays Inspired by a Life on the Move* (Hurst & Co., 2020).

31 Sam Durrant and Catherine M. Lord, eds., *Essays in Migratory Aesthetics: Cultural Practices between Migration and Art-Making* (Rodopi, 2007).

32 Josephine McDonagh, *Literature in a Time of Migration: British Fiction and the Movement of People, 1815–1876* (Oxford University Press, 2021). See also Josephine McDonagh and Jonathan Sachs, "Introduction: Literature and Migration," *Modern Philology* 118, no. 2 (2020): 204–12.

33 Elena Fiddian-Qasmiyeh et al., "Introduction: Refugee and Forced Migration Studies in Transition," in *The Oxford Handbook of Refugee and Forced*

their correction of the bias in the field towards current practices and policy development at the cost of history and lived experience, we no longer need to make a case for either a historical enquiry or a study that sets up "from below."[34]

While we are privileged to have the ground to build on, and a common place to speak from, our intervention is particular, using knowledge and form as its entry points. Questions of law, institutions, human rights, refugee protection, and policy are practical realities of forced migration that inevitably underpin many of the pieces in this book. But its dwelling is the interspace between encounter and ecology, where new conditions of knowing and unknowing come into play and new modes of expression are born; where the voices of migrants touch and change the voices of those who meet them; where a ruthlessly singular condition of being demands and exacts radical representation.

We attempt and enact more than we theorize. As we forge our own discursive modes, we consider the many meanings and operations of both migrancy and knowledge, including their imaginative remit, and explore pain and privation as well as joy and liberation. This confronts us with the knotty relation between ethics and aesthetics that such an approach entails as well as illuminates: We embrace the dilemmas that come with the territory to deepen our understanding of the stakes, even if we do not always find the perfect solution or register or mean. Our book is unusual in the methods it deploys in considering the past to understand the present and imagine a future. We make a start, albeit in an indicative and preliminary way, with bringing human and non-human migration into dialogue through considerations of elusive knowledge and singular forms. But all of this we do with a wide readership in mind — not just scholars and academics, but anyone interested in the subject, including those whose lives it is often about, some of whom feature in the

Migration Studies, ed. Elena Fiddian-Qasmiyeh et al. (Oxford University Press, 2014), 17.

34 Jérôme Elie, "Histories of Refugee and Forced Migration Studies," in *The Oxford Handbook of Refugee and Forced Migration Studies,* ed. Fiddian-Qasmiyeh et al., 30–31.

book. To this end, we have aimed to keep it readable and light on citation, while nevertheless providing sufficient mooring for readers to orient themselves.

Migrant Knowledge, Migrant Forms: The Collection

People, things, ideas, and languages have crossed borders since the earliest of times. Such passages have entailed epistemic shifts and encounters, transactions, and transformations. The knowledge that migrants carry with them is one manifestation of "migrant knowledge" — gained in the act of crossing. But it permeates receiving cultures too. Encounters with the strange disrupt our normal experiences of knowledge — because the other is unknowable, un-ownable, and disorienting. Such meetings demand and produce knowledges we are not accustomed to, about the self as well as the other. Then there is the inbuilt migrancy of knowledge which forms alchemies with particular experiences of mobility. But there is also the recalibration of "knowing" itself: when factual knowledge and its rationalizations become the preserve of a regime, an attunement or a quality of attention emerges as an alternative episteme. This book taps into these interconnected operations of mobile knowledge, thinking about migration and what it does with, and to, knowledge. Epistemic experiences that elude existing paradigms often come into play — such as knowingness, disknowledge, or the "migrant unknowledge" explored by Jonathan Gil Harris here — produced by "seeming familiarity" in unfamiliar terrain and casting light on the desires and fantasies at the heart of human knowledge projects. In its plural dimensions and functions, migrant knowledge is characterized by the connections it is at once formed by and mobilizes across disciplines, experiences, and practices, as Olga Demetriou, Efi Savvides, and Akid Hassan's collaborative essay demonstrates: the "common space of authorship" it examines is almost metonymic of the assemblage the book as a whole both embodies and probes.

But our volume offers more than critique: it is a creative intervention too. The deeper we explored migrant knowledge, the clearer it became that it has an intimate relation to form; seeking a commensurate expressive medium, it focuses a process and perhaps a habitus that are particular to the condition of migrancy. The book mines this interrelation, revealing and enacting this search, and at times finding or forging forms that are "migrant" in one of several senses. Certain art forms — say, stories or music — have an inherent migrancy; however stringently the borders are policed, they slip through. These speak naturally to the variously composite realities of migration in our lives. Others are generated by the condition of migration itself. Some of these have recognizable artistic contours (a sculpture responding to it, for example, or paintings from the frontline) — from Lili Andreiux's depictions of the Gurs transit camp in 1940 to the migrant Durgas of Kolkata. Others — from Christoph Büchel's *Barca Nostra* to mobile photos by migrants of relics of their abandoned lives — can be shaped into artifacts to mobilize their potential for cultural and political work. "Migrant" forms encompass both, along with the multiple agencies possible. It is this larger category that our volume posits, develops, and puts to work — arising out of the reality of contemporary migration and in response to the representational crisis it has created, the extreme discursive inadequacy it has presented us with. Simultaneously, the book tries to understand the dynamic between these forms and the knowledges they negotiate. The essays and artworks here — some of them discursive interventions that acquire aesthetic shape — are part of that larger community forming around the world, but as yet lacking a name. "Migrant form" brings into view an emergent generic formation, which cuts across established paradigms. Our book is a collective exploration of this possibility.

One of the questions the volume asks through practice is whether forms of art — writing, sculpting, photography, drawing, making of any kind — can provide radical, resistant alternatives which wrest forms of life from what Giorgio Agamben called forms of law.[35] Could they even provide a kind of asylum that does not need to be asked for? "An economy of the unlost," shorn of superfluities, whose contours develop out of absence and sparseness?[36] Could a sense of identity and belonging slowly take *form* out of the matter of estrangement and exclusion from known categories? Can a claim to rights emerge from a state of rightlessness? "Mysteries in the clarity of mind / Clear, sometimes, in their absence," to borrow the words of Yousif M. Qasmiyeh, as he writes the camp — writing out of his childhood in the Baddawi refugee camp at the northern border of Lebanon, finding space for hope in dislocation, a shape of the self in fragments, and a kind of home in writing at the crossing-point between atopia, dystopia, and utopia.[37] The poetry of the camp becomes a kind of negative image, as Yousif's prose-poem in this book intimates: "When we say the camp, we say what it is that is not a camp."

In tune with its subject, then, the volume dares its own crossings: across geographical as well as disciplinary boundaries, discursive worlds and genres, the scholarly and the personal. Its unorthodox shape pushes us to the limits of the habitual practice of making a book; somehow it both challenges and enables us to be true to the texture of lives in transit, and to the difficulty of assembling a collection on migrant knowledge and migrant forms. It is divided into sections, which feature — and mark — a variety of formats, clustered according to the preliminary principles of theme (such as human and non-human refuge), genre or medium (such as essays, poems, meditations, conversations and dialogues, interviews, multi-media memoirs), and embodied recollections or interventions (visual, verbal, aural, or mate-

35 See Giorgio Agamben, *Homo Sacer: Sovereign Power and Bare Life,* trans. Daniel Heller-Roazen (Stanford University Press, 1998), chap. 4 "Forms of Law," 49–62, and Giorgio Agamben, *The Highest Poverty: Monastic Rules and Form-of-Life,* trans. Adam Kotsko (Stanford University Press, 2013).

36 The phrase is from Anne Carson's *Economy of the Unlost: Reading Simonides of Keos with Paul Celan* (Princeton University Press, 2002).

37 Yousif M. Qasmiyeh, "'Time': Part VI," in *Writing the Camp* (Broken Sleep Books, 2021), 56.

rial, or, as with the migrant art of food, multisensory). But the larger structure allows resonances and synergies to spill over and across the thresholds, as they must, pointing up the fragility of boundaries even as it acknowledges our need for them: a duality that cuts to the experiential reality of migrancy. As Valerie Forman shows in her account of crossings at the southern borders of the US, migrants challenge border logic even while they appeal to it.

The origins of this book lie in a public event that we organized in Cambridge in late 2019: Migrant Knowledge, Early Modern and Beyond. This gathering — of talks, poetry readings, conversations, an exhibition, a game, a story-weaving workshop, and, unexpectedly, impromptu singing and dancing — not only grappled with the imaginative and ethical impact of encountering the other but also with the polysemy of "migrant knowledge" and its provenance, beginning in the early modern world and moving freely across periods to dwell on its urgencies in our own times. In the end almost an anti-conference in the unconventionality and spontaneity of its conversation, the occasion generated a field of energy that we wanted to channel into a book that translates and further activates that sense of community and possibility.

One of our ventures was to bring together artists, activists, and scholars responding to the reality of mass migration that touches all our lives, and refugees and migrants who are actually leaving, crossing, arriving, and negotiating a new reality with its human as well as legal demands. There were resistances and dilemmas to overcome. Well-meaning but pious compassion was one of them, as though the plight of poor, endangered, disenfranchised people braving the waves in places remote from us only served to measure our incommunicable difference from them; an over-wary reason for comfortable, middle-class respondents not to tune in, not to share a platform; an emotional palliative that ends up preserving the safety of the status quo. The risk we wanted to avoid was, instead, that of reinforcing division and precluding dialogue by insisting on radical difference. The payoffs — intellectual, human, and ethical — were immense. This book is committed to keeping that interspace open and dynamic, and not turning bridges into walls through sincere but ultimately facile benevolence.

Drowning the dykes between people-in-transit, asylum-seekers, refugees, economic migrants, settled migrants, artists, activists, and scholars, this collection does not stop at aesthetic humanitarianism — already available — but aims at a more radical intervention. It demonstrates the capacity of migrant knowledge and expressions to generate an impassioned reimagining of both the experience of migrancy and the possibility of creative, efficacious, and honest response. No wonder we resonated with the work of the Migration Museum — represented in the book by curators Aditi Anand and Sue McAlpine (with a response by Clair) — who invited a mixed cast of migrants to contribute to their exhibition, in order to rebelliously reconceptualize migration as a shared heritage while allowing space for individual or distinct experiences of it. The capaciousness of our concept of migrancy may seem to risk slippage between categories. But the available differentiations often map onto more dubious distinctions between deserving or forced refugees and undeserving or voluntary migrants, between "illegal" and "unauthorized," or "aliens" and "immigrants," or (à la Meloni) "migrants" and "shipwrecked people": distinctions currently subjected to an unconscionable and strategic twist in Britain's governmental rhetoric which labels refugees as "migrants" to deny them humanitarian protection.[38] How legible are the particulars of precarity to the taxonomic gaze? Faraj Alnasser, one of our interlocutors, who came from Syria and sought asylum in the UK, was fleeing a war-ravaged country. But he was also fleeing the specter of a sexual persecution that would inevitably thwart authenticity, identity, and self-expression, driven not

---

38 See asylum law specialist David Neale's article on the UK government's denial of asylum-seeking Albanian boys and men of the status of "real victims." David Neale, "Albanian Children Come to Britain for Safety. Instead, They Get Home Office Cruelty," *The Guardian,* February 8, 2023, https://www.theguardian.com/commentisfree/2023/feb/08/albanian-children-britain-home-office-asylum-seekers.

just by political exigency but bodily knowledge too.[39] Our use of "migrants" or "migration" is inevitably laced with the vexation around terminology, its contestability and manipulability. But it is not intended to be a homogenizing gesture, reducing difference to sameness; instead, it is a refusal to be complicit in the regimes of categorization, and to be alert to continuities as well as distinctions between different kinds of liminal experience, as also to the complexities of choice and enforcement.

"The Antinomies of Exile" and the Dilemmas of Response

Borders are fraught sites, places of paradox. Porous and rigid at once, they invite and resist crossings, conjoin home with unhome, and elicit unwonted kindness as much as they draw out ruthlessness of both predictable and unsuspected kinds. Governments strenuously shore them up, while for individuals and communities, they can be plots of invitation. As the humanitarian crisis in Ukraine has unfolded, Europe has seen spontaneous hospitality and warmth at several of its borders. In Poland, Ukrainian refugees have been received with compassion and open arms. Yet the same border force had violently pushed Kurdish, Syrian, and Afghan refugees back into Belarus in November 2021.[40] Non-white students (from Asia, Africa, and the Middle East) also fleeing the war have not only been repelled at

---

39 I mention this with Faraj's permission. One might compare the new demography of climate refugees who, although their numbers will no doubt expand exponentially in the near future, are nevertheless not currently covered by the UN's framework for deciding on refugee status (according to the categorization criteria of the UN Convention of 1951). On gender and employment migration, see Martin F. Manalansan IV, "Queer Intersections: Sexuality and Gender in Migration Studies," *The International Migration Review* 40, no. 1 (2006): 224–49, and on gendered bodies via-à-vis refugee law, see Sudeep Dasgupta, "Sexual and Gender-Based Asylum and the Queering of Global Space: Reading Desire, Writing Identity and the Unconventionality of the Law," in *Refugee Imaginaries*, ed. Cox et al.

40 See Lorenzo Tondo's moving coverage of what Europe would rather not look in the face: Lorenzo Tondo, "Embraced or Pushed Back: On the Polish Border, Sadly, Not All Refugees Are Welcome," *The Guardian*, March 4, 2022, https://www.theguardian.com/global-development/commentis-

borders such as Przemyśl, but deprioritized and sometimes left behind even by Ukraine's own evacuation efforts. Romani refugees from Ukraine have faced discrimination at every step of their journey: from the train station in Lviv to reception points at the Polish border and buses, cars, employers, and landlords in Kraków.[41] In the same week as Spain introduced an express system to take in refugees from Ukraine, we had to struggle not to blink as we watched the video of a young African man fearfully climbing down a border-fence from Morocco into the Spanish enclave of Melilla to be pepper-sprayed and beaten brutally to the ground by at least six armed policemen. The interior minister of Spain defended this act as "proportionate" to the aggression of border breaches: the video shows a bedraggled, defenseless Black youth being viciously thrashed by a gang of white men even before he lands on Spanish ground.[42] The rhetoric of those refugees who are like us versus those too different to count has hung like a cloud on borderlands otherwise made permeable by humanity and hospitality. Meanwhile, thousands of Ukrainian refugees have been stuck at airports in Iași, Warsaw, and elsewhere in Europe, waiting for the UK Home Office to reply to their applications. Problems and delays continue to trouble the official stance of open welcome.

As Regina Schwartz reminds us, with Rowan Williams's response, the economy of abundance that the "love command" of the Bible offers could be an alternative model to the policy of nation-states, and turn our encounter with strangers into a confrontation with our own vulnerabilities. It is just such a

free/2022/mar/04/embraced-or-pushed-back-on-the-polish-border-sadly-not-all-refugees-are-welcome.

41 As late as May 10, 2022, eighty Roma women and children from Ukraine were stuck in a hostel in Kraków. See Weronika Strzyżyńska, "'Meet Us Before You Reject Us': Ukraine's Roma Refugees Face Closed Doors in Poland," *The Guardian,* May 10, 2022, https://www.theguardian.com/global-development/2022/may/10/ukraine-roma-refugees-poland.

42 Sam Jones, "Spanish Minister Defends Police Accused of Brutality at Melilla Border," *The Guardian,* March 6, 2022, https://www.theguardian.com/world/2022/mar/06/spanish-minister-defends-police-accused-brutality-melilla-border.

challenge that we saw Thomas More facing his early modern Brexiteers with. But when resources are desperately stretched, love is a difficult gift. The unspeakable conditions at Manston asylum center, described in despicably agricultural terms as a "holding," nevertheless speak of the exhaustion of human and material supplies, even as it puts under a spotlight the gap between the anxiety and the facts, between perceived and real (and falling) numbers of asylum-seekers, between the institutional rhetoric and increasing processing delay of asylum-applications in Britain. There is indeed a long tradition behind the exaggeration of the limits to resources, going back to Elizabeth I's draft proclamation which has come under scrutiny lately. But the fear from which these distortions proceed is real, as is the perception of threat. Real strain can be politically manipulated by turning migrants into pawns: New York declared an emergency on October 8, 2022, when the number of migrants sent there by Republican states pushed the city to breaking point. One of the challenges facing the humanities, as well as the arts more specifically, is to accommodate difficult, unpleasant affects such as domestic insecurity, fear, and resentment, and to be unsentimentally attentive, if only to effect social change. Nor is this limited to current affairs. Even ancient Athens, known as the great hegemonic city, had carefully in-built transaction, calculation, and political interest at the heart of its hospitality and protection, as Euripides's *Heracleidae* shows, and the fear of refugees is never far from the asylum the *polis* offers.[43] Palermo, the Sicilian city which has committedly remained open to strangers as Italy has increasingly swerved right in our times, the liminal place which has been so conducive to plurality and mutual aid, has this statue ensconced in a central piazza (fig. 1.11): the Genio di Palermo, the protective deity of Palermo, a bearded old man with a serpent, embodying the alien in local lore, coiled round him and nursing at his breast.

---

43 See Angeliki Tzanetou, *City of Suppliants: Tragedy and the Athenian Empire* (University of Texas Press, 2012), esp. chap. 3.

Fig. 1.11. Genio di Palermo, Palazzo Pretorio. Source: Wikimedia Commons.

It is a fascinating emblem for a city which has for centuries been hospitable to foreigners, whether as traders, invaders, conquerors, travelers, or refugees. But welcoming the other has always been inseparable from anxieties about opening the self up to consumption. Several of the seven versions in the city have a motto wrapped around the figure of the Genio—a tough one: "Panormus conca aurea suos devorat alienos nutrit" ("Palermo [all port], golden basin, devours its own and nourishes the foreigner"). So this symbol of benevolent hybridity has an unassimilable adage, resonant of the tangle of feelings that encountering the other throws at us. This, too, is an artistic response to migration: take that.

Migrant forms that must counter such resistance have to enter dialogue with it. We cannot yet offer all the answers to this in the realm of art, but we can begin by registering the need to grapple with the irresolubles facing any responsible project of response. I saw a moving example in action at a public workshop arranged by Stories in Transit — an organization in Palermo which is committed to creating a space for cultural expression for young migrants — where teenagers from many places, speaking diverse languages, took up a local story embedded in Palermo's history and passed it round, each adding a line to it that brought in their own, foreign story, and history, grafting it onto the root. In the end it produced an interwoven narrative that was sung to drums and guitars, and then played by puppets, with a joy that was both disruptive and reparative in its performative crossing of cultural, national, and ethnic barriers. Valentina Castagna and Marina Warner, who founded Stories in Transit, converse in our volume with Saifoudiny Diallo and Clelia Bartoli about their consortium, Giocherenda, and give us insights into the "relational aesthetics" through which they negotiate belonging and indeed citizenship.[44] *Trade Winds,* the open-ended installation created by Susan Stockwell for our event in St. Peter's Church — part of Kettle's Yard, an art gallery in Cambridge — also created an environment where material and product were in service of encounter, as Carla Suthren's response here suggests, generating a collaborative questioning of the paradoxical symbiosis between money and movement, trade and tide, shore and sea, and containment and freedom. It consisted of a flotilla of boats made of paper currency and travel tickets from countries from which the bulk of the migration to

---

44 A term coined by Nicholas Bourriaud to describe art that works through encounter, inter-subjectivity, and social context, in Nicholas Bourriaud, *Relational Aesthetics,* trans. Simone Pleasance, Fronza Woods, and Mathieu Copeland (Les presses du réel, 2002).

Europe has taken place, crossing a sea made out of copper coins. As Derek Walcott wrote, "the Sea is History."[45]

The paradox of borders and border-crossings extends to our epistemic experience and manifests in our expressive practices. There is an undeniable imaginative yield in unsettled knowledge, caught in the act of passage; in living and thinking in multiple languages and time-zones; even in radical insecurity. In her part of her collaborative meditation with A.E. (Alicia) Stallings, Angela Leighton explores the inherent diaspora of language and the flow of art forms into one another, through the sound-crossings that map the "perpetual migrations" of poetry. What Amit Chaudhuri calls "mishearing" is a migrant form born out of the imaginative freedom, unique pleasure, even privilege, of being out of place, the aural counterpart of "a plurality of visions" that Said — significantly borrowing a term from music — calls "contrapuntal."[46] Amit suggests that when we hear a tune in a place where we have arrived, we remake a familiar tune from home, filtered and transformed by different notes from a new world of sounds. This is not fusion but a new form where both the original and the subsequently encountered retain their essence but interact to form a found music: produced by a sudden moment of contact and a conceptual crossing, revealing an unforeseen relation. What kind of knowingness and unknowing does this "form" comprise, and how does it inflect the temporality of the musical experience at both the artist's and the hearer's ends? Sound — like form, as form — is bound up in place and environment. After all, as the Anglophone Caribbean poet Kamau Braithwaite said, reflecting on "nation language," "the hurricane does not roar in pentameters."[47] Yet we might also remember Naipaul's response to Wiltshire through the lens of the colonial education in Trinidad that taught him Wordsworth in third grade, seeing an "immense Lake District solitude" in the

---

45 Derek Walcott, *The Star-Apple Kingdom* (Farrar, Straus and Giroux, 1979), 25.

46 Said, "Exile," 186.

47 Kamau Braithwaite, *History of the Voice: The Development of Nation Language in Anglophone Caribbean Poetry* (New Beacon Books, 1984), 10.

bent figure of an old farmer in Salisbury — "a figure of literature in that ancient landscape."[48] Is this culpably apolitical, as Salman Rushdie and Derek Walcott thought, or the deep politics of migrant double-seeing which complicates the relation between privilege and privation, owning and owing?

Migration as an act that straddles mind and body — and exile as a crossing of barriers not only of territory but of thought — has implications for spatial relations, exchanges, and movements in a variety of contexts. The theater is a particular one. As Pip Williams, dramaturg, director, and actor, shows, it demands that we migrate into the post-COVID-19 worlds with reimagined contracts and a recalibrated understanding of the porous borders between artist and participant, and between times, places, and spaces in the performance space. Angela ponders how poetry itself is a crossing in sounds — "from word to word […], mouth to ear, ear to memory." At times, even the boundary between matter and mind proves porous in the migrant condition: the "object" that Dine (Saifoudiny) — crossing over physically and hazardously from Guinea to Palermo — brought with him and presents to us in this book is a story; as Naipaul said about the drifters in 1950s London: "[their] principal possessions were their stories. And their stories spilled easily out of them."[49] Gabriel Josipovici's reverie takes us into a deeper blur: the inherent porosity of boundaries in the mind. The threshold between known and unknown, self and other, home and un-home, abundance and scarcity, is permeable, like narrative itself. We try to keep both the intransigence of borders and their penetrability in view.

But the sublimations of metaphor can be a treacherous shore. For, as Said wrote, "exile is compelling to think about, but terrible to experience."[50] The moment we acknowledge the poetic life of crossings, of what W.S. Graham calls "speaking withershins," "[so] that somehow something may move across / The caught

---

48 Naipaul, *The Enigma of Arrival*, 15.

49 Ibid., 155.

50 Said, "Exile," 173.

habits of language," *we* are caught between the human indignity of forced uprooting and the lure of migrancy as a resonant place in the mind (with the exhilarating risk of dwelling on thresholds, the pleasure and play it can entail).[51] The inverse relation we noted between the harrowing of crossings in life and the representational power and even joy of crossings in art has the potential to be freeing, because borders and barriers not only keep us out but hem us in too — safe enclosures can tip over into prisons. But it can also incur the risk that Said warned us to resist: the temptation to make exile a poetic condition or aesthetic capital, transforming and transvaluing its irredeemable estrangement into "a potent, even enriching motif of modern culture"; to "banalise its mutilations" by thinking of the content of exile literature as "beneficially humanistic." Our book looks this risk in the face and negotiates it by grappling with, rather than evading, the dilemmas and dualities of both the migrant condition and the act of expressing or registering it in the media available to us. It engages with what Said calls the "antinomies of exile."[52] But from where we stand, now, it approaches a middle ground between his stark alternatives. For Said, the experience of exile is "almost by design irrecoverable" between "the modest refuge provided by subjectivity" and "the abstractions of mass politics."[53] The interventions in this book, in their distinct ways, either present or intimate new ways of responding to forced migration, refugeedom, exile, emigration, and other kinds of movement that are scrupulously true to the experience itself; new registers that stake a place between obscuring impersonality and impotent or alienated subjectivity; and artifacts that situate themselves at the interface between the private and the collective, initiating a dialogue between the two. Indeed, the book dares, and is designed, to be an attempt at recovery.

51 W.S. Graham, "The Constructed Space," in *New Collected Poems,* ed. Matthew Francis (Faber and Faber, 2004), 162.

52 Said, "Exile," 173–74.

53 Ibid., 176.

Fig. 1.12. Barca Nostra by Christoph Büchel, Venice Biennale 2019.
Photo by Subha Mukherji.

Acts of salvage as a way of inscribing and animating disaster
are, of course, fraught with ethical risk. But could the alternative slip into what Maurice Blanchot calls the disaster of passiv-
ity with respect to the disaster?[54] Büchel's quickly controversial
Barca Nostra is a case in point (figs. 1.12 and 1.13). It was the
hulk of a huge boat which sank between Libya and Lampedusa
in April 2015, taking with it 1100 migrants on board, with only
twenty-eight surviving, displayed on the lagoon in the Venice
Biennale 2019. It landed badly in many quarters: there was an
understandable unease and a suspicion of the opportunism of
art feeding off other people's disasters. Is this a living thing being
turned into a woven thing?[55] Ironically, conscientious objectors
to the installation found themselves on the wrong side of his-

54 Maurice Blanchot, *The Writing of the Disaster,* trans. Ann Smock (University of Nebraska Press, 1995).

55 Categories used by Erasmus. See Desiderius Erasmus, *On Copia of Words
and Ideas,* trans. Donald B. King and H. David Rix (Marquette University
Press, 2012), 50.

Fig. 1.13. Barca Nostra by Christoph Büchel, Venice Biennale 2019.
Photo by Subha Mukherji.

tory, with the hard-right, anti-immigration Salvini condemning
the display — the very man who refused, that same summer, to
let a rescue boat with 150 migrants stranded for eighteen days in
perilous conditions off Lampedusa to dock, a boat which Spain
eventually took in on humanitarian grounds.[56] On visiting the
Barca Nostra, I found it strangely moving. The marks of battery
and violence on its body were vivid. It was not framed as art,

---

56 See Daniel Dombey, "Spain Offers to Take Refugee Boat Turned
Away by Italy," *Financial Times*, August 19, 2019, https://www.ft.com/
content/0b7a0aae-c1ab-11e9-a8e9-296ca66511c9. For supplementary
details, see Angela Barnes, "Spain to Allow Open Arms Migrants to Disembark in Mallorca," *Euronews*, August 18, 2019, https://www.euronews.
com/2019/08/18/open-arms-migrant-rescue-boat-rejects-spanish-offer-of-
safe-haven.

or perhaps framed as not-art. Parked in a remote corner of the lagoon, forlorn, open to the elements, it had been allowed to rust — and was hard to find. We took several boats and got lost many times. So it felt like something we had stumbled on, more found than made. Not so much parasitic as a fossil of experience, poised between a relic and an artifact, it stood there like a huge living presence that was at once an accusatory witness and a meditative object. Of course, those who were in the ship are not there — but they are the ones who haunt, animate, and confer meaning on it. And those are not pearls that were *their* eyes — the barge refuses the kind of sea-change that the invisible Ariel sings to Ferdinand, washed ashore alive, in Shakespeare's *The Tempest*: a song that both describes and effects an aesthetic transformation of the macabre into the exquisite as he sings of Ferdinand's father, supposedly drowned in a shipwreck.[57] It is, rather, a rich and strange *exuvia*, to use Gell's term for the traces and leavings harvested from a living body, which preserve personhood and even presence in a distributed form.[58] Such an uncanny remnant confounds our ways of knowing or making sense. So, divisive as it is — as it must be — it provokes us to ask what new vulnerabilities and confessions, and indeed what new deceptions of art, such formal negotiations of the precarious crossings of our time, make available. And, crucially, it raises questions about agency.

In this volume, forms that come out of the experience of crossings meet those that emerge from our encounters with it. But they are bound by a shared awareness, a responsibility. For it is not just critical or historical engagement that is answerable. Aesthetic practice itself needs to be repositioned if it is to rise to the political and human challenges of migration. "Migrant forms" are the vehicles and the means of this imaginative reorientation — or an "alter-aesthetics," to use Supriya Chaudhuri's term — variously presented or posited here. In

---

57 See William Shakespeare, *The Tempest*, in *The Riverside Shakespeare*, ed. G. Blakemore Evans (Houghton Mifflin, 1974), I.ii.397–402.

58 Gell, *Art and Agency*, 11–15, 116, and 146n.

Brian Cummings's reading of Erasmus, metaphor, or, in a larger sense, literary form itself, becomes a home away from home, a space of migrant domicile. So, the specifically excursive and discontinuous shape of the adages provides the perfect form for the ambiguity of home for Erasmus: the everywhere — and elsewhere — of the one little room into which he can disappear. It is no accident that in so many of our critical offerings, form becomes the very subject of contemplation, while in the creative negotiations, it either fractures or realigns into new shapes. The question of form, it seems, has always been inseparable from the experience of migrancy. Anupam Basu shows us in his historical essay how the mobility of early modern vagrants leaks into the narrative form of rogue pamphlets which become the vehicle for an emergent "unsettled subjectivity" and position themselves against the containing structure and fixing imperative of poor laws. In our own time, Alicia wrestles to find a literary form in which to write without exploitation about the Aegean Sea and its tragic load from a place of safety, and alights on the epigram and the epitaph, on lists, and finally on myth and music, to ponder and process both distance and closeness. Angela's complementary piece, even as it sails poetically across forms and languages, is brought up short against her knowledge of the bitterness of Luigi Pirandello's African sea and rests in the end on the precarious boundary between sound and muteness, with its own end-stopped poetic. Rachel Spence, encountering the great city of crossings, is moved to layer and blend image, poetry, and prose to meditate on the ultramarine beyond the sea that travels to Venice from far away to blend with its own blue. To capture the migrations that underwrite Venice even as they are erased, that make it a place vivid with absent elsewheres, no settled shape would do, but a splintered, refractive palimpsest. These experiments may seem, but are not, a world apart from the *non-finito* of the migrant Durga, its tentative, interim style blending modes that have not mixed before, miming search rather than arrival.[59]

And how do those who are speaking from the heart of the experience negotiate the wholeness and comfort of received form? Anthony Vahni Capildeo's multi-form poem in this book plays and twists and turns to trace the shape of "crossing time" along the "whaleroad swanroad path of exile" to disintegrate and find truth and collaboration, finally, in the understood loss of form, broken across blank space: "Just look how   /   I've lost form." Mina Gorji's fugitive forms forge a provisional home for the creatures in flight who are her subjects, evoking homes lost but stirring still in new, half-formed shelters, but her subject is also, perhaps, her own migrant subjectivity. Yousif's formally hybrid piece in the book is an irregular traversal, splicing time present and time past with a "future subject to many pasts," to capture the radical temporality of the camp. More immediately tied to the exigencies of asylum is the resistant form of Kurdish Iranian writer, journalist, and film-maker Behrouz Boochani's memoir, *No Friend But the Mountains* (2019). Tapped out on his mobile phone as a series of WhatsApp messages in Farsi during his five-year incarceration (without charge or trial) in Australia's offshore detention center on Manus Island for arriving by boat as a refugee, it compounds its obligatory position as outsider to both institutional law and the law of genre with a defiant mixture of formal fragments.[60] His very mode of mimesis is a refusal of ordinary realism, an estrangement from familiar reference, because in Manus, nothing is but what is not: Corridor M is "Little Kurdistan," the prisoner Reza is the Gentle Giant, and the magnificent mango tree is both of the island and of the author's

---

59 *Non-finito* is an Italian term of art, referring to an aesthetic of the unfinished, especially in sculpture.

60 Behrouz Boochani, *No Friend but the Mountains: Writing from Manus Prison,* trans. Omid Tofighian (Picador, 2019). His film *Chauka, Please Tell Us the Time* was likewise shot on a mobile phone inside the Manus prison; it was a form of counter-reportage when the Australian authorities were denying journalists access to Manus Island, denying the refugees held there any means of expression, and actively suppressing refugee history.

Kurdish hometown, as are Maysam The Whore and The Cunning Young Man — a sense of the uncanny that his translator Omid Tafighian calls "horrific surrealism" in his "list of guiding principles" for "a situated schema for reading" the work, as if it challenges reading itself to find new bearings.[61] Bertolt Brecht, a refugee writer who ceaselessly experimented with satire, diary entries, and autobiographical stories, and was hugely influenced by episodic travelers' tales and conversational forms, sat on his material for *Refugee Conversations,* waiting for a suitable form to emerge. Written in exile and never wholly finished, it was published posthumously as a weave of loose fragments with dialogues between two refugees from Nazi Germany in that most iconic of transitory spaces for fleeting encounters — a railway station café-cum-waiting-room.[62] Naipaul, writing out of his dislocated, fractured self, long wrestled with the received apparatus of the novel, exploded linearity because it felt false to his migrant trajectory, and created his own form — blurring the lines between autobiography, fiction, cultural commentary, reportage, and elegy: witness *In a Free State* (1971), *The Enigma of Arrival* (1987), or *A Turn in the South* (1989). "I have arrived at this form slowly," he said in an interview, "Because of my background and the nature of my life, because I was not given knowledge of where I came from."[63] It is as if prefabricated forms are like the ready-made homes in Theodor Adorno's *Minima Moralia,* written in exile in 1951, where "the house is past," like language.[64] To find a home in writing, refugees and emigrés — and perhaps travelers too — need to reject the com-

61 Ibid., 240–43, and Omid Tafighian, "No Friend but the Mountains: Translator's Reflections," in ibid., 366.

62 The book was written mostly in Helsinki and partly in the US, c. 1940–1941, and first published in German in 1961. The first English translation appeared in 2020; see Bertolt Brecht, *Bertolt Brecht's Refugee Conversations,* ed. Tom Kuhn, trans. Romy Fursland (Bloomsbury/Methuen Drama, 2020).

63 See Jason Cowley, "vs Naipaul," *Prospect Magazine,* June 19, 1998, https://www.prospectmagazine.co.uk/magazine/vsnaipaul.

64 Theodor W. Adorno, *Minima Moralia: Reflections from Damaged Life,* trans. Edmund F.N. Jephcott (Verso, 2020), 42.

modification of subjectivity of off-the-rack genres. So Natalya Din-Kariuki unpacks the function of early modern travel writing as a migrant genre — "extravagant," might we say? — that engages and transforms established paradigms of literary form, and indeed canon. John Gallagher, on the other hand, unearths an alternative zone of migrant knowledge and articulation to the predominantly male culture of printed travel literature: the incomplete, fragmented accounts of migrant women in early modern London — in testimonial, legal, or ecclesiastical documents — are shown to emerge as a form that registers and enacts migrancy and its distinctive, gendered knowledges. This book brings into view the prehistory of "the archive of statelessness" that Cox and others identify as taking shape in the middle of the twentieth century, as well as opening up its evolving and continually innovative formal range in our times.[65] Yousif asks elsewhere who writes the archives — a question that the reality of migration has thrown in the face of the world. His poetic answer suggests a continual process in a scene of writing: "Only refugees can forever write the archive. / The camp owns the archive, not God."[66]

But art about migration does not only need to assert its own experiential truth against what Adorno calls the "administered world."[67] It also needs to negotiate the points of friction between its own predilections and the matter of migration. The intersec-

---

65 Emma Cox et al., "Introduction," in *Refugee Imaginaries,* ed. Cox et al., 3.

66 Yousif M. Qasmiyeh, "Writing the Camp," in *Refugee Imaginaries,* ed. Cox et al., 323. But the essay also opens up the paradox and the spectrality of the camp as a scene of writing. It is interesting to read it against Urvashi Butalia's *The Other Side of Silence: Voices from the Partition of India* (Duke University Press, 2000), which rewrites the archive by replacing the written word with the unwritten, weaving her history of the Partition entirely out of oral sources.

67 Cf. Theodor Adorno, *Dissonanzen: Musik in der verwalteten Welt* [Dissonances: music in the administered world] (Vandenhoeck & Ruprecht, 1956). Adorno first used the term in a radio conversation with Max Horkheimer and Eugen Kogon in 1950, printed as "The Administered World, or the Crisis of the Individual," in Max Horkheimer, *Gesammelte Schriften,* vol. 13: *Nachgelassene Schriften 1949–1972* (Fischer, 1989), 121–42.

tion between the monumental and the evanescent in aesthetic engagements with migration illuminates a paradox at the heart of the migrant condition itself — wanting to belong, to settle, to become permanent residents on arrival, yet also being ineradicably mobile and irreducibly transitory, dependent on appliances and media that allow a fugitive status and its facilities. As Supriya reminds us, migrant experience takes place not just across but along boundaries. Using a range of images, installations, and records across time, she taps into the duality between mobility and stasis in migrant life: remember how our migrant Goddess and her family are portrayed as they wait, trapped out of place. The irresolution is political, and migrant forms are art's answers to this challenge — tuning into the representational impulses of selves in transit by holding this tension, negotiating it, and using it as a built-in ethical barometer. In a world full of "placeless people" (Stonebridge), they offer an alternative habitus for art which finds itself out of place in its traditional habitats. Yet in another sense, they also resist fixed habitation, whether deliberately or subliminally, remaining "unattached as tumbleweed" like Auden's Jewish exile Rosetta.[68] Banksy, who may seem to have crossed back over into institutional artspace, drew a mural, in 2019, of a migrant child in a lifejacket holding a pink neon flame on a rotting Venetian wall which was already fading within weeks as the lagoon lapped away at it. Bhanu Kapil's poetic translation of the ambivalence of home and the enigma of arrival is one of the voices in our book which tune into this provisionality. Issam Kourbaj, a Cambridge-based artist from Syria, has turned an Aleppo soap into an artifact — entitled *Don't Wash Your Hands* — inscribing in his artwork an urge to dissolve itself. And he has made palm-sized boats out of recycled bicycle mudguards and packed them with matchsticks held by watery resin, evoking the little leaden boats that sail out of Syria with huddling refugees, which he sets on fire again and again in a repeated performance of precarity (fig. 1.14). A small fleet of these, crowded with spent matches, now nestles in the

---

68 Auden, *The Age of Anxiety,* 45.

Fig. 1.14. A boat from *Dark Water, Burning World* by Issam Kourbaj being passed around at the Migrant Knowledge event, Cambridge 2019. Photo by Subha Mukherji.

Gallery of the Islamic World in the British Museum.[69] Miniature and fragile, they are a defiantly anti-monumental response to both the scale of the crisis, and the traditional aesthetic impulse towards the immense and enduring. Meanwhile, their reused, discarded materials — cheap and adaptable, with scars and dents from their past lives — offer a migrant provocation in the face of the surrounding display of precious textiles and gems, glazed ceramics and tiles, metal filigree and opulent marble. They also interrogate the emblems of power from the Sutton Hoo ship burial in the room that leads to this gallery.

---

69 Seven boats from Issam Kourbaj's series, *Dark Water, Burning World,* are in the Albukhary Foundation Gallery of the Islamic world, British Museum.

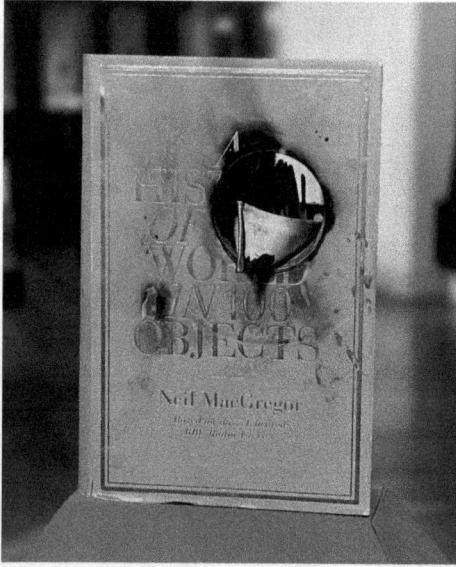

Fig. 1.15. Precarious Passage by Issam Kourbaj. Photo by Subha Mukherji.

Simon Goldhill's conversation with Issam in our book explores the dynamic between geography and artistic identity, assertion and transformation, in his work — the tension at its core between privilege and curse, settlement and exile, building and destruction, longing and belonging. Together, they probe the place of politics, loss, and repurposing in the material of migrant art, and the knowledges such art might carry, or bury.

Occasionally, the dissolution is turned outwards; indeed at times it turns on history, and the narratives of migration. Issam has just created a new work, "Precarious Passage," and donated it to the British Museum for Refugee Week (2023) (fig. 1.15). Here, one of his little boats perches on a hole burnt through the seven hundred pages of *A History of the World in 100 Objects* by Neil MacGregor.[70] Chosen as the 101st object in the updated

---

70 Neil MacGregor, *A History of the World in 100 Objects* (Allen Lane, 2011).

2020 edition of MacGregor's 2010 British Museum/BBC Radio 4 series of the same name, the signature boat is at once delicately placed in the burnt out hole, and enacts a violent disruption of the textual history of humankind (embodied here by the elegant blue cover of the book), as well as, perhaps, of museum practice. MacGregor was, after all, Director of the British Museum from 2002 to 2015. While the singed edges of the cavity are caused by the heat of the drilling, given the role of the boats in Issam's artistic practice, they play on a certain knowingness about traversals — as though the pages were scorched by the matches heaped into the boat, in the process of being extinguished in the prehistory of the artwork. "Precarious Passage" resonates intimately with us as we wrap up this almost anti-book with its own disruptive moves.

Courting dispossession to decline the sublimations and translations of aesthetics may be one of the ways migrant forms find their home. The Durga idol is a fascinating example of this, in its inherently dissoluble, clayey form. At the end of the week in October when Durga and her companions visit the earth, the idols are immersed ceremonially in the river Ganges, in a ritual that keeps alive the sense of transience at the heart of art and its living material. It has impermanence and unpossessability built into its very conception: thus, it offers a perfect vehicle for "migrant" artifacts. But in 2020, the Chief Minister of West Bengal, a secularist, declared that the migrant Durga would be saved from being dissolved and preserved in a protected space. The artist did not yet know which museum or space. Is "saving" an act of safe-making that is out of tune with migrant aesthetic? Or is it a necessary act of political co-option? The Behala Art Fest (from which fig. 1.7, the migrant mural featuring earlier in this piece, came) was begun with the governing principle of placing this new imaginary in the open street rather than the enclosed gallery. The inner process began when, some eight years prior to that, the convenor, Sanatan Dinda, an acclaimed artist, stopped doing gallery shows as he was overcome by the urgency of making art that not only speaks to a common reality but remakes it. As Leon Trotsky said (though the saying is often mistakenly attributed to Bertolt Brecht or to Vladimir Mayakovsky), art is not just a mirror which reflects but "a hammer which shapes."[71] When I went to see the wall with the migrant laborers in April 2022, the murals had been wiped out for new work for the next festival. Disappointed as I was, this felt peculiarly right and poignant. Similarly, The Good Chance's "Theatres of Hope" — so central to the artistic encounters and inventive forms they generated — were temporary geodesic domes built in areas of high refugee population. The Migration Museum had temporary spaces and a mobile life when they took part in our event — but then they acquired a semi-permanent venue, and are currently looking for a permanent one. What these necessary — and in many ways hopeful — moves augur about the mobile dynamic between agencies, ownership, and migrant art may only become clearer in time. Will Amal move into a gallery one day, and if so, would it feel like the home she is looking for?

Leaving Home, Moving Things

Art as a home for the homeless and narratives as possessions are almost truisms. But what happens to our belongings when we move? What material for migrant forms can bare life supply? What are the few things that are inalienably ours, which we carry with us and hold on to? Wider reflections on the role of mobile objects that accompany us on our journeys, or survive our departures and relocations, or act as formal exemplars of fragmentary lives, appear in and thread through several contributions to this volume. Rosita D'Amora, for instance, shows how nimbly the Turkish turban as a mobile fashion-object crosses borders in early modern Europe to act as an agent at once of othering and of domesticating foreignness, unmooring identities even when they are meant to fix them. But it is in our "Moving Things" section that the singular role of objects in our passages is distilled.

---

71 Leon Trotsky, *Literature and Revolution,* ed. William Keach, trans. Rose Strunsky (Haymarket Books, 2005), 120.

Fig. 1.16. Bhaager Ma: migrant Durga, stuck at the border with moving things. Photo by Rintu Das.

Here is a glimpse (figs. 1.16 and 1.17) of the suitcase that the 2021 Durga carries with her as she sits in limbo at the border, packed and ready to move — to a destination unknown. There are a few intensely personal objects that the opened lid reveals: Durga's red wedding saree spilling out of the case, a much-used utensil, and the children's early photos snatched from the chaos of eviction and stuffed into the box with desperate love. And here is little Lakshmi, goddess of wealth represented as a des- titute little girl clutching on to her owl — her divine carrier in traditional iconography, appearing as the favorite toy that she had time to quickly grab (fig. 1.18). Art and life enter uncanny

Fig. 1.17. Bhaager Ma: migrant Durga, stuck at the border with moving things. Photo by Rintu Das.

dialogue across multiple borders and trigger a double-seeing in viewers, migrant or not, when we look at Quique Kierszen-baum's photo of little Zaynab Ayoub playing with what remains of home — two rescued toys — next to the rubble of her demol-ished home in the Palestinian village of Fahit (2022) (fig. 1.19).

The stripping of possessions is especially stark in forced dis-placement. Even other kinds of migration — professional and circumstantial included — entail shedding, losing, learning to do without. When we are lucky, such departures allow for mea-gre choosing too, or snatching fragments from erasure. "Mov-

Fig. 1.18. Lakshmi in the making: from *Maarir deshe*. Photo by Pallab Bhowmick.

ing Things" is a sample photo-journal, consisting of a selection of photos of single objects that some of the migrants who are part of this book have carried with them from their old place to their new habitation. Whether shards or gleanings, these are neither perfect memorial synecdoches nor emblems of recognition; rather, they are tokens of the process of people discovering what they want to hold on to. Sometimes they make sense to the agents — in the moment or retrospectively. At other times we never understand why we snatched at a particular thing while leaving and losing. Exile and photo-artist Dragana Jurišić grabbed a huge leather-bound Bible and a pair of scissors when her family home in the former Yugoslavia was burnt down in

Fig. 1.19. Zaynab Mohammed Ayoub outside her demolished home in Palestine. Photo by Quique Kierszenbaum / *The Guardian.*

September 1991 after being taken over as a Croatian sniper nest. She says she still does not know why she clutched the heavy Bible: she was sixteen, and ungodly! But on being asked if she was a seamstress, she suddenly remembered that she had been going to a textile high school at the time: "[N]ever thought of that," she exclaimed. Who knows what matter in our daily lives matters, or constitutes us? And what knowledges the act of crossing itself bears, often unregistered? The things we carry are perhaps, above all, testimonies to an interruption, with all the significance and all the unassimilability of that moment of trauma in an ongoing life. They remain as witnesses to a history that resists assimilation even when we want, or need, to integrate to a new world. They carry the promise of stories about them, untold narratives waiting to leap into life when we touch such an object, or suddenly find it in an alcove or under our bed. Even where we keep them, how private or public we make them, tells us something about knowledges and memories we are able to own, and what of these we cannot bear or acknowledge ours. They are imbued with affects that find it hard to make their way into conventional critical discourse — such as embarrassment or secrecy, intimate pride, or half-owned longing. We want to give them a little space, and the power, to move, in our collection. And we want this space to make the range of our migrant voices and worlds vivid: stretching across, and connecting, Britain, Guinea, India, Israel, Italy, Kenya, Lebanon, Palestine, Poland, Syria, and the former Yugoslavia. This section provokes thinking not only about what objects do when we migrate, but what photography as a medium does to and for our memory, and what the act of photographing does for us when our worlds seem unpredictable and out of control. In turn, what knowledges and shapes does writing about photographs — a migrant form? — bring to the preserved or salvaged pieces of our lives that move with us?

If the "Moving Things" section is a miniature home, made out of things gathered and carried to shore against the "fallings from us, vanishings," as we cross borders,[72] Edmund de Waal's extraordinary installation, *library of exile,* is another kind of home for the unhoused. Founded on obliteration and contingency, it houses portable, fragile books and pots in a form that reaches towards permanence. It is in some senses almost emblematic of our book which itself is trying to find a home for particular encounters and transitory conversations, without closing the door to history, to memory, and to the future. Edmund's essay on his *library* begins by charting the journey of a collection of *netsuke* to meditate on home and homelessness.[73] Collecting itself emerges as an act of finding form and pattern in a chaotic and disintegrating world. These small Japanese ivory pieces, family possessions that carry knowledges about, and reanimate, his family's history of exile and dispossession as they migrate through worlds and times, lead Edmund to reflect on the genesis of his *library,* which began its life in Venice as part of the duet that formed the exhibition *psalm* (2019), stretch-

---

72 From "Ode: Intimations of Immortality," in William Wordsworth, *The Poems,* vol. 1, ed. John O. Hayden (Yale University Press, 1981), 528.

73 *Netsuke* are miniature sculptural objects developed in Japan from the seventeenth century onwards, often made of ivory or wood, used as ornamental toggles for personal items.

ing across the Venice Ghetto, a place of exile, and the Ateneo Veneto, a place of debate (but in times past also a liminal sanctuary for the condemned). Bringing together porcelain and poetry, Edmund layers erasure with inscription, archiving loss at the same time as he salvages, re-members, and preserves. The exterior of the *library*, first set up in the Ateneo, is porcelain layered over with gold leaves, written over with the names and histories of lost libraries, smudged in turn or brushed over with liquid porcelain. Inside, the migratory materials of his vitrines (gold, marble, and clay) are placed in dialogue with text — both the Talmud and three thousand books written by exiled writers from Ovid to the present, in seventy languages, from destroyed libraries across the world. Like its contents, the library itself has crossed many borders to Dresden, and will later move to Mosul, where the Babylonian Talmud was composed: exile and homecoming will touch each other. A Babel of longing, it enfolds absence at its heart — like Büchel's bark — but is alive and present as a space for translation and renewed inscription, inviting viewers to encounter, contemplate, and write into the books, extending the work of the writers and the artist. Lament is activated into agency, intimating the affective crossings and generic transformations that migrant forms can perform.

Translation: A Migrant Form

It is no surprise that translation should find its way to the heart of creative practice marked by migratory experience, as it does in Edmund's polyglot library. Translation, like migration, entails a form of mobility. While migration is mainly thought of as the movement of people — or, as we have seen, things — across boundaries, translation is usually conceptualized as the movement of texts across linguistic borders. But where borders are permeable to displaced people, languages, and texts, they are also open to the movement of cultures, sentiments, and structures of feeling and faith. No wonder, then, that points of overlap between human movement and the proliferation of hybridity through language practices have become anxious sites of state control and containment, as Loredana Polezzi succinctly summarizes (via Michel Foucault, Giorgio Agamben, and Cecilia Wadensjö).[74] So when the Carnatic singer and activist T.M. Krishna sang a patriotic, much loved Bengali song about the beauty of our land — "Dhana dhanyo pushpo bhora" — right after the Hindu-nationalist revocation of Article 370, which had long granted Muslim-majority Kashmir special status, it was a political act as well as an act of love. He got the declensions "wrong," often ignored the precise notation and the conventional *gayaki* (style) familiar to Bengal, yet dived into the emotional core of the song. The defiant anti-grammar of his rendering was a knowing musical translation across boundaries of language, state, style, politics, and religion: a sound-crossing that combined frisson, caress, and resistance, and used aesthetic estrangement to show up the homogeneity of national language as an ideological myth in plurilingual India. Later, at the anti-CAA protests by women in the working-class Muslim neighborhood of Shaheen Bagh in Delhi in 2020, he sang "Hum Dekhenge" in four different Indian languages — Tamil, Malayalam, Kannada, and Urdu (associated with Muslim native-speakers) — to the chagrin of the state. Originally a poem of resistance written by the great Urdu poet Faiz Ahmad Faiz in 1979 against Zia-ul-Haq's oppressive regime in Pakistan, subjected to a ban, and sung by Iqbal Bano in 1986 in defiance of the ban, it was adapted by T.M.'s many-tongued rendering as an agent of democracy. The same year, the launch of his book, *Sebastian & Sons,* was cancelled by the government-backed Kalakshetra Centre in Chennai, because it explores the history of making the *mrdangam,* a key percussion instrument in Carnatic music, and mines the inherent hybridity of the tradition. The *mrdangam* is made with cow-hide, and skin-work was the province of Dalit or "untouchable" Hindus, many of whom converted to Christianity — people on the fringes of the Carnatic community. Foregrounding a craft that involved a translation of musical concepts into a ma-

---

74 On the nexus between translation and migration, see Loredana Polezzi, "Translation and Migration," *Translation Studies* 5, no. 3 (2012): 345–56.

terial object made of a part of *Hindutva*'s sacred animal, and exposing the ironies of caste-hierarchy in the arts, the book was an inevitable target of state intervention. T.M. is also the artist who, in 2018, had been accused of defiling the purity of Carnatic music in using it to compose a hymn to Christ. Homogenization of culture is naturally resistant of translation except when it can be used for control, exclusion or ideological reduction. In conversation with me in this book, T.M. asserts the inseparability of his music from his activism, and the worlds of political possibility that musical and linguistic translations hold. We reflect on the defiant impurity of T.M.'s own understanding and practice of music: a refusal of cleanness that is a precise way of tapping into the inextricable entwinement that is the Indian aesthetic legacy, of tracing aesthetic pleasure and beauty to the messy material conditions of their production, and of mobilizing an inherent synergy between the condition of migrancy and the life of art.

It is translation in this wider sense that Giocherenda and Stories in Transit activate to create a space where their diverse community of *minorenni* (people who are under eighteen) can play, imagine, and be human, rather than simply being asylum-seekers trying to work out visas, employment, and subsistence. Their storytelling workshops use forms that are nonlinguistic, or have other elements to fill the gap, in the absence of a common language: song, puppetry, gesture, photographs, animation, and masking. Playwrights Joe Murphy and Joe Robertson, and Mohamed Sarrar, a refugee from Sudan, come together in this book to recount and reenact similar translations in the Calais Jungle refugee camp where they used drama and music to cross borders of language — an experience on which they founded the Good Chance Theatre (who made, or found, Amal). At a poignant and joyful moment in our event, Mohammad burst into a Sudanese song that most of us in the audience did not understand literally, but which brought us home to a shared place of encounter, of "something understood."[75] Nadina Christopou-

---

75 George Herbert uses this phrase to sum up the nature of prayer in his
    famous poem "Prayer I." See, e.g., George Herbert, *The Complete Poems*

lou and Alicia reflect, in their conversation about their creative community-building at the Melissa Network for Migrant and Refugee Women in Athens, on how translation is crucial but thorny, not least because the mother tongue is carried across borders in everyone's heads. Similarly, Angela recognizes, as she translates Pirandello, that it is a task that is "endless, impossible, yet necessary."

Said recounts in "Exile" how, one night in a Beiruti restaurant, he sat with Faiz, exiled from Pakistan, and Eqbal Ahmad, a fellow exile, reciting poems, till they stopped translating for Said at some point, but how "as the night wore on, it did not matter." The refusal of translation, or perhaps its shedding, was, to Said, "an enactment of a homecoming."[76] Yet in the same essay, Said finds a paradigmatic exploration of what for Hannah Arendt is the unbearability of strangers[77] in the failure of translation in Joseph Conrad's "Amy Foster" — a short story about Yanko Goorall, a poor central European emigrant washed up on the shore of Eastbay.[78] When, in his new life, he sits crooning to his little boy in his own language, he "sounded so disturbing, so passionate, and so bizarre" that Amy — the one person who had loved and pitied him enough to marry him — snatches the child from his arms; when, in the grip of a fever, he mutters in a language she "can't understand" — "though he may have thought he was speaking in English" — she feels nothing but "fear of that strange man," abandons him, and runs away with their child.[79]

(London, 1991), 45–46.

76 Said, "Exile," 175.

77 See Hannah Arendt, "Understanding and Politics (the Difficulties of Understanding)," in *Essays in Understanding, 1930–1954,* ed. Jerome Kohn (Harcourt, Brace & Co., 1994); Hannah Arendt, "Reflections on Little Rock," *Dissent* 6, no. 1 (1959), 45–56; and Hannah Arendt, "On Humanity in Dark Times: Thoughts about Lessing," in *Men in Dark Times,* ed. Hannah Arendt (Harcourt, Brace & World, 1968). See also Hannah Arendt, *The Origins of Totalitarianism* (Meridian Books, 1958), on the creation of unbearable strangers in Nazi Germany.

78 Joseph Conrad, "Amy Foster," in *"Typhoon" and Other Tales* (Oxford University Press, 2008).

79 Ibid., 172–74.

It is a stark story about the abyss of unknowing that a stranger can be plunged into, the knowledges they cannot communicate, and the effects of a foreign tongue without the facility of verbal translation. For translation can be a space of freedom, play, exchange, welcome, intercession, or intimacy, even while it feels, at times, like the measure of miles from home.

Annabel Brett captures the vexed if airy interspace of translation. Reading the fifteenth-century debate between Leonardo Bruni and Alonso de Cartagena over the dynamic between the local and the universal in the act of translation in tandem with the distinct approaches to it by Umberto Eco and Gayatri Spivak in our own times, Annabel shows how translation models the encounter between the familiar and the strange in our civic and political lives, stretched between erotics and ethics, surrender and agency, visceral and logical, and domination and negotiation. An intertextual migration of language, meaning and hermeneutics, translation is posited as an event in the world that at once mediates between the specific and the general, and constitutes those very categories in the process. It is shown, thus, to be an act of reading and a function of history which reveals history itself to be a migrant knowledge, and indeed a migrant form. The chronological and geographical thresholds inhabited and traversed in translation beget yet more thresholds, as Annabel's own "migratory reading" suggests. Do critical forms and historical agents have the capacity to embrace and extend the fraying of texts and selves that seems to be a function of the transactions of translation? Do they in fact have the responsibility of interposition, even as they must look its limits in the face?

Food from Home: Cooking Across the Border

Dante Alighieri, forced out of his beloved Florence in 1302, was in many senses a privileged exile. But the peculiar pain of banishment is vivid in the *Paradiso,* perhaps most minutely and viscerally when expressed in terms of an exile from the food of his motherland. The soul of his ancestor, Cacciaguida, prophesies how Dante will suffer when he "must depart from Florence":

Tu lascerai ogne cosa diletta
più caramente; e questo è quello strale
che l'arco de lo essilio pria saetta.
Tu proverai sì come sa di sale
lo pane altrui... (*Paradiso*, XVII, ll. 48; 55–56)[80]

Pane sciocco, the bread of Florence and indeed Tuscany, famously lacked salt — it still does. So, while there may also
be, in *sale,* a shade of the sense of "costly" or "rare" or "hard
to come by" that is implicit in *salato,* that sense of bitterness
about the exile's hard-earned bread is pinned to a deprivation
more immediate and sensory. Even the understood metaphor
for freedom — Florence's decision to abjure salt was part of her
self-freeing from Pisa's twelfth-century block on salt shipment
down the river Arno — feels secondary here to taste and smell,
among the most evocative sensations when one leaves home, or
the homeland.

When Faraj, now a unique food entrepreneur and chef,
crossed over to the UK as a refugee — by an "extravagant and
wheeling" course from Syria through Egypt, Turkey, Macedonia, Serbia, Hungary, Austria, Germany, and France — he found
himself in a temporary asylum in Huddersfield. One day he felt
an urge to cook *mujaddara.* And so he reconstructed a dish he
had never cooked, tracing a memory of taste and smell back
to his grandma's kitchen. That is when, he says, he realized
that he could create a sense of home anywhere. Food is what
had brought the world home to Faraj as he grew up in Aleppo.
But now, it was his vehicle for carrying a piece of home to the
world. An aspect of our lives that we take with us when we cross
boundaries, which no one can take away from us, is our sensory
apparatus, which holds our memory of food and our knowledge
of its material ingredients and production. Yet the body is a
culturally coded thing. The experience of migration demands a

---

80 "You will leave behind every thing you loved most dearly; and this is the
first arrow shot from the bow of exile. You will experience how salty is the
taste of other people's bread." Translation mine.

recoding on both sides of the encounter. Migrants' relationship with food, and society's relationship with their culinary cultures, are embodied negotiations of mobility. Faraj's conversation with me here asks what psychic and cultural realities come into view if we treat cooking — and recipes — as migrant art forms. As he started translating his memories into practice at the adventurous London restaurant, Honey & Co., his cuisine began to unsettle the gastronomic landscape of bourgeois London. His story — which, like Othello's, is also his history — shows how food is uncanny, both homely and unhomely, and how it is often the site of our first encounter with the strange. Our conversation probes these culinary passages, and re-embeds food in its stories in the context of human dislocation and relocation.

Faraj's journey shadows, in a geographical sense, the earlier journey of Claudia Roden, though hers was a privileged trajectory. My conversation with her in this book offers Claudia's account of the role of food in her childhood in Cairo, where her family were wealthy merchant-immigrants from Aleppo. It traces her journey from the cosmopolitan part of a culturally divided Cairo to Britain, and her transformative role in the British food culture of the fifties, introducing Middle-Eastern, Egyptian, and Jewish traditions at a time when available ingredients were far from cosmopolitan, and going on to write books that were at once cooking manuals, anthropology, personal memoirs, and histories of mentality. We go behind the gastronomic revolution she effected in her country of residence as an adult, and explore the relation between authenticity and innovation, the mobile and the immutable, in her experience of the evolution of migrant food and its recipes.

The enrichment of the culinary culture of a country by migration is a thing of joy and celebration. Yet Faraj still brings me apricot jam and muhammarra made by his mother in Cairo, with fruits and nuts ripened by a different sun. I still feel the thrill of buying and bringing *amshattva* (sun-dried mango pulp), *bori* (dried lentil croutons), and *nolen-gurer sandesh* (ricotta sweets with new-season molasses) from Kolkata every time I come back to Britain. We somehow want these items to remain inalienable from "home" and inaccessible elsewhere — for not everything is yet available everywhere, and I for one would feel a pang if they were. Nor do I believe that "ricotta sweets" transport half the complexity of sense, memory, and context that the very sound of "sandesh" evokes to a Bengali. Perhaps, like the *hüzün* Orhan Pamuk writes about in relation to his Istanbul, this is an intimate but collective longing we want to preserve — a "want" that we want, an ache that not only affirms but creates community.[81] Food, like other aspects of migrant experience, carries the duality between wanting to settle and needing to retain an element of unsettledness, to be true to the kindred points of both there and here. The paradox of migrant cooking may not be so different after all from the paradox of translation: home hovers between its practice and its occasional refusal.

Beyond the Bounds of the Human

Neither migration nor refuge is peculiar to the human species. Plant life holds its own intuition of seed, root, and movement; of both the opportunity and the cost of migration; and of what happens to knowledge at the edge of extinction when we tune into what Bruno Latour calls the "earthbound."[82] The journey of the kudzu, as Yota Batsaki uncovers in this book, is a fascinating example of how our designation of an "invasive species" is based on disknowledge. She shows how aesthetic intervention retunes us to find "ethical and ecological promise" in the very resistance of vibrant alien matter to the erasure of historical and political knowledges of oppression, its recalcitrance to facile epistemes. Form and knowledge dance around each other as the "migrant form" of William Christenberry's haunting photography is shown to recover, enshrine, and make visible a migrant form of nature. The abjection ascribed to the unwanted invasive

---

81 Orhan Pamuk, *Istanbul: Memories and the City*, trans. Maureen Freely (Faber and Faber, 2005), esp. chaps. 9 and 11, and chap. 26.

82 Cf. Bruno Latour, *Facing Gaia: Eight Lectures on the New Climatic Regime*, trans. Catherine Porter (Polity, 2017).

belies its uncanny power to evoke the human trauma buried in the depleted land under it and the human communities which have been forced to leave — so that the strange stirs at the heart of home, challenging to be known, acknowledged, and, indeed, represented. The small critters in Mina's poems have, like the kudzu, also made their way to strange shores by chance or human design. Mina imagines what emerging from containers into an alien environment might feel like, to these minute, non-human life-forms — parakeet or hall-wasp or ragwort, insect, plant, or animal — undesired or instrumental in their new habitats. The rhetoric of alienation and invasion, of course, crosses over from the human world to nonhumans we consider out of place, not least in the age of globalization — remember Cameron's "swarms."[83] As the Anthropocene undoes our inherited antinomies, opening us up to mutually constitutive entanglements, how might we cross the now perceptibly permeable border between nature and culture to carry knowledges over? How does it feel to be humans enclosed within bounds built for safety and for the preservation of the local?

Cornelia Parker's installation *Island,* on show at Tate Britain (2022), encapsulates a fragility that mirrors from inland the experience of these uncertain arrivals: a delicate, meshy, isolated greenhouse looking inwards, teetering to be "entire of itself" as the tides encroach and coastlines blur, with a bulb struggling to stay alight inside (figs. 1.20 and 1.21).[84] Built on reclaimed 1850s floor tiles from Augustus Pugin's House of Commons, but covered with countless tiny dots of chalk from the white cliffs of Dover, it embodies both the precarity and preciousness of refuge, and indeed of home — not just in the human world but

---

83 Cf. Banu Subramaniam, "The Aliens Have Landed! Reflections on the Rhetoric of Biological Invasions," *Meridians* 2, no. 1 (2001): 26–40.

84 Consider John Donne's famous phrase from his *Devotions Upon Emergent Occasions:* "No man is an island entire of itself." Cf. "Meditation 17," in John Donne, *Selected Prose,* ed. Neil Rhodes (Penguin, 1987), 126. I cannot believe that Parker did not have it in mind when naming the work.

Fig. 1.20. Cornelia Parker, *Island,* 2022 installation view, Tate Britain. Photo by Matt Greenwood.

across scales and orders of being, not just in post-Brexit Britain but in the "darkling plain" of a near-apocalyptic world.[85]

Prabhakar Pachpute's *Asylum Seeker,* on exhibition at the Frieze Art Fair 2022, is a poignantly postapocalyptic migrant form — one of his charcoal-on-plywood "travellers." It is a skin-and-bones farm animal with a machine inside it and an excavator for its head, trudging doggedly forward on exhausted soil estranged from labor, in search of a new home — its giant, glistening eye still as human as a cow's (fig. 1.22). A digger consists, after all, of various mechanical parts stuck to a rotating platform called "house": the conceit stretches outside-in as the engine that has infiltrated the "bull" includes a housetop, and loss and evacuation carry in their bowels a dream of home.

85 The phrase is from Arnold's poem "Dover Beach." Cf. Matthew Arnold, *Selected Writings,* ed. Seamus Perry (Oxford University Press, 2020), 437.

Fig. 1.21. Detail from Cornelia Parker, *Island,* 2022 installation view, Tate Britain. Photo by Matt Greenwood.

As Donna Haraway memorably put it, "right now, the earth is full of refugees, human and not, without refuge."[86] Can art help make the "shock of the Anthropocene" a bridge rather than a wall, and come up with a remedy that Christophe Bonneuil and Jean-Baptiste Fressoz do not quite get to?[87] Can it tap into

86 Donna Haraway, "Anthropocene, Capitalocene, Plantationocene, Chthulu-cene: Making Kin," *Environmental Humanities* 6, no. 1 (2015): 160.

87 The title of Christophe Bonneuil and Jean-Baptiste Fressoz's uncompromising book, *The Shock of the Anthropocene: The Earth, History and Us,* trans. David Fernbach (Verso, 2017).

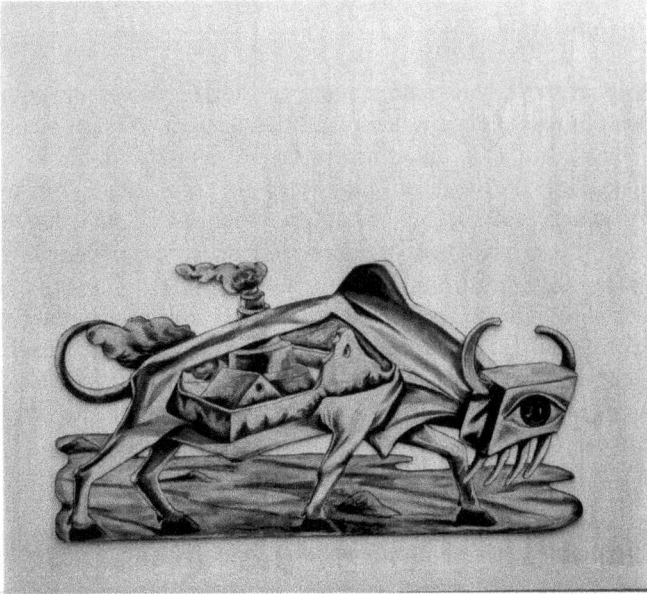

Fig. 1.22. Prabhakar Pachpute, *Asylum-Seeker,* 2020. Photo by JUD-DartINDEX/Andrew Judd.

a turn in the ecological plot which embraces tentacular knowledge and leads to a reimagining of kinship that can "replenish refuge" and imagine a new ecology of creaturehood?[88] Imagining goes hand in hand with representation. Will the varieties of artworks emerging from, and in response to, migration come together into a tribe? Could a book like ours play a role in clearing a space for such an assemblage? And in bringing together the seemingly loose web of art, environmental humanities, and migration studies under the umbrella of migrant forms, can we posit a new disciplinary formation, replacing traditional filiations with affiliations that are already functional but call out to be made knowable?

---

88 Haraway, "Anthropocene," 140.

In Conclusion

We have tried here to present our co-thinking as process, with truthfulness and rigor, but in an accessible way. We offer a collective meditation on an urgent theme, as well as a call for a larger life lived together, harnessing the imaginative yield of speaking, thinking, and moving across boundaries but doing so with ethical lucidity, in response to the new hybrid reality that we are all part of. Connecting our historical knowledge with the social, economic, and moral challenges of the contemporary world, this gathering of scattered selves and fledgling forms is both personal and political, an act of hope, and perhaps something of a tool for living. But it does not, and must not, expunge lament.

— June 2023

Bibliography

Adorno, Theodor W. *Dissonanzen: Musik in der verwalteten Welt* [Dissonances: music in the administered world]. Vandenhoeck & Ruprecht, 1956.

———. *Minima Moralia: Reflections from Damaged Life.* Translated by Edmund F.N. Jephcott. Verso, 2020.

Agamben, Giorgio. *Homo Sacer: Sovereign Power and Bare Life.* Translated by Daniel Heller-Roazen. Stanford University Press, 1998.

———. *The Highest Poverty: Monastic Rules and Form-of-Life.* Translated by Adam Kotsko. Stanford University Press, 2013.

Arendt, Hannah. *Men in Dark Times.* Harcourt, Brace & World, 1968.

———. "Reflections on Little Rock." *Dissent* 6, no. 1 (1959): 45–56. https://www.dissentmagazine.org/article/reflections-on-little-rock/.

———. *The Origins of Totalitarianism.* Meridian Books, 1958.

———. "Understanding and Politics (the Difficulties of Understanding)." In *Essays in Understanding, 1930–1954,* edited by Jerome Kohn. Harcourt, Brace & Co., 1994.

Arnold, Matthew. *Selected Writings.* Edited by Seamus Perry. Oxford University Press, 2020.

Auden, W.H. *Selected Poems.* Edited by Edward Mendelson. Faber and Faber, 1979.

———. *The Age of Anxiety: A Baroque Eclogue.* Faber and Faber, 1949.

Barnes, Angela. "Spain to Allow Open Arms Migrants to Disembark in Mallorca." *Euronews,* August 18, 2019. https://www.euronews.com/2019/08/18/open-arms-migrant-rescue-boat-rejects-spanish-offer-of-safe-haven.

Blanchot, Maurice. *The Writing of the Disaster.* Translated by Ann Smock. University of Nebraska Press, 1995.

Bonneuil, Christophe, and Jean-Baptiste Fressoz. *The Shock of the Anthropocene: The Earth, History and Us.* Translated by David Fernbach. Verso, 2017.

Boochani, Behrouz. *No Friend but the Mountains: Writing from Manus Prison.* Translated by Omid Tofighian. Picador, 2019.

Bourriaud, Nicholas. *Relational Aesthetics.* Translated by Simone Pleasance, Fronza Woods, and Mathieu Copeland. Les presses du réel, 2002.

Braithwaite, Kamau. *History of the Voice: The Development of Nation Language in Anglophone Caribbean Poetry.* New Beacon Books, 1984.

Brecht, Bertolt. *Bertolt Brecht's Refugee Conversations.* Edited by Tom Kuhn. Translated by Romy Fursland. Bloomsbury/Methuen Drama, 2020.

Butalia, Urvashi. *The Other Side of Silence: Voices from the Partition of India.* Duke University Press, 2000.

Carson, Anne. *Economy of the Unlost: Reading Simonides of Keos with Paul Celan.* Princeton University Press, 2002.

Donne, John. *Selected Prose.* Edited by Neil Rhodes. Penguin, 1987.

Ellis-Petersen, Hannah, Aakash Hassan, and Manoj Chaurasia. "Kumbh Mela: How a Superspreader Festival Seeded Covid Across India." *The Guardian,* May 29, 2021. https://www.theguardian.com/world/2021/may/30/kumbh-mela-how-a-superspreader-festival-seeded-covid-across-india.

Cohen, Gerald Daniel. *In War's Wake: Europe's Displaced Persons in the Postwar Order.* Oxford University Press, 2011.

Conrad, Joseph. "Amy Foster." In *'Typhoon' and Other Tales.* Oxford University Press, 2008.

Cowley, Jason. "VS Naipaul." *Prospect Magazine,* June 19, 1998. https://www.prospectmagazine.co.uk/magazine/vsnaipaul.

Cox, Emma, Sam Durrant, David Farrier, Lyndsey Stonebridge, and Agnes Woolley, eds. *Refugee Imaginaries: Research Across the Humanities.* Edinburgh University Press, 2020.

Dasent, John Roche, ed. *Acts of the Privy Council of England: New Series, 1542–1631.* Vol. 26: *1596–1597.* Mackie, 1902.

Dombey, Daniel. "Spain Offers to Take Refugee Boat Turned Away by Italy." *Financial Times,* August 19, 2019. https://www.ft.com/content/0b7a0aae-c1ab-11e9-a8e9-296ca66511c9.

Durrant, Sam, and Catherine M. Lord, eds. *Essays in Migratory Aesthetics: Cultural Practices between Migration and Art-Making.* Rodopi, 2007.

Eliot, T.S. *Collected Poems, 1909–1962.* Faber and Faber, 1974.

Erasmus, Desiderius. *On Copia of Words and Ideas.* Translated by Donald B. King and H. David Rix. Marquette University Press, 2012.

Fiddian-Qasmiyeh, Elena, Gil Loescher, Katy Long, and Nando Sigona, eds. *The Oxford Handbook of Refugee and Forced Migration Studies.* Oxford University Press, 2014.

Freedberg, David. *The Power of Images: Studies in the History and Theory of Response.* University of Chicago Press, 1989.

Gell, Alfred. *Art and Agency: An Anthropological Theory.* Oxford University Press, 1998.

Graham, W.S. *New Collected Poems.* Edited by Matthew Francis. Faber and Faber, 2004.

Haraway, Donna. "Anthropocene, Capitalocene, Plantationocene, Chthulucene: Making Kin." *Environmental Humanities* 6, no. 1 (2015): 159–65. DOI: 10.1215/22011919-3615934.

Hopgood, Stephen. *The Endtimes of Human Rights.* Cornell University Press, 2013.

Horkheimer, Max. *Gesammelte Schriften.* Vol. 13: *Nachgelassene Schriften, 1949–1972.* Fischer, 1989.

Hughes, Paul L., and James F. Larkin, eds. *Tudor Royal Proclamations.* Vol. 3: *The Later Tudors, 1588–1603.* Yale University Press, 1969.

Jones, Sam. "Spanish Minister Defends Police Accused of Brutality at Melilla Border." *The Guardian,* March 6, 2022. https://www.theguardian.com/world/2022/mar/06/spanish-minister-defends-police-accused-brutality-melilla-border.

Kerrigan, John. "Lampedusa: Migrant Tragedy." *Cambridge Journal of Postcolonial Literary Inquiry* 8, no. 2 (2021): 138–57. DOI: 10.1017/pli.2020.41.

Latour, Bruno. *Facing Gaia: Eight Lectures on the New Climatic Regime.* Translated by Catherine Porter. Polity, 2017.

MacGregor, Neil. *A History of the World in 100 Objects.* Allen Lane, 2011.

Manalansan, Martin F., IV. "Queer Intersections: Sexuality and Gender in Migration Studies." *The International Migration Review* 40, no. 1 (2006): 224–49. DOI: 10.1111/j.1747-7379.2006.00009.x.

McDonagh, Josephine. *Literature in a Time of Migration: British Fiction and the Movement of People, 1815–1876.* Oxford University Press, 2021.

McDonagh, Josephine, and Jonathan Sachs. "Introduction: Literature and Migration." *Modern Philology* 118, no. 2 (2020): 204–12. DOI: 10.1086/711142.

Mukherji, Subha. "'Footfalls Echo in the Memory': Displaced Durgas and Migrant Forms." *Humanities Underground,* October 2021. https://humanitiesunderground. org/2022/02/22/footfalls-echo-in-the-memory-displaced-durgas-and-migrant-forms/.

Munday, Anthony, Henry Chettle, Edmund Tilney, Thomas Dekker, Thomas Heywood, William Shakespeare, John Jowett, and Richard Proudfoot. *Sir Thomas More.* Bloomsbury Arden Shakespeare, 2013.

Naipaul, V.S. *The Enigma of Arrival: A Novel.* Penguin, 1987.

Neale, David. "Albanian Children Come to Britain for Safety. Instead, They Get Home Office Cruelty." *The Guardian,* February 8, 2023. https://www.theguardian.com/ commentisfree/2023/feb/08/albanian-children-britain-home-office-asylum-seekers.

Nyabola, Nanjala. *Travelling While Black: Essays Inspired by a Life on the Move.* Hurst & Co., 2020.

Pamuk, Orhan. *Istanbul: Memories and the City.* Translated by Maureen Freely. Faber and Faber, 2005.

Polezzi, Loredana. "Translation and Migration." *Translation Studies* 5, no. 3 (2012): 345–56. DOI: 10.1080/14781700.2012.701943.

Pollard, Alfred W., Edward Maunde Thompson, John Dover Wilson, and R.W. Chambers. *Shakespeare's Hand in the*

Play of Sir Thomas More. Edited by W.W. Greg. Cambridge University Press, 1923.

Qasmiyeh, Yousif M. *Writing the Camp.* Broken Sleep Books, 2021.

Said, Edward. *Reflections on Exile and Other Literary and Cultural Essays.* Granta, 2012.

Shakespeare, William. *Macbeth.* Edited by A.R. Braunmuller. Cambridge University Press, 2017.

———. *The Tempest.* In *The Riverside Shakespeare,* edited by G. Blakemore Evans. Boston: Houghton Mifflin, 1974.

Stonebridge, Lyndsey. *Placeless People: Writing, Rights, and Refugees.* Oxford University Press, 2018.

———. *Writing and Righting: Literature in the Age of Human Rights.* Oxford University Press, 2021.

Strzyżyńska, Weronika. "'Meet Us Before You Reject Us': Ukraine's Roma Refugees Face Closed Doors in Poland." *The Guardian,* May 10, 2022. https://www.theguardian.com/global-development/2022/may/10/ukraine-roma-refugees-poland.

Subramaniam, Banu. "The Aliens Have Landed! Reflections on the Rhetoric of Biological Invasions." *Meridians* 2, no. 1 (2001): 26–40. https://www.jstor.org/stable/40338794.

The Independent. "Suella Braverman Calls 'Broken' Immigration System an 'Invasion on South Coast." *YouTube,* October 31, 2022. https://www.youtube.com/watch?v=hG-E8GwWjYc.

Tondo, Lorenzo. "Embraced or Pushed Back: On the Polish Border, Sadly, Not All Refugees Are Welcome." *The Guardian,* March 4, 2022. https://www.theguardian.com/global-development/commentisfree/2022/mar/04/embraced-or-pushed-back-on-the-polish-border-sadly-not-all-refugees-are-welcome.

Trotsky, Leon. *Literature and Revolution.* Edited by William Keach. Translated by Rose Strunsky. Haymarket Books, 2005.

Tzanetou, Angeliki. *City of Suppliants: Tragedy and the Athenian Empire.* University of Texas Press, 2012.

Walcott, Derek. *The Star-Apple Kingdom*. Farrar, Straus and Giroux, 1979.

Wills, Clair. *Lovers and Strangers: An Immigrant History of Post-War Britain*. Allen Lane, 2017.

Wordsworth, William. *The Poems*. Edited by John O. Hayden. Yale University Press, 1981.

Yeats, W.B. *Selected Poetry*. Penguin, 1991.

II.

The Library of Exile

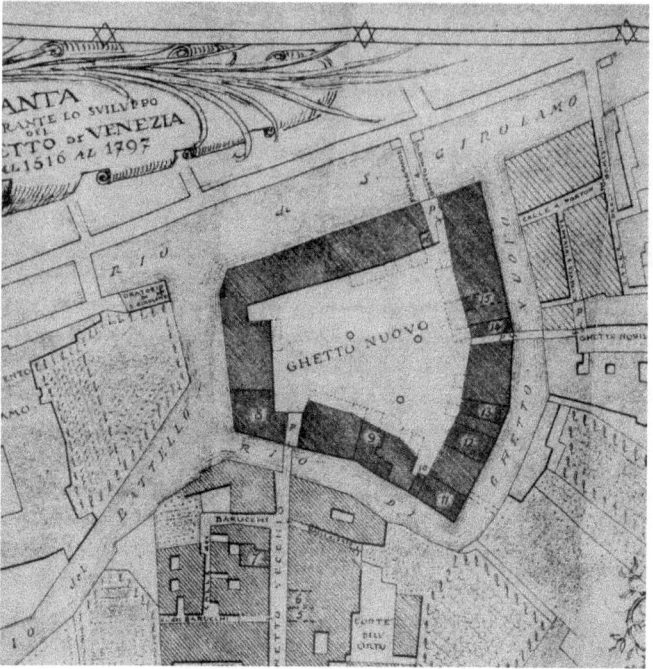

Fig. 2.1. Map of the Venetian Ghetto, 1797. Source: Art Critique.

2

Towards the Library of Exile

Edmund de Waal

I'll be talking about homecoming and homelessness. I start with an image of the ghetto in Venice (fig. 2.1), which is where we will end. But I want to take you on a different kind of journey about how I got to make a library and how I got to be in a ghetto.

This journey starts in West Norwood, a rather grotty but much-loved suburb of South London. When I go into my studio every day, there are two staircases I can take. One takes me up to a small and slightly monastic space, where I have my potter's wheel and a very uncomfortable bench which I have had since I was apprenticed almost forty years ago. I sit at this wheel, pick up one ball of white clay one after another, and make porcelain vessels. My clay comes from far away. It is migratory clay. It comes from Limoges. But porcelain clay is a different kind of long story, a different kind of migration, coming of course from China. It is a story of longing and belonging in itself. And I sit and iteratively make one vessel after another, often with the dog at my feet.

The other space that I go up to is a room full of books: piles of read, unread, to-be-read, re-read books, archival notes from all the way round the world from my travels, and shelves of shards, broken pieces of porcelain from my travels, things that I have stooped to pick up from the earth. Bits of clay, porcelain from Jingdezhen, from the Chinese mountains where porcelain was invented; broken shards of Meissen porcelain from Dresden; shards from the Cornish hillsides; shards that have been given to me; shards that I have found on my journey and other objects. In this shelf of stories in my studio are these small, tactile, hard, complicated, funny, erotic, beautiful ivory and wooden objects called *netsuke:* small Japanese sculptures made for the hands, made for touching, made for passing round, made for storytelling.

I was given this collection of tiny objects — "a very large collection of very small objects," as I put it in my book *The Hare with Amber Eyes* — by a beloved great-uncle in Japan, a Jewish Austro-Hungarian baron living in a flat in Tokyo. I inherited this collection of beautiful things twenty years ago, and I brought them back to London, and they sat in a vitrine in our flat in Camberwell in South London. And I realized that I had a choice to make: a choice whether to weave these objects from this beloved relative into anecdotes, or to try and work out what migratory story was embedded and en-storied in these objects. I talked to my wife Sue, and she said yes. I said it would take three months away from pottery to do the research.... It took me seven, biblical years. It was a story of how things get passed on.

This is a story of a Japanese collection, which begins in Odessa, with a Jewish family that was enormously, ridiculously, oligarchically, obscenely rich — who had cornered the market in grain in the nineteenth century — the Ephrussi family, my father's family. And like all good oligarchical dynastic Jewish families, they send their children out — in the middle of the nineteenth century — to conquer Europe, and to marry good Jewish girls. And half the family are sent to Paris, where they build a beautiful house in the Rue de Monceau, amongst other diasporic Jewish families. And the other half are sent to Vienna. And in the Paris house, there are children who become bankers. There's another son who becomes a lover of beautiful things and a lover of art, who collects extraordinary pictures by the Impressionists, is painted by Pierre-August Renoir, becomes friends with Marcel Proust, and collects small Japanese *netsuke,* to pass around in his salons. But he gets bored of this collection, and, in 1899, sends it as a wedding present to my great-grandfather, who is getting married in Vienna in a suitably grand house on the Ringstrasse. This is the house my father grows up in. It is a Ringstrasse Palais in Vienna 1899, gold encrusted ceilings, more naked nymphs on ceilings than you could believe possible. A house for a family of assimilated Jews who collect art, have an extraordinary collection and an enormous library, and are living in the greatest city in Europe, at the greatest moment there could possibly be. Every language is spoken in this house.

The four children grow up with English, French, German, they grow up with Spanish and they grow up with the classics. And they have the *netsuke* in a room in the Palais Ephrussi to play with, while their mother dresses to go out to balls. And the children run away, as children *should* run away. One gets married to a good Spanish banker, another runs away to America. My great-uncle Iggie doesn't want to become a banker. He's gay, and a fashion designer. He runs to America too, and my grandmother Elizabeth — literate, a friend of Rainer Marie Rilke — runs away to university, becomes a novelist, and marries and runs from Vienna. And you know what happens next, you know about the Anschluss, you know about the welcome given to the Nazis, the diaspora that happens, the destruction of the Jewish communities of Vienna. The house is broken into by the neighbors, one day after the Anschluss.

The Gestapo come the next day. The Kunsthistorisches Museum come the day after, and start cataloguing and dispossessing the family of their art collections. My great-grandfather Viktor — the great scholar in the family — sees his family's collection of books put on a truck, driven out from the Palais down the Ringstrasse, and disappear. My great-grandmother Emmy, seventy-five, is beaten up. My great-grandfather is arrested, and thrown into prison and threatened with Dachau. He signs away everything. And then begins the dispossession, the search for ways to exile and escape. Viktor finally makes it across the bor-

Fig. 2.2. Jewish boy is forced to write "Jew" on building's wall after the annexation of Austria by Nazi Germany, 1938. Source: Süddeutsche Zeitung Photo/Alamy Stock Photo.

der to Czechoslovakia with my great-grandmother — who commits suicide — and finally, finally, finally, this passport (fig. 2.3).

People become the documents of their longing. My great-grandfather, my grandmother, and my father arrive in England in May 1939: refugees with one suitcase. Viktor reads in front of a fire in Tunbridge Wells in their house and he recites *Lacrimae Rerum* — the great poems of Virgil — to my father. And he dies in Tunbridge Wells. Born in Odessa, childhood in Odessa, a student in Paris, becomes a citizen of the Austro-Hungarian Empire. A man who sees his wife die in Czechoslovakia, and he dies, and is buried in the crematorium outside Tunbridge Wells.

And after the war my grandmother goes back to Vienna, to a destroyed city, goes back to her house in the Palais on the Ringstrasse. And there is nothing there. There are no books. But she meets, there, her mother's maid Anna, who gives her back two hundred and sixty-four *netsuke,* which she hid away

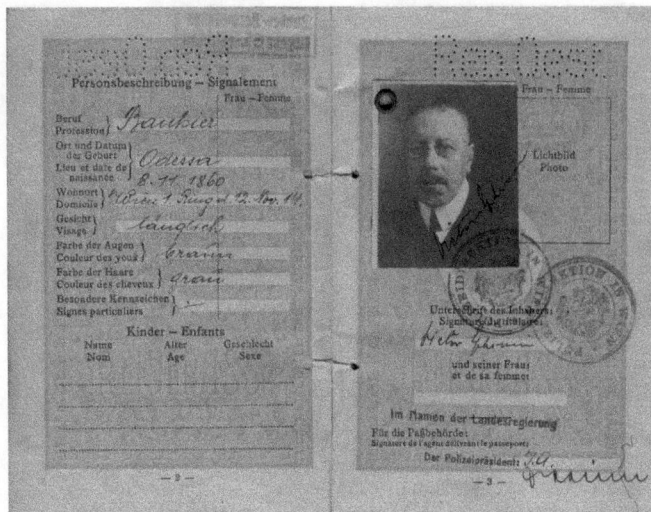

Fig. 2.3. Viktor de Waal's passport. Source: Edmund de Waal.

as the Gestapo ransacked the house. She has kept them secret from the art historians of the Kunsthistorisches Museum, who catalogued the rest of the collection, and sent it to Berlin, and to Goering: and she gives them back.

A small attaché case of stories, of objects, is brought back to England. And my great-uncle Iggie sees them on the kitchen table and says "I know what I'll do with them: I'll take them home." A man who could have lived anywhere looks at objects, and decides that the objects will take him home.

So in 1947, my great-uncle Iggie takes this *netsuke* collection and goes to Tokyo. There, he builds a house, and a vitrine, like the vitrine he remembers in Vienna.

And he meets his partner, Jiro, and they live together, and have very good dinner parties. And they open up their vitrines of *netsuke*. And there are storytellings like there were in Paris, in Rue de Monceau, and in the Ringstrasse. And when I arrive as a seventeen-year-old — having run away from school to become a potter — in Japan, because Japan is the potter's country, I end up on my great-uncle Iggie's doorstep. Jiro and Iggie open the door,

Fig. 2.4. Netsuke collection in Iggie de Waal's apartment. Source: Edmund de Waal.

and I'm given a huge hug, and a kiss, and a whisky sour. Iggie waves his hand at this vitrine, and says, "There's a story here...." Twenty years later, when I go and bury Jiro in the grave that he and Iggie had made for themselves in a Buddhist temple in Tokyo, and the Buddhist abbot recites the whole service of farewell, I say Kaddish for Iggie and for Jiro. Then I find that I have this whole suitcase to take home to London. So I write a book. And the book is about how you work out where you belong in the world; a book to try and connect storytelling, between one generation and another.

It's a book I write for my father, my father who is getting older. My father — who is a clergyman in the Church of England, who speaks with a strong Viennese accent, is Dean of Canterbury, but is Jewish — has never told us anything about Vienna. I decide that the only way that I can get my father to talk about what happened, and to talk to my children who are growing up, is to write a book and give it to him, and then tell him that he has the agency to say whether the book should be published or not. It's a very risky strategy, which I don't recommend to any of

Fig. 2.5. Iggie's apartment, Tokyo. Source: Edmund de Waal.

you! So I give Victor, my dad, this manuscript, and I don't hear from him for three days. Very long days. And then he rings me up, and he says, "it's OK," which is a big word.

So, you write a book, and it goes out into the world, and extraordinary things happen. Lots of connections and synapses in the world start to fire. And slowly, a diasporic family starts to talk. I get a phone call from Vienna. They have a temple, the Theseus Temple and it's on the Ringstrasse in Heldenplatz. Heldenplatz is a complicated place for anyone who has any Jewish ancestry. But it's a beautiful temple, and they do contemporary art installations, and it's my turn, they say. "Come and do something in Heldenplatz." So what I do is make an installation. I take a poem of Paul Celan called *Lichtzwang* (Light duress) — and I make two huge vitrines, with two hundred and sixty-four very small white vessels (fig. 2.6).

Celan haunts me. Celan has been part of my life since I sat having a conversation with Geoffrey Hill in 1983 about poetry, in his rooms in Emmanuel. He was a very wonderful man, and a very alarming man too. And he said "Why, Mr. de Waal, have you not read Paul Celan?" Celan is the great Romanian poet of

Fig. 2.6. Lichtzwang, installation view, 2014. © Edmund de Waal. Photo by Mike Bruce.

the German language, the great poet of the color white, the poet who breaks apart language, and puts it back together again, for whom poetry is exhortation and exhalation, who writes about white as the color of his mother's hair he will never see, and homecoming, and *Lichtswang*. And so I write the poem up on the walls, and for six months this is my way of being in Vienna. And then I go back and I make its pendant piece. Black porcelain, remembering the great black poem of Celan: *Todesfuge* (Death fugue). And then I get another phone call from Vienna. And this one is from the Kunsthistorisches Museum. So in these hallowed halls, what will I do in Vienna? I can't possibly choose my favorite things from these beautiful collections. It's a place haunted, haunted as the great epicenter for the looting and dispossession of the families of Vienna. And then I find this extraordinary watercolor by Dürer. It's an extraordinary picture of a nightmare. He writes during the night, "I was woken up between three and four, seeing the end of the world. I was utterly alone. I had no power. I saw the waters coming down. The waters rushing over me and I knew I had no power, no power in the world at all."[1] And when I saw this, I knew I had the centerpiece for my exhibition at the Kunsthistorisches Museum.

The exhibition was about nighttime in Vienna: I made an installation and called it *During the Night* and I chose all the objects in the museum that made me anxious. I chose images of shadows. I chose things from the Schatzkammer Corals, "Armedusa's Hair" in Renaissance early modern collecting. I chose images of "being looked at hard" and "things that keep poison away from you." I displayed them in almost total darkness and the critics hated my installation. But what I decided to do was to restitute anxiety back to Vienna. Because, actually, that's what objects can do. Objects aren't necessarily for your solace. Objects aren't necessarily just for the handing on of one benevolent story to another. They are also a way of re-energizing the force-field of history, and complicating it.

So I leave my exhibition there, in the Kunsthistorisches Museum.

And then I have one final demand from the museum — to close during the day, and open all night. Which we do. And in the watches of the night, all kinds of things happen. There are very strange liminal conversations that happen between objects, between memories, and between people. So I make an exhibition, which of course remembers all those difficult nights in Vienna. And in 2019 I sat with my family, my father and my children, and we decide there is one final act of restitution. We're not waiting for things to be given back to us; we're talking about restituting stories ourselves, taking stories back — which is what storytelling does. But with this beautiful and beloved collection, we're going to do two things. It is our inheritance — one hundred and forty-five years in the family. But we decide to sell part

---

1   Albrecht Dürer, *Traumgesicht* [Dream vision], 1525, Kunsthistorisches Museum Wien.

Fig. 2.7. psalm, The Jewish Museum, Venice, 2019 © Edmund de Waal.
Source: Edmund de Waal.

of this collection to raise money for unaccompanied minors in refugee camps. Some people write me letters saying, "How could you possibly, possibly do that?" And my answer is, "It's the right thing to do." But actually, collections are about passing things on, and making things happen. And so the other thing we do is to put the rest of the collection back in a briefcase, and take it to the Jewish Museum in Vienna.

That's how you work with a collection. And this takes me to the ghetto. Because for five years, I've been in conversation in this extraordinary, storied place. 1516 saw the establishment of the first ghetto: the walling up of the windows, the policing of the canals around the ghetto by Christian boats, the curfew bell, and then this extraordinary story of one community after another, a plural community from all over the Levant from North Africa, from all over Europe, being forced to live in this tiny space. I've been coming and going, and coming and going to the ghetto. Listening to its sonic atmosphere; trying to tune in to this particular place, and trying to work out what the ghetto means. My friends in the Jewish community in Venice don't talk about melancholy, don't talk about just stories of dispossession, but talk about the plurality of language, of literature, of music, of culture in this place. And so I ask, gently, whether or not I would be allowed to make a piece of work for them, for the synagogues in the ghetto. After five years of delicate, complicated, byzantine negotiation I start my project during the 58th Biennale, and it's called *psalm* (fig. 2.7).

The Psalms: because I've lived with the Psalms throughout my long Christian upbringing in cathedrals. The Psalms: because the Psalms are, and form, songs of exile, *Super flumina Babylonis:* "By the rivers of Babylon we sat down and wept." They travel with you wherever you go. All the Abrahamic religions have the Psalms.

So what I do is to make a series of installations in porcelain (try bringing porcelain to Venice, it's very complicated) and I make a project in two parts. You come in, go up these extraordinary dense staircases, and find a piece called *Adonai,* high up on a wall. *Adonai, Adonai, Adonai* — Lord, Lord, Lord. It's a tiny vitrine, with three things in it. A porcelain vessel: porcelain vessels are what I do. A piece of gold: gold is aura, and gold threads its way through the Psalms, and threads its way through the ghetto. And a piece of marble: because marble wasn't allowed in the synagogues. You could be Jewish, you could make your place of worship, but you could use no marble. I bring these three materials together into one, and call it *Adonai.* And then you turn the stair, and there's this piece which is based on an extraordinary poem — one of the extraordinary sonnets of Rilke. It's about waiting for God, waiting for the breath of God. It's a beautiful poem I've been living with all my life. And it's a series, you can just see it, on tiny slivers of porcelain, I've written "It's enough. It's enough. It's enough," in German. Bits of Rilke, fragments amongst the porcelain. And the light changes, and then you go up further into the gallery, just before you come into the canton Synagogue, which is five hundred years old. And here is

Fig. 2.8. tehillim, 2018. © Edmund de Waal. Photo by Mike Bruce.

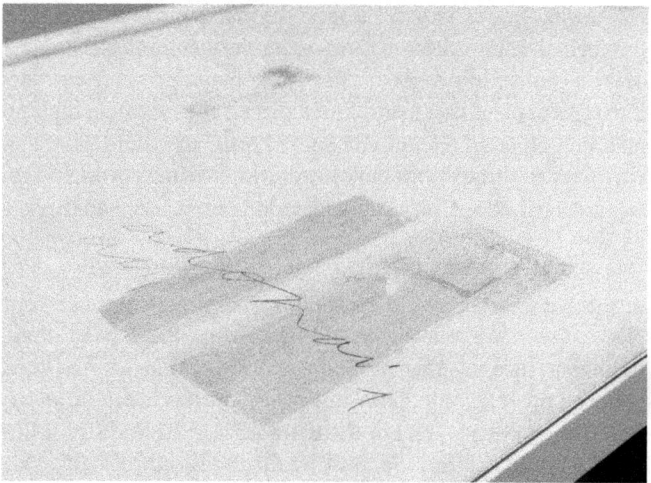

Fig. 2.9. a table for Sara Copio Sullam, 2019. © Edmund de Waal. Photo by Mike Bruce.

my piece, *tehillim* (psalm) (fig. 2.8). It's pieces of porcelain and pieces of gold, eleven vitrines one after another, after another.

It's a way of sounding porcelain. It's the thinnest porcelain I've ever made. There are no vessels. I've just taken clay, made it thinner, and thinner, and thinner, till it's "gold to airy thinness beat."[2]

This is the place where the psalms work, inside and outside of this incredibly beautiful sixteenth-century synagogue. You can sit there, and sit, and air comes in, and you can hear the sounds from the canals outside. And then you go further up, and there is one room where I've made a series of elegies: "Still beside me with your empty hands," poems of Mandelstam. Here are broken pieces of porcelain, because shards *matter*, fragments of poetry matter, you hold them together. And then I've made my first palimpsest. It's a table washed with porcelain. The text of Psalm 139 is written in Hebrew and in Latin, and in English, and then Latin on top, one layer of porcelain over another. *Tehillim*, written across the top. It's a table with gold, a table with porcelain, and it's a table for a wonderful Jewish writer, Sara Copio Sullam, who lived in the seventeenth century (fig. 2.9).

Finally, you go up to the highest room, and that's the sukkah. It's the space for the festival of Sukkot. The place where you celebrate the end of that extraordinary festival of being in transit, of being migratory, and you celebrate briefly this moment of bringing everyone together. And this is the *sukkah*, the highest space in the whole of the ghetto, with the prayers of the Sukkot all around you. And I've made another table, and nine tiny vitrines, which go up. Pieces of porcelain held very, very precariously here. And the light changes, and it is my way of talking about temporary shelter (Fig. 2.10).

And you look out of the window, and you remember that great short story by Rilke, about the elderly man in the ghetto in Venice, who wants to be moved higher and higher, and higher. He wants to see the sea. As he gets older, he's moved from one

---

2 John Donne, "A Valediction: Forbidding Mourning," in *The Complete Poems of John Donne*, ed. Robin Robbins (Routledge, 2010), 258.

Fig. 2.10. sukkah, installation view, 2019, The Jewish Museum, Venice. © Edmund de Waal. Photo by Fulvio Orsenigo.

room to another, and another, until finally, finally he can see the sea: and then he dies. So when you're in this room at the top topmost place, you're in this extraordinary space of looking down into the Campo di Ghetto Nuovo where there are all these kids playing football. And you remember there are all these extraordinary laws in the sixteenth century about not playing football on the Sabbath. And you remember all these extraordinary celebrations, and you hear voices, you hear all the plural languages that came together in the ghetto, not a place only of exclusion, but a place of plural language. You hear it, and that's why I made this piece, where all these things can sit together. And then finally, *psalm* in one place, but *psalm* somewhere else, across town, in the Ateneo Veneto. It's a beautiful sixteenth-century building, which was used as the place where condemned prisoners spent their last week. It's a place of another kind of liminality (fig. 2.11).

And this is where I've made my library — the library I promised you. It's a library of exile (figs. 2.12; 2.13).

Fig. 2.11. Ateneo Veneto, Venice. Photo by Edmund de Waal.

Fig. 2.12. library of exile, installation view, 2019, Ateneo Veneto, Venice.
© Edmund de Waal. Photo by Fulvio Orsenigo.

Fig. 2.13. library of exile, installation view, 2019, Ateneo Veneto, Venice. © Edmund de Waal. Photo by Fulvio Orsenigo.

You come in, and you see a small building. The walls are covered in porcelain slip — liquid porcelain. Around these walls I've written a text — a history of all the lost and destroyed libraries of the world (fig. 2.13).

It begins with Alexandria, but it goes through the lost Madrassah libraries, and Rabbinical libraries, the libraries of the Reformation and Counter-Reformation. It itemizes and anatomizes the book burnings. It goes through the whole of the twentieth century. Round the corner, I've written, "It is personal," and I've inscribed my grandfather's name for his destroyed, lost, looted, forgotten library in Vienna. I've written the haunting words of

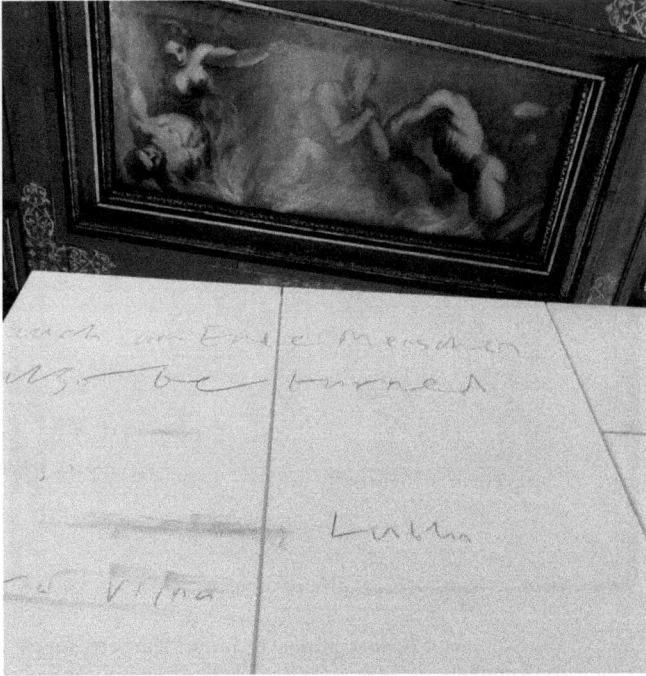

Fig. 2.14. library of exile, installation view, 2019, Ateneo Veneto, Venice. © Edmund de Waal. Source: Edmund de Waal.

Heinrich Heine, *"Auch am Ende Menschen"* ("Where there are books burned, in the end, people will also be burned") (fig. 2.14)[3]

Looking up after my inscriptions, I see this extraordinary image, unintentionally a conflagration above me. I have written the whole history, this threnody of loss, from Alexandria all the way through Sarajevo, and ending up with Mosul, with the destructions at Timbuktu and Mosul just that handful of years ago.

But you can't live with loss like this. It's not about melancholy, it's never about melancholy: melancholy destroys you, holds you

---

3   Heinrich Heine, "Almansor," in *Historisch-kritische Gesamtausgabe der Werke,* vol. 5, ed. Manfred Windfuhr (Hoffman und Campe, 1994), l. 244.

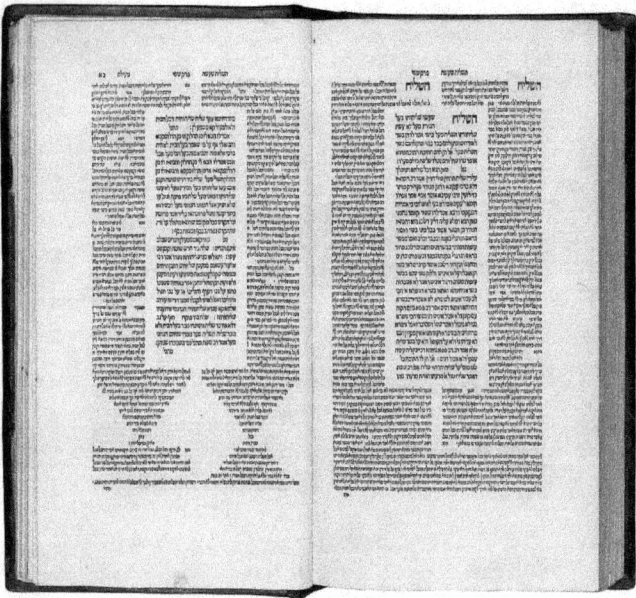

Fig. 2.15. The Babylonian Talmud, printed by Daniel Bomberg. Source: Wikimedia Commons.

viselike, and it makes you not work, preventing any agency in the world and leading you to nostalgia, which kills. So you go into the library of exile, and what do you find? You find four installations based on this great early printing by Daniel Bomberg, of the Talmud: the first printing of the Talmud done in Renaissance Venice, just one hundred yards away (fig. 2.15).

So I make four installations called *psalm,* where the holy word is suddenly left behind, and there are just empty spaces and shadows. And porcelain and marble take the place of commentary (figs. 2.16 and 2.17).

And these four installations sit in this space — and then? And then two thousand books, written by writers from Ovid onwards, two thousand years of exilic literature. Two thousand years of people, who have been forced across a border, who have been forced to flee.

Fig. 2.16. psalm, I, 2019. © Edmund de Waal. Photo by Mike Bruce.

So that when you go in, there are two thousand books, in eighty languages. And when you sit there, and reach down for a book, and open it up, you find that in every book it says "Ex libris – Library of Exile."

And you are invited to write your name in a book that matters to you. And I've seen so many people in tears, finding a book that matters to them, and being able to write their name, doing the things that you don't do in libraries: writing in the books. And I found that the book that has the most people claiming it in the whole of the library (we had two hundred people — one ex libris sticker on top of another) is Judith Kerr's *The Tiger Who Came to Tea* (fig. 2.19). Isn't that wonderful?

For three long months, we've had dozens and dozens of events there. We've had wonderful writers. We've had choreography, we've had music, we've had the Psalms day and night. We've

Fig. 2.17. library of exile, installation view, 2019, Ateneo Veneto, Venice. © Edmund de Waal. Source: Edmund de Waal.

had extraordinary encounters, we've had people leaving books on the doorstep, and it works. What works is the extraordinary experience of being alone in a library but being surrounded by voices, which is what libraries do. And it's my way of honoring that extraordinary moment, of crossing the threshold of the fact that actually, when we are surrounded by our books, *our* books, we're surrounded by people who have moved, that all language is diasporic, and the suggestions that have come in! There's this great big, wonderful table, where people tell us what we should be buying for the library. I hadn't budgeted for how many books I would have to buy. And it works not only because we have wonderful writers, but for the most marvelous reason of all: that it's not my library anymore. I set it going, and now it belongs elsewhere.

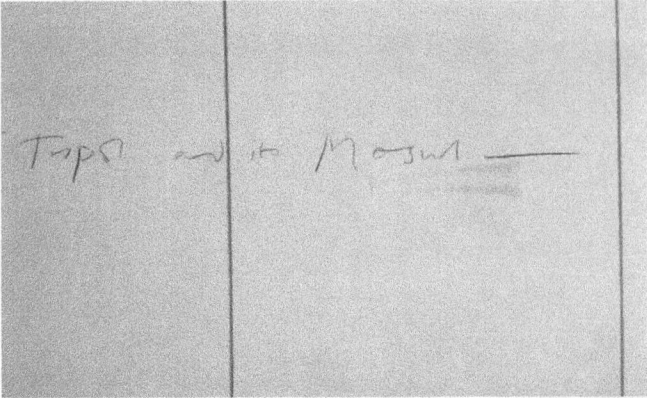

Fig. 2.18. library of exile, installation view, 2019, Ateneo Veneto, Venice. © Edmund de Waal. Source: Subha Mukherji.

So it's moving. From Venice, it moves in the winter to Dresden, it's going to occupy a place in the Japanisches Palais, where there was a great, great library destroyed in February 1945. It's going to Dresden at a difficult time for Dresden — with the toxic growth of the right-wing movement there. It's going to sit alongside a great room from Damascus that was brought in the nineteenth century; it will be near Damascus. Then in the Spring of 2020, it goes to the British Museum. And there's a huge program for writers, for children's groups, working with English PEN and other wonderful organizations. It's wonderful that it should be there. But the most moving thing of all is, that after it finishes, the panels on which I have inscribed the names of the lost libraries are being given to The Warburg Institute in London and the books are being given to Mosul, and are becoming the foundation of the new University Library of Mosul, which was destroyed by ISIS. It goes to the place where the Babylonian Talmud was written three thousand years ago, and it just tells you something about migrant knowledge. It tells you that you can't contain it, and that it goes on.

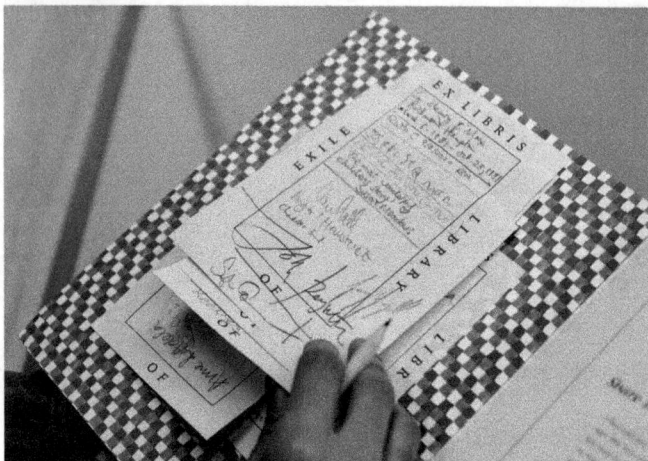

Fig. 2.19. library of exile, 2019, Ateneo Veneto, Venice. © Edmund de Waal. Source: Subha Mukherji.

Bibliography

Donne, John. *The Complete Poems of John Donne,* edited by Robin Robbins. Routledge, 2010.

Heine, Heinrich. *Historisch-kritische Gesamtausgabe der Werke.* Vol. 5. Edited by Manfred Windfuhr. Hoffman und Campe, 1994.

3

Response to Edmund de Waal

Gillian Beer

Edmund de Waal is a potter and a writer. One medium produces work that is stationary, its shape often enclosing hidden space; the other is implicitly narrative, sequential, migratory. But that is too simple a contrast between these two ways of being.

In this response to Edmund, I want briefly to connect his practice as a potter and as a writer in order to explore his passionate concern with exile and migration, destruction, and resurgence. Through his artistic practices he knows about loss and imperfection. He relishes shards and palimpsests. He is troubled by the history of porcelain, with its oppression of poor, working people and its association with wealth and dictatorships. The pure whiteness of the object has been produced by many marred lives. Yet he loves it. And we may love it too. His troubled feelings towards libraries are concentrated on their destruction, on the obliteration of past knowledge, the attacks on the experience of others. He is the champion of books and their power to embody lives and to sustain connection. He knows that the individual reader is part of a great unknown company of other readers across time and space.

Some of Edmund's work as a potter has been reserved—set high up in the ceiling at the Victoria and Albert Museum, and under a pavement vitrine at Sidgwick Avenue, Cambridge, both locations emphasizing the needs of eye and hand by denying their fulfilment. We long to touch pots. They are tactile objects, retaining the impression of human hands even when the maker may be absent or long dead. They are both plastic and immoveable. They have no legs. They do not move or migrate. But they can be set in relation to other pots, in clusters or distanced, tracing a kind of narrative, not linear but associative. And that clustering is one of the special features of Edmund's later work. New stories may flicker out from these nests or lines or ellipses.

Edmund has discovered implicit narratives among pots, through grouping and assembling, through spacing and distancing. These are shadow narratives, unstable because reliant on a hand to dispose them, and always capable of being rearranged by other hands into other meanings. This expresses affinity to writing, which is always reliant on being read, and which means anew in changed places and circumstances. The tiny Japanese *netsuke* given to Edmund by his uncle carry generations of family history for him, which he has opened to others of us through his writing and travels.

On the face of it, migration may seem then to be almost the opposite of ceramics. Pots can be carried but they are friable and may be among the first victims of travel. So Edmund's ambition to make a moving library composed of pots as well as books may seem quixotic. Scale may determine what survives. Very small squat objects like the beautiful *netsuke* can safely carry the almost obliterated memories of family members long dead. But their survival depended on human hands, on the housekeeper who hid them from the Nazis. In *The Hare with Amber Eyes* Edmund rediscovered, through travel and archives and writing, the profound and the contingent connections between people alive in the past and in the present, in books and in ceramics. He and his family have now sold half their collection of *netsuke* in aid of refugees, bringing a new phase of migration, and an emphatic real-world outcome, to the current story of these objects.

The event Migrant Knowledge, Early Modern and Beyond and Edmund's contribution to it took place in 2019. Over a longer time, his library of exile has moved across the world to lodge briefly at the British Museum and to experience the lockdown. So much has happened in these intervening months: Black Lives Matter, presidential insurrection in the USA, the pandemic which involves us all worldwide. During the current pandemic, Edmund's new ceramics have opened out into platters with low surrounding walls and a dark stripe of an insignia. Instead of a cloistered and inviolable inner space to which access must be denied if the pot is to remain unbroken, we now have work that lays itself bare to the eye. This is the artist's migration: it moves within and alongside events without being simply a commentary on them. It makes new.

III.

Essays

4

Travel Writing, Poetics, and the Early Modern Knowledge Economy

Natalya Din-Kariuki

The rise of travel and travel writing in early modern England precipitated an epistemological crisis. In presenting, or, at least, claiming to present new knowledge about the world, travelers' writings catalyzed debates about how knowledge should be defined, produced, and disseminated.[1] Fundamental to these debates was a distinction, one made especially explicitly by humanist pedagogues evaluating the educational benefits of foreign travel, between eyewitness "experience" and "book knowledge."[2] But the language of these debates is misleading: in practice, the distinction between "experience" and "book knowledge" was not quite so clear cut. This is because travelers often set textual witnesses — including the writings of other

---

1   An important volume on early modern travel and knowledge is Ivo Kamps and Jyotsna G. Singh, eds., *Travel Knowledge: European "Discoveries" in the Early Modern Period* (Palgrave, 2001).

2   For discussions of these debates, see Sara Warneke, *Images of the Educational Traveller in Early Modern England* (E.J. Brill, 1995), 41–104, and Melanie Ord, *Travel and Experience in Early Modern English Literature* (Palgrave Macmillan, 2008), 29–56.

travelers, works of natural philosophy and natural history, poetry, drama, ancient literature, and scripture — alongside their own eyewitness observations.

Early modern travel writing thus offers an especially striking illustration of migrant knowledge: knowledge which begins in one place and ends up in another, crossing geographical, historical, cultural, and textual borders along the way. It is also a migrant form, one produced through processes of textual allusion, citation, revision, and borrowing which transport ancient and vernacular texts across the globe, and, in so doing, transform them.[3] In what follows I examine two examples of such migrancy in seventeenth-century English travel writing. Although the travelers I discuss journeyed to different parts of the world and for different purposes, both turned to the affordances of literary form to understand and describe their experiences. By showing that travelers wrote in a self-consciously literary fashion, employing strategies drawn from rhetoric and poetics, I want to demonstrate the reciprocity of empirical and humanist modes of knowing as well as broaden the scope of what we understand early modern "literature" to comprise.

My first example is Henry Blount, author of an account on the Ottoman Empire titled *A Voyage into the Levant* (1636).[4] The purpose of Blount's travel is not certain, though it is possible that

---

3   I borrow the concept of "migrant form" from Subha Mukherji, in private conversation about ongoing work. She also discusses it at further length in the Introduction to this book.

4   For Blount's biography, see John Aubrey, *Brief Lives: with, An Apparatus for the Lives of our English Mathematical Writers*, ed. Kate Bennett, vol. 1 (Oxford University Press, 2015), 336–39; Nabil Matar, *Oxford Dictionary of National Biography*, s.v. "Blount, Sir Henry (1602–1682), traveller," https://www.oxforddnb.com/display/10.1093/ref:odnb/9780198614128.001.0001/odnb-9780198614128-e-2687; and Gerald MacLean, *The Rise of Oriental Travel: English Visitors to the Ottoman Empire, 1580–1720* (Palgrave Macmillan, 2004), 117–22. The following paragraphs draw on Natalya Din-Kariuki, "Reading the Ottoman Empire: Intertextuality and Experience in Henry Blount's *Voyage into the Levant* (1636)," *The Review of English Studies*, 74, no. 313 (2023): 47–63.

he was a spy.[5] He had interests in natural philosophy, and later became a member of the Royal Society.[6] In his introduction, Blount considered the relative merits of "travell"and "booke knowledge." He began by noting that "Intellectual Complexions have no desire so strong, as that of *knowledge*," and claimed that knowledge is best attained through eyewitnessing: because the eye has "the most immediate, and quicke commerce with the soule," an "eyewitness of things conceives them with an *imagination* more compleat, strong, and intuitive, then he can either apprehend, or deliver by way of relation." Travelling, and attaining an "ocular view," thus gives a better "impression" of things than reading accounts by others, which are like "dishes" better suited for "another mans stomacke." This is because the eye is selective: a traveler observes things that "his owne apprehension affects" and will "digest" these things into "experience" in a way that is most natural to him. By the same token, however, the mind is inclined to error; it tends to rely on existing knowledge, and to use its own, often flawed, perceptions as its main point of reference. Like a "false glasse," it represents objects in "colours, and proportions untrue," leaving the eye "dazled." To mitigate this, the traveler must come to places in a manner "fresh and sincere," judging other places on their own terms.[7] Blount ended these remarks by presenting the *Voyage into the Levant* as lines "registred to my selfe," intended to help him remember his travels in future.[8]

This passage borrows silently, but extensively, from Michel de Montaigne's essay "Of Experience," in John Florio's transla-

---

5 See MacLean, *The Rise of Oriental Travel*, 120, 128–29, 153, 158–59, 160, and 166.

6 See Esmond Samuel de Beer, "The Earliest Fellows of the Royal Society," *Notes and Records of the Royal Society of London* 7, no. 2 (1950): 190.

7 "Sincere" did not have its stable modern sense in this period. It connoted things that were clean, pure, unadulterated, or, relatedly, individuals lacking in dissimulation or pretense. See *OED*, s.v. "sincere, adj."

8 Henry Blount, *A Voyage into the Levant* (I.L. for Andrew Crooke, 1636), 3–4.

tion.[9] The opening of the *Voyage into the Levant* is a paraphrase
of the opening of Montaigne's essay, itself a paraphrase of the
opening of Aristotle's *Metaphysics*: "There is no desire more
naturall, then that of knowledge."[10] Blount shares Montaigne's
emphasis on experience, and, like him, understands experience
in Aristotelian terms, as an accumulation of memories.[11] His
commitment to recording his observations for memory paral-
lels Montaigne's conception of his essays as loose "memorialles,"
a record of past experience, while his use of the language of di-
gestion recalls the earlier writer's presentation of his writing as
"digested." The term "register," in Blount's "lines registred to my
selfe," is particularly important for Montaigne, who describes
his essays both as a register of self-knowledge, and as a mode of
coming to it. Blount thus positions the *Voyage* as another kind
of essay, in which the traveler's "selfe" is placed under scrutiny.

Nor is this the only borrowing in Blount's introduction. The
metaphor of the mind as a "false glasse" is ancient and conventional, but its formulation in the Voyage into the Levant is specifically indebted to Francis Bacon's *Advancement of Learning*.[12]
Here, Bacon explains that the mind "is farre from the Nature of
a cleare and equall glasse, wherein the beames of things should
reflect according to their true incidence." Rather, it is "like an

---

9   Michel de Montaigne, "Of Experience," in *The Essayes or Morall, Politike
    and Millitarie Discourses*, trans. John Florio (Val. Sims for Edward Blount,
    1603), 633.

10 Aristotle, "Metaphysics," trans. W.D. Ross, in *The Complete Works of Aris-
    totle: The Revised Oxford Translation*, vol. 2, ed. Jonathan Barnes (Prince-
    ton University Press, 1995), 980a15–16. For a discussion of Montaigne's
    engagement with Aristotle in "Of Experience," see Kathryn Murphy, "The
    Anxiety of Variety: Knowledge and Experience in Montaigne, Burton and
    Bacon," in *Fictions of Knowledge: Fact, Evidence, Doubt*, ed. Yota Batsaki,
    Subha Mukherji, and Jan-Melissa Schramm (Palgrave Macmillan, 2012).

11 Aristotle, "Metaphysics," 981a6–7, 981a13f.

12 For more general discussions of Blount's Baconianism, see MacLean, *The
    Rise of Oriental Travel*, 120, 123, 130, 134–35, 140, 165, and 176, and Gerald
    MacLean, *Looking East: English Writing and the Ottoman Empire before
    1800* (Palgrave Macmillan, 2007), 180. This language also has important
    biblical precedents, such as 1 Corinthians 13:12, and James 1:23–25.

inchanted glasse," predisposed to yield "false appearances."[13] Bacon employs this conceit elsewhere, including the *Novum organum,* where he uses it in reference to the "Idols of the Tribe." One of four "Idols of the Mind," the categories of error to which the mind is prone, the Idols of the Tribe represent the misguided assumption that human sense is the ultimate "measure of things." The intellect, Bacon says, is "to the rays of things like an uneven mirror which mingles its own nature with the nature of things, and distorts and stains it"; this unevenness can be attributed largely to the "dullness, inadequacy and unreliability of the senses," including sight.[14] Bacon's Idols are designed to help his readers to avoid or diminish the "false notions" which entrap the mind and, in so doing, to get closer to the truth.[15] Blount's understanding of the mind as false yet salvageable is in sympathy with Bacon's project.

Blount's introduction develops a philosophical account of experience and prepares the reader for the travel observations that follow. Yet this account is paradoxical: Blount asserts the necessity of eyewitness in the context of literary borrowing; his argument against "booke knowledge" is constructed through books.[16] The knowledge of the Ottoman Empire that he produces is inflected by his engagements with Aristotelian metaphysics, Florio's translation of Montaigne, and Baconian natural philosophy. It migrates between ancient Greece and early modern France, England, and the Levant, as well as between forms, crossing from the essay to the aphorism.

My second example comes from the writings of Edward Terry, who served as chaplain to Sir Thomas Roe at the Mughal

---

13 Francis Bacon, *Advancement of Learning,* in *The Oxford Francis Bacon,* vol. 4, ed. Michael Kiernan (Clarendon Press, 2000), 116.

14 Francis Bacon, *Novum organum,* in *The Oxford Francis Bacon,* vol. 11, ed. Graham Rees with Maria Wakely (Clarendon Press, 2004), 80–81.

15 Ibid., 79.

16 For a relevant discussion of Blount's engagement with his reading, see Eva Johanna Holmberg, "Avoiding Conflict in the Early Modern Levant: Henry Blount's Adaptations in Ottoman Lands," in *Travel and Conflict in the Early Modern World,* ed. Gabór Gelléri and Rachel Willie (Routledge, 2020).

court of Jahangir in 1616–1619.[17] Terry published an account of his experiences in India titled *A Voyage to East-India* (1655). In it, he acknowledged the "very great space of time 'twixt the particulars then observed, and their publication now," but insisted that "those remote parts," that is, India, have changed little in the intervening years; the reader should thus "look upon" his observations as if they had "been taken notice of, but immediately before it was here communicated." However, he added that the "Original Copie" of the account had been revised, and now included lengthy digressions on matters of scripture, "Divine truths that lie scattered up and downe in manie places of this Narrative" intended to capture those "who fly from a sermon, and will not touch sound, wholesome, and excellent treatises in divinity." As they travel through these pages, Terry says, readers will experience the "passage to East India" and be "brought [...] thither on shore" to "see" and "behold" the "riches and splendour" of Jahangir's court, as well as unexpected displays of "temperance, justice, and unwearied devotion" by "Pagans and Mahometans" alike, sights that should prompt Christians to "turn their eyes inward" to examine the depth of their own faith. For this reason, he says, he has designed the book "like a well form'd picture, that seems to look stedfastly upon everie beholder, who so looks upon it."[18]

Terry conceives of his writing in visual and topographical terms and relocates his observations from a position of spatial

17 For Terry's biography, see Michael Strachan, *Oxford Dictionary of National Biography*, s.v. "Terry, Edward (1589/90–1660), travel writer," https://www.oxforddnb.com/display/10.1093/ref:odnb/9780198614128.001.0001/odnb-9780198614128-e-27148. For Roe's own account of the embassy, see Thomas Roe, *The Embassy of Sir Thomas Roe to India 1615–19: As Narrated in His Journal and Correspondence*, ed. William Foster (Munshiram Manoharlal, 1990). For a study of Roe's embassy which discusses Terry, see Nandini Das, "'Apes of Imitation': Imitation and Identity in Sir Thomas Roe's Embassy to India," in *A Companion to the Global Renaissance: English Literature and Culture in the Era of Expansion*, ed. Jyotsna G. Singh (Wiley-Blackwell, 2009).
18 Edward Terry, *A Voyage to East-India* (T.W. for J. Martin, and J. Allestrye, 1655), sigs. A2r-A6v (unpaginated).

and temporal alterity to the "here" and "now," inviting the reader
to "see" and "behold" the scenes described. At the same time,
he makes it clear that they must carry out the most important
part of the journey themselves: the contemplative turn "inward"
that translates sight into insight. He thus positions the *Voyage to
East-India* as a spiritual exercise that reveals as much about its
author as it does about "everie beholder." Terry's conception of
the travel account as an extension of his ministry is made most
explicit in his reference to those "who fly from a sermon." This
phrase is an adaptation of a line in George Herbert's poem "The
Church-porch," which declares, "A verse may finde him, who a
sermon flies, / And turn delight into a sacrifice."[19] The connection to Herbert is reinforced by Terry's title page, which, like
Herbert's poem, recalls the Horatian sense of the poet's duty to
profit and delight by noting that the account of the voyage is
"Mix't with some Parallel Observations and inferences upon the
storie, to profit as well as delight the *Reader*." Terry thus makes a
claim for travel writing analogous to that which Herbert makes
for poetry: namely, that it has the potential to do the work typi-
cally performed by a sermon.

As we have seen, Terry claims that his digressions offer "Divine truths."[20] He specifically linked them to "application." "Application" is a technical term from preaching for the part of the
sermon in which the preacher explained the relevance of his
chosen scriptural text to the present auditory, helping them to
understand how they might apply it to their own lives. As Terry
explains in a sermon preached in 1646: "The life of Preaching is

---

19 George Herbert and Nicholas Ferrar, *The Temple: Sacred Poems and Private Ejaculations. By Mr. George Herbert.* (Thom. Buck and Roger Daniel,
1633), 1. These lines were widely quoted and adapted in the 1650s, during a
revival of interest and investment in Herbert who represented a version of
the English Church for which suppressed Anglicans were nostalgic.

20 For further discussions of Terry's digressive style, see Daniel Carey,
"Edward Terry's *A Voyage to East-India* (1655): A Chaplain's Narrative of
the Mughal World," *Études Anglaises* 70, no. 2 (2017): 200, and Richard
Raiswell, "Edward Terry and the Calvinist Geography of India," *Études
Anglaises* 70, no. 2 (2017): 167–86.

application, and the life of Application, is the applying of truths to our particular selves," "bringing home" the truths heard in the course of the sermon.[21] Terry first established a connection between application and his experiences in India in a sermon delivered to the merchants of the East India Company at St. Andrewes Undershaft in London in 1649, published the same year under the title *The Merchants and Mariners Preservation and Thanksgiving.* In this sermon, which was occasioned by the safe return of seven ships belonging to the East India Company, Terry applied Psalm 107:30–31 (one verse of which reads, in the King James Version that Terry was drawing on, "Then are they glad because they be quiet; so he brings them to their desired Haven") to the merchants' experiences of deliverance from the dangers of the sea, what Terry describes as a "Tempest." The sermon achieves a conventional preacher's goal (applicability) through unconventional means, adapting the tropes and conventions of travel writing — specifically, giving the circumstantial details of his journey including distance, climate, as well as reference to a specific person, the diplomat Thomas Roe — to a different generic context.[22]

Terry's sermon to the East India Company, which turns the auditory of a London church into virtual witnesses of India, thus anticipates the strategies he employs in the *Voyage to East-India.* As in the sermon, Terry analogizes his travel experience and the words of scripture. For example, in the section on "Soyl," Terry moves from a description of India's agriculture and husbandry to a rather problematic denouncement of the Indians' pride. Their pride, he says, is the reason that no *"Exhortations, Intreaties, Perswasions,"* not even the "strongest Arguments," will succeed in saving their souls. Quoting from Psalm 73:6, *"their Pride [...] compasseth them as a Chain,"* he concludes, "I would intreat my *Reader,* when he comes to this digression, to read it

---

21 Edward Terry, *Pseudeleutheria. Or Lawlesse Liberty* (Thomas Harper, 1646), 26. Emphasis in original.

22 Edward Terry, *The Merchants and Mariners Preservation and Thanksgiving* (Thomas Harper, 1649), 8–9, and 26.

over and over again."[23] By placing the psalm text within a highly localized passage, on foreign "Soyl" in more senses than one, Terry makes an implicit argument for its global, and eternal, applicability, while the request to the reader to return to this part of the text "over and over again" anticipates a reading experience both contemplative and iterative, analogous to the practice of a listener repeating the "use" of a sermon to themselves at home. Combining the topical approaches of preaching and travel writing, these texts enable his listeners and readers to experience India vicariously, and, by attending to Terry's digressions on scripture, to come to know God.

As the examples of Blount and Terry show, the opposition of "experience" and "book knowledge" which structured debates about travel in the early modern period does not hold in travel writing itself. Travelers' eyewitness experience is shaped, both structurally and conceptually, by textual witnesses, and when they journeyed across the world, they took their books in unexpected directions. These literary engagements, which situate works such as Aristotle's *Metaphysics* and George Herbert's collection *The Temple* in new geographical, cultural, and generic settings, reveal that travel writing is an inherently migrant genre, one which familiarizes the strange and estranges the familiar, transforming and retheorizing knowledge as it crosses borders.

---

23 Terry, *A Voyage to East-India,* 108–9. Emphases in original.

Bibliography

Aristotle. *The Complete Works of Aristotle: The Revised Oxford Translation,* Volume. 2. Edited by Jonathan Barnes. Translated by I. Bywater, L.D. Dowdall, E.S. Forster, H.H. Joachim, B. Jowett, F.G. Kenyon, T. Loveday, W. Rhys Roberts, W.D. Ross, J. Solomon, St.G. Stock, and J.O. Urmson. Princeton University Press, 1995.

Aubrey, John. *Brief Lives: with, An Apparatus for the Lives of our English Mathematical Writers,* Volume 1. Edited by Kate Bennett. Oxford University Press, 2015.

Bacon, Francis. *Advancement of Learning.* In *The Oxford Francis Bacon,* Volume 4, edited by Michael Kiernan. Clarendon Press, 2000.

——. *Novum organum.* In *The Oxford Francis Bacon,* Volume 11, edited by Graham Rees with Maria Wakely. Clarendon Press, 2004.

de Beer, Esmond Samuel. "The Earliest Fellows of the Royal Society." *Notes and Records of the Royal Society of London* 7, no. 2 (1950): 172–92. DOI: 10.1098/rsnr.1950.0014.

Blount, Henry. *A Voyage into the Levant: A Briefe Relation of a Journey, Lately Performed by Master H.B. Gentleman, from England by the Way of Venice, into Dalmatia, Sclavonia, Bosnah, Hungary, Macedonia, Thessaly, Thrace, Rhodes and Egypt, unto Gran Cairo.* I.L. for Andrew Crooke, 1636.

Carey, Daniel. "Edward Terry's *A Voyage to East-India* (1655): A Chaplain's Narrative of the Mughal World." *Études Anglaises* 70 no. 2 (2017): 187–208. DOI: 10.3917/etan.702.0187.

Das, Nandini. "'Apes of Imitation': Imitation and Identity in Sir Thomas Roe's Embassy to India." In *A Companion to the Global Renaissance: English Literature and Culture in the Era of Expansion,* edited by Jyotsna G. Singh. Wiley-Blackwell, 2009.

De Montaigne, Michel. "Of Experience." In *The Essayes or Morall, Politike and Millitarie Discourses,* translated by John Florio. Val. Sims for Edward Blount, 1603.

Din-Kariuki, Natalya. "Reading the Ottoman Empire: Intertextuality and Experience in Henry Blount's *Voyage into the Levant* (1636)." *The Review of English Studies* 74, no. 313 (2023): 47–63. DOI: 10.1093/res/hgac062.

Herbert, George, and Nicholas Ferrar. *The Temple: Sacred Poems and Private Ejaculations. By Mr. George Herbert.* Thom. Buck and Roger Daniel, 1633.

Holmberg, Eva Johanna. "Avoiding Conflict in the Early Modern Levant: Henry Blount's Adaptations in Ottoman Lands." In *Travel and Conflict in the Early Modern World,* edited by Gabór Gelléri and Rachel Willie. Routledge, 2020.

Kamps, Ivo, and Jyotsna G. Singh, eds. *Travel Knowledge: European "Discoveries" in the Early Modern Period.* Palgrave, 2001.

MacLean, Gerald. *Looking East: English Writing and the Ottoman Empire before 1800.* Palgrave Macmillan, 2007.

———. *The Rise of Oriental Travel: English Visitors to the Ottoman Empire, 1580–1720.* Palgrave Macmillan, 2004.

Murphy, Kathryn. "The Anxiety of Variety: Knowledge and Experience in Montaigne, Burton and Bacon." In *Fictions of Knowledge: Fact, Evidence, Doubt,* edited by Yota Batsaki, Subha Mukherji, and Jan-Melissa Schramm. Palgrave Macmillan, 2012.

Ord, Melanie. *Travel and Experience in Early Modern English Literature.* Palgrave Macmillan, 2008.

Raiswell, Richard. "Edward Terry and the Calvinist Geography of India." *Études Anglaises* 70, no. 2 (2017): 167–86. https://shs.cairn.info/article/E_ETAN_702_0167?lang=en.

Roe, Thomas. *The Embassy of Sir Thomas Roe to India 1615–19: As Narrated in his Journal and Correspondence.* Edited by William Foster. Munshiram Manoharlal, 1990.

Terry, Edward. *A Voyage to East-India. Wherein Some Things Are Taken Notice of in Our Passage Thither, But Many More in Our Abode There, Within That Rich and Most Spacious Empire of the Great Mogol. Mix't with Some Parallel Observations and Inferences upon the Storie, to Profit As Well As Delight the Reader. Observed by Edward Terry Minister* of the Word (Then Student of Christ-Church in Oxford, and Chaplain to the Right Honorable Sr. Thomas Row Knight, Lord Ambassadour to the Great Mogol) Now Rector of the Church at Greenford, in the Country of Middlesex. T.W. for J. Martin, and J. Allestrye, 1655.

————. Pseudeleutheria. Or Lawless Liberty.: Set forth in a Sermon Preached before the Right Honourable the Lord Mayor of London, &c. in Pauls, Aug. 16. 1646. Thomas Harper, 1646.

————. The Merchants and Mariners Preservation and Thanksgiving. Or, Thankfulnesse Returned, for Mercies Received: Set Forth in a Sermon of Thanksgiving, Preached at S. Andrewes Undershaft, Sept. 6. 1649. To the R. Worshipfull, the Committee of Merchants, Trading for the Eastern India, upon a Late Return of Seven of Their Ships Together. By Edvvard Terry, Minister of the Word, (Who Was Sometime in Their Service, There) Now Rector of the Church of Great-Greenford, in the County of Middlesex. Octob. 4. 1649. Imprimatur. John Downame. Thomas Harper, 1649.

Warneke, Sara. Images of the Educational Traveller in Early Modern England. E.J. Brill, 1995.

5

"Loitering Lusks and Lazy Lorels": Poverty, Vagrancy, and the Invention of Roguery

Anupam Basu

I

Mobility is in many ways one of the defining concerns of the early modern period. The early history of printed social and religious commentary was rife with caveats, trumpet blasts, admonitions, and dire warnings about the imminent and precipitous danger posed by people who are in some way or other *out of place*. In sumptuary laws and courtesy books, in formal church courts and informal networks of gossip, early modern social structures were deeply invested in reifying subjectivity as intimately and intrinsically connected to social position. From social upstarts who aspire for more than is their due, to uppity women who spill over the thresholds of domesticity, forms of dangerous mobility — social, economic, spatial, and semiotic — were imagined to pose a threat to the social fabric and at times the very foundation of the commonwealth. While a wide range of texts and genres including jests, ballads, pamphlets, sermons, and plays articulated concerns about mobility, the genre of pamphlet literature popularly called the "rogue pamphlets" dealt with migration, vagrancy, and homelessness in its most explicit form.

The genre arose out of the social and economic turmoil of the sixteenth century when a multiplicity of factors converged to cause an unprecedented displacement of people. These factors ranged from the Reformation and the abolition of monasteries, to the enclosure of the commons and agrarian reform, and extended further afield to the rise of exploration, overseas trade, and colonialism. Changing relations to land, new forms of labor, and a gradual desanctification of poverty led to the development of the first English poor laws and the poor relief system, as well as widespread cultural anxiety about vagrants. Significantly, while there was a rise in the number of vagrants, the perceived threat from mobile and homeless people as well as the cultural *fascination* with them was much more than the legal records from the period would justify.[1] Rogue pamphlets purportedly set out to warn readers about the devious ways of vagrants, such as their talent for disguise and their ability to mimic the "deserving poor." But such cautionary tales frequently ended up as comic capers where the shrewd criminal becomes a sort of anti-hero. Straddling the boundary between the stark objectivity of social documentary and the merry abandon of jests, rogue literature signals the early modern period's deep discomfort with mobility that coexisted with a fascination for the malleable, versatile figure of the vagrant — slipping in and out of social roles and economic positions as easily as they moved from place to place.

In this essay I want to read one of the most representative and popular pamphlets of the genre, Thomas Harman's, *A Caveat for Common Cursitors, Vulgarly Called Vagabonds,* to ask what ideological work this fascination with the literary representation of mobility performs. Harman organized the community of rogues and vagabonds into twenty-four categories. He took care to describe what kind of crime each type of rogue spe-

---

1 A.L. Beier, *Masterless Men: The Vagrancy Problem in England, 1560–1640* (Methuen, 1985), 123–26.

cializes in and their position in a supposed hierarchy of vagrant criminals. Further, he affixed a long list of "The Names of the Upright Men, Rogues and Palliards"[2] to his book along with a glossary of the "lewd, lousy language of these loitering lusks and lazy lorels,"[3] also known as "cant" or "Pedlar's French." These features indicate a preoccupation with cataloging and classification that has an affinity with the emergence of the criminal's body as a site of knowledge that we see in the penal practices of the period as well. However, the categorization of rogues is not specific to Harman's text but a feature of the genre as a whole. The *Liber vagatorum,* known in English as *The Book of Vagabonds and Beggars,* was one of the earliest works to introduce some of these familiar themes. Its organization exactly foreshadowed Harman's.

Harman's project on the other hand was predicated on a radically different notion of vagrancy as not only a physically itinerant condition but also a subjectivity that was inherently mobile and malleable. His text was not an extension of a project of penal semiotics designed to physically mark and control, but in fact presented a deep-seated and sustained critique of such a project. Branding or other physical mutilation — such as having one's ear cut off, or being scarred by the whip — or the social stigma associated with being "drawn at a cart's arse," or being put in the stocks were described in many contemporary laws, impressive not only in their precision but also in their emphasis on the significance or meaning of such punishment. For example, the act of 1572 prescribed for the able-bodied poor who did not seek work, "he or shee shalbe adjudged to bee grevouslye whipped and burnte through the gristle of the right Eare with a hot Yron of the compasse of an Ynche about, manifestinge his or

2   Thomas Harman, "A Caveat or Warning for Common Cursitors, Vulgarly Called Vagabonds," in *Cony-Catchers and Bawdy Baskets: An Anthology of Elizabethan Low Life,* ed. Gāmini Salgādo (Penguin, 1972), 140.

3   Ibid., 146.

her rogyshe kynde of Lyef."[4] The mark in this case becomes an external sign, a manifestation of one's criminality.

The *Caveat's* treatment of punishment differs markedly from such penal mechanisms. Unlike his meticulous detailing of the categories, methods, names, and language of vagabonds, Harman made no concerted attempt to describe the punishments that rogues and vagabonds might be subjected to. Punishments are only mentioned in passing, often to point out the failure of penal techniques to control vagabonds. The poem at the end of the pamphlet begins:

> A stocks to stay sure, and safely detain
> Lazy lewd loiterers, that laws do offend,
> Impudent persons, thus punished with pain,
> Hardly for all this, do mean to amend.[5]

Futhermore, Harman said of upright-men, one of the highest kinds of rogues in the hierarchy that he describes:

> These, not minding to get their living with the sweat of their face, but casting off all pain, will wander, after their wicked manner, through the most shires of this realm, [...] Yea, not without punishment by stocks, whippings, and imprisonment. Yet notwithstanding, they have so good liking in their lewd, lecherous loitering, that full quickly all their punishment is forgotten. And repentance is never thought upon, until they climb three trees with a ladder.[6]

Punishments only attempt to contain or confine vagabonds in particular locations (the stocks or the prison), or mark them (whipping), but were forgotten "full quickly." Hanging is the only form of punishment that Harman found effective. He went

---

4 "14 Eliz. c.3," in *The Statutes of the Realm,* vol. 4: *1547–1624* (Dawsons of Pall Mall, 1965), 591.

5 Harman, "A Caveat or Warning for Common Cursitors," 151.

6 Ibid., 117.

on to describe the formulaic speeches of repentance at the gallows. Such speeches were often represented in chapbooks and broadsheets and widely circulated, often in a modified and idealized form. The vagabond in the final poem, unaffected by all other forms of punishment, at last goes repenting to his death. An accompanying woodcut shows the execution with the gallows in the distance and a criminal with his hands tied being led towards it by the hangman while a crowd looks on. Harman's limitation of the possibility of repentance only to the absolute case of death by hanging, and his emphasis on its absence from all other forms of punishment, seems to suggest that he saw repentance as a means to an inward or ethical transformation.

This transformation is essentially a mis-recognition of a socioeconomic problem as an ethical one. The conception of vagabondage and poverty as the result of an unfixed, malleable subjectivity and moral corruption produced and conditioned the inattention towards vagabondage and poverty as a social problem. The *Caveat* proposed a notion of moral corruption as the cause of vagrancy in a way that foreclosed its emergence as an economic problem.

II

The case of Nicholas Blunt alias Nicholas Genings illustrates the limits of penal semiotics as an effective form of control, and of its incommensurability with Harman's conception of rogue subjectivity as inherently mobile. It is the most prominent instance in Harman and perhaps in all of the literature of roguery where such punishment is described in great detail. A.L. Beier cites Blunt as an instance of an "authentic rogue" whose existence can be verified from properly historical sources outside the literature of roguery[7]:

---

7   A.L. Beier, "On the Boundaries of New and Old Historicisms: Thomas Harman and the Literature of Roguery," *English Literary Renaissance* 33, no. 2 (2003): 194.

> Having one's portrait drawn and publicly shown seems novel,
> rather like F.B.I. Mugshots in the post office. The pamphlets
> include pictures of Blunt naked, in his real clothing, in his
> disguise as a false epileptic, being whipped at the cart's tail.
> Even the whips and manacles used are shown. A more com-
> plete recitation of the penal process would be hard to find in
> early modern literature.[8]

Beier's attribution of a photographic and literal authenticity fails
to recognize any significant difference amongst the various portraits of Blunt. However, as he himself notes, they vary significantly — one shows him naked, one in his real clothing, and one
in his disguise. We need to ask what in these very crudely executed woodcuts of a rogue in widely different attires produces
this certainty of verisimilitude, this photographic correspondence?

Blunt's "authenticity" here seems to lead Beier to draw a neat
opposition between the depictions of him in his "real clothing"
and as a "false epileptic" — a phrase resonating between the two
meanings of "false" as "not real" and "dishonest." This binary of
real and false recreates precisely the parameters within which
spectacular punishment functioned — it marked the body of the
criminal with a "real" identity that negates the false ones he cir-
culates. But does the illustration accompanying Harman's text
serve the same function? The woodcut in question depicts Blunt
as not one but two people simultaneously — as a well-dressed
person claiming to be a hatmaker, Nicholas Blunt, and as shabbily attired Nicholas Genings, a false epileptic begging for money in tattered clothes and complete with blood smirched on his
face. As if to emphasize the fact that these are not two pictures
but in fact simultaneous depictions of the same person, the two
figures both hold the same walking stick. Blunt is in an upright
position while Genings's pose is more servile, as if about to bow.
Neither figure is "real" in the sense that Beier uses the term, but
more importantly, neither can be depicted as simply "false" be-

---

8   Ibid., 195.

cause any construction of falsehood is posited on the possibility of a bedrock "real" or true self.

Harman's narrative, too, struggled hard to establish this true self by stripping away the layers of "deep dissimulation" that hide it. Upon Blunt's first capture as a counterfeit crank he was stripped of his clothes almost as if to emphasize his health: "Then they stripped him stark naked; and as many as saw him said they never saw a handsomer man, with a yellow flaxen beard, and fair-skinned, without any spot or grief."[9] On his next capture, "the printer sent his boy that stripped him upon Allhallow Day at night to view him."[10] Finally he was also "stripped stark naked" when taken to Bridewell. Nakedness is repeatedly equated in the text to the definitive condition of one's true self. One can detect a hint of jealousy in Harman's description of Blunt's body. However, the end of this episode undermined this trust on the truth of Blunt's naked self, as he ran away into the night "as naked as ever he was born" after the mistress of the house had let him out, strangely unsuspectful of his falseness. "This crafty crank, espying all gone, requested the goodwife that he might go out on the back-side to make water, and to exonerate his paunch. She bade him draw the latch of the door and go out, neither thinking nor mistrusting he would have gone away naked."[11] The goodwife's assumption, as well as Beier's, was undermined by Blunt's bold striding forth. For, his innate falseness and mobility are not to be deterred or contained even within the stripped down naked truth of an undeformed body. Harman's fourth edition of Caveat added a further woodcut of the naked Genings, in which he is not stripped down to his true self to show the falsity of his disguises, but innately false, escaping by running across the fields.

---

9   Harman, "A Caveat for Common Cursitors," 114–15.

10   Ibid., 117.

11   Ibid., 115.

III

Harman's description of certain classes of rogues betrayed a genuine sympathy for their condition at the same time that he struggled to objectify and distance them as fundamentally different and morally corrupt. The chapter on the "doxy" provides a telling example of this struggle. Harman's language in the description of a particular doxy who came to beg at his household betrayed the logic of transformation that produced this uneasy insensibility. Describing the woman, he said that she was "surely a pleasant harlot, and not so pleasant as witty, and not so witty as devoid of all grace."[12] As one skips through the self-conscious rhythm of the sentence, it is hard to miss the movement from the physical beauty of the woman to her intellect and finally to her utter immorality. Each step of the transformation is marked by an incommensurability — "and not so pleasant as [...] not so witty as [...]" — which is nevertheless elided by the relentless movement inwards. The physical aspects of the woman — as the sociological aspects of vagabondage as a problem — disappear, or rather are subsumed under the production of an essential subjectivity or interiority.

In the description that follows, however, Harman seemed to struggle to keep the external and internal, the material and the subjective, separate as binary opposites. His own language betrays a conceptual confusion that is further emphasized by his apparent unease and confusion in the face of the woman's way of rationalizing her experiences. "And before I would grope her mind," Harman said, "I made her both eat and drink well."[13] The suggestive metaphor seems to constitute interiority as not opposed to but rather as a continuation of the physical.

In the ensuing conversation, Harman pressed her to reveal the names of the upright-men and rogues she has "known and been conversant with,"[14] the insinuation clearly being directed

---

12   Ibid., 136.
13   Ibid., 137.
14   Ibid., 138.

at her moral failings and promiscuity. And although she seems to conveniently oblige, saying she has known "six or seven," the perspectives and expectations that she brings open up and challenge the logic of moral corruption that Harman was trying to impose. In other words, the doxy's responses destabilized Harman's monologic "extraction" of "information" about the rogues, producing instead a complex dialogic encounter with an entirely different set of material conditions and consequently an entirely different spectrum of moral values:

> "Then first tell me," quoth I, "how many upright men and rogues dost thou know, or has known and been conversant with, and what their names be?"

> She paused a while, and said, "Why do you ask me, or wherefore?"

> "For nothing else," as I said, "but that I would know them when they came to my gate."

> "Now by my troth," quoth she, "then are ye never the near, for, all mine acquaintance for the most part are dead."[15]

Harman persisted with the interrogation nevertheless, seemingly sensing an opportunity to underline the dreadful demise that awaits such corrupt lives, and the doxy admitted that they died not for "want of cherishing, or from dreadful diseases" but were in fact hanged.[16] She ignored Harman's apparent surprise and innuendo that if all her lovers were hanged, how come there are so many rogues about the country, implying of course, that this one single doxy must have taken all vagabonds as lovers. The woman plainly stated though that she had but six or seven lovers and they had been hanged at various times, some years ago and some just a week past. What follows is perhaps the most moving

---

15 Ibid.
16 Ibid.

articulation in Harman's text of the possibility of a genuinely alternative framework not only of morality but also of humanity. Hearing of their deaths, Harman expectedly swooped in with his moralizing agenda of sin, evil and repentance:

> "Why," quoth I, "did not this sorrowful and fearful sight much grieve thee, and for thy time long and evil spent?"

> "I was sorry," quoth she, "by the mass. For some of them were good loving men. For I lacked not when they had it, and they wanted not when I had it, and divers of them I never did forsake until the gallows departed us."

> "O merciful God!" quoth I, and began to bless me.

> "Why bless ye?" quoth she. "Alas! good gentleman, everyone must have a living."[17]

For this vagrant woman the ethical and the economic weren't distinct spheres as they were for Harman. He posit ethics as prior to and in fact as the cause of material suffering whereas she could easily think of both as functions of socioeconomic practices that are intimately interlinked. What was for Harman a question of inherent corruption, only purged by repentance at death, was easily reduced to one of material necessity and causality by the doxy's "everyone must have a living." And yet, the tenderness of her description of these apparently immoral relationships, echoing in places the language of marriage vows, created a disturbing counterpoint to Harman's logic. Harman's immediately following reduction of this episode to the formulaic framework within which he conceptualized and contained all vagrancy underlines both his uneasiness and the inadequacy of his framework to formulate vagrancy as a problem, "Other matters I talked of. But this now may suffice to show the reader,

---

17 Ibid., 137.

as it were in a glass, the bold beastly life of these doxies."[18] The connection between the need to make a "living" and vagrancy, while it seemed natural and self-evident to the doxy, as it might to many modern readers, was opaque to Harman. For the woman it was simply an articulation of the practical necessities of survival that the vagrant population must cope with.

Harman's consistent, willful misreading of migration and vagabondage in the Caveat sustained and contributed to the discursive refusal that foreclosed the analysis of poverty as a socioeconomic problem. Presenting the physical displacement of migrants as only an incidental manifestation of a far more dangerous, inherent problem — that of moral corruption — allowed Harman to perform his great sleight of hand, the displacement of the intersubjective and socioeconomic causes of poverty onto a relentlessly moral and essentialized conception of selfhood. Spatial mobility, instead of raising questions about the systemic causes of poverty, was mapped onto a set of semiotic and ethical parameters: the performative slipperiness and inherent moral corruption of the migrant. The displacement of the intersubjective and socioeconomic causes of poverty onto a relentlessly moral and essentialized selfhood preempts any understanding of poverty and mass migration as socioeconomic problems. Harman's notion of an essential, and essentially mobile, self was for him the central precondition of unsettledness, which did not allow him to conceive or articulate socioeconomic relations as anything but contingent circumstances or effects. It was the mystical shell which covered the irrational kernel of his inverted dialectic.

---

18 Ibid.

Bibliography

Beier, A.L. *Masterless Men: The Vagrancy Problem in England, 1560–1640*. Methuen, 1985.

————. "On the Boundaries of New and Old Historicisms: Thomas Harman and the Literature of Roguery." *English Literary Renaissance* 33, no. 2 (2003): 181–200. DOI: 10.1111/1475-6757.00024.

Harman, Thomas. "A Caveat or Warning for Common Cursitors, Vulgarly Called Vagabonds." In *Cony-Catchers and Bawdy Baskets: An Anthology of Elizabethan Low Life*, edited by Gāmini Salgādo. Penguin, 1972.

The Statutes of the Realm, Printed by Command of His Majesty King George the Third, in Pursuance of an Address of the House of Commons of Great Britain, Volume 4: *1547–1624*. Dawsons of Pall Mall, 1965. https://hdl.handle.net/2027/pst.000017915519.

6

Travel Testimonies: Migrant Women's Mobilities in London Consistory Records, c. 1560–1600

John Gallagher

In 1577, Lionne Foullon and her daughter were summoned to account for themselves at the French Church on London's Threadneedle Street. The two women had recently traveled to Bruges, a journey which the consistory — the church's governing body — believed to have been undertaken in the company of "scandalous and debauched people." Under questioning, Foullon's daughter told the consistory that she and her mother had gone to Bruges "to make a better living," but that in the end the pair had been forced to return to London. The consistory admonished both of them, but especially Lionne Foullon — as a mother, she was particularly to blame for her bad behavior and for the bad company she had kept during the journey.[1]

---

1   Anne M. Oakley, ed., *Actes du consistoire de l'église française de Threadneedle Street, Londres*, vol. 2: *1571–1577* (Huguenot Society of London, 1969), 199. Unless otherwise indicated, all translations are my own.

Lionne Foullon never wrote down the story of her travels: if she wrote letters or kept a journal describing where she went and what she saw, they have not survived. That she and her daughter undertook the journey to Bruges and back is only known from her answers to the questions of an all-male consistory. But her experience of traveling between England and the European continent was not an unusual one among the women of London's sixteenth- and seventeenth-century migrant communities. The consistory of the Dutch Church at Austin Friars would also hear the story of Mayken de Grave, who had traveled from London to the continent and back again and was suspected of having "fallen into popishness" while abroad.[2] They would show an interest in the woman who had traveled to London from the Low Countries with Jan Oosterlinck, and who he claimed was his wife.[3] And they would urge Janneken Schuttens to take a journey from London to Antwerp in order to "seek her right" in a case before the magistrate there.[4]

The women who migrated to England in the latter half of the sixteenth century were, by definition, travelers — but their experiences of mobility were not preserved in the same way that men's travel narratives in the period commonly were.[5] This essay argues that the consistory records of London's "stranger

---

2   A.J. Jelsma and O. Boersma, eds., *Acta van het consistorie van de Nederlandse gemeente te Londen 1569–1585* (Instituut voor Nederlandse Geschiedenis, 1993), 225.

3   Ibid., 391.

4   Ibid., 595.

5   On women as migrants and travelers, see Lotte van de Pol and Erika Kuijpers, "Poor Women's Migration to the City: The Attraction of Amsterdam Health Care and Social Assistance in Early Modern Times," *Journal of Urban History* 32, no. 1 (2005): 44–60; Eva Johanna Holmberg, "Introduction: Renaissance and Early Modern Travel — Practice and Experience, 1500–1700," *Renaissance Studies* 33, no. 4 (2019): 516; Patricia Akhimie, "Gender and Travel Discourse: Richard Lassels's 'The Voyage of Lady Catherine Whetenall from Brussells into Italy' (1650)," in *Travel and Travail: Early Modern Women, English Drama, and the Wider World,* ed. Patricia Akhimie and Bernadette Andrea (University of Nebraska Press, 2019), 124–26; and Amrita Sen, "Traveling Companions: Women, Trade, and the Early East India Company," *Genre* 48, no. 2 (2015): 193–214.

churches," which played host to the city's growing foreign Protestant communities from the latter half of the sixteenth century
onwards, can be used to reconstruct some aspects of these migrant women's experiences of mobility: what they did, what they
felt, what they knew.[6] The travel testimonies found in consistory records are often fragmented and incomplete: More often
than not, the stranger church consistories whose questioning
shaped them were not primarily interested in mobility itself, but
sought to investigate rumors, illicit sex, or marital disharmony
within their communities and beyond the seas.[7] The words spoken before the consistories are not transparent: different speak-
ers offered very different versions of events, tensions within the
community bubbled over, emotions ran high, and the record
that survives is one kept by male scribes serving all-male consistories.[8] But the women who were summoned to account for
themselves before the elders of London's French, Dutch, and
Italian churches — and those who presented themselves in order to state their own cases — frequently told (or had told about
them) stories of migration and mobility. Women's voices are rare
in the printed travel literature and manuscript accounts of travel
which form the basis for many histories of early modern mobility, but these consistory records can shed light not only on the
experience of travel for early modern migrant women, but also

---

6   There is no space here to summarize the rich historiography of London's
     stranger churches and migration to London in the sixteenth century. Key
     scholarship includes Owe Boersma, "Vluchtig voorbeeld: De Nederlandse,
     Franse en Italiaanse vluchtelingenkerken in Londen, 1568–1585" (PhD
     diss., Theologische Universiteit Kampen, 1994), and Andrew Pettegree,
     Foreign Protestant Communities in Sixteenth-Century London (Clarendon
     Press, 1986).

7   On social discipline in the consistories, see Pettegree, *Foreign Protestant
     Communities*, 182–214. On the archives of the "stranger churches," see
     Andrew Spicer, "Migration, assimilation et survie: Les archives des consis-
     toires du Refuge anglais," *Bulletin de la Société de l'Histoire du Protestan-
     tisme Français* 153 (2007): 671–93.

8   For an instructive investigation of the relationship between consistory
     business and the contents of consistory records, see Judith Pollmann, "Off
     the Record: Problems in the Quantification of Calvinist Church Disci-
     pline," *Sixteenth Century Journal* 33, no. 2 (2002): 423–38.

the ways in which networks, reputations, and personal histories could cross borders as they built a new life far from home.[9]

For men or women, journeys back and forth to the continent were physically taxing and fraught with danger, as the Dutch Church consistory recognized when it warned of the "great peril on the way" to the Netherlands.[10] Writing to his wife from Norwich in 1567, Pauwels de Coene told her to sell what she could and come to England. He sent her a barrel of herring with which to finance the journey and urged her to travel as soon as she could, "For the journey, as we understand is everyday becoming more dangerous, and will become [still] more dangerous because the devil will become more furious."[11] Some women undertook journeys to and from England while pregnant. Writing following his excommunication from the London Dutch Church and his "pilgrimage" to Emden, Adriaen van Haemstede wrote how his wife had had triplets — two boys and a girl, of whom the youngest boy had died.[12] In 1579, Tanneken van den Hove appeared before the consistory of London's Dutch Church, having recently come from overseas and seeking to have her child baptized in the church.[13] For other women, the journey must have been a substantial physical challenge: the mother of

---

9   Mary C. Fuller, "Afterword: Looking for the Women in Early Modern Travel Writing," in *Travel and Travail: Early Modern Women, English Drama, and the Wider World*, ed. Patricia Akhimie and Bernadette Andrea (University of Nebraska Press, 2019), 331.

10 Jelsma and Boersma, *Acta*, 716.

11 Pauwels de Coene to his wife in Ieper, Norwich, August 21, 1567. Alastair Duke, ed., "Private Correspondence Between Flemish Strangers in England and Their Families and Contacts in Flanders, 1566–1573," *Dutch Revolt*, https://dutchrevolt.library.universiteitleiden.nl/english/sources/english_sources-janssen-correspondence/. See also Alastair Duke, "Eavesdropping on the Correspondence between the Strangers, Chiefly in Norwich, and their Families in the Low Countries, 1567–70," *Dutch Crossing* 38, no. 2 (2014): 116–31.

12 J.H. Hessels, ed., *Ecclesiae Londino-Batavae Archivum. Tomus Secundus. Epistulae et Tractatus cum Reformationis tum Ecclesiae Londino-Batavae Historiam Illustrantes (1544–1622)*, vol. 2, part 1 (Cambridge University Press, 1889), 146.

13 Jelsma and Boersma, *Acta*, 538.

Jacobus Bucerus arrived in Sandwich in 1562, having renounced Catholicism and traveled to join her son and the stranger Protestant community in that town at the age of 72.[14]

Traveling alone was deemed to be risky for women. In 1561, the consistory of the London French Church debated at length how the wife of their minister, Nicolas des Gallars, should travel to England. The minister asked the consistory's advice on the best route, wondering whether it was best for her to travel through France or Germany. After some discussion, it was settled that the deacon Nicolas Binet was to be sent to collect her, since he was already planning to travel and see his parents.[15] Later, the consistory would deal with a mother's desire to go to Geneva in order to fetch her children: at her husband's suggestion, she was to be accompanied by a young man. The consistory demurred, unwilling to allow her to take such a long voyage with a lone man who was not her husband.[16] Some traveled with other family members, with children, or with friends, but even in a group, female travelers could find themselves and their enterprise treated with suspicion, as in the case of Lionne Foullon and her daughter with whom this essay began. The consistory's concerns about solo female travel were not only to do with physical danger, but also perceived threats to chastity and reputation. The suspicion and concern with which the all-male consistories viewed women's travel did not mean that they were implacably opposed to it. In 1596, a meeting of the Colloquy of England's French churches urged the wife of Jean Baudin to return to Holland in order "to prove the incestuous adultery of her husband before the magistrate of the place where he is."[17] In spite of its

---

14 Hessels, *Epistulae et Tractatus,* 195.

15 Elsie Johnston, ed., *Actes du consistoire de l'église française de Threadneedle Street, Londres,* vol. 1: *1560–1565* (Publications of the Huguenot Society, 1937), 26.

16 Ibid., 55.

17 Adrian Charles Chamier, ed., *Les actes des colloques des églises françaises et des synodes des églises étrangères refugiées en Angleterre 1581–1654* (Huguenot Society, 1890), 36.

dangers, women's mobility between London and the continent was a feature of the stranger churches' community life.[18]

Traveling in company was not necessarily safer for women. One journey where we have a little more information began in Arras in 1571 and took ten days to travel to England. The travelers were a group made up of Jeanne, the wife of Jean du Bois; Robert Bloquet and his wife Cateline Midy; a young man named Pierre, a baggage-carrier; and the group's leader, Jean du Quief. They left Arras on St. Christopher's day, July 25, and headed for the coast, spending the night in Hesdin before reaching Boulogne-sur-Mer, where they stayed for two nights before setting sail for England.[19] The reason we have more detail about this voyage is because of a scandal that emerged some months after the party had arrived in London. In December of that year, the consistory of the French Church first interrogated Jean du Quief about whether he had solicited Jeanne du Bois to engage in adulterous sex or slept with her. Du Quief attempted to stonewall the consistory, but there were more questions to come: Had he told her that she would pay nothing for her voyage if she agreed to sleep with him? Under pressure, he admitted that something had happened between the pair at Sandwich, but denied having initiated matters, claiming that she had told him to come and sleep on her bed.[20]

Interrogated the next day, Jeanne du Bois offered a rebuttal of du Quief's accusations. She told the consistory "that Jean du Quief had importuned her several times both beyond the sea and in England," describing how at Sandwich he had wheedled

---

18 Silke Muylaert argues convincingly that the term "exile" in this period "can divert us from the high mobility and socioeconomic opportunities underlying religious migration." Silke Muylaert, *Shaping the Stranger Churches: Migrants in England and the Troubles in the Netherlands, 1547–1585* (Brill, 2021), 17.

19 Oakley, *Actes,* 46. The du Quief case is considered by Susan Broomhall, "Authority in the French Church in Later Sixteenth-Century London," in *Authority, Gender and Emotions in Late Medieval and Early Modern England,* ed. Susan Broomhall (Palgrave Macmillan, 2015), 137–40.

20 Oakley, *Actes,* 41–42.

his way into her bed, promising not to do anything, but — when she eventually agreed — changing his manner and telling her that she would have to tell people she was his wife, and that if she said anything she would be thrown in prison.[21] When du Quief denied his actions, Jeanne du Bois fervently affirmed her words, saying "everything I've said is true, on the damnation of my soul."[22] Their companions in the voyage were called to give testimonies, which attest to the cramped, emotionally intense, and potentially dangerous experience of cross-Channel travel. On the first night of their journey, Cateline Midy recalled how du Quief hadn't dared to sleep "since someone had told the sergeant of the place that they were going to England."[23] The company often slept in close quarters, where Robert Bloquet could hear "the bed creaking loudly." Bloquet attested to having risen from bed with his dagger in his hand, "not wanting to permit such villainy in his company," before being talked down by his wife.[24] The witnesses attempted to speculate about Jeanne's motives and culpability and challenged both her narrative and du Quief's, but what emerges most clearly from the consistory's investigations into the case is that travel, for a woman like Jeanne du Bois, carried risks of pursuit by the authorities, physical and sexual violence or assault, and damage to reputation.

While the fear of physical assault colors some men's accounts of travel in this period, for women, the threat of sexual violence could loom large. The case of the fifteen- or sixteen-year-old Janneken Maldron was brought to the consistory of the Dutch Church in 1585.[25] Jan de Backer brought a written statement by Maldron which alleged that on the road between Oudenaarde and Tournai, Geeraert Truyen had "pushed his manhood into

21 Ibid., 43–44.

22 Ibid., 44.

23 Ibid., 46.

24 Ibid., 45.

25 Jelsma and Boersma, *Acta,* 756–57. On sexual violence and rape in early modern English sources, see Garthine Walker, "Rereading Rape and Sexual Violence in Early Modern England," *Gender & History* 10, no. 1 (1998): 1–25.

her hand and sought to have intercourse with her."[26] In the Green Lion in Tournai, Truyen had come naked to Maldron's bed while she slept and lain at her feet, pulling at her clothes and seeking the same. When she refused, Maldron said that Truyen had asked "why you wouldn't let me, you let the soldiers do it," a remark which, while not expanded upon in the hearing of the consistory, suggests the risks of sexual violence which came with the surveillance and policing of migrant routes in wartime.[27] On the road between Dover and Canterbury, Maldron had told the wife of Jan de Backer (with whom she would lodge in London) everything that had happened.[28] Janneken Maldron was not the only woman to report behavior of this kind on the road: Susanne, the widow of Phillips Janssen, was summoned before the Dutch consistory for her "immodest going overseas with Hans Walckneel," and because "people say that she has committed dishonorable acts with him."[29] Susanne countered by arguing that she had done nothing wrong, neither on the road nor in Antwerp, but recounted that Walckneel had come to her bed while drunk in her cousin's house, but that she had called out to her cousin and he had called the watch.[30] The consistories' concern with illicit sex meant that their records asked questions which other records of early modern travel did not, and may have ensured the survival of more information about sexual activity, sexual violence, and gendered experiences of travel than the more canonical accounts of elite male travelers.

Discussing one member who had spent time overseas, the Dutch consistory asked for witnesses to his good behavior, musing that while abroad he had been "out of our and the whole community's sight."[31] Susan Broomhall writes that overseas travel by members of the French Church "often separated husbands and wives, and youths from supervizing elders [...] and

---

26 Jelsma and Boersma, *Acta,* 756.

27 Ibid. For Maldron's further testimony, see ibid., 770.

28 Ibid., 757.

29 Ibid., 643.

30 Ibid., 643–44.

31 Ibid., 692.

left individuals freer (and more at risk) to apply their own moral codes."[32] Both consistory and community were intensely aware that when individuals traveled, so too did rumors and reputations, in spite of the efforts made by some migrants to leave their past lives behind them. In 1571, the Dutch consistory heard how Ebe, the widow of Rems Juyt, had promised to bring a document attesting to the life she had led while abroad. On reading the document, the consistory murmured about the "public shame" that attached to her by reason of some wicked deeds.[33] The power of a story that could follow a woman from beyond the seas is also seen in the case of Catherine de le Deulle, who first came to the attention of the French consistory in September of 1571 when the man to whom she was betrothed asked to be released from his promise of marriage, as he had learned that his fiancée had killed a man in Lille some years before. The consistory called a number of witnesses in order to investigate this shocking accusation.[34] But those who knew the story put a different spin on it, explaining that le Deulle had been the victim of aggression, and that her blow against her assailant had not caused instant death — in fact, some said that her assailant (a man, they said, of bad character) had been seen going around the town before he died some weeks later.[35] His family had not pursued le Deulle; in fact, when she was questioned by the consistory, she admitted having injured the man as described by the witnesses. She had been five years at Lille without being asked about the case, she said, and it was only since she had arrived in London that she had heard it spoken of.[36] The consistory's investigations offer some sense of the mobility of these rumors in London. Jan le Brun was admonished for having spread the story around the city, while Martin de Buisson told Jeanne le Cat that le Deulle was a murderer.[37] The next spring — after le

32 Broomhall, "Authority in the French Church," 137.

33 Jelsma and Boersma, *Acta*, 176.

34 Oakley, *Actes*, 16. See also Boersma, "Vluchtig voorbeeld," 151.

35 Oakley, *Actes*, 16–18, 56.

36 Ibid., 18.

37 Ibid., 33, 64.

Deulle's fiancé had sought to marry another woman in secret before himself dying of the plague — de Buisson would be admonished by the consistory for, among other offences, spreading rumors about the case "in houses and in the streets."[38] But by that time, le Deulle would be gone, having left London and headed for the Low Countries — whether still pursued by this mobile story, these sources do not show.[39]

The dislocation of migration could break relationships or offer an opportunity to start anew. For some women, this meant forging new relationships and seeking to marry, even though they might have a husband still living abroad.[40] The consistory concerned itself closely with investigating women's claims of the deaths of their previous partners.[41] Sara Ravets found herself in trouble for having been secretly married in an English church to a man "of reckless life" when it was not even clear that her first husband was dead.[42] A male member of the congregation was accused of living in "whoredom" with Eyken van Erckendale when, the consistory thundered, "a strong suspicion and rumor circulated that [her husband] was still alive."[43] Judith Janssens brought a man and a woman from 's-Hertogenbosch to attest to her husband's being eight years dead: the next year, she would remarry in London.[44] Cathelene Verhamme made her case for being allowed to remarry with the aid of a document signed by a notary in Middelburg stating that her first husband was dead.[45] In cases where reputation was at stake, words "out of the mouth

---

38 Ibid., 76–77.
39 Ibid., 76. Susan Broomhall considers the mobility of information in the French Church in "Authority in the French Church," 137.
40 On strangers' letters and separations among spouses and families in the migration context, see Duke, "Eavesdropping on the Correspondence between the Strangers," 118.
41 Jesse Spohnholz, "Instability and Insecurity: Dutch Women Refugees in Germany and England, 1550–1600," in *Exile and Religious Identity, 1500–1800*, ed. Jesse Spohnholz and Gary K. Waite (Routledge, 2015), 111–25.
42 Jelsma and Boersma, *Acta*, 135.
43 Ibid., 62–63, 72–73.
44 Ibid., 517.
45 Ibid., 497.

of a woman who had come from overseas" could be central to the consistory's deliberations. When these female migrants traveled, so too did knowledge — or speculation — about their pasts.[46]

For other women, time and distance meant that bonds had been broken, and some claimed not to know about the partners they had left behind. Janneken Cocq's husband had been absent for ten years and she purported not to know whether he was dead or alive. Her life had continued in his absence: she had become pregnant by Denys Denisschen but, the consistory was told, she had lost the child.[47] In August of 1581, Janneken Kramers was admonished for her dealings with her husband, who remained overseas. The Dutch consistory noted that "with many words" she had explained how she had tracked down her husband but that he had deceived her — it seems from her testimony that he was shacked up with a woman described in the consistory record (possibly by Kramers) as "the whore" — so she had returned to London. There, she found herself at odds with the consistory, who sought to urge her to return to her husband. She demurred, saying that she was not minded to follow their advice, at least before the winter. She declared her willingness to reunite with her husband, if he would leave the woman with whom he was involved, but she would not travel before the next summer.[48]

While consistory records can give some sense of the actions of some migrant women in early modern London, it is much more difficult to get a sense of their inner lives, and the impact that their experiences of migration had on them. Some moments of intense psychological distress stand out in the consistory records: a laconic mention in the records of the French church of a woman named Denette or Druette Barde, who "thought to throw herself in the river twice or three times," and was sum-

---

46 Ibid., 398.
47 Ibid., 399.
48 Ibid., 602–3.

moned to be admonished by the consistory.[49] Another member of the French congregation had not left her house for several years, "due to some trouble she has in her mind," and had not been seen at the church's services, even though she had shown herself "by her piety and charity to be a Christian woman."[50]

In September of 1567, Clement Baet wrote to his wife to tell her of the opportunities for them in Norwich, where he had settled, and urged her to set out for England to join him. She was to bring clothes for herself and her daughter, "for people go about decently dressed," as well as some furniture. Once she was ready to make the journey, her husband told her to "bring all this to the Nieuwe Dam and go to Nieuwpoort, to the Halve Maan: the woman there will help you."[51] Clement Baet's letter gave no further information on the identity or activities of the woman who could be found at the sign of the Half Moon, likely an inn, but the question of what kind of help she could offer remains tantalizing. She may have been a source of information, advice, or practical help for the onward journey, a moneylender, or an early modern migration broker. But while the exact nature of the "migrant knowledge" possessed by the woman at the Halve Maan is impossible to access, the travel testimonies found amongst the disciplinary records of London's stranger churches — however fragmented and contested their accounts of women's mobilities — trace what migrant women knew from experience in early modern Europe.

---

49 Oakley, *Actes,* 57.

50 Ibid., 17.

51 Clement Baet to his wife, Norwich, September 5, 1567, in Duke, "Private Correspondence Between Flemish Strangers."

Bibliography

Akhimie, Patricia. "Gender and Travel Discourse: Richard Lassels's 'The Voyage of Lady Catherine Whetenall from Brussells into Italy' (1650)." In *Travel and Travail: Early Modern Women, English Drama, and the Wider World,* edited by Patricia Akhimie and Bernadette Andrea. University of Nebraska Press, 2019.

Boersma, Owe. "Vluchtig voorbeeld: De Nederlandse, Franse en Italiaanse vluchtelingenkerken in Londen, 1568–1585." PhD diss., Theologische Universiteit Kampen, 1994. http://www.kerkrecht.nl/node/2027.

Broomhall, Susan. "Authority in the French Church in Later Sixteenth-Century London." In *Authority, Gender and Emotions in Late Medieval and Early Modern England,* edited by Susan Broomhall. Palgrave Macmillan, 2015.

Chamier, Charles, ed. *Les actes des colloques des églises françaises et des synodes des églises étrangères refugiées en Angleterre 1581–1654.* Huguenot Society, 1890.

Duke, Alastair. "Eavesdropping on the Correspondence Between the Strangers, Chiefly in Norwich, and Their Families in the Low Countries, 1567–70." *Dutch Crossing* 38, no. 2 (2014): 116–31. DOI: 10.1179/0309656414Z.000000000 54.

——, ed. "Private Correspondence Between Flemish Strangers in England and Their Families and Contacts in Flanders, 1566–1573." *Dutch Revolt.* https://dutchrevolt.library.universiteitleiden.nl/english/sources/english_sources_janssen-correspondence/.

Fuller, Mary C. "Afterword: Looking for the Women in Early Modern Travel Writing." In *Travel and Travail: Early Modern Women, English Drama, and the Wider World,* edited by Patricia Akhimie and Bernadette Andrea. University of Nebraska Press, 2019.

Hessels, J.H., ed. *Ecclesiae Londino-Batavae Archivum. Tomus Secundus. Epistulae et Tractatus cum Reformationis tum*

Ecclesiae Londino-Batavae Historiam Illustrantes (1544–1622), Volume 2, Part 1. Cambridge University Press, 1889.

Holmberg, Eva Johanna. "Introduction: Renaissance and Early Modern Travel — Practice and Experience, 1500–1700." *Renaissance Studies* 33, no. 4 (2019): 515–23. DOI: 10.1111/rest.12561.

Jelsma, A.J., and O. Boersma, eds. *Acta van het consistorie van de Nederlandse gemeente te Londen, 1569–1585.* Instituut voor Nederlandse Geschiedenis, 1993.

Johnston, Elsie, ed. *Actes du consistoire de l'église française de Threadneedle Street, Londres,* Volume 1: *1560–1565.* Publications of the Huguenot Society, 1937.

Muylaert, Silke. *Shaping the Stranger Churches: Migrants in England and the Troubles in the Netherlands, 1547–1585.* Brill, 2021.

Oakley, Anne M., ed. *Actes du consistoire de l'église française de Threadneedle Street, Londres,* Volume 2: *1571–1577.* Huguenot Society of London, 1969.

Pettegree, Andrew. *Foreign Protestant Communities in Sixteenth-Century London.* Clarendon Press, 1986.

Pollmann, Judith. "Off the Record: Problems in the Quantification of Calvinist Church Discipline." *Sixteenth Century Journal* 33, no. 2 (2002): 423–38. DOI: 10.2307/4143915.

Sen, Amrita. "Traveling Companions: Women, Trade, and the Early East India Company." *Genre* 48, no. 2 (2015): 193–214. DOI: 10.1215/00166928-2884844.

Spicer, Andrew. "Migration, assimilation et survie: les archives des consistoires du Refuge anglais." *Bulletin de la Société de l'Histoire du Protestantisme Français* 153 (2007): 671–93. https://www.jstor.org/stable/24309363.

Spohnholz, Jesse. "Instability and Insecurity: Dutch Women Refugees in Germany and England, 1550–1600." In *Exile and Religious Identity, 1500–1800,* edited by Jesse Spohnholz and Gary K. Waite. Routledge, 2015.

van de Pol, Lotte, and Erika Kuijpers. "Poor Women's Migration to the City: The Attraction of Amsterdam

Health Care and Social Assistance in Early Modern Times."
Journal of Urban History 32, no. 1 (2005): 44–60. DOI:
10.1177/0096144205279198.

Walker, Garthine. "Rereading Rape and Sexual Violence in
Early Modern England." *Gender & History* 10, no. 1 (1998):
1–25. DOI: 10.1111/1468-0424.00087.

7

Fickle Turbans and Mercurial Fashions: Blurring the Boundaries of Identities between Europe and the Ottoman Empire

Rosita D'Amora

In January 1479 the Republic of Venice and the Ottoman Porte signed a peace treaty ending a sixteen-year war. That August, a Jew named Simone arrived in Venice as special envoy of Mehmed II (1432–1481), the Sultan who, in 1453, had conquered Constantinople, the impregnable capital of the Byzantine Empire. Bearing letters from the Sultan, the envoy expressed the Sultan's wish for an artist to be sent to his court. This request was promptly met by La Serenissima who agreed to dispatch Gentile Bellini (c. 1429–1507), who was then, with his father Jacopo and his brother Giovanni, among the leading painters in Venice. Bellini travelled to the court of Mehmed II in September the same year and probably stayed in Constantinople until January 1481. During his residence, Bellini was commissioned to produce several works of art, of which only a few survive. These include a celebrated portrait of Mehmed II, now in the National Gallery in London, that is still considered one of the most iconic

Fig. 7.1. Gentile Bellini, *The Sultan Mehmet II,* 1480. Source: The National Gallery, London.

images of a Turk migrated to the West, and represents an equally famous turban.[1]

Bellini's Turban

It is generally assumed that this portrait preserved the likeness of Mehmed II's face that reappears in many other con-

---

1   On Bellini's stay at the Ottoman court and the wider patronage of Italianate art promoted by Mehmed II, see Caroline Campbell and Alan Chong, eds., *Bellini and the East,* exh. cat. (Yale University Press, 1988); Gülru Necipoğlu, "Visual Cosmopolitanism and Creative Translation: Artistic Conversations with Renaissance Italy in Mehmed II's Constantinople," *Muqarnas* 29 (2012): 1–81; and Antonia Gatward Cevizli, "Bellini, Bronze and Bombards: Sultan Mehmed II's Requests Reconsidered," *Renaissance Studies* 28, no. 5 (2014): 748–65.

temporary visual representations — both medallic and painted portraits — and also finds a strict correspondence in written sources.[2] Giovanni Maria Angiolello (c. 1451–1525), a traveler from Vicenza who, having been captured by the Ottomans, was in the service of the Ottoman court during Bellini's visit, describes some of Mehmed II's physical characteristics that can be also found in the painting: his prominent *naso aquilino* (aquiline nose), his *occhi gossi* (big eyes), and his *collo curto, e grosso* (squat neck).[3] The sultan's headgear, similarly, seems to be a faithful reproduction of a real turban. One of the earliest Ottoman chronicles, the *Tevārih-i Âl-i Osman* (The chronicles of the house of Osman) compiled by the Ottoman historian 'Âşıkpāşāzāde during the reign of Mehmed II, ascribes the introduction of a distinctive headgear to the reign of Orhan (1281–1362), the second Ottoman sultan, describing it as a *mu'akkad bûrma dülbend* (knotted turban with thick coils) that lords were required to wear when going to the imperial council. This description seems to correspond to the bulbous turban appearing in all the contemporary visual representations of Mehmed II.[4] Besides the correspondence between these sources, there is another element showing that Bellini had a clear understanding of the sultan's headgear. On the upper right and left corners of his painting, as well as on the reverse of the medal he designed, the

---

2   During his stay at the Ottoman court, Bellini also designed a medallic portrait of Mehmed II. Other medals were cast almost immediately before and after Bellini's arrival in Constantinople. See Julian Raby, "Pride and Prejudice: Mehmed the Conqueror and the Italian Portrait Medal," *Studies in the History of Art* 21 (1987): 171–94.

3   Angiolello's text, whose authorship was ascribed to Donado da Lezze, is reproduced in Donado da Lezze, *Historia Turchesca 1300–1514* (Carol Göbl, 1909), 122–23. The "truthfulness" of Bellini's portrait is discussed in Elizabeth Rodini, "The Sultan's True Face? Gentile Bellini, Mehmed II, and the Values of Verisimilitude," in *The Turk and Islam in the Western Eye, 1450–1750: Visual Imagery before Orientalism*, ed. James G. Harper (Ashgate, 2011).

4   Rosita D'Amora, "Alcune considerazioni sul valore simbolico del copricapo in ambito turco-ottomano," in *Scritti in onore di Giovanni M. D'Erme*, vol. 1, ed. Michele Bernardini and Natalia L. Tornesello (Università degli Studi di Napoli "L'Orientale," 2005), 344–45.

Venetian painter inserted a triple crown that has been regarded as a heraldic device which conveys the sultan's royal status.[5] This seems to indicate that the artist knew that the turban did not have the status of a crown. The turban did not attain this status in later periods either, though it gradually became understood as a politically significant object.

The connections between the visual and textual evidence from coeval Western and Ottoman sources seem to suggest that this turban, its shape and form, was not a product of the artistic imagination, but rather a faithful reproduction based on the direct observations of the real turban Mehmed II actually wore, or, at least, of a type of turban in use during his time. Bellini's, therefore, was a realistic and credible depiction which did not simply use a turban as shorthand for a "Turk" or to convey religious otherness. Bellini provided other contemporary artists with a reproducible and accurate model of a turban in a context in which, since the late Middle Ages, turban-like headgear was used as a device to represent not only Muslims but also Jews, Pagans, and Protestants, visually connecting them to Islam's presumed heresies.[6] The visit of Albrecht Dürer (1471–1528) to the workshop of Giovanni and Gentile Bellini during his first journey to Italy in 1494–1495, for example, while contributing more generally to the elaboration of Dürer's specific iconography of the Turk, allowed the German artist to borrow from Bellini the distinctive form of the Ottoman turban that he later used not only to represent Turks as Turks, but also to denote an anachronistically non-Christian other as an "extra-historical symbol of evil."[7]

---

5   Necipoğlu, "Visual Cosmopolitanism," 34.

6   Ruth Mellinkoff, *Outcasts: Signs of Otherness in Northern European Art of the Late Middle Ages,* vol. 1 (University of California Press, 1993), 60–61, 73–74.

7   Heather Madar, "Dürer's Depictions of the Ottoman Turks: A Case of Early Modern Orientalism?," in *The Turk and Islam in the Western Eye, 1450–1750: Visual Imagery before Orientalism,* ed. James G. Harper (Ashgate, 2011), 159–61, 165. Madar shows how Dürer's use of turbaned figures delivers a message on the impending danger of the rapid westward

Migration to the West

To the fifteenth-century viewer, the turban was already presented as a complex object loaded with connotations. A proper
knowledge of the turban, though, had not yet migrated to the
West. A hint of this comes from the small Italian city-state of
Mantua through an epistolary exchange, at the beginning of
1492, between the Marquis of Mantua, Francesco II Gonzaga
(1466–1529), and one of his agents, Giorgio Brognolo.[8] On February 16 Francesco II, who was fascinated with Ottoman culture
and had established friendly diplomatic relationships with the
Sultan Beyazid II (1447–1512), ordered Brognolo to find for him
in Venice a turban *a la turchesca, et bello* (in the Turkish style,
and beautiful).[9] The reason for the request remains unclear, but,
interestingly, Brognolo met the Marquis's demand with equiv-
ocation, sending him a "tulimano" (inner robe)[10] and pointing out how, despite his "diligent investigation," none of the
people he had consulted in Venice, including some Turks and
"stradioti,"[11] knew what a "turbante" was. In a subsequent letter
the Marquis would specify that the turban is a *capello aguzo che
usano [i] turchi* (pointed hat used by the Turks) made of cloth
wrapped around the head, of which he heard there were many
beautiful examples in Venice.[12] Once the agent understood what

advance of the Ottoman Empire. See also Julian Raby, *Venice, Dürer and
the Oriental Mode* (Islamic Art Publications, 1982).

8   Molly Bourne, "The Turban'd Turk in Renaissance Mantua: Francesco II
Gonzaga's Interest in Ottoman Fashion," in *Mantova e il Rinascimento
Italiano: Studi in onore di David S. Chambers,* ed. Philippa Jackson and
Guido Rebecchini (Sometti Editoriale, 2011).

9   Ibid., 62. On Francesco II Gonzaga's passion for turbans, see also Antonia
Gatward Cevizli, "Portraits, Turbans and Cuirasses: Material Exchange
between Mantua and the Ottomans at the End of the Fifteenth Century," in
Global Gifts: The Material Culture of Diplomacy in Early Modern Eurasia,
ed. Zoltán Biedermann, Anne Gerritson, and Giorgio Riello (Cambridge
University Press, 2018).

10   "Inner robe," from the Turkish word "dolaman."

11   Mercenary units from the Balkans in the service of Venice and other
central and southern European states.

12   Bourne, "The Turban'd Turk," 63.

a turban was, he seems not to have had any trouble fulfilling the Marquis's desire.

Although Brognolo's bewilderment may seem odd in the context of cosmopolitan Venice, there are similar examples of European writing on the Ottoman Empire which does not always assume readers' familiarity with the turban. Theodore Spandounes (d. after 1538), belonging to a Byzantine refugee family that had settled in Venice after the conquest of Constantinople, refers to the Turkish turban as a headgear that has been seen in Italy in his account of the rise of the Ottoman Empire (published in three different editions between 1509 and 1538), but nonetheless describes what it looked like in detail.[13] In later periods, though the Western public had acquired greater familiarity with the turban, European travelers' attention would still be caught by the variety of headgear in use within the multi-ethnic and multireligious Ottoman society. In particular, they continued to be intrigued by turbans: their often voluminous proportions, distinctive shapes, and different models that could immediately reveal, to those who knew how to interpret the taxonomy, the role and position each individual had within the community.

These descriptions become a trope in travel narratives even after Mahmud II's (1785–1839) 1829 clothing law imposing the fez as the official headgear of the empire.[14] Significantly, the Italian author Edmondo De Amicis (1846–1908), who visited Istanbul in 1874, would still nostalgically lament the lack of turbans in his widely translated travel account *Constantinople* (1877–1878), noting how the "old enormous turbans of the age of Suleiman [the Magnificent] shaped as the dome of a mosque" could then

---

13 Spandounes's work entitled *Discorso di Teodoro Spandugino Cantacusino Gentil'homo Costantinopolitano Dall'origine de' Principi Turchi,* originally written in Italian, is also available in English: Theodore Spandounes, *On the Origin of the Ottoman Emperors,* trans. and ed. Donald M. Nicol (Cambridge University Press, 1997).

14 On how the fez came to be the prevalent headgear in the Ottoman Empire, see Youssef Ben Ismail, "A History of Ottoman Fez before Mahmud II (ca. 1600–1800)," *Muqarnas* 38, no. 1 (2021): 155–83.

only be admired "on the head of decrepit men in the darkest little shops of the most secluded narrow alley of the Gran Bazar."[15] It is clear in his travelogue that an attentive observer could still gather information about people's social position from the vast array of dress and headgear in use. However, after Mahmud II's reforms, the age of the Ottoman turban was clearly coming to an end.

Marking Identity and Status

The Ottoman Empire had clear norms regarding clothing whose use was often regulated by the issue of different sumptuary laws.[16] Dress was for the Ottomans an essential part of the presentation of the self as well as of the perception of the other. In this act of mutual recognition, turbans had particular roles and multiple symbolic values. Since it was considered a symbol of Islam, its use was mainly reserved for the Muslim population of the empire; its different colors, shapes, and dimensions stated a person's social status, their ethnicity, profession, or affiliation to a particular Sufi order. Among the elite, one's rank and position within the court hierarchy was also shown by the particular model of turban they wore. Until the issue of Mahmud II's clothing law relegating the use of turbans only to clergymen, their characteristics were visible markers of identity, social position, and ethnic or religious affiliations. Each model of turban had its own category of wearers, specific contexts of use and particular proper names, such as *mücevveze, selīmī, kallāvi, perīşānī, kātıbī,* or *örfi.*

The turban was an important marker of identity and status not only in life but also in death. Ostentation in gravestones and funerary monuments was considered reprehensible in Islam. Death was supposed to level human beings in the face of God.

---

15 Edmondo De Amicis, *Costantinopoli* (Touring Club italiano, 1997), 76.

16 On Ottoman sumptuary laws, see Donald Quataert, "Clothing Laws, State, and Society in the Ottoman Empire, 1720–1829," *International Journal of Middle East Studies* 29, no. 3 (1997): 403–25.

Yet turbans were used on tombstones, becoming a central element of a peculiar Ottoman funerary tradition that emerged in the sixteenth century and continued well into the nineteenth. This clearly signified a desire to inscribe a visual clue of the deceased's status in life. However, these markers were unstable: the conventional boundaries delineating who could wear the different types of turban were constantly crossed, especially at the borders between different socio-economic and cultural groups, or when the different meanings the turban could convey were translated or migrated elsewhere.

To Put on a Turban

Although wearing the turban has always been a shared practice among different cultures and religions, in the Christian West the turban was, and to an extent still is, perceived as having strong religious connotations and almost exclusively associated with Islam.[17] Indeed, many early modern European languages used the expression "to put on the turban" to mean embracing Islam, "to turn Turk." With a few noticeable exceptions — such as Bellini's portrait of Mehmed II — the turban became the main visual device through which the Muslim other was depicted either as a fearsome infidel or a defeated enemy.

A good example of this is a late work of Titian (c. 1488/1490–1576) entitled *Philip II Offering the Infante Fernando to Victory*. Painted between 1573 and 1575, it was commissioned by Philip II, King of Spain. It was conceived as an ex-voto to commemorate

---

17   In the aftermath of the 9/11 Twin Towers bombing, a Sikh–American entrepreneur, Balbir Singh Sodhi, was murdered because he was mistakenly believed to be a Muslim. According to a report by The Sikh Coalition, founded in response to the violence emerging in the US after 9/11, thousands of Sikhs were victims of hate crimes, workplace discrimination, school bullying, and racial and religious profiling, especially in airports. The Sikh Coalition, "Fact Sheet on Post-9/11 Discrimination and Violence Against Sikh Americans," https://www.sikhcoalition.org/images/documents/fact%20sheet%20on%20hate%20against%20sikhs%20in%20 america%20post%209-11%201.pdf.

Fig. 7.2. Tiziano Vecellio, *Philip II offering the Infante Fernando to Victory,* 1573–1575. Source: Museo del Prado, Madrid.

the Christian victory over the Turks at Lepanto on October 7, 1571, and the birth of Philip's son Fernando on December 5 of the same year, two events that were viewed as gifts from heaven. The Battle of Lepanto is in the background, while in the foreground the King raises his newborn son towards an angel who holds a palm and the inscription *Maiora Tibi* (More triumphs awaiting you) in one hand, and a laurel — symbol of victory — on the other. By contrast, the Ottoman defeat is represented by a Turk seated half-naked and in chains, deprived of his weapons and military insignia, and with his head bowed, looking in dismay at his turban lying on the floor, right at the center of the painting. In a context in which Ottoman expansionism and military might seemed unstoppable, the turban knocked off of the Turkish soldier's head embodies most vividly the severe blow dealt by the Christians to the Ottoman fleet.[18]

---

18 Also in the famous painting *Pala Pesaro,* realized between 1519 and 1526, Titian resorts to the representation of a head-bowed Turk wearing a white

Blurring the Boundaries

Despite its strong symbolic values both in the Ottoman Empire and in Europe, the turban is an object over which many different meanings were constantly negotiated de facto. This is evident, for instance, where the use of the turban is associated with liminal personas shifting, voluntarily or involuntarily, between Islam and Christianity: travelers, merchants, or slaves returning to Christian territories after having been in contact with the Turks.

Many travelers noted that it was considered wise to dress as an Ottoman when in Ottoman lands and this, sometimes, included using turbans. Between the sixteenth and nineteenth centuries there are many instances in which the Ottoman state issued dress concessions allowing non-Muslim merchants to bear arms and to wear Muslim clothes for additional safety when they were passing through dangerous areas. These concessions would include the possibility of wearing a white turban, whose use was customarily restricted to Muslims. Thus, a symbol perceived and employed to mark the differences between Muslims and non-Muslims was used instead to conceal such differences and blur boundaries of identity and religion.[19]

In a different but equally liminal context, the turban often appears in paintings of Christian prisoners of the Turks. They are represented in distress, shabbily dressed, bound in shackles and chains, and waiting to be freed, wearing a turban-like headgear hinting at their dangerous proximity to Islam. Analogously, the turban was also associated with manumitted Christian slaves. The fear that close contact with the infidels could have left some indelible traces on the freed slave's morals and religious integrity

---

turban to represent the victorious battle against the Ottomans at Santa Maura in 1503.

19 Charlotte Jirousek, "More than Oriental Splendor: European and Ottoman Headgear, 1380–1580," *Dress* 22, no. 1 (1995): 25, and Matthew Elliot, "Dress Codes in the Ottoman Empire: The Case of the Franks," in *Ottoman Costumes: From Textile to Identity,* ed. Suraiya Faroqhi and Christoph K. Neumann (Eren, 2004).

was a constant concern for the community to which the slave returned. The impending danger of conversion to Islam, which according to Christian propaganda all slaves experienced during their captivity, and the suspicion that these conversions might have actually happened, was unremitting. When the Italian polymath Count Luigi Ferdinando Marsili (1658–1730) returned in 1684 to his hometown of Bologna after almost a year as a slave of the Turks, malicious gossip spread. In particular, rumor had it that he had embraced the "Alcorano" and converted to Islam. This accusation of apostasy was accompanied by the circulation of anonymous portraits depicting Marsili dressed "alaturca" and wearing, of course, a turban.

The turban, then, can offer a valuable point of entry into the complex and multilayered migration and circulation of knowledge between Europe and the Ottoman Empire. Although the turban could be perceived, understood, and represented as an unambiguous marker of identity and status within Ottoman society, and would become one of the most powerful visual tools in Europe to represent the other, it was also in fact a source of potential ambiguities. The meanings and symbolic values the turban assumed would constantly change over time and according to the place, identity, and expectations of the user, as well as the interpretations of the public. Thus, it should be approached as a negotiable object rather than a symbol, almost intrinsically inclined to continuous redefinitions and new forms of use, able to represent at once a visual and tangible divide between opposing worlds and a domestication of antagonistic foreignness.

Bibliography

Ben Ismail, Youssef. "A History of Ottoman Fez before Mahmud II (ca. 1600–1800)." *Muqarnas* 38, no. 1 (2021): 155–83. DOI: 10.1163/22118993-00381P06.

De Amicis, Edmondo. *Costantinopoli*. Touring Club italiano, 1997.

D'Amora, Rosita. "Alcune considerazioni sul valore simbolico del copricapo in ambito turco-ottomano." In *Scritti in onore di Giovanni M. D'Erme,* edited by Michele Bernardini and Natalia L. Tornesello. Università degli Studi di Napoli "L'Orientale," 2005.

Bourne, Molly. "The Turban'd Turk in Renaissance Mantua: Francesco II Gonzaga's Interest in Ottoman Fashion." In *Mantova e il Rinascimento Italiano: Studi in onore di David S. Chambers,* edited by Philippa Jackson and Guido Rebecchini. Sometti Editoriale, 2011.

Campbell, Caroline, and Alan Chong, eds. *Bellini and the East.* Yale University Press, 1988. Isabella Stewart Gardener Museum. Exhibition catalog.

Cevizli, Antonia Gatward. "Bellini, Bronze and Bombards: Sultan Mehmed II's Requests Reconsidered." *Renaissance Studies* 28, no. 5 (2014): 748–65. DOI: 10.1111/rest.12059.

———. "Portraits, Turbans and Cuirasses: Material Exchange between Mantua and the Ottomans at the End of the Fifteenth Century." In *Global Gifts: The Material Culture of Diplomacy in Early Modern Eurasia,* edited by Zoltán Biedermann, Anne Gerritson, and Giorgio Riello. Cambridge University Press, 2018. DOI: 10.1017/9781108233880.

Elliot, Matthew. "Dress Codes in the Ottoman Empire: The Case of the Franks." In *Ottoman Costumes: From Textile to Identity,* edited by Suraiya Faroqhi and Christoph K. Neumann. Eren, 2004.

Jirousek, Charlotte. "More Than Oriental Splendor: European and Ottoman Headgear, 1380–1580." *Dress* 22, no. 1 (1995): 22–33. DOI: 10.1179/036121195805298172.

da Lezze, Donado. *Historia Turchesca 1300–1514*. Edited by Ion Ursu. Carol Göbl, 1909.

Madar, Heather. "Dürer's Depictions of the Ottoman Turks: A Case of Early Modern Orientalism?" In *The Turk and Islam in the Western Eye, 1450–1750: Visual Imagery before Orientalism*, edited by James G. Harper. Ashgate, 2011.

Mellinkoff, Ruth. *Outcasts: Signs of Otherness in Northern European Art of the Late Middle Ages*. University of California Press, 1993.

Necipoğlu, Gülru. "Visual Cosmopolitanism and Creative Translation: Artistic Conversations with Renaissance Italy in Mehmed II's Constantinople." *Muqarnas* 29, no. 1 (2012): 1–81. DOI: 10.1163/22118993-90000183.

Quataert, Donald. "Clothing Laws, State, and Society in the Ottoman Empire, 1720–1829." *International Journal of Middle East Studies* 29, no. 3 (1997): 403–25. DOI: 10.1017/S0020743800064837.

Raby, Julian. "Pride and Prejudice: Mehmed the Conqueror and the Italian Portrait Medal." *Studies in the History of Art* 21 (1987): 171–94. https://www.jstor.org/stable/42620181.

———. *Venice, Dürer and the Oriental Mode*. Islamic Art Publications, 1982.

Rodini, Elizabeth. "The Sultan's True Face? Gentile Bellini, Mehmed II, and the Values of Verisimilitude." In *The Turk and Islam in the Western Eye, 1450–1750: Visual Imagery before Orientalism*, edited by James G. Harper. Ashgate, 2011.

Spandounes, Theodore. *On the Origin of the Ottoman Emperors*. Translated and edited by Donald M. Nicol. Cambridge University Press, 1997.

The Sikh Coalition. "Fact Sheet on Post-9/11 Discrimination and Violence against Sikh Americans." https://www.sikhcoalition.org/images/documents/fact%20sheet%20on%20hate%20against%20sikhs%20in%20america%20post%209-11%201.pdf.

8

Migrant Unknowledge:
A Vision of the Virgin in
Fifteenth-Century Kozhikode

Jonathan Gil Harris

Let me go out on a limb and make a claim that I will put to the test here. One of our most significant experiences of time is a time beyond linear time: an everyday experience of what I can only characterize as timeless time. Despite the fact that the world changes, and time's arrow moves forward, we are often confident that, as sure as the sun will rise tomorrow, X or Y or Z is the way of the world, time and time again. Please note I'm not making any truth claim about this time actually existing outside our experience of it. But it is an experience common to many people across history and cultures. We could call this time metaphysical time, holy time, or (as I have done) timeless time. But whatever we call it, it is a time that usually provides a measure of existential comfort, by promising a meaningful world that operates according to certain transcendent principles and laws that abide across time.

What interests me is how this sense of timeless time is formed. Even though it gestures to a realm of truth beyond the protean material world, it is often shaped through the ritual repetition of embodied practices within it. No matter how metaphysical this time may often seem to be, its effect is paradoxically produced through physical engagement with matter that serves a mnemonic function, creating the recursive impression that this is how things are, this is how things have been, and this is how things will be, all the time. Sensuous interaction with matter is thus the gateway to a meta-temporality, a time that emerges in time yet supposedly exists beyond time.

But matter can also disrupt, or obstruct, this meta-temporalizing maneuver. It becomes *migrant* matter — at least in the instances I will examine — because of its power to move us away from symbolization and the reassurance of meaning. I could get Lacanian or Žižekian and call the effect of this movement "The Real." But I will allow migrant matter to speak to us in its own unsettling terms, in a space of cultural encounter where what we think we know tends to fall apart as we interact with objects that we'd assumed would orient us towards the familiar and the understandable. And there, in a space where we meet objects from worlds new to us, matter all too often resists our attempts to orient ourselves towards timeless time. It produces what we might call migrant un-knowledge.

* * *

In the summer of 1498, the first Portuguese fleet of Vasco da Gama landed in southern India at what Westerners call Calicut, and its residents call Kozhikode. The local ruler welcomed da Gama and his men in hospitable fashion, dazzling him with a procession of three thousand armed Nair warriors. The Indians asked the Portuguese what they had come to Kozhikode for; one of the general's men is said to have replied, "Christians and spices."[1] Vasco da Gama's search for spices is well known; it prompted the aggressive Portuguese takeover of Indian Ocean trade routes previously controlled by Malayalis, Gujaratis, and

---

1   See Sanjay Subrahmanyam, *The Career and Legend of Vasco da Gama* (Cambridge University Press, 1997), 129.

Arabs, which led in turn to the formation of the Portuguese Estado da Índia and its various Indian and Indonesian colonies. But da Gama's search for Christians has been bypassed by straightforwardly economic and political histories of early modern Portuguese colonial expansion.

Vasco da Gama had certainly been lured around the Cape of Good Hope and the Horn of Africa to India in search of the wealth associated with the lucrative spice trade. But he was also on a mission to find potential allies who might assist the Portuguese in their ongoing battles with Islam following the Christian *reconquista* of the Iberian Peninsula. Marco Polo had written of the Christians of South India who had been converted long ago by St. Thomas — a story reiterated by Sir John Mandeville.[2] Mandeville also added credence to the legend of Prester John, an Indian Christian king who ruled over seventy-two provinces and seven tributary kings. Europeans had long dreamed that Prester John's wealth and power might prove invaluable assets in the war against Islam. It was precisely the dream of Prester John that prompted da Gama to insist on meeting with the "king of Calicut," despite his counsellors advising against it. And his conviction of the Christianity of the locals led him to accept an invitation to visit, along with eleven other Portuguese, a place of worship near Kozhikode.

Some fifty years later, the sixteenth-century Portuguese chronicler Fernão Lopes de Castanedha recounted da Gama's visit.[3] According to Castanedha, the building was an impressive one: Its exterior boasted a bell-tower with seven bells, and its

---

2 See Marco Polo, *The Travels of Marco Polo*, trans. R.E. Latham (Penguin, 1958), 274–76, and John Mandeville, *The Travels of Sir John Mandeville*, trans. Charles Moseley (Penguin, 1983), 124–25.

3 All references to Castanedha's report, *História do descobrimento e conquista da Índia pelos Portugueses*, are from Shankar Raman, ed., "Fernão Lopes de Castanedha — Excerpts from História do descobrimento e conquista da Índia pelos Portugueses. 1582. English Translation by Nicholas Lichfield, published as *The First Book of the Historie of the Discoverie and Conquest of the East Indias*," in *Travel Knowledge: European "Discoveries" in the Early Modern Period*, ed. Ivo Kamps and Jytosna G. Singh (Palgrave Macmillan, 2001).

ornate exterior was complemented by a dazzling interior fes-
tooned with holy icons. Priests, wearing petticoats and threads
that reminded the Portuguese visitors of the attire of monastic orders in Europe, welcomed them by burning incense and
sprinkling holy water. The building's most revered icon was a
portrait of the Virgin, aloft in the nave near the bells, and the
Portuguese clambered upstairs to be in her presence. Amidst
the smell of incense, the sound of bells, the cooling sensation
of holy water, and the sight of the Virgin, the Portuguese settled
happily into the task of performing their ritual worship of God.

But something about this church wasn't quite right. Castanedha tells us that one of the Portuguese, João de Sala, realized that the figures depicted on its walls didn't look like the
religious icons he was used to back home. The figures had wide
open mouths with long teeth. Even more strangely, several of
them had multiple arms. Slowly panic overtook de Sala. And he
began to wonder about the identity of the "Virgin" icon. Fearing this church was, in fact, a satanic perversion of a house of
God, de Sala fell to his knees, shouting, "If this be the devil, I
worship the true God!"[4] Da Gama started laughing — perhaps
a little nervously — at de Sala's panic. Yet he continued to pray.
His decision was sneeringly glossed in Nicholas Lichfield's 1582
English translation of Castanedha's narrative: "the General, deceived, committed Idolatry with the devil."[5] For, as you may have
gathered by now, this was not a Christian church at all: it was
what we would now call a Hindu temple, presided over by Brah-
min priests.

In the case of the Protestant Lichfield, the story was a pre-
text for deriding the devilish idolatry of a Roman Catholic too
beholden to matter that he could no longer tell the difference
between true religion and paganism. But for the Catholic Castanedha, writing in the 1540s long after da Gama's visit, it was a
story of how the Hindu residents of the Malabar coast were not

---

4   Ibid., 129.
5   See Marco Polo, *The Travels of Marco Polo,* trans. R.E. Latham (Penguin,
    1958), 274–76, and Mandeville, *The Travels of Sir John Mandeville,* 124–25.

the trustworthy Christian allies da Gama had hoped they would be. João de Sala emerges as the true Christian hero of Castanedha's account: he had been right about the temple's non-Christian objects. The matter of the "church" included the typical appurtenances of a Malabar Hindu ambalam or temple. Its priests were Brahmins wearing sacred threads; its bells were rung as part of pujas in which incense was burned; its holy water was sprinkled to purify the temple devotees as well as given to them to drink; and the figures with long teeth and multiple arms were certainly icons associated with Bhagavathi, one of the female deities worshipped in south Indian Hindu temples, especially in what is now the state of Kerala. Although the Goddess is sometimes worshipped as an un-representable presence — the Pisharikavu temple in Kozhikode district, for instance, depicts her obliquely through the figure of a sword — she is often embodied as a large multi-armed female icon in a sanctum sanctorum. The honored "Virgin" worshipped by da Gama and his men was probably one such icon.

I am interested, though, less in correcting the error of da Gama and his men — an impulse shared by the Protestant Lichfield and modern cultural historians alike — than in understanding the emotional response of de Sala. It isn't too much of a stretch, I think, to call his response a breakdown. It isn't simply that he feared he was in the presence of the Devil. A physical object that had at first seemed familiar to him had now become fundamentally unfamiliar, confusing him so profoundly that it rent apart his sense of the world. De Sala had been confronted by strange matter — a strange Mater — that deeply disrupted his sense of holy time, a time that promised the comforting reassurance of communion not just with God but also an entire realm of meaning.

There were probably many reasons why da Gama and his men were so susceptible to believing they were in a church. They were already happily inhabiting a narrative of a Christian India. But the Portuguese visitors' belief that this was a Christian church must have been fortified further by their sensory experiences inside the ambalam. Walking into a church was, for da

Gama, not just about moving into a physical space. It was also about moving into an experience of time — a sense of holy time that transcends the vanities of the everyday. It was founded in the illusion of a fullness of meaning, or rather, in a guarantee that meaning is *here*. Entry into the church is also entry into the time of God, the time of logos, the time of that which is and always will be.

For a Portuguese Christian in the fifteenth century, this sense of time was no disembodied abstraction. It was pointedly produced through repetitious material practices. Some of these practices were trained ritual movements on the part of the church-goer, such as kneeling, singing, folding hands in prayer, and crossing oneself. Many more were sensuously involuntary — smelling incense, feeling and tasting holy water, hearing bells, and seeing holy icons. It is hard to underestimate the effect of these embodied experiences in creating the sense of holy time. We might describe the space of the church as a memory machine driven by the body's sensuous interaction with material elements during ritual practices. These practices could produce aches, pains, and other embodied annoyances like creaky knees, stuffed noses, or ringing eardrums. But they also transported the body out of linear time and into an experience of timeless communion with God. It was precisely this experience of time that must have been activated in the encounter of the Portuguese men with the matter of the ambalam. Its bells, water, incense, and icons were all spurs to embodied memory, spurs to the performance of practices remembered as much through muscle memory as through conscious recollection.

Yet it was the matter of the ambalam that also punctured that assurance. Da Gama's experience confirms that, in a strange place, one will see (and smell and hear and feel and taste) what one expects to find. But the unfamiliar matter of the temple also resisted the projections of familiarity performed on it. Indeed, what seems to have prompted de Sala's collapse was precisely his intuition that the Virgin — Mother Mary, *Mater Dei,* maternal figure of comfort — had suddenly morphed into something unfamiliar, something unfamilial. De Sala's term for the agent of this transformation was the Devil. But adding to his panic was surely his multisensory experience of the sound of bells, the feel of holy water, and the smell of incense. All these were no doubt initially reassuring: they must have sounded and felt and smelled, quite literally, like home. But as the "Virgin" resolved into a demonically unfamiliar apparition, de Sala's sensory over-load became literally unbearable, to the point where he could no longer trust the evidence of his eyes, ears, and nose. Here we see how strange matter functions unpredictably in the cultural contact zone, both as *aide-mémoire* of home and as physically overpowering irruption of the foreign and unexplainable.

If this sounds like a version of the uncanny, so be it. But the uncanniness here is not confined to the simultaneous familiarity and unfamiliarity of the Virgin mother, or to the realization that the good-breasted maternal nurturer is equally a bad-breasted demonic denier. The Freudian or Kleinian family romance nar-ratives may capture something of the emotional crisis de Sala felt. But they cannot capture the deeply embodied dimension of de Sala's experience. This dimension points to the uncanny power of matter as the ground of holy time. De Sala's breakdown is a reminder that, at home as much as abroad, what seems to guarantee one's unmediated access to metaphysical or holy time is physical matter. And this matter is always fraught with the risk that it might not successfully signify its metaphysical ref-erent. The cognitive maps that we produce of the spiritual, the holy, the transcendent unravel without warning. No matter how many times we deploy familiar matter to perform our repetitive rituals of devotion, matter keeps estranging our attempts to sub-ordinate it to the spaceless space of signification, to the timeless time of logos. It keeps producing migrant un-knowledge.

* * *

Let me now situate a little my reading of de Sala's response to the Virgin who wasn't, to the familiar Mater who became unfa-miliar matter. I am writing as a recent immigrant to India. And amongst the many experiences of disorientation I have suffered there, perhaps chief among them concerns my relation to matter.

As someone who grew up in mountainous New Zealand, and then spent thirteen years living in the rugged Finger Lakes district of upstate New York, I often navigate using hills. These are not just spatial markers. They are temporal markers too. I can usually make out how far away I am from somewhere I am travelling based on the blueness of a hill on the horizon: the bluer it is, the further away it is, and so I can track my anticipated progress from here to there accordingly. That may seem like a very linear conception of time. But the sense of comfort I derive from being able to measure distance belongs to a different order of temporality, one founded in repetition. I know my way through space, and I know the time it takes to get from A to B, because I have over time repeatedly navigated this way, positioning my body in relation to hills, internalizing them within a cognitive mind-map that has been re-externalized in my movements on foot or behind a steering wheel. This may not be the holy time craved by the Christian visitors to Kozhikode. But it is, like that time, a mode of temporality produced through the ritual repetition of orientations towards objects. And it again offers a great sense of comfort. Growing up in mountain-dotted Auckland, my pantheon of saints weren't religious but volcanic, cones that reassured me where I stood in the larger scheme of things.

In Delhi, which is completely flat, I have lost this sense of time. And that has been terribly disorienting for me. Often I simply feel lost in the city, as I have no visible compass points to navigate by. So imagine my joy one day when, driving north of Delhi, I saw a misty blue hill on the horizon. Something in my heart soared. And it looked like a huge hill, far in the distance, because it was a particularly hazy blue. Without consciously realizing it, I placed it around ten kilometers — twenty minutes away in Delhi traffic — by car. But I reached it much more quickly, in about two minutes. My sense of disorientation was compounded at that point. Because the hill turned out not to be something made of rock and soil. It was a 200-foot-high mound of trash. And it was misty because the members of the human scavenger caste who live on top of it are perpetually burning the day's newly dumped trash, in search of metals they can sell at the local markets. The mistiness of the hill, in other words, was not the mistiness of distance but of smoke and human activity. But I was to find all that out only much later. For now, I was in a state of utter disorientation.

This disorientation had nothing to do with linear time being disrupted. If anything, there can be something deeply consoling about the disruption of linear time. That consolation is a feature of Shakespearean romances like *The Winter's Tale* or *The Tempest,* in which familiar yet strange matter — a statue, a storm — allows us to go back in time and repossess what we have lost. Death is not our only destination, romance assures us, because we can move back as well as forward, at least in fantasy. But the disruption of our orientations to space and time in a zone of cultural contact bring us face to face with another kind of death: the death of mastery, of sense, of knowing. We who know that the Strange Mater of Kozhikode was probably the Goddess Bhagavathi can laugh at the panic of the horror-stricken João de Sala and the devotion of the worshipful Vasco da Gama. But we laugh from a position of knowledge. And that's the problem. Perhaps we should also sympathize a little with de Sala's experience of time disintegrating into horrifying inexplicability. We might recognize ourselves in him, and recognize in particular the misrecognitions prompted by the seemingly familiar matter he interacted with. For familiar matter has the power to become strange when it refuses to do what we expect it to do, when it punctures our sense of a world that abides through time, and when we find ourselves, and our bodies, in a state of migrant un-knowingness.

Bibliography

Raman, Shankar, ed. *"Fernão* Lopes de Castanedha — Excerpts from *História do descobrimento e conquista da Índia pelos Portugueses.* 1582 English Translation by Nicholas Lichfield, published as *The First Book of the Historie of the Discoverie and Conquest of the East Indias."* In *Travel Knowledge: European "Discoveries" in the Early Modern Period,* edited by Ivo Kamps and Jytosna G. Singh. Palgrave Macmillan, 2001.

Mandeville, John. *The Travels of Sir John Mandeville.* Translated by Charles Moseley. Penguin, 1983.

Polo, Marco. *The Travels of Marco Polo.* Translated by R.E. Latham. Penguin, 1958.

Subrahmanyam, Sanjay. *The Career and Legend of Vasco da Gama.* Cambridge University Press, 1997.

9

Knowledge in Translation:
Between the Local and the Universal

Annabel Brett

In the early years of the fifteenth century, a heated debate over
the correct principles of translation blew up between the celebrated Italian humanist Leonardo Bruni and the Spanish bishop of Burgos, Alonso de Cartagena. This famous episode is of
more than purely antiquarian interest. It resonates with all the
perplexities we encounter today, as translators, historians, and
citizens, as we try to create pathways of comprehension between
what is familiar and what is different with tools of reasoning that
threaten to collapse that difference the moment we pick them
up.

My title is prompted by the opposing starting-points taken
by the two protagonists — on the one hand, that correct translation depends on a specific knowledge of language comparable to a local knowledge of place, and on the other, that correct
translation depends instead on universal reasoning capacities,
universal in the sense of "common to all nations." I think that
these two poles say something about translation more generally.
Translation can be seen as a movement from one kind of local to
another kind of local — from Italian to Spanish, say. But transla-

tion is not centrally from language to language, as Umberto Eco insists in his own writing on translation, *Mouse or Rat? Translation as Negotiation.* Rather, it is from text to text.[1] As such, translation involves interpretation, a creative act of making sense of a particular text in and through another. In order to *make sense,* we have to move out of the local entirely in some way, drawing not only upon specific knowledge but also more general tools of reasoning such as analogy and comparison, which in turn involve our more general human experience.

That movement out of the local into whatever it is that is not local — that is the kind of migration I am interested in here. It's a movement that is compromised in the sense that the local and the nonlocal do not stably preexist our translation, but are constructed in, and on, the very path that we choose between them. This makes translation a kind of migrant knowledge — not a knowledge that preexists the pathway, knowledge *of* the way, but knowledge *in* and *on* the way. Knowledge *of,* with its apparently stable coordinates between the local and the universal, bends to knowledge *in* as we traverse what Gayatri Chakravorty Spivak in her essay on the politics of translation calls "the spacy emptiness between two named historical languages."[2] What I am essaying is a migrant reading, in this sense, of the Renaissance debate between Bruni and Cartagena.

In 1416/1417 the renowned humanist scholar Leonardo Bruni published a new translation of Aristotle's *Nicomachean Ethics.* It includes a preface in which he systematically rubbished the old one. He did not know the identity of the old translator, but we know him as Robert Grosseteste, the great thirteenth-century Oxford scholar. Perhaps the anonymity helped Bruni with his invective against "the man of iron" who massacred Aristotle's

---

1   Umberto Eco, *Mouse or Rat? Translation as Negotiation* (Weidenfeld and Nicolson, 2003), 25–26.

2   Gayatri Chakravorty Spivak, "The Politics of Translation," in *Destabilizing Theory: Contemporary Feminist Debates,* ed. Michèle Barrett and Anne Phillips (Polity, 1992), 178.

text.[3] Bruni developed his polemic in a later work, written between 1424 and 1426, on how to translate properly, *De interpretatione recta.* Here he extended his criticism to an old translation of Aristotle's *Politics,* the author of which was, as we now know, William of Moerbeke rather than Grosseteste. In both cases, Bruni compares the medieval translation to the defacement of a picture: like someone throwing feces at a painting by Giotto, as he later put it.[4] There's no doubt Bruni felt very strongly. But his new translation of the *Ethics,* together with its preface, provoked equally strong feelings on the part of Alfonso de Cartagena, the Bishop of Burgos. For Cartagena, Bruni's crime was not merely to have denounced the old translation in too vehement and unseemly a manner. It was to have denounced it as *not a translation at all,* but rather an annihilation of the old.[5] Cartagena's defense of the old translation came, in turn, into the hands of Bruni. He wrote two letters to Francesco Pizolpasso, Archbishop of Milan, expostulating against this man who claimed to be able to judge between his new translation and the old *without knowing any Greek.*

The outlines of this controversy are fairly well-known.[6] Bruni argues from a position that all but the most recondite vocabu-

---

3   Leonardo Bruni, "Praemissio quaedam ad evidentiam novae translationis Ethicorum Aristotelis," in *Leonardo Bruni Aretino: Humanistisch-philosophische Schriften mit einer Chronologie seiner Werke und Briefe,* ed. Hans Baron (Teubner, 1928), 78–79.

4   Leonardo Bruni, "De interpretatione recta" [On correct translation], in *Leonardo Bruni Aretino: Humanistisch-philosophische Schriften mit einer Chronologie seiner Werke und Briefe,* ed. Hans Baron (Teubner, 1928), 83, and Leonardo Bruni, "Leonardus archiepiscopo Mediolanensi salutem" [First letter to Francesco Pizolpasso, 1436], in *Humanismo y teoría de la traducción en España y Italia en la primera mitad del siglo XV,* ed. T. González Rolán, A. Moreno Hernández, and P. Saquero Suárez-Somonte (Ediciones Clásicas, 2000), 284.

5   Alfonso de Cartagena, "Liber Alphonsi episcopi Burgensis," in *Humanismo y teoría de la traducción en España y Italia en la primera mitad del siglo XV,* ed. González Rolán, Moreno Hernández, and Saquero Suárez-Somonte, 202.

6   For further details, see chapter 6 in Eckart Schütrumpf, *The Earliest Translations of Aristotle's* Politics *and the Creation of Political Terminology*

lary can be translated from Greek into Latin. It is not clear that this is a thesis that will hold for any two languages, since Bruni's defense of the possibility of translating into Latin is premised upon the riches, the opulence, of the Latin language. Given this wealth, though, there is no excuse whatsoever for leaving Greek words in the original, as the medieval translators frequently did; and still less for making up new Latin words — that's "Latin" words — that have no meaning in any language. As for knowledge of the original language, Bruni argues that it can only come through reading widely in its literature. You have to come to know in precise detail the way that people talk, including figurative usage and idiomatic expressions. Once you have the requisite knowledge of both languages, however, there is such a thing as *interpretatio recta* (correct translation), in which both sense and style are translated precisely from one language into another.[7]

Cartagena, for his part, frankly confesses that he doesn't know any Greek, so he isn't going to argue on those grounds. That would give Bruni an unfair advantage! He insists, however, that reason is common to all nations, however they speak.[8] Thus, in translation as an act of interpretation, or making sense, what we are doing is using our reason to reconstruct the reasoning of the original, on the presumption that the original is reasonable in the same way as we are. You wouldn't even try to translate a text that you did not think was rational — why would you bother? You couldn't learn anything from it. For Cartagena, the peculiarities of one historical language versus another are incidental to this process of understanding which takes place between one person's reason and another's. And, if historical language actually gets in the way — say there's no equivalent word in one or other of them — well, then, by all means make up a new word. The reader, who is also rational, will understand that new word.

(Wilhelm Fink, 2014).

7   Bruni, "De interpretatione," 83; cf. 78, where he cites as evidence for his position the possibility of translating comedy accurately, as the Latin playwright Terence shows with his translations of Attic new comedy.

8   Cartagena, "Liber Alphonsi," 204.

In short, when we translate, we translate the thought, not the words, and we access the thought through universal reason, common to all three parties: author, translator, and reader.

Two very, very different conceptions of translation, then. Later Renaissance translators of Aristotle, despite their humanist allegiances, would have some sympathy with Cartagena — believing that when you translate philosophy, you have to translate the philosophy, precisely — and they criticized Bruni for his rhetorical translation that blurs the philosophical sense of the Greek original. They did at least know their Greek, however. Cartagena's understanding of the philosophical sense of the text is entirely from the Latin text itself, supplemented by what is effectively *his own* reasoning. No wonder Bruni accuses him of some mystical practice of divination, and ridicules his appeal to *reasonable conjecture* in the establishment of meaning.[9] It's as if, he says, I were to go to France or Spain and tell some people I meet that a certain church is on a hill overlooking Bologna.[10] They've never been there, don't know the place at all; but they don't think that's likely, since it would be risky to build a church on top of a hill. It's a much more *reasonable conjecture* that the church is at the bottom of the hill. But, says Bruni, I've been there and I *know* it's on top of the hill. Why are we even having this conversation??!!

I think we are all familiar, from our own experiences, with the peculiar mix of arrogance and defensiveness that characterizes both positions. On the one hand: I have the local knowledge, you don't, so you can't understand anything and have to defer to my interpretation. On the other: I don't need any local knowledge, it's all to do with being rational, so your local understanding is just that — small and pedantic. But translation is, in fact, impossible on either assumption. And indeed, when we get

---

9   Bruni, "Leonardus archiepiscopo Mediolanensi salutem," 274, and Leonardo Bruni, "Leonardus archiepiscopo Mediolanensi salutem plurimam dicit" [Second letter to Francesco Pizolpasso], in *Humanismo y teoría de la traducción en España y Italia en la primera mitad del siglo XV,* ed. González Rolán, Moreno Hernández, and Saquero Suárez-Somonte, 290.

10   Ibid., 314.

into the more detailed texture of the argument between Bruni and Cartagena, we see both of their positions beginning to slip and morph into something much more flexible.

One of Bruni's examples of making words up is Moerbeke's *honorabilitas* for the Greek *timēma*.[11] The correct Latin translation, he writes, is instead *census*. But his marginal note defends this translation by comparing political organization in Greece and Rome. Here, then, the knowledge is not purely local, but involves an understanding of the relationship between two historical cultures. Behind that note lies Bruni's first exposure both to history and to translation through the *Parallel Lives* of the Greco-Roman author Plutarch. This text was introduced to him by the Byzantine scholar Manuel Chrysoloras, whom Coluccio Salutati had invited to Florence in 1397. Chrysoloras promoted Plutarch's *Lives* because of the commonality it posited between Greek and Italian cultures. So one of Bruni's principles for translating Greek into Latin was a function of a moment of encounter, of migration, between Byzantium and early Renaissance Italy. In the hands of Chrysoloras, that encounter involved a specific politics of cultural rapprochement that in turn inflected Bruni's politics of translation, providing the poles within which his comparison operates.[12]

Just as Bruni does not, in practice, appeal to local knowledge alone, neither does Cartagena, in fact, appeal to universal reason alone. He too uses history to make sense. But his is a very different history. Instead of there being two different languages, two different cultures, that can be known historically, Cartagena starts with a historical understanding of languages as mixed rather than pure. Again, it's not clear that this is universal proposition, but it's certainly true for Europe, in which not only is Greek mixed in with Latin — and was so even in

---

11 Bruni, "De interpretatione," 94.

12 See Paul Botley, *Latin Translation in the Renaissance: The Theory and Practice of Leonardo Bruni, Giannozzo Manetti, and Desiderius Erasmus* (Cambridge University Press, 2004), 15, and Marianne Pade, *The Reception of Plutarch's Lives in Fifteenth-Century Italy*, vol. 1 (Museum Tusculanum Press, 2007), 89–100.

antiquity — but both languages sit alongside the vernaculars into which they have also seeped.[13] Take "philosophy" itself as an example. Is that a Greek word? A Latin word? A Spanish word — or, we might add, an English word? Translation takes place, not between one pure language and another, but inside this mix within which the two poles cannot be fully distinguished from one another. That mix is a function of history, as languages leak out of chronological as well as geographical boundaries. Unlike Bruni's, Cartagena's history is not something past, of which you have historical knowledge like the geographical knowledge you might have of something over there. Rather, Cartagena's history is continuous with the present. And this is the frame in which he makes his own comparative moves.

Let me illustrate that with one of the more fun episodes in the debate. A passage of Grosseteste's *Ethics* translation that aroused Bruni's particular ire was the straight transliteration whereby Aristotle is made to say that the virtuous mean in conversational wit or humor is "eutrapely," the excessive vice "bomolochy," and the negative vice "agrichy." (I have anglicized the form so you get the picture.) "O iron man!," cries Bruni. "You call that *translation??*" A *bomolochus*, he says, is in fact a Latin *scurra*, which means a kind of comic parasite, so Latin has the perfect word for the excessive vice: *scurrilitas*.[14] No, says Cartagena. A *bomolochus* is not a *scurra*, because a *bomolochus* is not a parasite, making obscene jokes for money. That kind of person is called in Spanish an *alvardano*. But, he says, warming to his theme, I've known quite well-off and prominent men who display this vice of excess in humor, so it can't be something peculiar to scroungers. In view of the fact, then, that Latin does not have a word for *bomolochus*, Grosseteste was quite right to leave it in the original — but actually it's precisely not in the original: it has been written in Latin as *bomolochus*, and declined in that form, so now it *is* Latin, and we all know what it means.[15]

13 Cartagena, "Liber Alphonsi," 208–10.
14 Bruni, "Praemissio," 78–79.
15 Cartagena, "Liber Alphonsi," 216–18; cf. 212.

Cartagena's willingness to dip into vernacular language and present-day culture to make sense is in the sharpest possible contrast to Bruni, who calls the vernaculars "barbarian" in the same sense as did the Greeks and the Romans, and rejects the mixing of languages not only as a chaos, but also as a kind of impurity or defilement.[16] The difference between the two positions is reflected in the figurative expressions each chooses for the Latin language. Bruni uses a metaphor of money, and, with that, of social hierarchy. As we've seen, Latin for him is a wealthy language. But the old translator does not own that wealth. Rather, he's a beggar, scrounging or at the very least borrowing scraps of Greek vocabulary even in the midst of linguistic opulence.[17] Cartagena's similes are quite different. Moral philosophy in Latin, he writes, is like a noble maiden marrying in a far-off land, who brings some of her handmaidens with her — Greek words, which she keeps with her "among Latin men" as a comfort and to remind her of her origins. Will Bruni, he asks, force her to deport them out of her borders? Moreover, the fact that Latin continually accepts words from Greek and also from other foreign languages is not, for Cartagena, an index of poverty. Rather, it represents the peculiar preeminence of Latin as a "space without borders." It brings alien words into its domain as if captured from the enemy under the law of nations.[18] Cartagena's similes evoke a social and linguistic inclusivity that may seem appealing to us in contrast to Bruni's aversion to mixing as defilement. But they nevertheless invoke the very real violence involved in the migration of Latin through Europe and beyond: the violence of war and the gendered violence of intermarriage, in which the young girl is a commodity in the transaction.

Such thoughts take us back to our starting point, to our two modern translators, Gayatri Spivak and Umberto Eco, and to our underlying question of movement between the local and

16 Bruni, "Leonardus archiepiscopo Mediolanensi salutem," 280, and Bruni, "Leonardus archiepiscopo Mediolanensi salutem plurimam dicit," 326.

17 Bruni, "Praemissio," 77; cf. Bruni, "De interpretatione," 85.

18 Cartagena, "Liber Alphonsi," 210.

whatever it is that is not local. Not surprisingly, neither Spivak nor Eco thinks of translation in the same way as either Cartagena or Bruni. But it is nonetheless suggestive to read their differences within this longer history of difference between translators. Eco's conception of translation as negotiation reminds us in some respects of the transactional elements in Cartagena. For Eco, however, the translator as negotiator is a non-violent figure, brokering a fair exchange between the integrity of the original and the legitimate expectations of the reader. A shared space does not preexist the transaction, but is created as a new place in which the original and the reader can meet, even if neither party can do so entirely on its own terms. In this process, both the agency and the ethics of the translator are central to building a viable bridge of sense between the two parties.

Spivak, by contrast, thinking about translation from a post-colonial perspective, writes of a kind of surrender of translator to text, a position more erotic than ethical. In this we are reminded of Bruni, for whom the translator is "carried away by very force" into the style of the original, and must bend and turn himself rather than the text.[19] For Spivak, the process of translation needs to hold both the agency of the translator, and the expectations of the audience, at bay. It is only through this surrender that one can translate for rhetoricity, the specific voice of the text, rather than for verbal logic. To use logic as a crowbar to engineer intelligibility *to* others is only to perpetuate, in translation, a logic — and a history — of the domination and suppression *of* others. In translating for rhetoricity, by contrast, the translator instead "frays" the edges on both sides, a fraying of language that also, implicitly, frays the self of both translator and reader.

For all our translators, for all their differences, history runs through language just as language runs through history. The very possibility of translation is embedded in that nexus, which is why we cannot translate, nor can we write history, without challenging our own complicity within that process. But it

---

19 Bruni, "De interpretatione," 87.

would be a false move both in language and in history to force a choice, to insist on one universal theory of translation or one universal way of writing history. As historians we juggle our alignment with our sources and with our audience, caught between intimacy and ethics. We are conscious of fraying the edges of past and present on the "spacy emptiness" between them, and of the fraying of identity that comes with that. We do not want to engineer intelligibility at the cost of perpetuating the suppressions of the past. We want to be alive to the silence that Spivak identifies as the unspoken heart of rhetoricity. But at the same time we must accept that we are agents, bridge-builders, and negotiators, with a responsibility towards both our sources and our audience that we cannot shrug off. We have so much to learn from migrants, who know more about the fraying, more about the silence, more about the spacy emptiness, than anyone else, but who, at the same time, find a new agency, and a new position of bridge-building, in a new commons that does not preexist but is instead created by their own migration. For it is in just this sense that history itself is a kind of migrant knowledge.

Bibliography

Botley, Paul. *Latin Translation in the Renaissance: The Theory and Practice of Leonardo Bruni, Giannozzo Manetti, and Desiderius Erasmus.* Cambridge University Press, 2004.

Bruni, Leonardo. "De interpretatione recta." In *Leonardo Bruni Aretino: Humanistisch-philosophische Schriften mit einer Chronologie seiner Werke und Briefe,* edited by Hans Baron. Teubner, 1928.

———. "Leonardus archiepiscopo Mediolanensi salutem." In *Humanismo y teoría de la traducción en España y Italia en la primera mitad del siglo XV,* edited by T. González Rolán, A. Moreno Hernández, and P. Saquero Suárez-Somonte. Ediciones Clásicas, 2000.

———. "Leonardus archiepiscopo Mediolanensi salutem plurimam dicit." In *Humanismo y teoría de la traducción en España y Italia en la primera mitad del siglo XV,* edited by T. González Rolán, A. Moreno Hernández, and P. Saquero Suárez-Somonte. Ediciones Clásicas, 2000.

———. "Praemissio quaedam ad evidentiam novae translationis Ethicorum Aristotelis." In *Leonardo Bruni Aretino: Humanistisch-philosophische Schriften mit einer Chronologie seiner Werke und Briefe,* edited by Hans Baron. Teubner, 1928.

Cartagena, Alonso de. "Liber Alphonsi episcopi Burgensis." In *Humanismo y teoría de la traducción en España y Italia en la primera mitad del siglo XV,* edited by T. González Rolán, A. Moreno Hernández, and P. Saquero Suárez-Somonte. Ediciones Clásicas, 2000.

Eco, Umberto. *Mouse or Rat? Translation as Negotiation.* Weidenfeld and Nicolson, 2003.

Pade, Marianne. *The Reception of Plutarch's Lives in Fifteenth-Century Italy.* Museum Tusculanum Press, 2007.

Schütrumpf, Eckart. *The Earliest Translations of Aristotle's Politics and the Creation of Political Terminology.* Wilhelm Fink, 2014.

Spivak, Gayatri Chakravorty. "The Politics of Translation." In
Destabilizing Theory: Contemporary Feminist Debates, edited
by Michèle Barrett and Anne Phillips. Polity, 1992.

10

Internal Migration:
The Letters and Adages of Erasmus

Brian Cummings

Did Erasmus long for home? Or was he always avoiding going back? In July 1514, in one of his most confessional letters, he wrote from near Calais to the Prior of his old monastery, Servaas Rogerszoon. It is well over twenty years since Erasmus left the cloister, but Servaas has suggested it may be time to return. Servaas, it appears, has urged that Erasmus belongs with his brethren, his countrymen, and that it would be to serve God in one place. "But I know the Dutch climate," Erasmus replies — literally the "Dutch sky" (*et novi coelum Hollandicum*).[1] Home made him ill: the diet disagreed with him, as did the cold and wet; he got fevers, or the stone (the priory is at Steyn).[2] Holland will be the death of him. Maybe, he suggests slyly, that is

---

1 Epistle 296, Erasmus to Servatius Rogerus, Hammes, July 8, 1514. *Opus epistolarum Des. Erasmi Roterdami* [EE], 12 vols., ed. P.S. Allen, H.M. Allen, and H.W. Garrod (Clarendon Press, 1906–1958), 1:567. Translation from *The Collected Works of Erasmus* [CWE], 86 vols. (University of Toronto Press, 1974), 1:296.

2 The Latin word for gallstone is *calculus;* the Dutch (*steen*) is morphologically identical to the placename.

CROSSINGS

Servaas's motive: preparation for death by means of a return to the place of birth. Yet perhaps migration is a more natural human estate than home, Erasmus counters. Did not Solon travel, or Pythagoras, and Plato? Were they not praised for it? The apostles were endless vagabonds, especially St Paul. Even the monk Jerome turned up now in Rome, now in Syria, now in Antioch. Like Jerome, Erasmus lives *nunc alibi atque alibi,* now here, now there. He is welcome everywhere: "There is not a single realm, neither Spain, nor Italy, nor Germany, nor France, nor England, nor Scotland, which does not invite me to be its guest."[3]

No region is foreign to him: he can live anywhere in Europe, from Skye to Salamanca, from the Atlantic to the Danube. Yet Erasmus in this passage represses something as well as proclaims the virtue of cosmopolitan experience and political neutrality. Although he paraded under the patrimonial designation "of Rotterdam," it is possible he never saw his city again after infancy. Indeed, he barely stayed overnight in the northern Netherlands after 1500. Meanwhile he lived in Brussels, Paris, Louvain, and then in England several times (in Oxford, London, and more often Cambridge). Yet it is hard to call anywhere his "home" till Basel in his fifties, followed by Freiburg-im-Breisgau in his sixties. He is the twentieth-century migrant before its time. His letters migrate as well, sometimes written in one city and posted in another.

Παρεπιδημία τίς ἐστιν ὁ βίος, *id est Peregrinatio quaedam est vita.* "Life is a time of exile": thus *Adagia* IV x 74.[4] Erasmus added the adage in 1533, the penultimate edition of his lifetime, although the idea is proverbial in him from the first experimental edition of Paris in 1500 and the expanded one from Venice in 1508. It is a difficult line to translate. The word *peregrinatio* sug-

---

3 CWE 1:297; Nec vlla est regio, nec Hispania, nec Italia, nec Germania, nec Gallia, nec Anglia, nec Scotia, quae me ad suum non inuitet hospitium, EE, 1:568.

4 *Adagia,* from vol. 2 in Erasmus, *Desiderii Erasmi Roterodami* Opera omnia [ASD], 9 vols., ed. J.H. Waszink et al. (Brill, 1969–), 2/8:258; CWE, 36:527. The full text of this adage is supplied at the end of this chapter, in the original languages and in translation.

gests a context from the Hebrew scriptures, as Erasmus quickly
elucidates via 1 Chronicles 29:15, Psalm 119:19, and in the New
Testament, 1 Peter 2:11 and Hebrews 11:13. "For we are strangers
before thee, and sojourners, as were all our fathers"; "I am a
stranger in the earth: hide not thy commandments from me."[5]
The Jewish language of eternal exile fitted into the early Christian self-image of persecution in the temporal state. In an adage
of just seven lines, Erasmus creates a miniature prose poem of
dislocation, alienation, or inevitable exile: *vitam hanc esse exilium, esse incolatum et peregrinationem.*[6] Human beings do not
belong anywhere. They are born out of nowhere and die into
nowhere. Meanwhile they patch out an existence that is homeless and placeless.

The *Adagia,* printed all over Europe in ever larger and more
complex collections, are the lifework of Erasmus, his last published work in 1536 as well as his first in 1500. They provide a
kind of encyclopaedic knowledge of the ancient world, citing an
eclectic range of sources from Hesiod or Sappho to the church
fathers. What lies within is a storehouse of metaphor combined
with a subtle and playful commentary. Erasmus twists and turns,
encouraging the reader to do the same, in the process creating
a source for self-invention (for author and reader alike) along
with an imaginary of the other, in the endless encounter with the
peoples, myths, quirks, anxieties and desires of literature, history, politics, as well as the pagan, Jewish, Persian, Zoroastrian, or
Christian religions. A constant lodestone of self-identification
for Erasmus is Ulysses the wanderer, the home-loving home-
avoider, the trickster, the mind's interior inventor. Θάλασσα
κλύζει πάντα τἀνθρώπων κακά, "the sea washes away all mortal
ills" (*Adagia,* III iv 9).[7] Or we are like Ulysses's crew — *Ulyssis
remigium* (*Adagia,* II x 62), who "did not abstain from Circe's

---

5   Erasmus freely paraphrases a cento of these verses, picking up words from
    the Latin Vulgate translation without quoting exactly; here I give 1 Chroni-
    cles 29:15 and Psalm 119:19 using the KJV.
6   "This life is life as an exile, life as an alien, life in a land that is not our true
    home," CWE, 36:527.
7   ASD, 2/5:245; CWE, 35:8.

drinks, who could not be torn away from the Lotus-eaters, who would not keep their hands off the oxen of the Sun."[8] As with Joyce, Erasmus makes Ulysses the carrier of an intertextuality of almost indeterminate temporality, from Homer until today. Our folly is our undoing, in the endless Joycean swell.

Poetic meditation and mystic speculation, however, takes place alongside a much grittier political and religious context. *Peregrinatio* (or "pilgrimage") in the world of Erasmus has a specific resonance very different from its Hebrew roots. It conjures up the cult of the saints, a world that is highly rooted and full of a sense of place. The relics of the martyrs have been translated all over the world, and pilgrimages map routes in a religious line of purposeful direction. Erasmus is ambiguous at best about this sense of pilgrimage. *Peregrinatio religionis ergo,* or "A Pilgrimage for Religion's Sake," his *Colloquy* first published in 1526, makes ample mockery of the world of Chaucer's pilgrims. Indeed, it is based on actual English visits Erasmus made to Our Lady of Walsingham in the summer of 1512 and with John Colet to Canterbury sometime before 1514. In a fabricated letter, he makes the Virgin Mary complain of her endless travails from pillar to post, conjured into apparitions of virginity and childbirth, becoming reembodied in her afterlife in an endless metonymic stream of transitional relics, her clothes or her milk, then prayed to by pilgrims whether for continence or fertility, financial success or abstinence. What would she give for a settled place of burial and permanent monumentalized retirement.[9]

Pilgrimage involves a paradoxical relationship between the translation of the body of the saint and the fixedness of the cult once established. Prayer can be done anywhere but appears more meaningful in some places than in others.[10] Erasmus approves the omnipresence of devotion while demurring an insistence

---

8 ASD, 2/3:316; CWE, 34:151.

9 CWE, 40:624–28. There are of course no bones of the Virgin, following her Assumption; her surviving milk is described in flowing prose by Erasmus in CWE, 40:632–6.

10 Peter Brown, *The Cult of the Saints: Its Rise and Function in Latin Christianity* (University of Chicago Press, 2009), 90–91.

on sacred sites. His vision of religion as of knowledge in general is one of mobility. Translatability of sacredness corresponds to translatability of texts: unlike other religions, the Bible has moved between languages, something Erasmus imitated in his parallel texts of Greek and Latin in the 1516 New Testament. A third meaning of the Latin word *translation* — metaphor — suggests another Erasmian piece of thinking. Knowledge is carried across (the literal meaning of the Greek *metaphora*) from person to person, place to place, just as it is translated from one language to another. Yet he sees the ambiguity of this. A rare trilingual adage (I ix 26) notes that proverbs, like wines, do not always travel well: "For it is a property of most proverbs that they require to be uttered in the language in which they originated, and if they migrate into another tongue, they lose much of their charm."[11] The migration from one language to another (*quod si in alienum sermonem demigrarint*) is perhaps untranslatable. Yet he says this while translating Hebrew into Greek and then Latin.

The satire in Erasmus of the religious sense of place is highly controversial and his humour shows an anxiety and suppressed violence that demonstrate how exile and pilgrimage are not at all entirely figurative. Meanwhile, the Greek word chosen by Erasmus to exchange for the Latin *peregrinatio* in the 1533 adage, Παρεπιδημία (parepidēmia), has a wholly different but equally pressing context. It refers to a practice in ancient Greece of providing temporary residence to aliens from foreign cities. In a world of city-states political exile was commonplace, with the need for migrant domicile (we might say pre-settled status) a concomitant necessity. This was absolutely the sixteenth-century world Erasmus came to occupy. His eternal vagrancy was not fancy free. He first settled in Basel when his associations with incipient Lutheranism made life in Louvain uncomfortable. The imperial legate in the Netherlands — ironically his former bed mate from Venice, Girolamo Aleandro — began a full-scale inquisition which threatened books and increasingly lives. Yet as

---

11 CWE, 32:196.

Erasmus aligned increasingly against the Lutheran heresy, Basel became too forthrightly Protestant for him. Even though he rather despised the *Gemütlichkeit* (warmth or home comforts) of Freiburg — complaining of being stuck in the Black Forest far from the Rhine (the river is really only a few miles away) — he welcomed Catholic anonymity. Yet by the end of his life, he moved back to Basel seeking another alternative neutrality. All over Europe, as religion changed back and forth, confessional migrants moved too, from place to place.

The term *innere Emigration* — "internal emigration" — William Outhwaite writes, seems to have been coined in Germany, for obvious reasons, soon after 1933. Many were forced to leave, many were pressed to stay. Many who stayed died as a result, although some died through leaving. This was the terrifying fate of German Judaism. Yet there was also a weird fate for non-Jewish anti-Nazi Germans in staying. As Outhwaite writes: "In the years following World War Two, the term *innere Emigration* was the focus of acrimonious exchanges in West Germany between exiles and those who had remained in Germany or Austria, notably Thomas Mann in the former category and Frank Thiess in the latter."[12]

Asked whether he was an exile, W.G. Sebald later wrote, "you cannot call it exile when Europe has become such a small country."[13] It is a deeply ironic statement, based around ideas both of speed of travel and yet also a narrowing of political ideology. Sebald, a voluntary migrant from Germany to England, implied that exile is never exactly an act of free will. His choice of language — he wrote his novels in an old-fashioned German, while teaching in English — became part of this ambiguous recognition. This mirrored the legacy of the wartime generation of

---

12 William Outhwaite, "Internal Emigration Revisited," conference paper, Sussex Centre for Migration Research, University of Sussex, Falmer, UK, October 2017.

13 "Von Exil kann man nicht reden, weil dieses Europa ja ein so winzig kleines Land geworden ist." In a 1993 interview with Sigrid Löffler, quoted in Robert C. Hauhart and Jeff Birkenstein, eds., *European Writers in Exile* (Rowman & Littlefield, 2018), 233.

his parents. Whether to remain in an abandoned Germany of the memory while fleeing to the UK or USA, or else to maintain a position of internal exile while living on inside the Reich, were both positions of imprisonment and alienation.

Something like this became the life of Erasmus. The Dutch regarded him as a foreigner. He disowned his own Dutchness, while retaining a sense of *nostos* in adages on the theme — most famously in *Auris Batava,* "a Dutch ear" (IV vi 35), which for long occupied the last space in the *Adagia*.[14] The Dutch are hopelessly common and vulgar, the adage begins, as if Erasmus is not a Dutchman. But he includes himself, before then claiming the Dutch as superior to the Greeks and Romans, precisely because they are not so sophisticated, or politically superior.[15] They know their own place and do not invade other countries as a result. Meanwhile he said ruefully that the English think I am German, while the Germans think I am too French. He lived in a kind of *tussenland* — one of the places in between. Politically the Netherlands lay between the kingdom of France and the German Empire. The counts of Holland historically were party to the Empire; in 1433 they devolved to the Burgundian Netherlands, and from 1481 the Habsburg hegemony. Burgundy itself is a fertile in-between-land, an alternative geopolitical space that has been written out of nationalistic modern history yet in Erasmus's time was Europe's richest and most powerful place. Ulysses the imaginary Burgundian avoided the sea (fearing sea-sickness and pirates, drowning and pickpockets) and instead made his life a river journey, a migrant bird of the Rhine on the wing from the delta at Rotterdam to the falls at Schaffhausen to the lake at Constance.

In 1522, offered the citizenship of Zürich through the mediation of Huldrych Zwingli, Erasmus replied (ironically) that he was already *mundi civis* (citizen of the world).[16] It is a boast,

14 ASD 2/7:36; CWE, 36:235.

15 CWE, 36:235–7.

16 Epistle 1314, Erasmus to Huldrych Zwingli, Basel, September 1522; EE, 5:129; CWE, 9:183.

but not an idle one; for it carries with it the modern threat that a citizen of the world is also a citizen of nowhere. Homelessness endows him with disempowerment and statelessness, wanderlust with willed *Auswanderung* (emigration). Partly this is belligerent choice. Someone else put him in late childhood in a monastery meaning for him to stay forever. Evading the cloister became an existential quest. Freedom is impossible in the monastery, he stated. It regulates your food, your dress, your sex life, imprisons you socially and geographically. As a Calais migrant in 1514 he writes back to Prior Servaas that he is still better off out than in, since: "I had been forced into the kind of profession which was utterly repugnant to my mind and body alike: to my mind because I disliked ritual and loved freedom, and to my body because, even had I been wholly satisfied to live such a life, my bodily constitution could not tolerate its hardships."[17]

Yet his defence of personal freedom contains its own ironies. Although he fought hard to be freed from the habit, he clung to it in private dress so much that it became a cliché of his appearance. While claiming no longer to be an Augustinian Canon Regular he often chose to reside within the walls of one of the order's houses, such as in Haarlem or Oxford. While he knew where he did *not* want to live, he was less good at deciding where to go. In the letter to Servaas he excused himself from returning to Gouda while also expressing a powerful will never to return to Cambridge, despite earnest entreaties. He carried on telling everybody into the 1520s that he was wanted urgently in Rome, but despite writing about Italy as his destiny before and after his three-year stay from 1506 to 1509, he never went back. He never got to Spain at all.

The reason for that was obvious enough: if he went to Spain he might never get out. This is where internal migration became a useful excuse for him. Erasmus was wise enough to know that the charge of heresy was permanently possible for him. To the Lutherans he was a Catholic and to the Catholics a Lutheran. Enemies on both sides accused him of temporizing, fence-sit-

---

17 CWE, 1:295.

ting and fudging. He showed cunning in this. For several years, he claimed not to have read more than a few lines of Luther. Yet he also evinced a kind of courage in defending the rights of others accused of heresy. He was accused of bad faith in writing against Luther, although he replied that he owed Luther nothing, and was never thanked by Luther's opponents either. Erasmus managed to please nobody but he hardly cowered from the fight. The list of his formal opponents in print is a dictionary of Reformation biography on all fronts. The schools in Paris, Louvain and Valladolid denounced him, and in the end, after his death, his name was included in the Index of Prohibited Books. Yet conspicuously, he never came close to dying for his faith, for which posterity has barely forgiven him.

Meanwhile his letters show an extraordinary sensitivity to exile, internal and external. One of the most remarkable survives only in a holograph draft, found by P.S. Allen in Erasmus's surviving papers in Copenhagen Royal Library.[18] It is dated March 22, 1525 although it is only through Allen's detective work that its recipient can be named: Jean, cardinal of Lorraine and Bishop of Metz. A young friend of Erasmus, Pierre Toussaint, a canon in Metz, had migrated from cloister to various universities in order to study scripture and theology. Now Pierre is a guest at the house of the heretic Oecolampadius in Basel, while fellow canons in France petitioned the bishop for his urgent return to Metz, with obvious enough implications. Erasmus appealed emotionally to the bishop to allow exile to continue and to forbid the brother from returning home. Pierre is called a heretic; but by that standard, Erasmus replies, *sum hereticus,* "I am a heretic myself."[19] It is not something Erasmus says lightly. The only evidence against Pierre took the form of notes he made into books. But notes in books mean nothing, he says: Erasmus had to make notes from Luther in refuting Luther. Now Erasmus comes home to his theme via a digression in ancient Ath-

---

18 Copenhagen, Kongelige Bibliotek, MS GKS 95, fol. 241.
19 Epistle 1559, Erasmus to Jean de Lorraine, March 22, 1525; EE, 6:54, CWE, 11:78.

ens: "When Alcibiades was summoned to face trial before his fellow Athenians, he chose to leave the country; and when he was advised to trust his fate to the jurors, he said he would not trust himself to his own mother for fear she might substitute the black pebble for the white by mistake."[20] Alcibiades chose exile in order to protect himself from his fellow citizens. It is clear that Erasmus was telling Jean de Lorraine that he was asking the same freedom of migration for his young friend Pierre. Pierre was lucky, and grateful: he never went back to Metz. He was still alive forty years later in Montbéliard near the Swiss border. He outlived Michael Servetus in Geneva, although the fate of Servetus shows how close he was to death.

By writing about Alcibiades Erasmus shows another side to internal migration: irony and allusion. Ancient Athens is his parry to avoid any talk of modern Paris. Just let Pierre be, he argued, while reserving judgement on the charge of heresy. *Non hec eo tendunt vt damnem necessaria quibus opprimuntur heretici deplorati* ("This does not mean that I condemn measures to suppress the incurable heretic"). In this wording, Erasmus resorts, as so often, to *praeteritio* (a rhetorical device where the speaker mentions a topic while claiming not to). Erasmus avoids saying what he means by asserting he does not mean the opposite. Rhetoric is another kind of internal exile. In this way, if exile is metaphor for him, metaphor is also a short cut to exile. I am like Ulysses, Erasmus keeps saying. Not only because is he always on the move, but also that he shares with Odysseus another feature: he is a shape-shifter, a user of tropes, or as the first line of the *Odyssey* puts it, πολύτροπον (many-turning). This is cited in the adage *Proteo mutabilior* ("More changeable than Proteus," *Adagia,* II ii 74).[21] Adagiastic writing is always digressive, elusive, fragmentary. Perhaps the most beautiful figure for Erasmian self-disappearance is the adage *Gygis anulus* ("The ring of Gyges," I i 96). The story is taken from Lucian's *Wishes,* merged with a passage in Plato's *Republic.* Gyges the herdsman has a

---

20 CWE, 10:79.
21 ASD, 2/3:188; CWE, 33:113.

ring which he discovers has magical properties. "If he happened
to turn inwards the jewel set in the ring," he becomes invisible,
although he can still see everyone around him.[22] If he turns it
back, he becomes visible again, "and they all talked about him
just as if he had not been present." In all his portraits by Holbein
and Dürer, jewelled rings are highly prominent. In his will, Erasmus left dozens of them, including one still in the museum in
Basel. Did Erasmus turn the bezel in his ring whenever he did
not want to be seen? Or is it a metaphor for the way that reading
and writing offer temporary internal space, even when external
authorities wish to find us? Erasmus never wants to be found.
He is never at home. But if he allows, we can wander into the
room with him, in his figures of speech, as he decides whether
to let us in or keep us out. We should let him stay there, allowing
him to speak for himself:

Παρεπιδημία τίς ἐστιν ὁ βίος, id est Peregrinatio quaedam est
vita. Socrates in Axiocho Platonis adfert hanc sententiam ut
vulgo apud omneis decantatam, quanquam is dialogus hab-
etur inter nothos. Videtur esse potius hominis Christiani qui
Platonem voluerit imitari. Haec enim sententia frequenter
occurrit in sacris voluminibus, vitam hanc esse exilium, esse
incolatum et peregrinationem, quanquam et Socrates Pla-
tonicus narrat animas hominum e coelo fuisse delapsas, quo
sibi per philosophiae studium parant reditum.[23]

Life is a sort of time in exile. In Plato's *Axiochus,* Socrates
adduces this sentiment as a popular saying known to everybody—though this dialogue is considered spurious. Its author was more likely a Christian who wanted to imitate Plato,
as this sentiment is often found in Holy Scripture, namely,
that this life is life as an exile, life as an alien, life in a land that
is not our true home. Though even Socrates as depicted by

---

22   CWE, 31:138.

23   ASD, 2/8:258.

Plato does say that the souls of men have fallen from heaven and endeavour to return there by the study of philosophy.[24]

24 CWE, 36:527.

Bibliography

Brown, Peter. *The Cult of the Saints: Its Rise and Function in Latin Christianity.* University of Chicago Press, 2009.

Erasmus, Desiderius. *Desiderii Erasmi Roterodami Opera omnia.* 9 Volumes. Edited by J.H. Waszink, Jean-Claude Margolin, M.L. van Poll-van de Lisdonk, Otto Herding, Clarence H. Miller, Jacques Chomarat, Antonius Gerardus Weiler, Maria Cytowska, H.J. de Jonge, Jan Bloemendal, and K.A.E. Enenkel. North-Holland Publishing Co., 1969–.

———. *Opus epistolarum Des. Erasmi Roterdami,* 12 Volumes. Edited by P.S. Allen, H.M. Allen, and H.W. Garrod. Clarendon Press, 1906–1958.

———. *The Collected Works of Erasmus.* 86 Vols. University of Toronto Press, 1974–.

Hauhart, Robert C., and Jeff Birkenstein, eds. *European Writers in Exile.* Rowman & Littlefield Books, 2018.

Outhwaite, William. "Internal Emigration Revisited." Conference paper, Sussex Centre for Migration Research. University of Sussex, Falmer, UK, October 2017.

11

Out of Place:
Migration, Knowledge,
and What Remains

Supriya Chaudhuri

In late March 2020, the start of what became the pandemic year, a series of surprising images began to circulate in India, and soon achieved global visibility. Against a nationwide lockdown announced at four hours' notice on March 24, with public transport withdrawn; interstate movement banned; schools, universities, and workplaces closed; and a population of 1.38 billion people urged to shelter in place, long lines of men, women, and children formed along national highways and railway tracks, heading out of India's crowded cities. Images of these travelers — on foot, precariously balanced on bicycles, crammed into auto-rickshaws or trucks, dragging bundles or cheap cases on which the odd baby might be perched — brought home, as nothing else could, the reality of migrant labor in urban South Asia. It was the largest population movement the subcontinent had witnessed since the 1947 Partition of India, when 16.7 million people, displaced by religion, had crossed, over a period of four years, the newly-formed borders of independent India and Pakistan. Nearly seventy years later, similar numbers were in transit within India's borders during six months.[1] On September 14, 2020, India's Labour and Employment Minister stated in Parliament that nearly 10 million migrant workers had attempted to return home during the COVID-19 pandemic and subsequent lockdown. Asked about the numbers who had died in the attempt, the Minister said that the government had no data on this, though Right to Information (RTI) applications filed by independent news agencies indicated that the railways and other ministries *had* collected data on migrant deaths. Real migration numbers during lockdown were probably far in excess of official estimates.

But was this migration? In fact, it was the reverse. Termed a "migrant crisis," a tragedy of epic proportions that drew public attention to the plight of migrant workers, these heart-breaking processions on India's highways, crowds held back by police at state borders, were actually people attempting to *return* to their homes in distant villages. They were migrants, but they were not migrating. Stranded by government fiat in places that had overnight become unproductive and hostile, their only hope was to go back to where they had come from. Around 120 million of India's 470 million workforce (of which nearly 80% belong to the informal, or unorganized sector) are seasonal or longer-term migrants from rural to (largely) urban markets, without assured wages unless they can work. Unprotected by contracts or labor laws, they either lack or leave behind in their native districts the "ration cards" that might entitle them to subsidized grain under India's public distribution system. Despite official reassurances, most received no wages during lockdown and could not pay rent or buy food. The Modi government's promises of free meals and shelters proved largely illusory.[2] Shortly

1   *Citizens and the Sovereign* (Migrant Workers Solidarity Network Publication, November 2020), and S. Irudaya Rajan, P. Sivakumar, and Aditya Srinivasan, "The COVID19 Pandemic and Internal Labour Migration in India: A 'Crisis of Mobility,'" *The Indian Journal of Labour Economics* 63 (2020): 1021–39.

2   Hari Vasudevan, "Food Is a Necessity, So Is Making It Available," *Newsclick,* April 22, 2020, https://www.newsclick.in/Food-Necessity-Making-

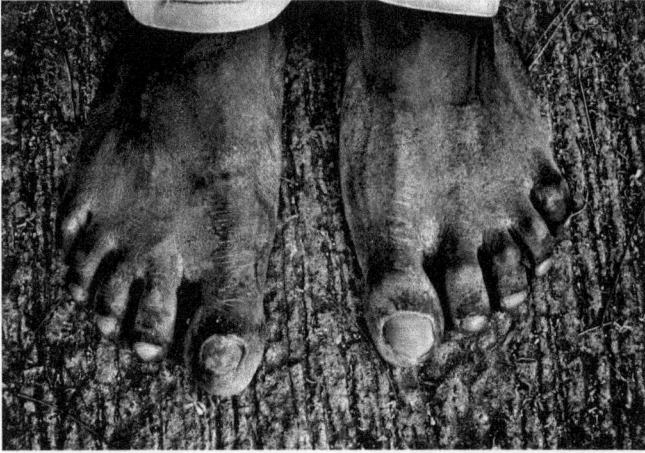

Fig. 11.1. Migrant laborer's scarred feet, May 2020. Source: Shome Basu.

after the lockdown was announced, huge numbers of migrant workers, with their families, embarked on the long walk home.[3] Such was the public outrage at the appalling scenes in print and digital media that the Supreme Court of India demanded a status report. On March 31, the Solicitor General, Tushar Mehta, stated on oath that not a single migrant was on the road any longer: all had received food and shelter.

Not only was this untrue, but it grossly ignored the human cost of the crisis. By early May, forty-two migrant workers had been killed in road accidents alone. On May 7, Krishna Sahoo and his wife Pramila, trying to ride a bicycle home with their two young children from Lucknow to Bemetara in Chattisgarh, a distance of 700 kilometers, were run over and killed almost immediately by an unidentified vehicle. Many others died of heat and exhaustion on the road, like twelve-year-old Jamalo

---

Available.

3   See Ishan Chauhan and Zenaida Cubbinz, eds., *India's Long Walk Home* (Paranjoy, 2021).

Makdam from Chattisgarh, who had been working in the chilli fields of the southern state of Telengana. After walking 150 kilometers, she collapsed on April 18, in sight of her native village. Migrant workers were detained in camps, picked up by police and crammed into container vans, stopped at state borders, stranded at railway stations, and forced to pay enhanced fares for the few buses and trains that started running from May 1. Unsurprisingly, protests and violence erupted at transit points. Mounting public anger was transformed to horror when on May 9, press photographs showed charred *rotis* (flatbreads), slippers, and clothes, strewn on the railway line between Jalna and Aurangabad where sixteen Adivasi laborers, having dozed off on the tracks during an 850 kilometer walk home, were run over by a freight train.[4] Tragically, they had used the railway line for direction, assuming that trains did not run during lockdown. Migrants who managed to reach their villages said they would never go back to the brutality and exploitation of urban labor contractors.[5] But when the season turned and the lockdown eased, the logic of want forced them to return. Always temporary, "contractual" yet unlegislated, and in ever-changing, distant locations, they went back to work as masons on urban construction sites, as artisans in small manufacturing units, as hired porters or cleaners, or as agricultural laborers in alien fields.[6]

The point here is not the migrant crisis itself, but the nature of migrant life, defined not by purposive travel for work and

---

4 Supriya Chaudhuri, "The Working Person's Right to Life," *The Economic Times,* May 12, 2020, https://economictimes.indiatimes.com/news/economy/policy/view-the-working-persons-right-to-life/articleshow/75683761.cms.

5 Roli Srivastava and Anuradha Nagaraj, "'I Will Never Come Back': Many Indian Migrant Workers Refuse to Return to Cities Post Lockdown," *Scroll.in,* May 30, 2020, https://scroll.in/article/963251/i-will-never-come-back-many-indian-migrant-workers-refuse-to-return-to-cities-post-lockdown.

6 The rights of migrant workers in India are still covered by the Inter-state Migrant Workmen Act 1979, one of the most poorly implemented of all laws in the country. Four new labor laws, passed by Parliament, have not yet been implemented.

livelihood, but by political and psychological *abandonment*. Migrancy is an estranged condition, as Julia Kristeva puts it, "Toujours ailleurs, l'étranger n'est de nulle part" (always elsewhere, the stranger belongs nowhere).[7] A migrant life is *always* out-of-place. It is marked as much by arrest as by movement, by a periodic blocking, and by being stranded or left behind as an unexamined surplus in contemporary narratives of citizenship and the state. The entirely avoidable tragedy of migrant labor in India during that pandemic year was one of internal migration within the country's borders, not a crisis of cross-border refugees driven by political oppression, climate catastrophe, or economic hardship. It was a tragedy uniquely produced by the lockdown, which robbed citizens of the right to free movement, and trapped migrant workers as outsiders and aliens *within* the nominal framework of citizenship. In India's federal system, even interstate borders posed a legal barrier. Returning workers were forcibly stopped at state borders, sprayed with disinfectants, and confined in camps. Such events are powerfully depicted in the film *Bheed* ("Crowd," 2023), directed by Anubhav Sinha, about a police officer charged with stopping a crowd of migrant workers from crossing a state border.

The plight of migrant workers in those terrible months, from March to September 2020, cast more than one retrospective political shadow. Just before the lockdown, India had witnessed country-wide protests against the Citizenship Amendment Act (CAA) and the National Register of Citizens (NRC), through which the Hindu majoritarian Bharatiya Janata Party (BJP) government sought to link citizenship to religion. Made law on December 11, 2019, the CAA focused entirely on cross-border entrants into India from neighboring countries, facilitating citizenship for some categories of asylum-seekers, but excluding Muslims. The NRC proposed draconian measures to check the citizenship papers of all Indians, with the threat that resident

---

7   Julia Kristeva, *Étrangers à nous-mêmes* (Librairie Arthème Fayard, 1988), 21.

Muslims might be rejected as illegal immigrants.[8] Ironically, the first NRC exercise in the eastern Indian state of Assam ended up excluding far more Hindus than Muslims, with 1.9 million residents unable to prove their status, and facing the prospect of imprisonment in newly constructed detention camps. Country-wide agitations against these repressive laws culminated, just before the pandemic was officially proclaimed, in the North East Delhi riots of February 2020, killing fifty-three persons (mainly Muslims), and destroying their properties and businesses.

Thus the figure of the migrant as bogey and scapegoat had been vividly present to the national imagination even before the lockdown. In a country that still bore, seventy years after political independence, the unhealed trauma of its 1947 Parti-tion — the drawing of borders across a living and working pop-ulation — citizenship was already a critically fraught concept. Citizenship involved questions of history, geography, and politi-cal will, entangling *time* (different "cut-off" dates for entry into India), *place* (of birth or domicile), and *law* (different Citizen-ship Acts applicable in each case). In late 2019, these questions assumed an ominous urgency, even foreboding, that brought thousands of people (this writer included) out on the streets to protest what seemed a gross violation of India's secular Consti-tution. The paranoia and animus against migrants deliberately stoked by the government affected even the COVID-19 climate. When attendees at an international Islamic gathering, the Tab-lighi Jamaat, were stranded in Delhi in March 2020, they were accused of carrying the virus and infecting the local populace. Hysterical outrage over this event was not replicated for larger political gatherings elsewhere, like the welcome for Donald Trump in Ahmedabad on February 24, political rallies during state elections next year, or the 9.1 million devotees at the Hindu Kumbh Mela. The bogey of the "illegal" migrant was replaced

---

8   Supriya Chaudhuri, "La question de la 'nation hindoue' est au coeur des manifestations," *Le Monde,* December 23, 2019, https://www.lemonde.fr/idees/article/2019/12/23/inde-la-question-de-la-nation-hindoue-est-au-c-ur-des-manifestations_6023874_3232.html.

Fig. 11.2. Mother and child by roadside during long walk home, May 2020. Source: Shome Basu.

during the pandemic by another figure, a figure that India appeared to have forgotten or never recognized. This was the migrant worker, a stalled, arrested, abandoned *internal migrant,* both *at home* and *far from home*: a citizen, but a citizen without rights. It was as if a huge, critically important part of the country's workforce, rendered invisible by political and economic neglect of its vital function, had suddenly begun walking down the highways or squatting by the roadside in full public view, forcing its *stay-at-home, work-from-home* counterparts to look at it for the first time. Given that 70% of internal migrants in India are female, though their representation in the paid workforce is much lower, there was a troubling parallel here with the state's failure to "see" women's labor.

That failure was itself inscribed within the visual imaginary created by public art, when, during the Hindu festival of Durga Puja in Kolkata, the sculptor Pallab Bhowmick and the artist Rintu Das depicted the goddess Durga herself as a migrant worker with her children, gazing back at the worshipper-spectator as if to remind us that this huge, popular festival celebrated the homecoming of a "migrant" goddess, visiting her natal home,

Fig. 11.3. Partition transport, part of the Durga Puja installation by
Pradip Das, 2021. Source: Pradip Das.

children in tow.[9] The following year, 2021, Das collaborated with
Debayan Pramanik to produce an openly political piece of anti-
NRC religious art, representing the goddess as a displaced woman with her four children, confined, in a posture of profound
abandonment, between the barbed-wire fences and watchtow-
ers of the India–Bangladesh border, with a small golden image
of the Dhakeśvari Durga (transported from Dhaka to Kolkata
during India's Partition) in her lap.[10] For the same festival, the

9   Durga Puja, Barisha Club Kolkata, 2020. See Tapati Guha-Thakurta, "The
    Migrant Worker and the Goddess," *Indian Cultural Forum*, October 30,
    2020, https://indianculturalforum.in/2020/10/30/migrant-worker-god-
    dess-durga-puja-sculpture/.
10 "Durga Puja 2021: When Pandals Depict Political Themes," *Outlook*,
    October 13, 2021, https://www.outlookindia.com/website/story/india-news-
    durga-puja-2021-when-pandals-depict-political-themes/397565. For a
    discussion of these and other images see Subha Mukherji, "'Footfalls Echo
    in the Memory': Displaced Durgas and Migrant Forms," *Humanities Un-
    derground*, October 2021, https://humanitiesunderground.org/2022/02/22/
    footfalls-echo-in-the-memory-displaced-durgas-and-migrant-forms/. See
    also Mukherji's Introduction in this volume.

Fig. 11.4. Abandoned suitcases, part of the Durga Puja installation by Pradip Das, 2021. Source: Pradip Das.

artist Pradip Das also drew upon memories of India's Partition, evoking the railway carriages and abandoned suitcases that bore silent witness to the migrants' trauma.

In *Border as Method* (2013), Sandro Mezzadra and Brett Neilson argue that the material proliferation of borders in today's world invites a rethinking of the nature of borders "between inclusion and exclusion." Borders do not obstruct the flow of global capital, blocking "global passages of people, money, or objects," but sort, filter and articulate them. Arguing that, "Borders play a key role in the production of the heterogeneous time and space of contemporary global and postcolonial capitalism," they posit multiplicity and heterogeneity as crucial to the composition of Karl Marx's "contemporary living labor," and instance the complex systems of bordering that internally divide the Indian labor market. Thus the "dyadic figure of the citizen-worker," that had so long monopolized the political imagination of the Left, is progressively diffused by processes of division and multiplication initiated by the movements and struggles of internal and

external migration.[11] The sedentary metaphysics of colonial geography are paralleled by the sedentary politics of the nation-
state, its linking of citizenship with place. Yet, by a paradox,
the emergence of that nation-state coincides with the spread of
global capitalisms that require the extraction and movement,
not just of raw materials and goods, but also of human bodies.
The migrant worker, whether citizen or non-citizen, determines
the contours and internal structures of globalization, producing
both transnational and transregional social spaces, and complicating relations between migration, citizenship, and labor
markets. The authors therefore contest both the new globalizing
vision of a borderless world (like that of the Internet) and that of
repressive state boundaries (the Wall, Brexit), proposing instead
a complex interplay of markets and labor where borders define
subject-positions, articulate time, and configure the world.[12]

Mezzadra and Neilson's notion of differential exclusion,
through which they consider the varying temporal experiences of, say, the commuter, "the detained migrant, the former
peasant who runs a tea shop, or even the benched body shop
worker," allows them to project migrants not as marginal subjects, but as "central protagonists in the drama of composing the
space, time, and materiality of the social itself."[13] However, the
authors' main concern is not that drama, but the figuration of
borders as both geo-political and epistemological, showing how
they shift, overlap, cut across, and undermine each other in an
era of global capitalism. As a result, the figure of the migrant,
whether domiciled in the Parisian *banlieue* (suburb), huddled in
the Indian refugee slum or "service village," confined in the detention camp, herded behind a barbed-wire fence, holding on to
a sinking boat, or stranded on the long road home, is relatively
less vivid and urgent than the theorization itself. So too, Thomas
Nail's philosophical and historical study, *The Figure of the Mi-*

---

11 Sandro Mezzadra and Brett Neilson, *Border as Method: Or, the Multiplica-
    tion of Labor* (Duke University Press, 2013), viii–x.
12 Ibid., 243–80.
13 Ibid., 158–59.

grant (2015), offers a powerful abstraction of the migrant, the human being-in-motion, not as a "type of person" or fixed identity but a "mobile social position or spectrum that people move into and out of under certain social conditions of mobility."[14] In this history of human movement, new subjectivities are engendered, with migrants as stateless, mobile, surplus populations. In consequence, as Arjun Appadurai suggests:

> The spectacle of the precarious migrant endangers the "host body" of the Heimat [homeland], bringing liquidity, formlessness, and vulnerability into the nation, threatening to turn the phantom limb into the phantom Heimat. Guests, strangers, and migrants expose the precarity of the nation, its fabricated kinship, its ersatz solidarities, its derivative sacrifices, and the artificiality of all its limbs.[15]

But how can we know the texture of actual migrant experience? Acts of experiencing and witnessing are our sole recourse here, like the Kurdish journalist Behrouz Boochani's *No Friend but the Mountains,* written in Papua New Guinea's Manus Island detention camp as a series of WhatsApp texts in Farsi on a smuggled mobile phone. Translated into English in 2018, it won a number of major literary awards despite the author's continuing incarceration by Australia's infamous border protection forces.[16] Much literature, art, documentary, and narrative film draws upon migrant experiences in borderlands like those of eastern India, witness to prolonged population movements across as well as forcible confinements along political boundaries — from the huge two-way migrations during the 1947 Partition to the

---

14 Thomas Nail, *The Figure of the Migrant* (Stanford University Press, 2015), 235.

15 Arjun Appadurai, "The Phantom Heimat," in *Whose Land Have I Lit on Now? Contemplations on the Notions of Hostipitality,* ed. Federica Bueti, Bonaventure Soh Bejeng Ndikung, and Elena Agudio (Savvy Contemporary, 2020), 102.

16 Behrouz Boochani, *No Friend but the Mountains: Writing from Manus Prison,* trans. Omid Tofighian (Picador/Pan Macmillan, 2018).

more restricted entry into India of Chakma and Hajong refugees, members of the "Chittagong hill tribes" (so described by
British colonial administrators) from East Pakistan/Bangladesh,
and Rohingya Muslims from Myanmar. Malini Sur's recent work
on the borderlands of eastern India indicates that the time experienced by border dwellers is not linear.[17] The migrant's life and
the migrant's time are thus a new political, social and aesthetic
configuration. If time and space are compressed and speeded up
for the privileged global citizen, they are stalled, prolonged, and
disjointed for the migrant who inhabits a precarious non-space
and non-time.[18]

Boochani's narrative, documentary and cryptic in equal
measure, a poetic, philosophical bricolage creating new epistemologies out of the experience of incarceration and statelessness, is exemplary for another reason as well. Borders or
interfaces, and the figure of the migrant (a category both mobile
and arrested) bear witness to the instability of artistic form as
well as the fragility and impermanence of expressive medium, as
it transitions between paper or electronic book, still or moving
images on film, digital representation, video, sound, and installation art. As art struggles to interpret a world marked by conflict, catastrophe, and state violence, where prisoners, detainees,
illegal migrants, and asylum-seekers must daily work out new
equations between risk, survival, and the law, the aesthetics of
representation are also under stress. Thus the exiled Chinese
artist Ai Weiwei's German film on the European refugee crisis, *Human Flow* (2017, shown in the main competition section
of the 74th Venice Film Festival) offers a politics of witnessing
from locations in at least twenty countries. It shows Ai and his
film crew as they travel around the world documenting refugee
life (with iPhones, drones, and film cameras) but also simply
being with the refugees. Ai appears on screen intermittently, di-
recting, cooking, using his cellphone, cutting a man's hair, walk-

---

17 Malini Sur, *Jungle Passports: Fences, Mobility, and Citizenship at the North-
    east India–Bangladesh Border* (University of Pennsylvania Press, 2021), 8.
18 Nail, *The Figure of the Migrant*, 235.

ing to a makeshift graveyard; at the same time, there are aerial shots of destroyed cities and expanses of water to be crossed. The film is an open call to action on the migrant crisis, and Ai Weiwei is himself a refugee, confined in a camp in China until being allowed to leave in 2015, living then in Berlin, and, from September 2019, in Cambridge, England.

Migrant knowledge is not a knowledge that travels, so much as it is an epistemology bred in the experience of the migrant, "the new political figure of our time," an experience of being — whether static or in motion — *out-of-place*.[19] Such forms of knowing require new ways of seeing, an alter-aesthetics. One of the most distinctive of these forms is the film or video installation, viewed in an art gallery on endless loop, unmooring narrative through the mechanics of repetition, and fitting Ranajit Guha's categorization of migrant time as "a whirlpool for the strangeness of the arrival to turn round and round as a moment of absolute uncertainty."[20] Instead of the static viewer and moving image of classic cinema, we have the moving viewer and bounded screen of video, as well as a completely altered sense of blocked or arrested time. This was my own experience of viewing two very different films. The first, *Passage,* was a twenty-six-minute video installation by the UAE artist Nujoom Alghanem at the Venice Biennale (2019), depicting the journeys of a displaced woman, Falak, and of the director (Alghanem) and actor (Amal), through a two-channel video on opposite sides of a shared screen and soundtrack. The other was the Bangladeshi artist Naeem Mohaiemen's feature film, *Tripoli Cancelled* (2017, ninety-five minutes, Documenta 14 Kassel/ Experimenter Gallery Kolkata, shortlisted for the Turner Prize, 2018) about a man stranded in Athens's abandoned Ellinikon airport. The actor Vassilis Koukalani's brilliant solo performance took off from the experience of the director's father, who once lost his passport en route to Tripoli and was stranded in Athens for nine days.

19 Ibid.

20 Ranajit Guha, "The Migrant's Time," in *The Migrant's Time: Rethinking Art History and Diaspora,* ed. Saloni Mathur (Yale University Press, 2011), 5.

Fig. 11.5. Still from Naeem Mohaiemen, *Tripoli Cancelled* (2017), commissioned by Documenta 14. Source: Naeem Mohaiemen.

In Mohaiemen's rendering, the episode becomes an extended, non-naturalistic take on the refugee-migrant's state of suspension outside national borders, in an airport, the chronotopic paradigm of postmodernity. The protagonist writes to his wife, enacts charades, identifies himself to an imaginary bartender as a Mussalman — implicitly, *der Muselman* of Primo Levi's *Survival in Auschwitz* (1947) — carries a stewardess-mannequin on a grounded aeroplane, boogies to the song "Rivers of Babylon" (1979), and reads aloud from Richard Adams's novel about migrant rabbits, *Watership Down* (1972). While Adams's allegory explores collective liberation struggles through flight, heroic survival, and resettlement, Mohaiemen's stranded protagonist invites reflection on the liminality of migrancy itself, its stateless, placeless stasis.

Viewed, as I saw it several times, endlessly looping on a wall at the Experimenter Gallery and on a larger screen at the Tate Britain, as audiences milled around, stayed to watch or left midway, it offered a sense of time quite distinct from that of the traditional cinema hall, one of Michel Foucault's modernist heterotopias.[21] In the gallery, the "emancipated spectator" (the

---

21 Michel Foucault, "Of Other Spaces," trans. Jay Miskowiec, *Diacritics* 16, no. 1 (1986): 22–27, and Laura Mulvey, *Death 24x A Second: Stillness and the*

phrase is Jacques Rancière's) can choose her mode of looking, whether stationary before the screen or wandering away at will, to take in other scenes or objects.[22] On screen there is stalled or arrested time, an endless vacancy inhabited by the protagonist, who fills it with activities that are alternately banal and quirky; in the gallery, there is the spectator's viewing time, mentally apportioned according to interest, curiosity, and leisure. Temporarily, the two are drawn together by the immersiveness of the screen experience, projecting its stasis, its being "out-of-place," profoundly unlike the heterotopic viewing time of the cinema theater. Just so, we may feel, do we glance at press photographs in a newspaper, or watch television footage about drowning migrants off the coast of Lampedusa, herded behind fences on the Mexican border, stranded on a national highway in India, or leaving rotis on a railway track: figures inhabiting a time that is not ours, a placelessness that only the migrant can know. This is migrant knowledge, a knowledge towards which art can gesture, yet one that it can never reproduce.

Moving Image (Reaktion Books, 2006).

22 Jacques Rancière, *The Emancipated Spectator,* trans. Gregory Elliott (Verso, 2009), 17.

Bibliography

Appadurai, Arjun. "The Phantom Heimat." In *Whose Land Have I Lit on Now? Contemplations on the Notions of Hostipitality,* edited by Federica Bueti, Bonaventure Soh Bejeng Ndikung, and Elena Agudio. Savvy Contemporary, 2020.

Boochani, Behrouz. *No Friend but the Mountains: Writing from Manus Prison.* Translated by Omid Tofighian. Picador/Pan Macmillan, 2018.

Chaudhuri, Supriya. "La question de la 'nation hindoue' est au coeur des manifestations." *Le Monde,* December 23, 2019. https://www.lemonde.fr/idees/article/2019/12/23/inde-la-question-de-la-nation-hindoue-est-au-c-ur-des-manifestations_6023874_3232.html.

———. "The Working Person's Right to Life." *The Economic Times,* May 12, 2020. https://economictimes.indiatimes.com/news/economy/policy/view-the-working-persons-right-to-life/articleshow/75683761.cms.

Chauhan, Ishan, and Zenaida Cubbinz, eds. *India's Long Walk Home.* Paranjoy, 2021.

Foucault, Michel. "Of Other Spaces." Translated by Jay Miskowiec. *Diacritics* 16, no. 1 (1986): 22–27. DOI: 10.2307/464648.

Ghosh, Deepanjan. "Durga Puja 2021: When Pandals Depict Political Themes." *Outlook,* October 13, 2021. https://www.outlookindia.com/website/story/india-news-durga-puja-2021-when-pandals-depict-political-themes/397565.

Guha, Ranajit. "The Migrant's Time." In *The Migrant's Time: Rethinking Art History and Diaspora,* edited by Saloni Mathur. Yale University Press, 2011.

Guha-Thakurta, Tapati. "The Migrant Worker and the Goddess." *Indian Cultural Forum,* October 30, 2020. https://indianculturalforum.in/2020/10/30/migrant-worker-goddess-durga-puja-sculpture/.

Kristeva, Julia. *Étrangers à nous-mêmes.* Librairie Arthème Fayard, 1988.

Mezzadra, Sandro, and Brett Neilson. *Border as Method: Or, the Multiplication of Labor.* Duke University Press, 2013.

Migrant Workers Solidarity Network. *Citizens and the Sovereign: Stories from the Largest Human Exodus in Contemporary Indian History.* Migrant Workers Solidarity Network Publication, November 2020. https://sanhati.com/wp-content/uploads/Citizens-and-the-Sovereign.pdf.

Mukherji, Subha. "'Footfalls Echo in the Memory': Displaced Durgas and Migrant Forms." *Humanities Underground,* October 2021. https://humanitiesunderground.org/2022/02/22/footfalls-echo-in-the-memory-displaced-durgas-and-migrant-forms/.

Mulvey, Laura. *Death 24x A Second: Stillness and the Moving Image.* Reaktion Books, 2006.

Nail, Thomas. *The Figure of the Migrant.* Stanford University Press, 2015.

Rajan, S. Irudaya, P. Sivakumar, and Aditya Srinivasan. "The COVID19 Pandemic and Internal Labour Migration in India: A 'Crisis of Mobility.'" *The Indian Journal of Labour Economics* 63 (2020): 1021–39. DOI: 10.1007/s41027-020-00293-8.

Rancière, Jacques. *The Emancipated Spectator.* Translated by Gregory Elliott. Verso, 2009.

Srivastava, Roli, and Anuradha Nagaraj. "'I Will Never Come Back': Many Indian Migrant Workers Refuse to Return to Cities Post Lockdown." *Scroll.in,* May 30, 2020. https://scroll.in/article/963251/i-will-never-come-back-many-indian-migrant-workers-refuse-to-return-to-cities-post-lockdown.

Sur, Malini. *Jungle Passports: Fences, Mobility, and Citizenship at the Northeast India–Bangladesh Border.* University of Pennsylvania Press, 2021.

Vasudevan, Hari. "Food Is a Necessity, So Is Making It Available." *Newsclick,* April 22, 2020. https://www.newsclick.in/Food-Necessity-Making-Available.

12

One and Three Knowledges: Displacement, Art, and Anthropology

Olga Demetriou, Efi Savvides, and Akid Hassan

Three Knowledges

Migrant knowledge can enable and oppress. As knowledge that migrates, it creates bridges between disciplines, experiences, and practices that enable action and resistance. As knowledge about migration and about migrants, it mobilizes those connections in the determination of how lives are lived. And as knowledge possessed by migrants, it becomes an object entangled in the power relations that determine those lives. This contribution is a sketchy attempt to grapple with these various migrant knowledges by foregrounding different media and different connections that produce it, and assembling them in a common space of authorship. It integrates artworks, depictions of artwork, and textual commentary on artworks, in asking what such assemblies mean (assemblies we often find in both art and social analysis related to migration), and what authorships and collaborations they may entail, imply, or obscure. We do this by tracing the connections between knowledge fields that these formats speak to: between displacement and art, between art and anthropology, and between anthropology and displacement studies. Through these connections, this contribution proposes a pondering on forms of knowledge that might be placed against oppressive regimes of migrant knowledge. Previous work,[1] which showed how mechanisms of knowledge production in the migration regime utilize data such as statistics and complex legal instruments to account for restrictive policies and excuse failures to protect people, is used as a springboard for the exploration of art as a resistive possibility.

In 1965, Joseph Kosuth produced *One and Three Chairs,* an iconic piece of conceptual art, hosted at the Museum of Modern Art.[2] The work is an assembly of a wooden chair, a photograph of a wooden chair, and a dictionary definition of "chair": three things that he did not actually produce but instead brought together in the exhibition space. The installation is meant to invite contemplation on the nature of art: not merely whether this is art, but how we know art, where to locate it between thinking and making, and what to make of the thinking of these questions. The title of this essay takes its inspiration from this exemplary artwork and its simultaneous querying of positivism (what is a chair?), institutions (what is art?), and knowledge regimes (how do we know either?). Knowledge of the chair migrates from object to image to text, and in that migration, materiality, interpretation, and definition, the three knowledges, simultaneously merge and remain separate. The three "chairs" pose together the question of what and who makes a chair, really, and in posing it under the sign of "art" also pose the question of the role of art and, more importantly, our position towards it. In this essay we borrow Kosuth's technique in an attempt to trace connections between ways of knowing "migration" and to pose the question of what "migrant knowledge" might be. In the process we also

1   Olga Demetriou, "Complementary Protection and the Recognition Rate as Tools of Governance: Ordering Europe, Fragmenting Rights," *Journal of Ethnic and Migration Studies* 48, no. 5 (2022): 1264–85.

2   Museum of Modern Art, "Joseph Kosuth, *One and Three Chairs,* 1965," https://www.moma.org/learn/moma_learning/joseph-kosuth-one-and-three-chairs-1965/.

reflect on the positionalities that migrant knowledge might attempt to shift — and, in failing, expose productive disciplinary discomforts.

The three of us have each come to know displacement in different ways: an artistic theme, the focus of academic enquiry, the result of statelessness and a hunger-strike cause. These experiences are "partial truths" as anthropologists might say,[3] but in being so they are also (b)ordering devices. They maintain the differences between refugee and citizen, knowledge and experience of the law (and its functions), empathy and corporeality in the claiming of rights. Our first encounter, during a solidarity march at the height of a hunger strike by the Hassan family in 2017, exposed these separations: interaction was minimal. Later encounters represent attempts to acknowledge and speak across these divides; however, they cannot purport to undo them. Indeed, in assembling these knowledges here, we do not propose answers to the Kosuthian question. The knowledges we seek to assemble do not necessarily blend into a whole that is more than its parts. They do not necessarily complete each other. They rather show the fissures as well as the inevitably insufficient attempts to fill them — much like our writing is punctuated by the visuals that represent the different contributions.

They also stunt the writing between the first person the anthropologist (Demetriou) would have otherwise used and the depictions of conversations that produced them. These conversations, with the authors of the visuals below, as well as the artworks themselves and their depictions in print, are an integral part and not complementary to the text, the reason for its existence — and hence, they call for acknowledgment of collective authorship. The written text frames the visuals, which are themselves produced through the interactions of the video-artist and photographer (Savvides) and the protester-artist (Hassan). But this collective creation also results in uncomfortable uses of the

3   James Clifford, "Introduction: Partial Truths," in *Writing Culture: The Poetics and Politics of Ethnography*, ed. James Clifford and George E. Marcus (University of California Press, 1986).

Fig. 12.1. Akid Hassan, *untitled*, 2017, site-specific installation, variable dimensions. Source: Efi Savvides.

third-person and passive voice, punctuates conventional forms of writing, and arrests the flow. The effort in "co-production," a term mired by the neoliberal connotations of academic funding cultures, is centered on exploring the discomforts of traversing fields: describing an artwork, retelling a memory, framing a still. Under academic conventions, these are often practices we take in our stride as anthropologists, for example, anonymize informants by default[4] and consider the ethics of participant observation. In this short intervention, we have instead tried to experiment with the assembly of these knowledge forms, placing the artworks more integrally into the text and into the authorship of this assembly. The result is more punctured than seamless, and for that reason less assertive. But in precisely this sense, it occasions a contemplation on the difficulties of migrant knowledge as the tracing of a journey punctuated by power barriers, imperfect translations, and discomforting displacements.

---

4   Jason De León, "The Indecisive Moment: Photoethnography on the Undocumented Migration Trail," in *Photography and Migration*, ed. Tanya Sheehan (Routledge, 2018).

Displacement and Art

Akid produced this untitled piece in 2017 while on hunger strike outside the Ministry of Interior in the Republic of Cyprus, in the parking lot of which he had camped, together with his parents and siblings, demanding citizenship after years of their living and working in the country as stateless persons. Inspired by conversations with Efi on *arte povera* (the artistic movement named after the Italian phrase meaning "poor art") and the significance of using cheap, everyday materials in the production of art, it was an attempt to create an imaginary space, a space of respite from the stresses of the strike and the inescapable anxiety it created. The piece also marked the beginning of an engagement with the art scene in Cyprus in general, and Nicosia in particular, a place experienced as quite distinct from the rest of society, a place where racism seemed not to exist. This art had been difficult to recreate elsewhere, after the end of the strike and the return to the village (where the family had initially settled on arrival to Cyprus in the 2000s), where this milieu was absent.

The work was created at the height of the strike, which Efi followed closely on a daily basis and supported in various ways, one of which was through conversations with the family and Akid in particular, contemplating the condition of being stateless and the impasses of living in Cyprus in that insecurity. Art here provided a space to think outside this impasse, an opportunity to create a space other than the grounds of a governmental building and a time other than the hunger strike.

The piece recreated another space, the village that had been left in Syrian Kurdistan, where holidays were spent with grandparents. Under a tree like this, one of the old eucalyptuses in the Ministry's parking lot, childhood parties were held with friends from the village. There was an open fire in the vineyards outside the village where the group of boys were allowed to play; there was roasting of onions, potatoes, cracking of pecan nuts produced in the area, sharing of bread, and talk. Never meat; that was a goal for the group that never materialized. Pinecones were

Fig. 12.2. Efi Savvides, *Judgment Day,* 2017–18, single-channel video, color, with sound, 50' [still at 12.20]. Source: Efi Savvides.

used as kindling, similar to the ones found around other trees in the parking lot. There was no money to buy pecan nuts; a friend would steal them from home and offer them — everyone would bring something from home. Were the piece to be given a title it would be "Talaswad/Gire Resh," after the name of the village (in Arabic and Kurdish).

The photograph reproduced here is missing a coat that was later hung on the tree trunk. It was a representation of grandparents' overcoats that they wore in the fields. The grandmother's coat continued to hang on the tree in Gire Resh long after she died, a reminder of her presence and an interlocutor in silent conversations of private moments.

The eucalyptus in the Ministry grounds was singled out almost on arrival at the spot and Akid's chair was placed there as soon as the protest tents went up. Its shade that summer became a personal space for contemplation. Later, as the grounds became more familiar in the development of the protest, a bed was assembled between two other eucalyptus trees and that became a resting spot.

The shade of the tree made exposure difficult for the representation used here, making the left side of the photograph much darker. The day the work was made was strangely overcast, exacerbating the problem. This image is therefore corrected. Of all the photographs of the art piece, this one contains a background that includes the sign of the Ministry and the Republic's logo in the distance, at once locating the context of the piece in the strike and echoing the shift of focus and priority on the art and its recuperative potential over the context that produced it.

Art and Anthropology

Efi produced the film *Judgment Day*, from which the still is taken, while the protest was ongoing. The film is an attempt to document and artistically present the everyday processes involved in the hunger strike. It was assembled as a triptych of scenes unfolding in parallel over the sounds of the setting and interviews with the family, mostly Akid. The materials that sustained the hunger strike, both in the enabling sense of sustaining life (water, tents, boiling pots, family interactions), and in the suppressive sense of sustaining its cause (governmental structures, unresponsiveness to claims, societal indifference) are meant to be juxtaposed in these parallel scenes.

Much of the film records Akid's thoughts on the condition of hopelessness that spurred the protest, his contemplations on stateless as a state of being that feels less than human, and the injustices of forever waiting for a decision — a judgment on "status" that places life on this side of citizenship or that. A tree becomes a point of identification: "I felt that if I was a tree, a tree would have a better life than me. The gardener comes and looks after it, trims it, waters it," he says of these injustices in the film. The thoughts recorded then articulated an emptiness, the evacuation of dreams and expectations: the sole focal point in the future became that day of judgment, which would bring at least some rest.

The conversations provided relief, of sorts, but also a pivot point for the despair that seemed ever present in those days.

They offered diminishing room for escape as that judgment day moved further away. They also prompted a contemplation of the complicities that such definitive separations between citizenship and its lack create: tents on this side, homes to return to at day's end on that.[5] Reflections on these complicities of un-care were discomforting, as they prompted an unwelcome affinity with a society perceived by the protesters as unconcerned with their lives and frailties: the society of Greek-Cypriots who drove past, shielded in their cars, on each of the sixty-seven days that the hunger strike lasted.

Art offered respite from an ever-draining cycle. The eucalyptus providing the setting elicited an ambivalent relation: "I relax, with these trees — why do I relax with these trees? Because on these trees they come sit, I see the birds that come sit on them; I mean the bird, it has its freedom, I'm a person and I don't have my freedom," Akid says at seventeen minutes (17:15–17:56). The childhood scene the piece recreates perhaps allowed some possession of that elusive sense of freedom. The work of the film aligns with and amplifies the installation piece, emphasizing its conceptual premises as it elucidates them.

Displacement and Anthropology

An important aspect of Kosuth's conceptual art was his work — across domains of knowledge, and particularly his employment of anthropology to aid artistic reflection — on remedying the threat of marketization that photorealism was suggesting in the 1970s. For Kosuth, art could learn from anthropology how to reflect, and on that basis it would then engage with the culture it was situated in. Kosuth advocates an art that makes culture abstracted and rethought anew as unfamiliar but for that reason better understood, for an audience that is a public: a politically aware and thinking public. Kosuth's essay could be described as a text of art. It is a depiction of thinking in process — made up

---

5   Also, Efi Savvides, "[Untitled Chapter]," in *Drone Vision: Warfare, Surveillance, Protest,* ed. Sarah Tuck (Art and Theory, 2022).

of selections of passages from anthropological and other texts, interspersed with the author's thoughts, organized in note form and developed through critical and self-reflexive statements. A notebook and manifesto at the same time. The assemblage of knowledges in this note form provides an escape from the liberal conundrum which makes of art an assembly line of consumer culture.

Fast-forward two decades, and these connections across disciplinary knowledge became themselves integrated into the assembly line, instead of providing answers. In a scathing critique of site-specific art, Hal Foster[6] found fault with the proliferation of art that attempted to speak to other cultures by studying them superficially and treating ethnography as something to be consumed. The study of others had been roped into the mechanized process of flying in the artist, setting up local encounters, and coming out the other side with site-specific art as the product. Otherness had been commercialized. In this context, it could no longer function as a platform for thought. The implication of art in capitalist production and alienation, Foster argued, had spread across knowledge domains and instrumentalized the knowledge of the other.

This worry has particular relevance for a consideration of "migrant knowledge" as applicable to the anthropology of displacement today, not least because of the emergency frames within which migration has emerged as a major political issue. Even though these framings are not necessarily new,[7] what is happening in recent years, and particularly since 2015, is that migration and displacement policy has been developing and relying on ever more complex instruments of knowledge.[8] While this knowledge is created through fields such as statistics and law, there is a parallel proliferation in ways of knowing migra-

---

6   Hal Foster, "The Artist as Ethnographer?," in *The Traffic in Culture: Refiguring Art and Anthropology,* ed. George E. Marcus and Fred R. Myers (University of California Press, 1999).

7   Saskia Sassen, *Guests and Aliens* (New Press, 1999).

8   Demetriou, "Complementary Protection and the Recognition Rate."

tion from perspectives that mobilize the visual, particularly art. And thus, the industry of migration works through images instrumentalized for funding for development[9] but it is also questioned and resisted by images that can instrumentalize otherness for similar reasons, even if causes are nobler.

In the face of this impasse, perhaps one thing we can do is to acknowledge the difficulties of migrant knowledge, and to experiment with ways of making interactions more visible, knowledge journeys more complex, and processes of production more open. From the safe distance of citizenship now acquired, and the hunger strike now an ambivalent memory of pain and perseverance, the contemplation of the interactions that happen in emergencies and their significance to very different projects that may be indeed, ultimately, self-interested, serves at least to underscore the discomforts of appropriating knowledges. The politics of migrant knowledge entail that we become uncomfortable in our disciplines and perhaps welcome that discomfort for what it can allow us to see.

---

9 Ruben Andersson, "Europe's Failed 'Fight' Against Irregular Migration: Ethnographic Notes on a Counterproductive Industry," *Journal of Ethnic and Migration Studies* 42, no. 7 (2016): 1055–75.

Bibliography

Andersson, Ruben. "Europe's Failed 'Fight' Against Irregular Migration: Ethnographic Notes on a Counterproductive Industry." *Journal of Ethnic and Migration Studies* 42, no. 7 (2016): 1055–75. DOI: 10.1080/1369183X.2016.1139446.

Clifford, James. "Introduction: Partial Truths." In *Writing Culture: The Poetics and Politics of Ethnography,* edited by James Clifford and George E. Marcus. University of California Press, 1986.

De León, Jason. "The Indecisive Moment: Photoethnography on the Undocumented Migration Trail." In *Photography and Migration,* edited by Tanya Sheehan. Routledge, 2018.

Demetriou, Olga. "Complementary Protection and the Recognition Rate as Tools of Governance: Ordering Europe, Fragmenting Rights." *Journal of Ethnic and Migration Studies* 48, no. 5 (2022): 1264–85. DOI: 10.1080/1369183X.2019.1682979.

Foster, Hal. "The Artist as Ethnographer?" In *The Traffic in Culture: Refiguring Art and Anthropology,* edited by George E. Marcus and Fred R. Myers. University of California Press, 1995.

Kosuth, Joseph. "The Artist as Anthropologist." In *Art after Philosophy and After: Collected Writings, 1966–1990,* edited by Gabriele Geurcio. MIT Press, 1991.

Museum of Modern Art. "Joseph Kosuth, *One and Three Chairs,* 1965." https://www.moma.org/learn/moma_learning/joseph-kosuth-one-and-three-chairs-1965/.

Sassen, Saskia. *Guests and Aliens.* New Press, 1999.

Savvides, Efi. "[Untitled Chapter]." In *Drone Vision: Warfare, Surveillance, Protest,* edited by Sarah Tuck. Art and Theory, 2022.

13

Migrants' Narratives: Challenging the Border Logic of the United States

Valerie Forman

In October of 2018, a migrant caravan that started in Honduras was dominating news headlines. It had crossed through Guatemala and was making its way through Mexico to its southern border with the United States. Reports containing images of crowded bridges and thousands of people walking together on roads flooded mainstream media. It was not the first caravan; caravans had been coming to the US from Central America since at least 2017. But it was the largest, with estimates of up to 10,000 people. One of the primary reasons people who migrate travel in a caravan is safety. In their journey of over 2,700 miles from Honduras to Tijuana (about 2,500 miles of which is through Mexico), people who migrate confront many threats, from cartels and gangs to corrupt police and military. The trains that thousands of migrant people ride on top of every year, commonly known as *la bestia* (the beast), claim numerous lives and limbs.[1] The caravans are thus a means of collective survival.

The journey of people migrating, however, is far from over when they reach the border with the United States, and the safety they create within caravans is challenged when they finally arrive at the US border. In January of 2019, I decided to go to Tijuana, not sure what I would be doing, but hoping that my ability to speak Spanish would allow me to support the migrants' pursuit of justice and greater safety. I found my way to Al Otro Lado, a legal services organization in Tijuana that was expanding its border rights projects to provide "know your rights" workshops and consultations conducted by volunteer advocates and lawyers. The project's primary goal was to provide participants with more information about both the risks they would face in the United States and the strength of their asylum cases. They could thus make informed decisions about whether or not to wait in Tijuana, considered one of the most dangerous cities in the world — a wait that, at the time, was about two months due to illegally imposed metering systems.[2]

What follows are reflections and concerns based on that and other more recent experiences that have transformed my understanding of not only migration from Central America and Mexico to the US, but also of the immigration system within the US.[3] At first, my primary role at Al Otro Lado was to translate

---

1   For a detailed and insightful discussion of the dangers and complexities of the journey through Mexico for Central Americans, see Óscar Martínez, *The Beast: Riding the Rails and Dodging Narcos on the Migrant Trails*, trans. Daniela Maria Ugaz and John Washington (Verso, 2013).

2   According to international and US law, migrants have the right to cross the border and state their fear of returning to their home country. This metering system, which relies on a list of those waiting, was first implemented under the Obama Administration in 2016.

3   I want to express my gratitude for the following organizations for the work that they do and for allowing me to participate in it: Al Otro Lado, Cara Pro Bono Project at the Dilley Family Residential Center (a detention center for woman with children), New Sanctuary Coalition (especially their Accompaniment program), The Ark Immigration Clinic at Congregation Beit Simchat Torah, Freedom for Immigrants, and NYC DSA Immigrant Justice Working Group. My deepest thanks go to the many

what the person planning to seek asylum was saying into English, and then translate what the volunteer lawyer said back into Spanish. I quickly realized, however, how forms of translation not only of language but also of experience and forms of collective knowledge would be central to this process.[4]

All of these forms of translation are necessary from the first and central question asked of people seeking refuge: Why are you afraid to return to your country? Past persecution, or a well-founded fear of persecution, is central to asylum laws. In 2019, Yolanda told me that she was afraid for her and her son's life because her husband had been tortured and murdered two years earlier by gang members.[5] Given the length of time between his murder and when she left her home, I thought there might be more she was afraid of, and a strong asylum claim would likely require more recent threats or harms. When I asked, she added that gang members came to her home asking her to sell drugs for them. She refused. They came back. They threatened to kill her and her son if she said no. She still said "no." As a mother, she could not get involved in that kind of activity. When she said "no" the second time, they grabbed the son. After a tense standoff, they let the son go. But their threat before leaving was clear: They would be back and kill the son if she refused them again. Yolanda and her son fled as soon as they could get the money together to make the journey to the US.

Asylum laws and regulations provide a much narrower window for refuge than we might expect. Being in the clear, explicitly life-threatening danger Yolanda faced is not enough. To be granted asylum in the US, past or future persecution needs to be the result of five protected grounds: nationality, race, religion,

---

people on the move who have shared with me their histories, experiences, and concerns.

4 Over time, and at some of the other places mentioned above, I would speak with people seeking asylum one on one and then consult with a supervising lawyer afterwards.

5 I have changed the names of those with whom I spoke and combined or altered details in order to prevent anyone from being identifiable. For this reason, I have also not provided their country of origin.

political opinion, or membership in a particular social group. To determine the connection between the threats and a possible protected ground (the "nexus"), I asked Yolanda why she thought the gang had chosen her to sell drugs, and why they threatened her in particular. This question is often the most difficult, and answers are rarely simple or straightforward. She returned to what she said at the beginning of our conversation: "because they killed my husband." When asked about why he was afraid, her nine-year-old son gave a similar answer: he said he feared the people who killed his father would kill his mother too. For both of them, the recent threats by the gang and the murder of their husband/father in the past are not just linked; they are part of the same experience. After more conversation in which she continued to foreground the husband's death, I realized that from her perspective a question about why she was targeted that is not related to his death was inscrutable. But foregrounding his death in her claim would require a detailed explanation of how his murder was explicitly connected to the threats they were currently receiving.

My role then was to "translate" the narrow logics of the asylum system to her. I explained that asylum for her and her son would depend primarily on threats or harms they received directly. While trying to be respectful of her experience, I also had to communicate clearly that she would have to translate her experience into a narrative that would be legible to a US asylum officer. The new version went something like this: she feared returning to her home country because the gangs threatened to kill her when she refused to sell drugs for them. When she refused a second time, they threatened to kill her son and even tried to kidnap him, because she had refused on the grounds that as a mother she could not sell drugs. Only then would it be relevant for her to add that her husband was murdered by the gangs two years ago. She, therefore, knows that the gangs act on their threats. This account deemphasizes her husband's death and disaggregates what is a single source of fear for her into two distinct events. Essentially, none of the "facts" had changed, but to attempt to meet the legal requirements, she would have to offer a narrative that did not match her felt experience and discredited her memory and knowledge regarding her own safety. Under the stress of the interview, would she remember to provide a linear account of a layered experience in which the profound connections between life-threatening events do not conform to the logic of cause and effect?

Many scholars and advocates who have written about asylum have spoken of the ways it problematically demands a narrative of victimization — of suffering and desperation — to prove merit of humanitarian relief.[6] People seeking asylum or other forms of relief also face additional narrative challenges. People who migrate must transform histories that are experientially complex, even within their own contexts, into a coherent narrative that makes sense to an official outside their context.[7] But how can they seem "credible" when they are translating their experiences into a form that might not feel immediate? How do they recount their stories, as Yolanda needed to do, while deemphasizing something so painful and significant like the murder of a family member? To shift the burden, how do we match a legal system with the realities and fears of those actually in danger and how they understand their experience? How can we create an asylum process, and one of migration in general, that values the knowledge and experience of the very people it is set up to engage?

Many people who migrate, especially those traveling from what is referred to as the Northern Triangle (Honduras, El Salvador, and Guatemala) have resisted one of the two main gangs, MS-13 and Barrio 18.[8] They might have refused to pay extortion,

---

6   For a thoughtful engagement with the complexities of asylum, see John Washington, *The Dispossessed: A Story of Asylum at the US–Mexican Border and Beyond* (Verso, 2020).

7   In addition, more often than not, they do so without lawyers, who are allowed but not provided.

8   Since the writing of this essay, the presence of gangs in El Salvador in particular has changed dramatically. In March of 2022 President Nayib Bukele declared a state of emergency that has reduced considerably the amount of gang violence, but did so through the dismantling of demo-

join the gang, work for the gang, or be the girlfriend of a gang member. They might have refused to accept the gang's authority by denouncing them, or by trying to find out what happened to a loved one at the hands of the gang. "Requests" from gangs are effectively demands. They come with a threat. The choices are: do as they say, leave, or suffer the consequences.[9] In Mexico, the same is often true, though the source of the threat might be the even more powerful cartels.

Gustavo, a young man traveling with an adult nephew, told us that gang members had approached him and two of his nephews, insisting they allow the gang to use their newly inherited home for its meetings. They refused. Within a couple of days one of his nephews was shot and killed while running an errand. Knowing they were in the same danger, Gustavo and his other nephew joined the caravan. At the end of our conversation, Gustavo showed me two photos: one of his nephew when he was alive and another of his memorial. The photos could serve importantly as a form of proof. But I do not think that is primarily why he showed them to me. He was showing me a material representation of his memory of his cousin and his own relationality to family and neighborhood networks. That relationality forms a primary basis of his knowledge — the knowledge that he needed to flee his home.

When I consulted with one of the volunteer lawyers, she told me Gustavo did not have a strong case. Maybe he would pass his credible fear interview (CFI), but she thought it just as likely that he would not pass. Refusing the request of a gang does not provide a clear protected ground. I explained this to him and also needed to tell him that if he did not pass the CFI, he would

---

cratic institutions and human rights violations on a grand scale with over 85,000 people swept up and arrested without due process. In March of 2025, US President Donald J. Trump deported without due process over two hundred Venezuelans accused of belonging to gangs, though most had no criminal records. Trump's government will be paying that of Bukele to keep them in his notorious mega-prison, CECOT, which he opened in 2023.

9 See Óscar Martínez, *A History of Violence: Living and Dying in Central America*, trans. Daniela Maria Ugaz and John Washington (Verso, 2016).

likely be deported. His immediate response was that he would be killed if he were deported. A short while later, we waited as another volunteer made sure he would be able to access a copy of his documents in case they were lost, stolen, or taken from him by Custom and Border Patrol. I noticed a slight tremor in his hands; he looked at me with incredulity and said, "they will deport me if they know I will be killed." It was partially a question and partially a statement of disbelief — something that to him seemed implausible, absurd even. His incredulity is, of course, warranted. What does it mean to have an asylum system that will send someone back to certain death? How as a country can we accept these norms as "natural"? How has it come to be that offering refuge to people in life-threatening danger, regardless of its source or why someone was targeted, is a radical position?

All of these experiences are complex, and in some cases, with further probing, a "nexus" between the persecution and a protected ground can be found. But this is often "luck" or arbitrary. Not finding one doesn't necessarily mean someone's life is in less danger, or that they have less reason to fear returning to their home country. Thus, for US asylum law to function for refugees, it needs to shift its focus away from the hard line around nexus, to instead address the problems of those who are seeking asylum, and acknowledge the role of the US in producing the conditions from which people are fleeing. This is stating the obvious. Yet, the logic of borders and nation states based on the sovereign right to exclusion discourages countries who "receive" refugees from imagining themselves in this kind of relation to people seeking refuge.

I want then to reframe the way we think about this process. There is an important question which countries need to ask refugees individually and also collectively. What is it about their lives and the context of their lives that they want those making decisions about their migration status to understand? How do they understand their fear of persecution and its relationship to their subject positions and the reasons they are being targeted? This kind of shift would unsettle at least one of the fictions that serve as the basis for asylum law: that the "receiving" country is the source of knowledge.

Lack of knowledge of larger structural issues often has severe negative impacts on people who are seeking asylum. Even the ways structural issues are engaged derive from our self-beliefs as a nation: for example, that there are not systemic problems with the police or other authorities here as opposed to "over there." While I am not equating our conditions, I make the connection to raise questions about what happens when we represent the contexts of people who are migrating as radically outside our own conditions of possibility. Holding the difference as absolute exacerbates misalignments and can increase the burden of proof (by law, on the refugee) and even undermine credibility. Doing so also scripts "sending" countries as violent, chaotic, and "underdeveloped." These representations matter because they allow the US to perpetuate its self-narrative as separate from "sending" countries and thus their citizens who seek refuge here, as if we live in completely different worlds.

This narrative of separateness functions in very problematic ways. It allows the US to frame granting asylum to individuals as an act of generosity, as humanitarian rather than as a form of justice. Doing so perpetuates the disavowal of complicity with the root causes of migration.[10] People who migrate are thus seen as victims of a context far removed from our own, rather than potential actors in our world.[11] Moreover, the resulting reliance on a narrative of victimhood serves to create a division between deserving and undeserving migrants. This latter distinction produces a number of harms, but one of the most common is the production of the category of "economic migrant." Politicians and mainstream media alike often make the distinction

---

10 The gangs that have spread through Central America are native to the US, having first formed in Los Angeles. The United States also plays a primary role in creating the conditions that propel migration through political, military, and economic intervention in the Northern Triangle and elsewhere.

11 See E. Tenday Achiume, "Migration as Decolonization," *Stanford Law Review* 71, no. 6 (2019): 1509–74.

between people seeking refuge and those who are *just* seeking economic opportunity. Economic need or the impossibility of providing for oneself or one's family does not in most instances provide people migrating with a "legitimate" claim to refuge, nor any path to residency. Claiming an opportunity to make *a living* is denigrated as choice and opportunism, rather than actively seeking a life with possibilities, the latter of which is paradoxically at the heart of the ideology of being "American." That ideology, however, exists alongside the right of "Americans" to determine who has access to those possibilities.

What is the difference between fleeing poverty that does not allow your community to thrive or survive, and fleeing violence? Is it even possible to disentangle economic conditions from other forms of persecution? Diego said he had come to the US because he could not make a living at home. This response places him in the category of "undeserving" migrant. Part of the informal economy in his lakeside community, his business could no longer support his family. Like other small businesses in his town, his was regularly vandalized. In addition, some of the owners who organized to form a watch had been threatened with violence if they reopened their businesses. When we asked more questions about why people would want to get rid of these businesses, we found out that the threats came from parties who wanted to privatize the desirable land and develop it, thus connecting his struggle with a long history of expropriation and exploitation of land. Finally, we could tell him that his case aligned with asylum regulations after he spoke of the involvement of members of local government in these privatization efforts and his own participation in local community organizations. Clearly the poverty he is fleeing is inseparable from the persecution at the hands of the government that provides him with possible grounds for asylum. Though the details of the case might be relatively unique, the entanglement is not.

Our challenge is to find a way to reframe how we think about migration and the dangerous restrictions that impede it by centering the knowledge and experience of people who migrate. Can unveiling the absurdity and incongruity of certain requirements for asylum from the perspectives of people who migrate lead to a transformation of both law and discourses of migration? Can Yolanda's understanding of the relationship between past and present challenge the temporality by which asylum claims are adjudicated, while also foregrounding the importance of memory and local knowledges? Can the experience of Diego interrogate the very idea of dividing people who migrate into discrete categories by which they will be judged? Does the incredulity of Gustavo, who questions the rationale behind deporting someone to their certain death, challenge the right to exclude? He insists upon a claim to well-being as part of a collective that acknowledges the interdependence of nations and of our interconnectedness as beings. How might the knowledge of people on the move demand a rethinking of the world and its beings as divided into discrete units?

The caravan, as a whole, models solidarity that makes visible its members' collective claim as a political group to migrate. When as a group they chose to go through Veracruz because the terrain would be less arduous for the children, even though it was more dangerous, they put out a public statement holding the government of Veracruz and federal authorities responsible for their safety.[12] People imprisoned in migrant detention centers, too, challenge the abominable conditions and their lack of freedom collectively through hunger strikes and by sharing knowledge they gain while fighting to be free. They file complaints and petitions individually and jointly, while articulating the connections they have to communities within the US and outside of the US as well, thus challenging the exclusionary logics of belonging that the border instantiates. Within the caravans and detention centers, people who migrate center themselves as collectives, interconnected and interdependent with those who inhabit the spaces they leave, travel through, and to which they arrive and stay — either temporarily or permanently. As we as a

---

12 Jesús A. Rodriguez, "How the Migrant Caravan Built Its Own Democracy," *Politico*, December 12, 2018, https://www.politico.com/magazine/story/2018/12/12/migrant-caravan-tijuana-border-government-222856/.

country navigate the complexity of our relation to people who migrate, we need to center their forms of knowledge and, in particular, their collective ways of knowing and acting.

Bibliography

Achiume, E. Tenday. "Migration as Decolonization." *Stanford Law Review* 71, no. 6 (2019): 1509–74. https://www.stanfordlawreview.org/print/article/migration-as-decolonization/.

Martínez, Óscar. *A History of Violence: Living and Dying in Central America.* Translated by Daniela Maria Ugaz and John Washington. Verso, 2016.

———. *The Beast: Riding the Rails and Dodging Narcos on the Migrant Trails.* Translated by Daniela Maria Ugaz and John Washington. Verso, 2013.

Rodriguez, Jesús A. "How the Migrant Caravan Built Its Own Democracy." *Politico,* December 12, 2018. https://www.politico.com/magazine/story/2018/12/12/migrant-caravan-tijuana-border-government-222856/.

Washington, John. *The Dispossessed: A Story of Asylum at the US–Mexican Border and Beyond.* Verso, 2020.

14

"You're Back in the Room": Theatrical Borders in a Post-COVID-19 World

Pip Williams

In March of 2020, about a week before the first COVID-19 lockdown in the UK, I began work on an article for my website, in which I intended to review three shows I had seen at Camden People's Theatre (CPT), one of my favorite London venues, as part of their Sprint festival. The shows were Shepard Tone's *Coming Out Of My Cage (And I've Been Doing Just Fine)*, Nathan Ellis's *work.txt*, and Anorak's *Experimental Prototype Community of Tomorrow* (henceforth *EPCOT*). I enjoyed them all hugely, and they were all made by people I'm lucky enough to be able to call friends and acquaintances. My review article was supposed to be about audiences, the roles these shows cast their audiences in, and the degree to which those roles presented dramaturgical or more broadly political challenges to us. It was going to begin with an observation about an amateur production of *The Winter's Tale* that I saw two weeks before life froze, which featured a child actor who kept looking at the audience and grinning, despite all the grown-ups doing their best to pretend we weren't there. I thought this was a neat way to look at audience interaction, and what we understand by the audience-performer trans-action, the border that exists between the two parties.

However, I did not write this article. Because, as we all know, a week or so after I saw those shows, the government called a lockdown, all the theaters shut, my livelihood and the livelihood of most of my friends was thrown into complete chaos, and suddenly it seemed churlish and insensitive to be writing about audiences, about the importance of being in rooms together, of sharing space. Because there were no longer spaces to share.

In the piece I did end up writing, I went through those three shows and tried to consider what they might have to offer us going forward, in a moment of collective uncertainty, fear, and loneliness; how we could use their provocations and challenges to reflect on what it was we actually wanted theater to do, when it came back, and whom we wanted ourselves to be within it.

It is nearly a year since I saw those shows, and therefore nearly a year since I've actually been to a theater. Those considerations are even more pertinent and pressing now — the arts are fighting for their very existence every day, with countless theaters closing for good, freelancers hemorrhaging money and time, and certain government figures advising us, helpfully, to "retrain." Especially pertinent is this idea of a border — the "fourth wall" — separating us from the action onstage. In this COVID-19 world, we live within any number of borders, borders which mostly atomize and isolate us, even if they are totally necessary for our safety — borders both ideological and material. Very real. How are we to rebuild and rethink ideas of audience, of how we make meaningful exchanges between viewer and performer, in a world where it is dangerous to go anywhere near each other? How are we to reach out to each other, as we certainly need to do in these strange and trying times, when every exchange is mediated through masks, plastic screens, and hand sanitizer?

I'd like to look again at the three pieces of theater I saw at CPT, a year ago, in 2020, before the end of the world, and reconsider what they might have to tell us in the coming years.

Shepard Tone's *Coming Out…,* I suggested, was sort of theater-as-party, with the audience as guests. It was a show without a bad bone in its body, an ongoing exercise in finding commonality and shared experience. It was a show about song, and specifically about people singing, together. It was a show about community. It set out to explore the reasons for the enduring popularity of the song "Mr. Brightside" by *The Killers;* it included karaoke, throwing things at the actors, and the audience deciding what the name of their band would be (which changes every night). In a series of gentle instructions and provocations, we were told to close our eyes, then "open up [our] eager eyes" (in a nod to the lyrics of the song) in response to certain questions — to open our eyes if we'd prefer to be remembered as kind rather than successful, for example, or to look at someone in the room you'd like to say hi to. They were exercises in finding common ground — they emphasized the fact that we had all, separately, made the decision to come to this building at this time because of a thing we all liked. Fundamentally it emphasized the fact that, actually, it should be *fun* to be in a theater — that we were sitting there because of what we shared. We were in a room where we could play loud music, watch videos, and make the lights go all flashy. It was right and proper for the theater to be fun. And, as one of the performers suggested at one point, "the theater can be a good place to meet people." It's a social activity, and *Coming Out…* really emphasized that idea. It was a show geared towards our, the audience's, enjoyment — we were rewarded generously for simply being there, and guided gently to look at what we all had in common and to sing. The show ended with a sound clip of Brandon Flowers (lead singer of *The Killers*) talking about how "Mr. Brightside" doesn't belong to him anymore, but to all the people who sing it with him every night, to the crowds who chant it. It was a show about how art belongs to communities, not to individuals. A piece of art is a baby we raise together, that we unriddle and share and live with together, in the theater building, yes, but in bars and bedrooms and seminars and coffee shops, together, for hours and days and years afterwards. It is enough for a show to bring a group of likeminded people together and establish that we are all there for the same reason.

It is vital, going forward, that we remember what we share. The theater should be a space for play and freedom, and a place where we can own something together. Sadly, one suspects that this aspect of the theater, the act of congregating, will be one of the last aspects we regain post-COVID-19, but at a time where our experiences as humans are so vastly differentiated, when we are so separate, when we are wrestling with so many different kinds of grief and misery, theater's capacity for creating shareable, communal joy must not be overlooked. The theater of the future must be an exercise in community, and in the joy of that. God knows we've missed it.

Nathan Ellis's *work.txt* presented a very different spin on the idea of "audience participation." Taking the form of a series of prompts and instructions, projected onto the back wall of the theater, it was a play for no actors, performed entirely by the audience. Ostensibly about the gig economy, about how late capitalism has effectively blurred the lines between work and pleasure, how technology has rendered the two inseparable (we can check our social media at the office, we can shop for clothes on our work computers), the piece was also a subtle and wry look at the place art has in that world. Should art be the absence of labor, something distracting and relaxing in a busy and hectic time? Or should it be something we wrestle with using our creative brains, something we really have to engage with, something we work to understand? Like *Coming Out...*, *work.txt* presented a series of provocations to find what the audience had in common — pieces of text to be read by "People Who Like Swimming," or "Geminis," or "Someone Who Doesn't Like Experimental Theatre." This switched between groups and individuals in an exciting and often very funny way, gradually inching us towards a place where we were given the instruction, "A member of the audience comes onstage." To introduce this element too early would be to scare us off, to prioritize only the most confident or stage-happy audience members, but Ellis managed to cook the room at just the right temperature and for just long enough to create a truly collaborative and ultimately playful atmosphere.

But why should we participate? It is one of the piece's central questions — why should we have to work for art? Shouldn't art be doing the work for us? "Yes," seemed to be the show's answer, but then we live in a world where *everything* is work. Where we are doing work every second of our days, be that financially, be that physically, be that mentally. Like a mantra, we are instructed to repeat, "Work is being done." All *work.txt* did was lay this reality bare, reminded us that even in a theater we were doing work of a sort, the work of not working. The work of having fun.

However, one of the piece's central images was of an act of protest. An individual (with the name of an audience member, of course) lay down in the lobby of a big building and refused to get up. It baffled her co-workers and prompted a rhapsody about modern art and meaning from an art critic. And still, all around them, relentlessly and eternally, "work was being done." So what we took from *work.txt* was that we, the audience, were a powerful body. We were not made just for work. It was an act of power to stop and opt out, and it was our right to lie down — our right to protest through rest. In work.txt we, the audience, were given the means of production. And though we were invited to play an active part in a pre-existing structure, written by someone else to be performed by us, it became incumbent on us to move things forward, to drive the action of our enjoyment. It empowered us to feel as though we were sufficient; that we could rely on ourselves and each other to create something meaningful. The power to start something was as present within us as the power to stop it.

The theater reminds us, then, not only of our commonality but of the energy that rests within it. Particularly at a time when more and more people are recognizing the problems inherent in so many structures, the evils present in so many of the systems we lived by, pre-pandemic, the power of groups and congregations must not be underestimated. Likewise the knowledge that has come for many over this time is that we are not just creatures

CROSSINGS

made to work — that we have the potential to be sufficient, full individuals on our own terms.

It is also, I think, worth considering what it is we want from art, moving forward. Are we looking for escapism? Are we looking for plays and pieces that allow us to forget the miseries of 2020–2021, to pretend that what's happening outside the theater isn't happening? Or should we be seeking to make plays that can change the world? The two probably aren't mutually exclusive, but this is another vital question that *work.txt* posed — are we willing to work, or not? And what form should that work take?

At the end of *work.txt* we watched the world end. God took voluntary redundancy; the universe retired because "it has become too big." But in Anorak's *EPCOT*, we were invited to rebuild the world, together. And it is this piece I think that has the most to teach us about the borders we need to cross together, when all this is done. More a thought experiment than a play, the start of a conversation rather than a thing we experienced as observers, *EPCOT* cast the audience as a kind of focus group, a collective of creators, as, under the gentle guidance of James Nash and Hannah-Louise Batt, we were invited to picture the future, a future that takes place in our individual imaginations after we have left the theater and gone to bed, and yet seemed to come to life before our very eyes. The whole show was addressed to "you" (that is, us), couched in a state of provisionality, an endearingly deferential future conditional. "What do you think the future looks like?," we were asked, and later, more clearly, and maybe more angrily, "What do you want?" Nash and Batt lay out a collection of objects (empty bottles, floppy discs, cardboard boxes) and we were invited to map our version of the future onto them. It was a slyly efficacious device, and certain images still stay with me: a Perspex box slowly filling with steam from a humidifier; the shock of a cardboard tower suddenly falling; the glowing white orb that took center stage, a warm little electronic planet. We realized how quickly we as humans map stories onto things, how fast and adaptable the human imagination is. There was beautiful care in the way Nash and Batt set out these perfectly ordinary little objects and created their world, and it was a care that radiated through the piece, short as it is.

But while the piece was intimate and even, to a degree, soothing, it never let its audience off the hook. While it did not inscribe audience participation, it gave us the tools for active reimagination. Nash and Batt told us two subtly different stories about the future we could wake up in. Nash's future was a sort of endless, carbonless, socialist utopia, where destructive systems had been toppled and humanity was reconciled to itself; Batt's was no less politically idealistic, arguably, but was socially lonely, a far-off and alien time dominated by lost friendships and a befuddled nostalgia for a barely remembered past. In one desperately sad image, Batt, in a futuristic museum, looked into a glass case and saw a polaroid (itself, even in 2020, a relic of a past most of us don't remember) of her and her friend, the friend now long gone, hundreds of years in the past, their friendship now an artifact. "What do you want?," we were asked at the end, "What do you want?" It was the most confrontational and forceful part of the show, but it was only right that we were asked it; if we were being asked to imagine the future, and indeed to collaborate imaginatively in the creation of it, it was right that we asked serious questions of ourselves. Is it progress that we want? The exponential advancement of the human race, the creation of a politically, ecologically perfect superworld that we tend like gardeners? Or is it something a bit more like the present? Is it a safe place where we have all the things we have now but don't have to worry about them — forward motion, but getting to keep polaroid cameras and vinyl records?

I would argue that this is the most important thing a piece of art can give to us; perhaps it is too much to ask for change to happen in the theater building, contingent as that is on the congregation of certain people, at certain times, in a certain place. Perhaps it must happen in our minds in the days, months, years afterwards. Perhaps it is enough for a piece of art to suggest to us a way that we might co-imagine, a way to map meaning onto meaningless objects, a way to create rooms that are big enough to hold all of our futures.

But this is the problem we face, at time of writing. We cannot create rooms, as we recognize them. We cannot congregate, and we cannot share art in the way that we're used to doing. What will the audience-performer border look like when the world emerges looking different? How willing will we be to pretend that we are looking into a room, containing people who cannot see us? To pretend that there is an invisible wall, separating us from other people, when we have spent so long in the company of walls? Will we be up for sitting quietly and pretending we're not there? The theater must, surely, expand and open its arms, create space, like the little girl in *The Winter's Tale,* to look into the audience and smile. It must face us, and address us with the energy and vitality of our shared, finally reunited humanity. To make the responsibilities and motions of the play the responsibility and motion of the whole theater, of its very brickwork, of all the people in it. We must leap over the border that separates us, and create art that draws us all together. We must be allowed to have fun; to sing, dance, and throw things; to make active change and decisions; to imagine together the world we could live in.

When we are allowed back in the room, it must be big enough for all of us, and all of our futures.

IV.

Conversations

15

Communities and Stages: Conversation with Good Chance Theatre

Mohamed Sarrar, Joe Murphy, and Joe Robertson

MOHAMED SARRAR: How did I end up in the Jungle? That's a long story.

When I left Sudan, I didn't have a specific target. I ended up in Paris, via Italy. I'd heard people say Paris is a beautiful city and France is a beautiful country and good for human rights. Lots of high hopes. But no. Same police as in Italy. Same treatment as I used to get back home. I met someone in La Chapelle — a neighborhood where lots of refugees live on the streets — and he told me about the Jungle. He told me, just go. It's easier, it's better when you get to the UK.

So I went. When you get there, it's difficult to go back when the target is really close and you can see the white cliffs, but it's difficult to stay because it's not a great place to be. And you just keep trying.

JOE ROBERTSON: We ended up in the Jungle because we'd been watching the news images in summer 2015 of people arriving in Greece and Italy in the tens of thousands. We saw the picture of Alan Kurdi, the Syrian boy whose body was washed up on a beach in Bodrum. The news at the time was hysterical; the basic questions about who these people were, why they were travelling, where they were travelling to weren't being answered.

So we decided to fill the car with clothes and pots and pans, and drive to Munich to find out. We planned to stop for a day in Calais on the way, and ended up staying for eight months.

We knew that there were people waiting while they tried to cross to the UK, but we didn't know that there were restaurants, cafes, churches, mosques — but no government agency, no United Nations, no big NGO running things. It was a huge, makeshift, self-governing shantytown of about 8,000 people, twenty-two miles from Dover. We couldn't believe it. After a few hours of wandering around, meeting people, it started to get dark and a few nice Kuwaiti guys built us a tent and cooked for us, and we sat around a campfire and told stories until they went to try for the UK. I'll never forget that day.

JOE MURPHY: When you arrived, Mohamed, what was that like?

MS: Tents everywhere, and of course restaurants, like a city, and you can find everything, even night clubs. I didn't expect that. You want a drink, you'll get it; you want a night club, you go, you want mosque, you go, I even found a shisha bar in one of the restaurants. It was amazing.

JM: What shocked us was seeing people from over twenty-five different countries. Not just Syrians, who we had expected to find there, but also people from Sudan, Afghanistan, Eritrea, Iraq, Iran, Kurdistan, Ethiopia, Kuwait, Palestine, Somalia....

JR: What was it like being surrounded by different languages, different kinds of people, different colors, backgrounds, religions?

MS: A bit scary. I'd never met Afghan people or Kurdish people. I thought, "OK, it will be Syrians, it will be Iraqi, it will be

Sudanese and maybe Eritreans." Then when I found out there were more than twenty-five nationalities, I thought ... wow.... So many people have travelled. Not only me.

JM: We heard so many different stories. It seemed to us that the need to tell stories, the need to express what was happening, was fundamental. Before you even found out someone's name, you'd heard about their journey, their hopes for the UK, their families back home. Being playwrights, who live in stories, this really affected us. We thought about how we could contribute. There was already a community of European volunteers providing food, clothes, medicine, shelter materials. And because winter was drawing in, and the nights were getting closer, we thought that a place where stories could be told and shared in warmth and safety could be genuinely useful. And of course, for us that place is called a theater. So we raised enough money to buy a geodesic dome, the strongest temporary structure. But it's also a democratic space which can't be built without the collaboration of many people.

We spent a whole day building the Dome with 100 people from different countries. So by the time it was finished, it was already owned by everyone. And then the first night, we had a party. People came from all across the camp to dance to music from every different country. People passed their phones to the DJ table to play songs from their country. A huge release of energy.

JR: Then we were in all the British newspapers the next day — "British Activists Build Night Club in the Jungle" — and we said, "no, it's a theater, we promise!" And they published pictures of refugees dancing — as if they didn't deserve that one moment of enjoyment.

MS: We came from different places and had terrible times travelling, so they think we are traumatized and we can't have fun. Even if you are traumatized you need sometimes just to forget, to live in the moment.

JR: That sums up for me what the Dome was for. I had some of the best nights in a theater in my whole life there. So electric, people doing music or dance or circus, and it wasn't about charity, it was about having an amazing time together as human beings.

MS: I'll tell you something, I sometimes miss the days there, everyone dancing, having fun with everyone. Obviously, we've done it here (in the UK) since then with the Jungle family.... But you know, when it was there — because everyone was welcome, and you would meet different people, you could find new friends and new members of the family; new songs and music, hearing stories, seeing performances....

JR: What was it like when you first came across the Good Chance Dome?

MS: When my friend Halaf and I used to go to Jules Ferry (a French-government-run center on the site) for food, we would pass the Dome and wonder, because it was one of the biggest tents, "what is that"? And the shape of it — in Sudan, in Khartoum, we have many buildings similar to the dome. One day we decided to go in. And I found people singing and dancing, so I went again, and I found Milan (a musician from Iran who has since collaborated with Good Chance many times) with his guitar, singing Iranian songs. I loved this.

JM: And you were already writing songs in the Jungle?

MS: I was writing and singing some traditional Sudanese songs. I had a few songs that I had already composed, or hadn't finished writing which I wrote back home. But some songs like "Abbas Hallas" I wrote in and about the Jungle. I kept writing whatever came into my mind, just typing on my phone.

JM: I remember you telling us how you wrote "Abbas Hallas."...

MS: So, one day with some friends we went to try. It took three hours to walk from the Jungle to the train station. If you don't find good chance, this will be six hours of walking, plus the time you stay there, trying. Your day is gone. And that day we went and we managed to get across the first fence, and then the second, the third, the fourth.... Twelve fences we crossed, one by one. And after the twelfth — the security guard saw us and came at us with dogs, and we started running, everyone in different directions, and I hid in a kind of big underground drain, with dirty and disgusting water. We stayed there for hours. We tried to leave, and when we couldn't reach the train, we went back to this place, and ended up staying there two whole days.... So when we couldn't do anything, with no food and water, I decided to deliver myself to the security and let them call the police. I thought the police would take me back to the Jungle, but they just left us outside the train station instead. So during the three-hour walk back to the Jungle, I made up the song. "Abbas Hallas, adeena chance." Hey officer, give us a chance. We were hiding ourselves for a day, and then another day came.... All this with the security guard walking around, and he caught us before the train was leaving. So yeah, then I mentioned that I was missing parents, brother, sister.... That's how I made the song. It was a long walk. My phone was dead so I couldn't write it and so I was just doing the song in my head, and singing it, and when I arrived at the Jungle, I forgot half of it! So what I remember is what I sing now.

JM: What was the point of art in the Jungle and the art that we do together now? Why are songs important? What does it mean to step out of reality into art?

MS: In the Jungle people were from more than twenty-five countries. Although some people, maybe half, speak more than one language, there's still a lot who won't understand if you want to express something. But through art they can express whatever they want. So Yasin (another friend and collaborator of Good Chance whom we met through the Jungle) — he's Kurdish and

Iranian — can express what he wants through his martial art. I'm Arab Sudanese, and I can say it through the music. Milan speaks through the music too. Or you can do it through a play. Everyone can do their own thing, express their feelings through their art, it connects everyone.

JM: So you arrived in England in November?

MS: I arrived December 17, 2015. That was the day I was born in the UK. I was supposed to perform in the dome in Calais that day, with my friends, Halaf and everyone! Instead, I sat in the truck all night, till we crossed over. When we arrived at Dover at 7 a.m., touching British land, I knew there is no way they could take us back, even if we were caught — it was a really small chance to get caught because of the noise of the trucks and the sea and the sheep. No one was going to search the back of the truck while it's there. So I called Halaf and said: "I've got it. I'm in UK." And he said to me: "Oh, but you've got your performance today!" I said I didn't care!

JR: [Laughing] It absolutely ruined our show, that you got safely to the UK!

MS: We got caught in Birmingham. But we just got on with the process, waiting for the interview, and another one, the brown letters coming — what is it, do they trust you...? It was scary because you don't know what's going on and what's going to happen, it's just waiting; they send you a letter by post, and then you just come to the place at the time. I stopped in Birmingham for just twenty-four hours, at the police station, and then got moved to Croydon for a week, and then Wakefield for another two weeks, then Bradford, where I got my asylum.

JR: And while you were going through this we were still in the Jungle. We stayed until March, until it all burned down. It was terrible, traumatic, and the police came in and evicted people, we left, and took the dome down and quickly got out. I think we met again — maybe May, June 2016?

MS: I think May was the first workshop for *The Jungle,* for the play. I was still in Bradford — I went to Manchester for the workshop.

JM: So you've arrived in the UK, you're going through the asylum process, and then we all get together and you see people again whom you haven't seen since the Jungle. What was that like?

MS: You know, through the time I was in Bradford, I had a Burmese person next to me. Neither of us spoke perfect English, so we couldn't understand each other well. But there was another Eritrean guy who spoke Sudanese Arabic, so we could communicate. And then another Kurdish guy who had perfect English. So it was a bit difficult for me to click with everyone. All of a sudden I got invited to the workshop, and it meant everyone was there, I had such a good and lovely time. It was my first time in Manchester. I hadn't been out at all, just staying in Bradford. On the way out I didn't even know where to go, I had no friends there, some of my friends were still in Calais. And then I got invited to the workshop. You booked my tickets and everything and I thought, ok, let's go. And for the first time, I met people I hadn't met in a long time.

JR: And then we spent maybe two years workshopping, meeting up again and again. Joe and I would go away and write and then we'd do a workshop and find out how much work we needed to do, and then we'd go away and write more. And then we performed it, *The Jungle* play, at the end of 2017. That was at the Young Vic, and then the play was transferred to the West End in summer 2018, New York later that year, and San Francisco in 2019. It was due to return to New York in spring 2020 and embark on a tour of the US, but then the pandemic struck.

JM: What was it like telling that story to a London audience — because the set was very like one of the restaurants, maybe quite similar to the one where you smoked shisha in the Jungle? What was it like, having to recreate that every night?

MS: When you get on the stage of the play, *The Jungle,* you feel like there's a spirit taking you to the real Jungle, not just a play, because of the nature of the stage and the theater and the floor and everything.

JR: The floor. That always made me really think I was in the camp again because the floor was mud and like, rubbish in the mud....

MS: And the only thing that tells me that I'm not in the real Jungle is that I can have a shower every day after the play! Because back then the Jungle was just tents with your mud.

JM: And then you were meeting audiences every day and we often thought how weird that must be: you've always been a star, but actually being a *star* and people coming and wanting your autograph and asking about your experiences, all very much in your face. That must have been overwhelming.

MS: You know some people just watch what's in the media. The media doesn't give you everything. And when you don't get the full image you can get a negative idea about what it is. In the play we showed the reality. When people come and talk about that, I feel like they care now and want to know what's going on. And of course, I keep telling what I always want to tell, what they need to know, and they can talk about this and keep working and offer a helping hand. After the play, many people decided to go there.

JR: That was weird, when I went back to Calais when the show was on, and Help Refugees (a grassroots NGO which also formed in the Jungle) was being funded by donations made by audience members after the play. Seeing all these volunteers who were there because they had seen the story you were telling on stage was amazing.

MS: I think that's the success of the play, when you have more people who think about what's going on there, and they try and work on that.

JM: Let's talk about Sounds of Refuge, because we also made an album together. In Abbey Road.

MS: When I arrived, I never thought that I would really carry on doing music, because I write songs in Arabic, though I am willing to write in English. At that time my language didn't help me. I got other Arabic songs as well, they were ready just to record and I didn't know how to do it, and how to start. And then I remember when Joe and Joe and John Falsetto (an actor and musician who was in The Jungle) said to me that we need to do something after we met in The Jungle workshops; that we need to sing together. Then all of a sudden we were going to do something and Good Chance was joining us — and that was it! We made it there in Abbey Road. And that was like the biggest thing that happened to me in my life. I never thought I would be in that studio. For me, starting in Abbey Road studios meant getting me to do other things, getting me writing more in English.

JM: How does it feel writing in English?

MS: It's completely different. Sometimes when I write something in Arabic and then I try to translate it into English and make a song of that, it's difficult to get it the way you want it to be. I can change the rhyme and put in different words with the same meaning, but this depends on my vocabulary. The expressions I use in Arabic, they don't work in English. And then, second thing, writing in English is difficult and of course I'm scared to make something that doesn't ... show where I am now.

JM: Could you ever imagine writing in both English and Arabic?

MS: I've done something like this, actually. When I started with John I did an Arabic bit, and he did a Shona bit, so I represented the Arabic and my culture and my language, and John represented his (from Zimbabwe). But for me, when I do the Arabic one and the English together, I'm representing the English identity as someone who lives here and got into English culture, and at the same time I'm bringing my Arabic self to the UK, and mixing them together and doing the same work on my own.

JR: It's been a true privilege knowing you and working together over the last six years, Mohamed. We can't wait to hear your next album, and to carry on collaborating for the next six years and beyond.

16

Stories in Transit

*Dine Diallo and Clelia Bartoli in conversation with
Marina Warner, transcribed and translated
by Valentina Castagna*

MARINA WARNER: I first met Saifoudiny Diallo, who goes by
Dine, in September 2016 when he had just arrived in Sicily on
one of the boats making the crossing from Libya, and was taking
part in a Stories in Transit workshop in Palermo. With two of
his friends — Ibrahim Ture and Gassimou Magassouba, known
as Maga — he gave a talk about their hopes and ambitions; they
also introduced the other workshop participants to the concept
of *giocherendan,* a Fula word for an ideal principle governing
civil life, social and personal responsibility, and justice. The
three of them were impressive — eloquent and ambitious and
determined. They were in a school where Clelia Bartoli, one of
their teachers and a campaigner for human rights, found there
was as yet no furniture or books. Clelia and other colleagues
from the University of Palermo had argued passionately about
what needed to be done in their region, which was receiving
thousands of men, women, and children fleeing to Europe from

Fig. 16.1. Saifoudiny (Dine) Diallo on stage. Courtesy of the artist.

civil conflicts, border wars, famine, and drought, all of these consequences of ecological devastation.[1]

Valentina Castagna, a university lecturer, had worked as an interpreter in the law courts for asylum seekers. Her experiences of hearing their stories inspired us both to organize the Stories in Transit project as a series of story-making, storytelling workshops with local schools and young migrants like Dine, Maga, and Ibrahim. Dine and several others threw themselves into the process with imaginative exuberance. The word "giocherenda" sounds as if it could be formed from the Italian *giocare,* to play — a fortuitous connection — and so Giocherenda became the name of their group.[2] During the very first Stories in Transit workshop in Palermo, which we held in the atmospheric set-

---

1   See Carola Rackete and Anne Weiss, *Il est temps d'agir,* trans. Catherine Weinzorn (L'Iconoclaste, 2020) for an impassioned argument about the ecological causes of displacement and migration.

2   See Marina Warner, "Living in a Country of Words," in *Others: Writers on the Power of Words to Help Us See Beyond Ourselves,* ed. Charles Fernyhough (Unbound, 2019).

Fig. 16.2. Saifoudiny (Dine) Diallo on stage. Courtesy of the artist.

ting of the International Puppet Museum Antonio Pasqualino,[3] Dine told a story he had heard during his childhood; this fable inspired later performances, with puppets and live action and animation, "The Huntsman and the King's Son" (fig. 16.1).

Dine also starred as Gilgamesh with Maga as Enkidu when the Stories in Transit group worked on the Babylonian epic during another three-day workshop[4]; the result[5] — a kind of pageant — combined music, masks, costumes, and procession and took place in the Botanical Gardens of Palermo, and later in the grounds of a primary school. (fig. 16.2)

Since those days, the approach of Stories in Transit and the success of the workshops inspired Dine and Clelia, and several other colleagues and friends, to set up Giocherenda, an asso-

---

3   *Antonio Pasqualino Museo Internazionale delle Marionette,* https://www. museodellemarionette.it/en/.

4   "Stories in Transit VI: 'One for You, One for Me', 'The Old Man and the Serpent' & 'The Huntsman and the King's Son,'" *Stories in Transit,* http:// www.storiesintransit.org/workshops/storiesintransitvi/.

5   Stories in Transit, "Stories in Transit IV - Giocherenda Workshop September 2018," *YouTube,* October 22, 2019, https://www.youtube.com/ watch?v=LXdttrPkEoE.

ciation where they carry on their work. They make storytelling games on the premises, as well as laptop sleeves, backpacks, and bags. The pandemic has curtailed the group's activities, but Stories in Transit has managed to hold two workshops online, in collaboration with Compass Collective[6] and some new members of Giocherenda. As Stories in Transit, we are also developing an exhibition exploring methods and ideas for playing and generating stories which will feature Giocherenda's games, artifacts, and animations. Dine presented Giocherenda to the Migrant Knowledge event and led a very engrossing game of *La Ronda dei Desideri* (The Wheel of Wishes).[7] For this interview, Dine Diallo, Valentina Castagna, and Clelia Bartoli joined me on February 20, 2021. Valentina has transcribed and translated the conversation, which I have edited for publication.

MW: Can you tell us something about your story?

SAIFOUDINY DIALLO: My name is Saifoudiny Diallo but I am always called Dine. I was born in Conakry, Guinea, on May 2, 1999, and I grew up there, and studied French, Arabic, and religion. I worked with my father and had the opportunity to meet many important people. When I was in Fouta Djallon [a mountainous region of central Guinea], I met many with a deep knowledge of both culture and religion and was able to sit with them and gain some experience from their hands. Meeting other people allows you to confront different cultures. So I didn't only learn at school, but also through meeting different people.

MW: That's how you first heard about this principle of giocherendan?

SD: Yes, giocherendan means real sharing, a human exchange. Making giocherendan is making a network that you can't see,

---

6 *Compass Collective,* https://www.compasscollect.com/.

7 Giocherenda, "Scopri la Ronda dei Desideri," *Facebook,* August 31, 2020, https://www.facebook.com/watch/?v=344753083317460.

but we are all connected by it. We should live our lives feeling each other's happiness, even each other's sadness. The world of giocherendan is not a world of selfishness, of violence, of evil: it is a world that creates great good. I'll tell you about an episode in which giocherendan even saved my life. One night, while I was in the desert on my way to Libya, I fell off the pickup. The car drove directly over my foot, after ten seconds my foot became as big as two feet. The people in the car didn't know me, but they told the driver to stop and come back for me. They said that if he didn't stop, they would all rather get off the pickup and die with me in the desert. This strong solidarity that they showed they had inside, their sharing of the pain I felt, really made me understand the strength of giocherendan. And afterwards, when they took me back into the pickup, I couldn't even sit down. All these very tired people let me sit on top of them. They accepted this suffering to help me. That's an incredible thing that happened to me.

MW: Do you still hear from them or have you lost touch with them?

SD: Of those people, there's only one person I still have contact with. All the others, I don't know if I'll ever hear from them again: even if I saw them, I don't think I'd recognize them. Only giocherendan can do this kind of thing: imagine a person you don't know at all, you meet them by chance, and immediately you put yourself in their place, you defend them, you save them. They could have easily gone ahead and not given a damn, but they stopped. And then one day I returned the favor: I was in Libya and about to leave in a dinghy. However, just before we left, some criminals came and attacked the place where we were. They were shooting at us. I wasn't hurt, but one boy was badly wounded, they shot three bullets in his hands and feet. That evening a trafficker arrived and said we had to leave immediately with the dinghy. Even though I was weak, I picked up this boy on my shoulders who couldn't walk and carried him to the dinghy. I was supposed to get into the dinghy and leave, there were three of them that had to leave that night. All my friends got into the first dinghy. The first group of wounded people, those who had been shot at, all got on the first dinghy. I was supposed to get on that one too, with my friends. But one of the traffickers said to me: "Wait, you won't embark here. Wait for the second one." While waiting for the second boat, I asked him: "My friends have all gone there, why can't I go up?" I had that boy on my back, who couldn't even walk, couldn't even put his feet on the ground. The man said, "Look, I'm not putting you in the first one, I'm not putting all the wounded on the same boat. I'm putting this wounded man in the second boat." The first boat left, made it across. My boat, the second boat, couldn't go. After an hour we came back, but the dinghy was taking on water, it was full of water. Luckily, God made sure we could get back, otherwise I would have died. But there was no way I could leave there. I had to stay in that place for three months, with all the suffering of that place. But I did not regret what I did: that injured boy had to get back. He didn't come to Europe, though — the next day they had to take him to Niger to extract the bullets from his body. In all this suffering, people would come up to me and ask: "Are you still alive, are you still here?" It was almost as if I belonged there. But in the end, I really managed to get through it. They would ask me, "Why don't you go back?" I would reply, "I have nowhere to go back to, my only option is to move on. As long as I am alive, I'll go forward." These are some of those moments when you live giocherendan, not only in times of peace and tranquility: that's when you really have to commit and show this thing that you have inside, even if it's difficult. A lot of those guys didn't care about injured people. But there were volunteers, too, five of us, who took it upon ourselves to bring these people, to help them.

MW: Thank you, Dine, for telling us these difficult things. At the beginning of Stories in Transit, Dine, Ibra, and Maga gave a presentation about the principle of giocherendan. Clelia, you were very instrumental in forming the group which took the name Giocherenda. When did you first hear them talk about it?

CLELIA BARTOLI: It was when we started this beautiful educational experiment, Polipolis, which contained this principle without knowing it. One of the goals we had set ourselves was to create a link between the students and the city, not just to transmit knowledge. Not only for the benefit of our students but also of the city. One day we were going to see some students from a local high school, to get them to do things together and create an opportunity for young people who were mainly born in Palermo to meet our school, which was mainly attended by young migrants who had recently arrived here by crossing the Mediterranean. While we were on the metro train, I remember Maga saying, "there is a real need for giocherendan here." And that intrigued me. He explained something that I've heard from all the young people from West Africa: that in Europe there's a bad habit of not greeting people you don't know, as if there's little willingness to create new relationships. Trying to explain what this giocherendan was, they explained that it is not simply solidarity: solidarity can have the meaning of "I who have more give to you who have less," affirming a moral superiority through giving ("I have more money, I can give to you, and I am also better than you, I can afford to be good to you"). And "taking care" often entails controlling the lives of others. Instead, giocherendan comes from the awareness that there is an invisible network that binds us, as in Dine's story. I receive from someone or I give to someone, and it is a wider exchange between humanity and perhaps beyond. I give and then I receive, but also from others, third persons. There is an awareness of an immense, joyful power that comes from being able to do things with others. They realized that this awareness was lacking in Europe, leading to a lot of loneliness and depression. There may be poverty, but there's also a form of wealth that doesn't make you profoundly happy, because it lacks this element of sharing. So they felt somehow invested in the need to become ambassadors of giocherendan and thus we created the association. Westerners have often had the presumption of wanting to export values, such as democracy or development, without realizing (or without having the humility to see) how much they have to learn.

This is an inversion of the typical way of seeing Africa and its inhabitants, as the ones who should receive help, charity, and knowledge. Instead, the members of Giocherenda realized that there are people in need in Europe, and that young people with sensitivity, depth, and solid experience can really bring values that make the place where they have arrived grow.

MW: I have seen examples of this. Dine, can you tell us about a case in which Giocherenda's work has been effective in Sicily? For example, when you went to these schools in the difficult areas of Palermo?

SD: Yes, for example, as Clelia said before, for us who come from Africa, not answering greetings is a very strange thing, because for us it is not just a duty. When one says hello, the most joyful way of interacting is to say it back. If I see an African person, he or she will say hello to me: we will make a reciprocal gesture. So we felt it was a very important loss of value.

MW: Have you managed to get the people of Palermo to say hello even if they don't know each other?

SD: Many of them have now understood the mission of Giocherenda. We put a lot of effort into it. Maga and I used to organize meetings. We've been to the Galileo Galilei high school and various other schools, even the ZEN district in Palermo [the most disadvantaged part of the city, with multiple problems]. With Anna Starapoli of the Pedro Arrupe Institute, we've worked a lot in difficult neighborhoods in this city where many Palermo residents don't go easily.

Some people come to the shop and say, "A friend of mine suggested I come." We explain what we do and so these people are now helping to spread giocherendan. A lot of people today are living according to this principle. I can see the fruits of what we have brought together with Clelia. Many people in different areas remember us. If we look at this pandemic, it has made us reflect a lot on how important giocherendan is. We often say that if I am ill, it means that you also feel this pain that I have inside. If it doesn't matter to you whether I'm well or not, it's no good: COVID-19 was only carried by one person at the beginning, but this person transmitted it to the whole of humanity. This is the human connection that we were talking about: without knowing it, we depend on others, we are connected. Without others we have no strength. Our paths are connected. This is the most practical way of defining giocherendan.

CB: I agree with Dine. During the lockdown, if I went down to throw out the rubbish and met strangers in the street, we would say hello and smile at each other, even behind a mask. And why did you say hello when before you didn't pay attention to others? Because somehow this situation made people more aware that this giocherendan, this invisible thread that unites us, is there. You recognize in the other someone involved in the same adventure and this makes you greet them even if you didn't know them. Now it is fading a little, but when there is a common fragility greeting one another is instinctive.

MW: When you go to these places, Dine, with people who are in very difficult situations, what do you do? Do you use games or do you just talk? Do you create stories?

SD: We use our cooperative games to show this thread that connects us. They are tools we can use. We have also studied the methodology of Philip Zimbardo's Heroic Imagination Project (HIP). By going to these places, we encourage people to play, we play together, we share experience. For example, with our *Cubi Contafiabe* (Storytelling Dice), when I roll the dice and start the story, the others must listen. If they don't listen, they can't connect their story with the previous part. They have to pay attention to the others; they can't get distracted. We always say you need to turn on the engine that connects us and helps us capture the stories of others so we can tell something together. Sometimes we meet people who are desperate, who can no longer cope with their daily difficulties. They think that their life is ruined. So we intervene at that moment by giving examples from our own lives, we tell them about the obstacles we have encountered. People like Philip Zimbardo, Clelia, many of you in Stories in Transit, have managed to achieve success but it was certainly not easy. If one also talked about the difficulties, all the pressure, others would understand. I met a girl in the ZEN neighborhood. She had a dream of becoming a singer. Her father had died, she only had her mother, and their economic situation was not very good. She said to me: "I've thrown my dreams away. I know they are no longer feasible." So I said to her, "Listen, we can compare ourselves a little bit. Because I haven't thrown my dreams away, and if I tell you about them you won't believe me. I'll tell you about myself and what I've had to face. If I'm here in front of you now, talking to you, it's because I never thought 'I can't make it.' No way. I always have to try to move forward. Maybe you could reach top levels. As this HIP module shows us, there are always higher levels. In order to reach them you must never give up." When I finished explaining a little bit about what I had to face, the girl was crying. She thought that no one had been in the situation she was in. She was crying, she came to hug me. She told me: "I'm going to start studying again, from now on I'm sure I'll make it, I'll work hard to make it." That strikes me very much when there are these moments of sharing.

MW: Bello. Dine, can you tell us a bit about the workshop, what you do there, the things you are making. Can you also tell us something about your grandfather's stories?

SD: As Giocherenda, even during this pandemic, we have managed to get closer to people. First of all, we tried to make some face masks, which we initially gave away for free to help people when there were none available. We also started making online connections with people who were far away so that we could be close by playing together online. It was a great success — we played with the *Carte Acchiapparicordi* (Memory Catcher Cards). We are continuing with this plan, but at the moment, we are working more on the making of the masks, which must still be worn.

As for the stories, we have collected many. I also did an online workshop with a middle school during the pandemic. With Clelia, we got in touch, we organized the materials on gender education, discrimination against women. I was one of the facilitators of this workshop. It went well. At the end, I also transcribed the story of the first Black African woman pilot for the students, Fatoumata Binta Diallo, who was always known as Binta Pilote. She had to wait so long. She died in Paris two years ago. I think she was born after the Second World War; she was quite young but she was not well. She is one of the women who fought for our independence.

MW: As you know, I am very interested in the stories you told us, that you know from your grandfather, like the one about "The Huntsman and the King's Son." They're traditional but you have developed them, taken them in different directions.

SD: Those stories I heard from my grandparents always offer something to learn. I didn't understand that before, as a kid, but when I got older, I realized that there's a big lesson behind what seemed to us like just an evening story, to put us to sleep. We listened to lots of stories — it's a moment of sharing, when you finish dinner. Before they used to tell stories, now you watch television.

MW: Tell me a bit about all your friends from Giocherenda. How many of you are there now?

SD: There are twelve of us now.

MW: How many countries?

SD: At present, we represent six countries — Guinea, Gambia, Mali, Sierra Leone … and there's a girl who's originally from Morocco but raised here. And there's Italy.

MW: Have any of them now left Palermo?

SD: Maga is now in France but still part of Giocherenda. We travel for the association, too. Last April I was supposed to go to Orleans in France for Giocherenda, but this has been postponed because of the pandemic. We are now planning a trip to Senegal, to train teachers in a school there, show them how to teach children using these tools, how to create a job starting with these artistic ideas.

MW: When you arrived, not everyone spoke the same language. Now what language do you speak among yourselves?

SD: Most of us now speak Italian, that's how we communicate.

MW: You speak Italian very well but do you have nostalgia for your mother tongue?

SD: I do, but you know we don't all have the same mother tongue. If I'm with Amadou [Diallo], we speak Fula (also known as Pular, spoken in twenty countries in west Africa), because we both know it. But learning the language of the place where you live is essential to be able to express yourself and make yourself understood. That's why we chose Italian. But you know what, Marina, we've lost a lot. Colonization, globalization have made us lose a lot. Our ancient languages are no longer spoken, they have been mixed with the languages of the colonizers. That is why we are now often trying to teach our mother tongues more in schools.

MW: Also the cultures, the stories.

SD: That's why I say I live in 1800 BCE. I am no longer part of this era because I remember the values, the stories, the cultural principles of the past. I see that all this globalization is making everyone lose many things.

MW: Do you think that in this moment of such a serious situation in the world with all these dictators, the murders of people in America, such upsetting events, do you think Palermo is a good place compared to North America, or have you suffered racism in Palermo as well?

SD: Yes, not physically, but I have had friends who have also been attacked because of racism. As far as racism is concerned, I always repeat what Nelson Mandela said: racism hurts the person who is racist the more. The racist person is affected with a bad disease, so we have to free racists from racism.

The problem is not only what happened in the US, the death of George Floyd. The problem is historical. Until today the white person still thinks that the Black person has to be subaltern, that we have less value. I said before that all people have flaws, but do you know what they say in Africa about whites? That they never tell lies. When you make an appointment with a person, in Africa they say to you, "please be like a white man." They think that white people respect their commitments, that they would never be late. But when I came here, I met a boy who had had so many difficulties in Palermo: he was from my country and wanted to be repatriated and the lawyer told him that I could help him, explain some things to him. And this boy told me that since his arrival here in Europe, the only real thing he ever heard was: "Lunch is ready." He said that nobody had ever told him anything true. When this guy goes back to Africa, and they'll tell him again, "you have to be like a white man," he will answer, "I am as I am. Where I have been, no white person has been able to tell me things to my face, directly." I think it is very important to understand these diversities, the values that we are losing. We are connected. But on the other hand, globalization is damaging us too much.

When Sekou Touré, former president of Guinea, went to France, he said that he was not there to extend his hand to be helped, but to make real agreements, to relate as a human being. He said that the image of Africans abroad is of those who always extend their hand to beg, because without that they cannot go on. No country can make it on its own. So humanity must remember that we are all equal and we must all put our cultures together, our knowledge, to fight hatred and hunger. We all have to put ourselves at the same table, knowing that nobody is perfect and that we all have to see each other as people.

MW: Clelia, as founding member of Giocherenda, do you want to comment?

CB: Yes, I myself feel that I have benefited so much from my experience with Giocherenda. They have nourished me, they have made my life much more exciting than it would have been. We are making a mistake by putting migrants in the category of those who need to be helped. We are getting it completely wrong. People don't just need bread, they need fantasy. That's the beautiful thing about Stories in Transit. People don't just need to receive; they always need to give. And if you really remove the obstacles so that everyone can give to each other, then you get much more out of it and paradoxically even economic development is much greater if you allow people to give. Those who carry out development cooperation see that the benefactor gets rich, not the beneficiary. We should reverse this process: we should give money to the poor so that they can help people who may be well off but in a situation of senselessness and depression. The poor will be better off because they will have dignity. The rich will be better off because they may be richer in the world. There has to be an exchange. Giocherenda is pioneering this role reversal. Dine said a few days ago, "I want to give; I don't want to receive." He knows that he has plenty to offer, but if this remains inside you, you become disheartened because you know that it is an asset that will perish if you don't share it with others.

MW: I agree, these are the ideas that underlie our work on Stories in Transit and I am very happy that our collaborators and friends in Giocherenda are continuing in this spirit. Dine, you have hopes for the future?

SD: Sometimes I also have moments of difficulty to overcome. But there is hope, it's always with hope that we can move forward. If we are alone, we lose ourselves. Each one of us is very rich, but to be able to contribute you have to be listened to. If you imagine that I am useless, that I am of no use, what can I give you? What can I tell you? If, on the other hand, you go beyond that, as with Giocherenda, if we reverse the roles, there will be mutual enrichment. At all these meetings, I do not only go there to teach, people also teach me, in these neighborhoods where many never go. As I told you at the beginning, if I share my life, I am enriched by others. Today I am talking to you and this has come from a desire for mutual enrichment. Otherwise we would never have met, but we were all willing to.

Bibliography

Giocherenda. "Scopri la Ronda dei Desideri." *Facebook,* August 31, 2020. https://www.facebook.com/watch/?v=344753083317460.

Rackete, Carola, and Anne Weiss. *Il est temps d'agir.* Translated by Catherine Weinzorn. L'Iconoclaste, 2020.

Stories in Transit. "Stories in Transit IV - Giocherenda Workshop September 2018." *YouTube,* October 22, 2019. https://www.youtube.com/watch?v=LXdttrPkEoE.

"Stories in Transit VI: 'One for You, One for Me', 'The Old Man and the Serpent' & 'The Huntsman and the King's Son.'" *Stories in Transit.* http://www.storiesintransit.org/workshops/storiesintransitvi/.

Warner, Marina. "Living in a Country of Words." In *Others: Writers on the Power of Words to Help Us See Beyond Ourselves,* edited by Charles Fernyhough. Unbound, 2019.

17

"Sea of Hope": The Poetry Circle of Melissa Network's Women

Nadina Christopoulou and A.E. Stallings

I cannot hope, I cannot think of that. It has been so long that all
I experience is difficult and hard, that my brain cannot hope.
— Nozi, 15, Afghanistan

In the beginning I wondered: what was I, a Filipino maid,
doing here in a poetry class? What would I have to contribute?
Shouldn't I be doing something else in my limited free time?
But now, if I were to describe it, I feel as if I am speeding on my
bicycle, with wings on my back.
— Karen, 24, Philippines

There's a red, rectangular table in the heart of Athens, where
women from around the world sit, read, write, talk to one another, eat, knit, thread their eyebrows, and pick up the threads
of lives interrupted. It stands in the middle of a 1928 neoclassi-
cal building, now the home of Melissa Network. Every second
Tuesday afternoon, it becomes a secret bridge.

After 3 p.m., the living room beside the hidden, leafy terrace is cleared of all other action, strong coffee is brewed, herbal tea is prepared, and fresh cakes and biscuits are set on the table beside flowers, pens, pencils, and colorful writing pads. The women who take their places around the red table are not always the same — though some have been constant presences throughout their time in Greece — nor are they similar to one another. Khadidja, an English literature teacher from Latakia, started coming in by train from the very beginning, when she lived in a tent at the port of Piraeus, while Nuha, a hairdresser also from Syria, walks in from the "assisted accommodation" next door, because she feels isolated and wants company. Suha runs in after her restaurant shift. She is usually the first to finish writing, ready to recite. Then she packs up and runs to catch the next bus home, where her elder daughter babysits three younger siblings. Alia brings in the pages she has already written and kept hidden, Roya writes about the wedding veil she never wore. Fereshteh brings in the freshly baked flat bread she made for her brother who died suddenly in Kabul, while Elize, owner of a small restaurant in Gabon, shares the cake for her baby's first birthday. Maryam writes about the mountains of Afghanistan, and Mahboubeh about her blind mother's recipe for fragrant rice, while Razie, who has decided to become a writer, today stands on an empty page.

In the course of that hour, they pour their hearts out on paper, and then recite in their language, voicing their desire. Pages fill with calligraphic writing and ornate patterns and colors, the words transferred to the whiteboard by long-time Greece resident, American poet Alicia E. Stallings, with the help of the interpreters — mostly refugees themselves — to be shared in the group. For some of them, in whose country poetry is forbidden for women, this is an act of rebellion and resistance, while for others it is an act of gratitude and self-love. The common denominator is uprootedness and nostalgia, uncertainty, anxiety, and fear mixed with limitless hope. And then the page — and the whiteboard — become a mirror of their souls, and of the world to come. Every Tuesday afternoon, in that brief hour before dusk, they open the window of their imagination and take a leap of faith into the world they want to be in.

Crossing Paths and Building Beehives

Greece itself is a bridge between the West and the East and South. For over one million refugees on their way to Europe, Greece is not a destination but a crossing.

Since its launch in 2014, Melissa, a small organization co-founded by women of diverse origins, sought to bring together, support, and empower migrant and refugee women arriving or living in Greece, promoting integration and social cohesion. Amidst the haze of the overlapping crises that Greece has witnessed in recent years, and the open-ended cycle of precarity faced by women on the move, this quiet and safe space — a garden of forking paths in the words of Jorge Luis Borges, a castle of crossed destinies in Italo Calvino's words — serves as a sanctuary and a reminder of humanity, hope, and desire.

The name "melissa" — the Greek word for honeybee — was chosen as a metaphor for women coming from all over, bringing along their countless stories of uprooting, pain, and separation but also of strength, hope, and resilience, as well as their dreams, their talents, their skills, and their commitment to building a better future. Melissa was created first and foremost with the purpose of sharing stories — the stories of women settling in, permanently or temporarily, and contributing to the well-being of the host society in countless ways, visible and invisible. Its social vision was that of an open beehive of communication and creative exchange, instead of a set of isolated cells: a safe space where women learn and share, seek strength and support in each other, build trust and community.

Located near Victoria Square, a central but now rundown part of Athens with a cosmopolitan past and a tense and polarized present — at once a multicultural neighborhood and a stronghold of the neo-Nazi Golden Dawn party — Melissa's building has lived many lives. It was previously home to a film production company, a gambling salon, and a maternity clinic, before becoming a safe womb. The opening of the small day-center coincided with the massive influx of refugees in 2015–2016, and the subsequent humanitarian emergency. Victoria Square became the first continental stop in the long journey that brought to the doorstep of Europe the largest number of displaced people since World War II. In those days, it was the Casablanca or Ellis Island at the dawn of the twenty-first century — a place at the crossroads of fear and hope. The almost one million people who passed through Greece in that first year, and all those who followed, were coming from blazing war zones or sites of protracted oppression — places that turned into "the mouth of the shark."[1]

Melissa Network responded to the urgent needs in the surrounding streets. Solidarity was created spontaneously between women who were underprivileged and doubly marginalized and women who had even less. In the words of one of Melissa's co-founders, Deborah Carlos Valencia, "you give not because you have more but because you know how it is not to have anything." Women from all communities, religions, and ethnic backgrounds took to the the city streets and squares that had turned into makeshift camps, delivering aid. Cakes baked overnight were handed out in the early morning with milk and hot tea. Backpacks for the journey were packed with a mother's care, filled with essentials along with things that may be less — or more — essential: a torch, a tube of hand lotion, a hand-knit toy, a card with words of welcome written in different languages. They also contained pens and notepads, in the hope that when the time would come for the history of this journey to be written, it would be in their own words.

Soon after the closing of the northern borders and the Balkan route in 2016, with thousands bottle-necked in the country, refugee women started arriving at Melissa's doorstep, seeking sup-

---

1   Verse from British Somali poet Warsan Shire's poem "Home": "no one leaves home unless / home is the mouth a shark." Warsan Shire, "Home," *Amnesty International,* https://www.amnesty.ie/wp-content/uploads/2016/06/home-by-warsan-shire.pdf.

port or a moment of peace. The newly arriving women entered with broken wings and unsmiling faces, uncertain about what they would encounter, devastated from their ordeals and carrying the heavy burden of their anxiety about the future. They came from countries including Syria, Somalia, Afghanistan, Iran, and Iraq, and violence was the grammar many had learned throughout their lives. In passing through the sanctuary of Melissa, they started remembering themselves, resuming their lives, reclaiming their future, gathering their thoughts, standing on their own, and moving forward.

Amidst the escalating efforts of the international humanitarian community, Melissa Network realized that they had a unique potential: a combination of experience and community resources that allowed them immediate access, feedback, and insight into the needs and hopes of the women on the move. Backed up with academic and clinical expertise, they came up with a unique, innovative integration scheme, in order to facilitate the first steps of a new life in a new place. The aim was to shift the focus from aid to agency, from victimization to resilience, and from addressing urgent needs to building sustainable life strategies for integration. Education modules were designed and taught interactively, combined with mental health support, art, information, leadership, advocacy and media training, self-care, and community engagement. Activities and workshops ranged across drama and movement therapy, music, dance, poetry, writing, film and photography, storytelling, crafts, and cooking. Melissa's program developed into the first and longest culturally-aware, trauma-informed integration program in Greece, bringing together approximately 150 women and children from over forty-five countries every day; employing people of twenty different ethnic origins; relying on the skills of community leaders as well as a vast range of experts, artists, and intellectuals; earning international recognition and awards; and building a robust, transnational beehive buzzing with creativity and coexistence.

Empowerment was thus conceived as a winding path, where trauma can only begin to heal through building a sense of belonging and community. Migrant and refugee women are active agents in the co-creation process, not passive recipients of aid. The purpose was to forge a compass and a toolkit they could carry along the journey. In mere weeks, the newly arriving women started expressing and affirming themselves, proposing ideas, opening up to one another, going out in the community and in the city, and claiming a role and the right to be heard. Most importantly, they transitioned from recipients of emergency services to "givers" — supporting one another through mutual understanding. It was in this context that poetry came to play its part, not only as expression, but also as a liberating practice.

Found in Translation: Poetry at the Crossroads of Languages and Experience

A poetry workshop might seem an unlikely way to develop mutual empathy among women from various cultures who have undergone historical and personal trauma, but it proved popular and successful. Women navigating asylum services must fill out bureaucratic forms; subject to prying interviews, they must repeat over and over the most traumatic details of their life history, and make personal narratives conform to the narrative of fear that narrowly defines the asylum seeker. Poetry offers another way to define the self: poetry gets to ask the questions, and to speak in the first person singular; poetry does not tick the boxes of preconceived categories, but explores all aspects of human experience, including pleasure, humor, and joy. If the language of bureaucracy is dehumanizing, the language of poetry is subversively human.

Translation itself — literally, to "carry across" — became a bridge for understanding. The poetry course was taught in English, but women, from Syria, Iraq, Congo, Palestine, Afghanistan, Iran, and elsewhere were encouraged to write in their mother tongues. Some of the most interesting, and laughter-filled, conversations around the red table involved attempts to define words, discover universal metaphors, and also acknowledge what was stubbornly untranslatable.

Yet if poetry is, as Robert Frost says, that which is lost in translation, how can it be found in the borderlands between languages? We began with list poems. In lists, there is no grammar or syntax to navigate, yet the simple accrual of items builds meaning and narrative. Working as a group, with translators and whiteboard on hand, but also with Google Translate and online dictionaries, each woman's phone a powerful tool, we began with "home." What must it contain? At first, it was basic necessities — a shower, a bathroom — then other kinds of needs: school, English lessons. Soon, however, the women understood this as an exercise in the imagination. The list for "home" included television, music, books, make-up, kisses. Home had a goldfish, and birdseed ("for the bird").

Another of our early exercises were acrostic poems. The letters of a thematic word would be thrown out, and we would play a game of coming up with words beginning with those letters. "I" was sometimes the first person, sometimes "island," and often "ice cream." "G" might be "Greece" or "gratitude" or "generous" or "God." "F" might stand for "freedom" or "fear." "W," "wonderful," or, more often, "war." Consider the concision of the poem "Safety," by Zahra: "Still Afraid For Everything? Trust Yourself."

Acrostics of the women's own names were often among the most moving artifacts, as women produced brief self-portraits, catalogues of fears or hopes, and personal narratives. Witness the playfulness of 16-year-old young Sakina from Afghanistan,[2] a fan of rock-and-roll and Jackie Chan movies:

Suddenly —
Action!
Kung-fu
In the

---

2   The women at Melissa give informed consent that in participating in the poetry workshop their work may be shared. I attach first names to the poems, but not always family names, as many of the women were or are in the middle of delicate legal proceedings, or in other precarious positions, where a degree of anonymity is prudent.

Night
Am I a good girl?

Sometimes we used our names to discuss other topics, such as the self we are today, or the self we hope to be tomorrow. For this, Fatemah had written these lists: Today: "Free Alone Tent Education Music Eager Happy"; Tomorrow: "Fate America Top Embassy Mother End Happy."

Punning upon one's name is a feature of traditional Persian and Arabic poetry. We were reminded of this when, one rainy day, the prompt was the rain: rain, that recognizes no borders, and that falls everywhere on everyone alike. An Afghan woman named Hashti Hashemi wrote a poem in Farsi that, with the interpreter, we translated as:

Rain

I am like the rain
because rain is the start of deep feeling
because rain is clean sadness
because rain is filtered weather
because I am the universe
because I dance on glass.

In the penultimate line, the workshop leader wondered, did Hashti perhaps mean "because I am everywhere"? During the conversation, we came to understand that her name, "Hashti," means "existence," or the "universe." She had "signed" the poem with her existence, her name.

Becoming the author and subject of one's own narrative is about recovering a range of memories, not simply trauma. In a workshop based on smell and memory, Alicia brought in an array of items: coffee, chocolate, lemon, cumin, oregano, rose petals, nail polish, jasmine, saffron, cinnamon, and other distinctive aromas. We passed these around the red table in a darkened room, inhaling the scents.

Baran wrote of the Iranian brand of "Fahramond Chocolate" from her childhood. Another woman wrote of "Ghorme Sabzi that my mother cooks and it reminds me of rice fields and orange and lemon trees of my grandfather's garden, where we used to drink saffron tea under the lemon tree." An Arabic speaker confessed simply that, "The smell of the food reminds me of the days of the war — in that time the food was less. The smell of the garden reminds me of my childhood and the smell of my children reminds me of my mother."

Another woman wrote:

Unforgettable memories:
Roses
I miss my home and my family and being together
Coffee
The sea
Sweet and sour
I am waiting for it.

The donation of a huge stack of postcards of famous paintings and images inspired another successful prompt, for ekphrastic poems: poems based on art work. Each woman selected an image of a painting that "spoke" to her.

By far the most popular images were of the sea (almost all of the women had come over the dangerous sea route from Turkey to the islands of the Eastern Aegean), in particular Hokusai's iconic print of the "Great Wave off Kanagawa." The women put themselves into the picture.

Mujabe wrote:

I see the refugee life in this picture.
When they decide to travel, they don't know
about the dangerous ways
and the other things coming
after this event,
They drowned in this sea.

Another woman reacted to the same image:

> The first time I saw this boat I was afraid.
> I thought I would die with this unsafe boat,
> Because it was the first time I saw
> This kind of transportation and that kind of sea.

Sakina, the same poet who had written the playful acrostic poem about Kung Fu, flooded a full notebook page with blue ink, including the following words:

> Fear, terror, anxiety, death but hope…

> …

> Remember your goal wasn't to shipwreck and die;
> You came to make your future.
> This picture reminds me of the day
> We wanted to come to Greece from Turkey in the boat.

For most of the women, Alicia titled the poem on the white board after the Hokusai print, "The Great Wave." But Sakina titled her own poem "The Sea of Hope," a metaphor where the vehicle of the sea conveys its fragile vessel onto another shore and a new life; the sea of hope is the crossing, and the bridge.

As the participants became more confident in self-expression and more trusting of group projects, we embarked on writing collective pantoums. The pantoum, originally a Malay form, is written in quatrains, braids, and pairs of lines; each line is repeated in a new context, down through the poem. Everyone in the class had to come up with two lines about a chosen topic. As women contributed their lines to the poem, it grew and deepened, pivoted, and prismed. Somehow a real poem would happen, with only the slightest nudge or reordering from the workshop leader. The pantoum had room for private griefs and gnomic statements, but always added up to more than the sum of its parts. Consider these stanzas about autumn:

The third autumn in Greece is coming. I miss autumn in my country
Autumn is the season of many colors — red, yellow
O wind, take me to Iran
It is the season of my daughter, when she came

Autumn is the season of many colors — red, yellow
The war — I hope it will fall from my country like the yellow leaf.
It is the season of my daughter, when she came.
I hope to meet my old love, like leaves that stayed on the tree.

The war — I hope it will fall from my country like the yellow leaf.
Autumn is the happy season.
I hope to meet my old loves, like leaves that stayed on the tree.
I hope to leave for another country.

Or a stanza from this Spring pantoum:

Hyacinths, we put on the tablecloth of New Year to welcome the spring.
My childhood memories have the smell of my grandmother's chador, with its flower-print design.
Flowers make me feel happy
The smell of the damask rose next to the fish pool

Somehow, the text of the pantoum, woven seemingly at random out of specific, individual memories, general statements, and lyric images, takes on its own life. The form itself — taking one step forward, two steps back, but always expanding and deepening — becomes almost a metaphor for the women's own journeys. Even the seemingly unpoetic topic of International Woman's Day produced some startling lines: "In Farsi, the first letter of 'woman' means 'life,'" and "Woman is the myth of stamina."

Poetry — the process of *poiein* (making) — has become a sacred hour at Melissa, a way of creating life anew. Ultimately, this is what Melissa Network is: a bridge to cross, and the first solid ground underneath the feet. It connects, opens windows, and reignites the capacity to imagine. It explores how meaning is created when language — literally and metaphorically — is broken. It is an attempt to pick up those broken pieces, and to trace the ways in which desire is gently, quietly, almost secretly nourished.

18

Curating Migration:
A Conversation with The
Migration Museum

Aditi Anand and Sue McAlpine

ADITI ANAND: The purpose of the Migration Museum is to reflect, in a moving and inspiring way, on the long history of migration that has shaped the United Kingdom from its beginnings — its culture, politics, economics, and physical landscape. Discussions about migration tend to focus on contemporary, postwar migration, but we are interested in putting that into perspective. We wanted to create a place for a historical and contemplative, rather than polarizing, discussion of it, driven by the ethos that migration is a story that belongs to all of us. To explore that shared heritage, we collect personal testimonies, and use a number of different formats. Early on, we asked people to contribute their stories by filling out disks to record their family's history of migration.

Here is a sample response: "My parents brought me here from Afghanistan, they paid a smuggler and carried me across borders. It took us 3 years to reach Calais, and we arrived in Dover in 1999. I still have the backpack I was wearing on the journey. I am now a medical student at UCL." Another traces

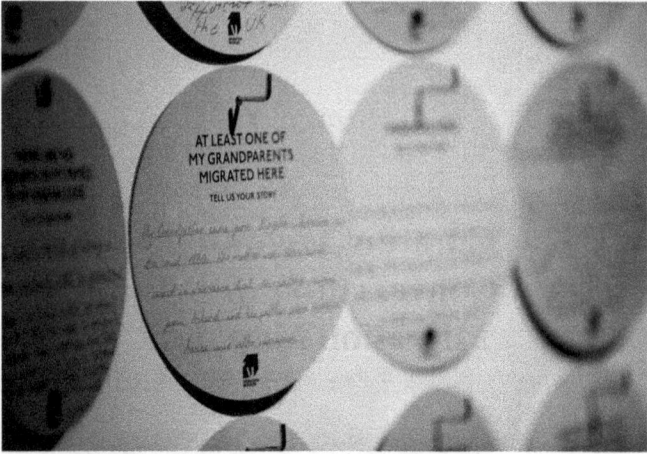

Fig. 18.1. Migration story discs filled in by visitors. © Migration Museum.

the route taken by the respondent's ancestors from Jamaica and Ireland to Britain. We've collected a huge range of these stories, nearing 10,000. From the beginning, our focus on ordinary stories is what set us apart from other museums. Sharing these makes people feel that they belong to the fabric of this country.

The oral histories, on the other hand, feel fresh because there's no real formula for how to make it happen. When we collect oral histories specifically for an exhibition, we ask fairly targeted questions rather than asking for an entire life story. But the impetus is to enable people to remember that emotion that's related to those spaces and memories, rather than just deliver a narrative.

Alongside our exhibition *Call Me by My Name* about the Calais Jungle camp, we organized a day with music, art, food, and performance around experiences of the Jungle. PSYCHEdelight Theatre Company presented "Borderline," a satire on the camp performed by a group of people who had lived in the camp and European actors. We do things that are unusual for a museum, engaging people and letting them tell their stories. For example, we held cooking classes inside our exhibition *Room to Breathe,*

Fig. 18.2. Norma's penny. Source: Migration Museum.

working closely with Migrateful, a charity who organize cookery classes run by migrant chefs. Because the story of migration exists all around us, we take our work outside the walls, doing multiple walking tours around London, looking at all the fabric of migration stories on our streets and buildings. But migration is not just a London story, so we partner with the National Trust and the Museum of Liverpool, among others, to have it told in a variety of institutional contexts.

We are a museum without a permanent collection. We set out to visualize the theme of migration by running a competition with *The Guardian,* based on an open call for people to submit images that spoke to them about migration. We received about 700 submissions, from a mix of professional photographs, amateur photographs, and family album items.

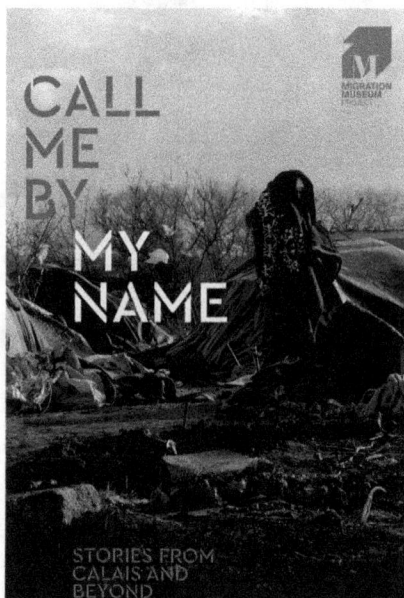

Fig. 18.3. Poster for the exhibition *Call Me By My Name*. Photo by Paul Evans.

A different project in our early days was around keepsakes that people carry with them. Its proposition was that some of the most incredible stories and objects might not be in museum collections, but hidden in people's attics and in their drawers. I love this one.

The penny shown in figure 18.2 belongs to a woman called Norma from the Caribbean. Her mother gave it to her on the ship, wrapped up in a handkerchief, a sort of lucky penny to ensure she would always have riches when she arrived in Britain. She kept that penny in her handbag for fifty years and this was the first time it had ever left her bag, to be part of our temporary display.

SUE MCALPINE: We don't actually have a permanent venue. Like migrants, we move from one meanwhile space to another. We

Fig. 18.4. Portrait of Ahmad Al Rashid. Source: Hannah Thomas.

have done three major exhibitions in the time that we've been thinking about setting up our permanent site, and because we have no collection, we have to start from scratch each time. Because we're not an accredited museum, we also want to explore how far we can go with making exhibitions experimental and rebellious. We want to make sure our contributors get their voices heard, and that our visitors can be included and involved.

Call Me by My Name — our first exhibition, in a warehouse in Shoreditch — was about the Calais Jungle refugee camp. This was designed to give the people who lived in the camp an opportunity to tell their stories in the way they would want their stories to be told. The media headlines were talking about refugees in derogatory terms, as "swarms" and "floods" and "vermin." We wanted to humanize them. We wanted our visitors to understand that refugees have professions, they have families,

Fig. 18.5. The Wanderers. © Migration Museum.

they have love stories, they have children, they have aims and ambitions. This exhibition gave refugees the opportunity to tell us their name. But we wanted the stories to be told from every angle. So we explored the idea that sometimes refugees cannot tell their real names. We asked smugglers what it was like to be a smuggler, and lorry drivers what it was like to have refugees in the back of their lorry. We asked paramedics, cooks, and volunteers to tell us stories. We wanted to show the camp in Calais as a complex social structure with a transient population, with people who are courageous, strong, and ambitious, suffering and surviving. Thus, the exhibition acted as a vital platform for us as a museum to question our national responsibility towards refugees. We did not want to present a kind of voyeuristic, emotionally laden exhibition. We tried, rather, to represent the subjects in the way they would want to be represented. On our several visits to the camp, the question we asked was, "what would you like people in the UK to know about you?," giving them choice of what they wanted to tell us.

Like all exhibitions, we used all media, photography, art, presenting the oral histories that we collected in the forms of text,

Fig. 18.6. Painting by the Mauritanian artist ALPHA. © Migration Museum. Source: Migration Museum.

audio, and installations. We commissioned portrait artists, as with this oil painting of Ahmad Al Rashid, a Syrian refugee (fig. 18.4), showing that oil paintings are not just for rich and settled people.

We were also very fortunate to be able to show the work of the Danish artist Nikolai Larson.

Figure 18.5 is a piece called *The Wanderers,* consisting of over 400 human figures made of black, plasticine-like material, was the first thing visitors saw as they entered the exhibition. It had an immediate emotional impact. It was also important that we showed the art of the inhabitants of the camp, including children, who would not consider themselves as artists but were making art.

In figure 18.6 you can see a painting by ALPHA, an artist from Mauritania, saying "my art can go to the UK, but I can't."

The piece shown in figure 18.7 is made up of the gas canisters that the French police chucked at everybody in the camp.

And in figure 18.8 is an artist from Afghanistan called Habib, painting a temple right in the middle of the dome, which was

Fig. 18.7. Gas canisters. © Migration Museum.

where the Good Chance Theatre — fellow interlocutors in this book — had located themselves within the camp.

While the fires were burning around him, and the French police were doing what they were doing, Habib continued to make his art. When we unpacked his Sudanese camp-mate Yasin's paintings for the exhibition, we could smell the fire.

Among the many telling oral histories we collected, here is an example — from a Sudanese man called Samer upon his arrival in this country: "I went back to Calais at the end of March this year. It's crazy what a passport can do. With that little book in my hand I made the crossing in twenty minutes, a journey that once took me ten months. It seemed to me that these little books control our lives, more than humanity, more than kindness, more than right and wrong. Without them, we are like pawns in a game of chess."

Fig. 18.8. Habib painting. Source: Suzanne Partridge.

Our second exhibition, *No Turning Back,* took its seeds from the Brexit referendum. We decided to use the Brexit moment as a springboard for looking back in history. How far have migrants been welcomed into Britain, and to what extent they have been rejected? We took seven moments, kind of random yet not really, to explore historical junctures in which people have come in or gone out, which still reverberate today. We feel that exhibitions should be at once about history, today, and the future.

Among the historical moments we looked at was 1290, when the entire Jewish population was expelled from this country; 1607, which marks the first East India Company voyage from England to India; the arrival of the Huguenots — the first refugees — in 1685, so that we could compare their experiences with

Fig. 18.9. Humanae. © Angélica Dass. Photo © Juan Miguel Ponce.
Source: Migration Museum.

those of the Kindertransport children and their reception here
in 1939; bringing it up to date, with Syrian children and their experience of not being welcomed immediately into this country.
We showcased art which offers the perspective of those who suffer — such as the colonized or the alien. We looked at the 1905
Aliens Act, when people were first officially labelled as "alien,"
"illegal," and "good immigrants" and "bad immigrants." And we
explored the Rock against Racism movement of 1978.

In the 2011 census, which we examined, there were a great
number of people defining their ethnic origin as mixed. So we
worked with a Brazilian photographer called Angelica Dass
whose Humanæ project takes photographs of people and compares the color of their skin with a Pantone color, making you
see that everybody has a slightly different color-tone, and nobody is just black or white. Our invitation of people from local communities to talk about the extent to which they identify
themselves with the particular color of their skin took off from
Dass's work and extended it to generate revealing conversations
about identity.

Fig. 18.10. Bands of Colour. © Hormazd Narielwalla. Source: Migration Museum.

Hormazd Narielwalla is an Indian artist whose art uses tailoring and old sewing patterns. We showed Hormazd an illustration of the yellow pieces of felt Jews were forced to wear by Edward I in 1274, and asked him to create a work for us to illustrate the 1290 expulsion of the Jews. That badge, after all, was the heritage of the Nazi yellow star which Jewish people were forced to wear. He went away to think about it, and came up with a multimedia piece, *Bands of Colour,* which has no yellow in it at all. He said:

I didn't want to work with yellow because I didn't want to celebrate that decree. I came across the blue city Chefchaouen in Morocco, where Jewish settlers painted all the houses in

Fig. 18.11. The Chart of Shame, by Liz Gerard. © Migration Museum.
Source: Migration Museum.

shades of blue, and I decided that the artwork would be made
in shades of blue, to celebrate Jewish culture and contributions.

He added, "the 1274 decree could have been aimed at any peoples
or race, and as a minority, being a Zoroastrian Indian gay immigrant, it could easily be me forced to wear a badge of shame,
instead of celebrating my contributions to British culture." An
artist never does exactly what you want them to do.

In figure 18.11, you see an image of the "Chart of Shame,"
which had a real effect on our exhibition.

This bar-chart was compiled by Liz Gerard, a journalist
who put together all the national newspaper headlines on immigration for the year 2016 — 297 by her count. And most of
them — like the *Sun* and the Star — feature horrific, racist headlines.

We like to engage our audiences in conversations in our exhibitions. An interactive event in 2011 began with someone saying
that they were having a mixed-race child, and asking the assem-

Fig. 18.12. Room to Breathe. © Migration Museum. Source: Migration Museum.

bled group how they should bring this child up. This led to an extraordinary sharing of personal experiences.

Figure 18.12 is our exhibition, *Room to Breathe.*

It was intense and emotional, and brought people to tears. This is probably the exhibition of which I, as a curator, am most proud. Here, we wanted to encourage people to tell their ordinary stories of settling into this country, what it was like when they first arrived, how they managed without a word of English, negotiated the Home Office, found somewhere to live, found somewhere for the kids to go to school, and found work. *Room to Breathe* comprised a series of rooms, which visitors walked through. We wanted to make the first room an uninviting place — one we jokingly called the Home Office — by using some of the incomprehensible bureaucratic jargon like "non-suspensive appeal," "non-compliance grants" — and other categories that you are placed in during your immigration journey. At the other end of the room, there are hundreds of files with numbers on them, each representing a person. But we also wanted visitors to really immerse themselves in the exhibition. So, unlike most museums where you can't change, move, or even touch things, we wanted our visitors to sit on the bed, at the desk, in the chair, and at the kitchen table; to make art, to contribute their story, to open drawers and read others' stories. They had the agency to change the exhibition if they wished.

We had an art studio in this exhibition: six artists-in-residence made it their own and brought the place alive. We also turned a part of the space into a barber shop, where people could sit in the chair, and instead of seeing their own face in the mirror, see someone else and hear their stories. We wanted to include the barber because immigrants and barbers — and barbers are often immigrants themselves — have a curious rapport, which can generate conversation.

We also had a school room where we asked children about their experience of arrival. And then there was a kitchen — where we put the plates on the table and projected an animation of food stories. We hope we can continue to make such exciting projects and work closely with many people who have come and gone from the UK well into the future.

19

Response to The Migration Museum

Clair Wills

A few days before the Migrant Knowledge event in Cambridge in September 2019, I returned from the island of Lampedusa in the southern Mediterranean, where on a clear day you can see Tunisia. It was my second visit to the island. Eighteen months previously I spent Easter there, and I was struck by how similar the place seemed to a small West Ireland town I knew in the 1970s — bar the weather, of course, and the food. At mass on Easter Sunday the old women sat towards the front, the kids turned somersaults, and the teenagers chatted and checked their hair. The men hung around in groups at the back of the church and didn't wait for communion — the only difference I could see was that in Skibbereen the men were farmers in their Sunday suits, and on Lampedusa they wore the uniforms of the coast-guard, the military police, and the border patrols.

Returning in the tourist season in the summer of 2019, the population had swollen from 6,000 to 25,000, but the military presence was still palpable. Several times a week the coastguard picked up small groups of migrants, often travelling in their own boats from Tunisia, and sometimes in smugglers' rubber din-ghies from the Libyan coast. They were (and still are) landed in the militarized section of the harbor, a few feet from the tourists — mostly from northern Italy — queuing for their dolphin-watching tours. When I was there no one seemed to notice.

One of the boats that often docks in the harbor by day is a small fishing boat that was used to save forty-five migrants on the night of October 3, 2013. It's a boat that usually holds six people. Most of the migrants crossing that night — 350 of them — were not saved. And this small fishing boat, and a man who was out fishing — Vito Fiorino — who piloted it, have become the storytellers for the people who died that night. I mean this quite literally: journalists from around the world turn up to cover the "migrant crisis" and they like to get the human story. But Lampedusa is a not a place where migrants stay for any length of time. So the journalists hire translators and interview Vito to get the story of how he and a few friends had decided to sleep on his boat that night because of the fine weather, how they were woken up by cries in the night, how they alerted the coastguard and the coastguard didn't come, and didn't come, and how they tried to save as many as they could. It's a story about migrants, certainly, and it needs to be told. But it is not the migrants' own story.

The Migration Museum — Britain's first national institution dedicated to the history and experience of migrants and refugees — seeks to come at experience from the other side. Curators Aditi Anand and Sue McAlpine explain that their exhibitions start from the conviction that migration is a story that belongs to all of us. It is ordinary. This in itself is a challenge for any commemorative project, and perhaps a museum in particular. How can an experience that is not only part of everyday life, but forms the deep background to contemporary British society, be made visible in a manner that remains true to its unexceptional nature? How can we document and represent the histories and experiences of migration to Britain without creating exceptional characters, or focusing too much or disproportionately on remarkable narratives? This is only one of the difficulties facing an institution dedicated to the movement of individuals and populations. To many people, who consider themselves settled, that movement in itself is to be decried rather than explored and commemorated. There is a strong media-driven narrative around migration, and vested interests that don't really want the narrative to change. The story of migration is personal and subjective as well as public and political, yet there are ethical challenges to collecting, editing, and displaying peoples' personal stories for public display, or even for entertainment. How can a museum break down the barriers between those who visit, and those whose stories are represented? In the current, highly polarized, political atmosphere around migration, exacerbated by the manner in which immigration to Britain was weaponized during the Brexit referendum, these are not theoretical or abstract questions, but have real-life effects.

The Migration Museum curators have chosen not to depoliticize the history of migration, but to tackle underlying prejudice directly. Their first exhibition, on the Jungle in Calais was, they explain,

> designed to give the people who lived in the camp an opportunity to tell their stories in the way they would want their stories to be told. The media headlines were talking about refugees in derogatory terms, as "swarms" and "floods" and "vermin." We wanted to humanize them.[1]

And, as they say explicitly, such "humanizing" was aimed at helping visitors to the exhibition question national responsibility towards refugees. The exhibitions have employed a number of imaginative practices for situating the contemporary experience of individuals and families travelling across the Mediterranean (from Turkey, Libya, or Morocco), through Lesbos or Lampedusa, to Calais and then across the English Channel, within the long history of migration to Britain. These include gathering nearly 10,000 personal testimonies from both individual migrants and their descendants, encouraging visitors to the museum to become involved by adding their own stories to those represented in the exhibits, setting up events, workshops,

---

1   See the conversation with the Migration Museum, in this volume.

CROSSINGS

and walking tours to break down the boundaries between the inside and the outside of the museum. A large part of the attraction of the exhibitions lies in the dynamic relation between oral history and personal testimony on the one hand, and artistic transformation on the other. Paintings, photographs, poems, sculptures, videos, and stories, created by migrants, or by others in response to migrant testimonies, shape the experience of the visitor to the exhibitions. And the museum itself is currently a migratory project — without a permanent site — so that the exhibitions can respond to and be shaped by local contexts, and local communities.

Still, the practice of "humanizing" migrants is fraught with difficulty, as the curators themselves acknowledge. Recent research commissioned by the museum has emphasized the challenges such institutions face in resisting stereotypes of "good," or deserving migrants and refugees, those who will contribute to British society in positive ways. Museums, argues Domenico Sergi,

> have participated in the construction of an ambivalent moral economy around asylum: on the one hand romanticising the "heroic" nature of refugee displacement, and on the other pathologising refugees as "traumatized" subjects. This extreme formulation has effectively placed refugees "outside the ordinary," subjugating human rights discourses to a form of conditional belonging whereby refugees may exert their right to protection so long as they are mentally fit and can positively contribute to British society.[2]

It's the double bind of the migrant success story. Even though stories of achievement (from contributions to the NHS, to sport-

2   Domenico Sergi, "Exploring the Potential of Museums and their Collections in Working Practices with Refugees" (PhD diss., University of East Anglia, 2016), quoted in Hannah Tendler and Cathy Ross, *Migration and Museums*, 2020–2021, https://www.migrationmuseum.org/wp-content/uploads/2020/08/Migration-and-Museums-%E2%80%93-A-review-for-the-Migration-Network-2020_21_compressed-3.pdf.

ing prowess or entrepreneurial drive) undercut the negative portrayals of refugees often seen in the media, the negative stereotype itself is left untouched. It may be precisely through reaching for the "human" or personal element in migrant or refugee experience that broader legal questions of human rights and responsibilities become harder to access.

One of the books I had with me in Lampedusa in 2019 was Amelia Gentleman's *The Windrush Betrayal* — an account of the effect of the policies designed to create a "hostile environment" for illegal immigrants on long-term legal residents who do not have all the papers to prove their right to remain in Britain. Gentleman is good at describing the deliberately dehumanizing processes that people caught up in the hostile environment are subjected to — from the practice of describing individuals as "Migrant" in official documents, rather than using their names, to the tortuous requirements to report to officials at various centers and the officials' refusal to listen, to the experience of detention itself. It is easier to deny someone citizenship if you no longer regard them as a person. Yet the very notion of a betrayal of Windrush migrants suggests an immigrant hierarchy. It implies that postwar migrants who came to Britain from the Caribbean because they were British citizens should not have been treated with hostility — not that hostility in itself is a problem.

Several meanings get attached to the idea of the "good" immigrant, and very often they contradict one another. Good can mean the most "desirable," the most like us, or the most "deserving," those who have suffered most. Today's stereotypes and prejudices tend to foster sympathy for refugees from war and conflict over economic migrants, but that wasn't always the case. In the late 1940s there was a debate in Britain about whether the displaced persons in refugee camps on the continent would make "better" or "worse" immigrants to the UK than economic migrants from southern Italy, India, Ireland, and the Caribbean. People expressed fears that a camp mentality meant that the refugees would find it hard to be "productive" members of society.[3] They preferred the idea of economic migrants, and even here there was a hierarchy—Germans, Latvians, Lithuanians were considered hard workers (which was often code for more middle class and Protestant), and likely to be more productive members of society than, for example, southern Italians.

On Lampedusa I discovered that those currently designated "good" immigrants are the ones from Somalia or Eritrea, who have struggled through famine and war and the hellhole of the Libyan camps. They elicit sympathy. By contrast the Tunisians who arrive under their own steam are more strongly disliked. They are reasonably well-dressed; they arrive with backpacks; they look remarkably similar to Italy's regular inhabitants. In effect they are perceived as being "too Western" to be truly "deserving" immigrants. They haven't suffered enough. It is a failure not so much of sympathy, but of empathy—a failure which in Britain was encapsulated in the United Kingdom Independence Party's 2016 "Breaking Point" poster.

Britain is patting itself on the back for belatedly waking up to the effects on its own citizens of the active government policy of creating a hostile environment for immigrants. The popular outrage over the Windrush betrayal is read as proof that, despite the racism experienced by Black immigrants to Britain in the 1950s and 1960s, they are now accepted—by their neighbors, if not by the government. On this reading, they were "good immigrants" all along. It is of course the wrong lesson. It should be read instead as proof of the need to treat migrants with dignity, however they arrive, and wherever they have come from.

By focusing on the ordinariness, and the ubiquity, of Britain's story of migration, the Migration Museum attempts to avoid the trap of turning the migrants of fifty years ago (the Windrush and other postcolonial and Commonwealth migrants, as well as refugees from the Second World War and the postwar Communist bloc) into good migrants, whose successful assimilation and contribution to British society retrospectively legitimates them.

---

3 See Clair Wills, *Lovers and Strangers: An Immigrant History of Post-War Britain* (Penguin, 2017).

In the 1950s and 1960s, migrants from the Indian subcontinent and from the Caribbean who came to Britain and found work as cleaners in Heathrow Airport, or in mills and foundries, or in the NHS, were not fleeing for lives. They were economic migrants. But the other legitimating factor for Britain's postwar, postcolonial migrants is that they were citizens of the British Empire, who had the right to live and work in Britain — a fact highlighted in many of the vignettes in the Migration Museum's *Room to Breathe* exhibition. Although the legal definition of British citizenship was progressively narrowed during the 1960s and 1970s, nearly all the migrants who now come to Britain through Calais (or who get stuck in Calais) leave countries that were at one time under British rule. There is still a feeling of belonging, even if it is denied by Britain.

It is divisions like these between deserving and undeserving, and between refugee and economic migrant, that the work of Migration Museum and its Migration Network seeks to undercut, by placing the stories of contemporary migrants in dialogue with Britain's long, complex, and shared history of migration. Perhaps the hardest division to break down is that between migrants whose journey is over — who have arrived, whether that was in 1850, or 1950, or 2000, and settled, and made a home in Britain — and those who are still travelling. It is the division between a story of successful immigration (successful simply because it has been completed), and one of hope for a new life. It is a division encapsulated in the painting by the Mauritanian artist ALPHA, of his art travelling across the Channel from Calais to Britain (planted with oak trees) while he remained stuck on the other side of the border. In a culture and an environment where the Royal National Lifeboat Institution has to put out a video defending its humanitarian work in rescuing migrants in danger in the English Channel, and explaining why individuals and families should not be left to drown,[4] the Museum has its work cut out for it.

---

4   Rachel Hall, "Donations to RNLI Rise 3,000% after Farage's Migrant Criticism," *The Guardian,* July 29, 2021, https://www.theguardian.com/

Bibliography

Hall, Rachel. "Donations to RNLI Rise 3,000% after Farage's Migrant Criticism." *The Guardian,* July 29, 2021. https://www.theguardian.com/world/2021/jul/29/rnli-donations-soar-in-response-to-farages-migrant-criticism.

Sergi, Domenico. "Exploring the Potential of Museums and their Collections in Working Practices with Refugees." PhD Dissertation, University of East Anglia, 2016.

Tendler, Hannah, and Cathy Ross. *Migration and Museums,* 2020–2021. https://www.migrationmuseum.org/wp-content/uploads/2020/08/Migration-and-Museums-%E2%80%93-A-review-for-the-Migration-Network-2020_21_compressed-3.pdf.

Wills, Clair. *Lovers and Strangers: An Immigrant History of Post-War Britain.* Penguin, 2017.

world/2021/jul/29/rnli-donations-soar-in-response-to-farages-migrant-criticism.

324

20

"Don't Wash Your Hands"

Issam Kourbaj in conversation with Simon Goldhill,
curated by Subha Mukherji

SIMON GOLDHILL: Issam, you describe yourself as an artist from Syria, not as a Syrian artist. Could you explain what you mean by that?

ISSAM KOURBAJ: I prefer to think of the multiplicity of identity, rather than its oneness. I am, of course, Syrian-born, but being Syrian is not one thing. So, Syrian-born, Cambridge-based, I am equally a visual artist and a painter, a walker, a cyclist. There are many adjectives that could describe me, but having that geography somehow limits the description.

SG: Your uncle took bombs and beat them into spoons, a lovely biblical image of how the ploughshare can be made out of weapons. Do you see art, then, as a form of transformation of identity?

IK: Definitely. My studio in Cambridge is next door to the ADC Theatre. I collect props that are thrown away and I make things out of them. My uncle was incredibly resourceful, thinking in the time of hardship, how one could use whatever is available.

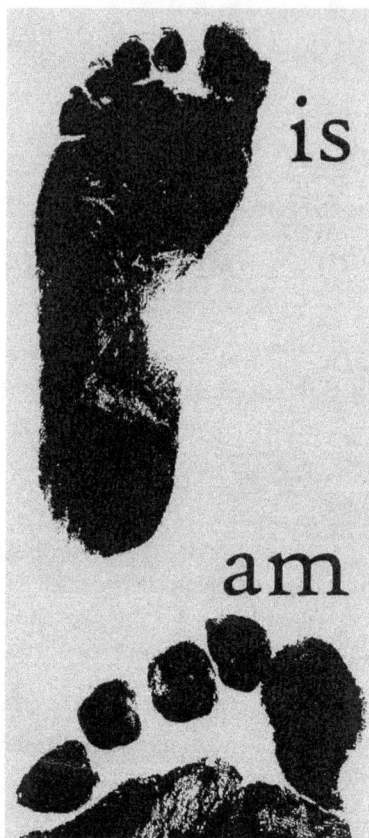

Fig. 20.1. is am. © Issam Kourbaj.

To transform bombs to spoons is to turn a weapon of destruction into a tool of nurturing. If I could achieve that quality of resourcefulness in my artwork I would be very delighted.

SG: Yet one of your most moving pieces is a print with two feet of different sizes, and next to them are two words: "is," and "am" (fig. 20.1). This seems to me to be a strong statement of identity. So are you, in some senses, moving away from transformation into assertion, perhaps to a political statement, or, in this case, a statement about family life?

IK: Actually, the minute you have a child, suddenly you become a child again; your child-self surfaces. This was my first exhibition with my son Mourad, who was three at the time. The privilege, for me, was to follow in his footsteps, with his freshness, without boundaries — and not being confined by the rectangular. For three weeks, he was the master, and I was the technician. I was taken by his primal vision of the world, and then I exhibited my work next to his. To my delight, visitors were confused whose was whose. I called the show *Is/Am:* Is, Am.

SG: Every parent in England will know that one of the first things you do with a child and paint at school is put their hand or foot in the paint and then put it on the paper. The print marks identity. It has two existential statements, "IS" and "AM." You're the third person *and* the first person. The second person is missing in that there's no address. But the first and the third person *also* spells your name, Issam. So you have put your name, divided, in the middle of the picture, and you tell me that it's not a statement of anything?

IK: I like the way you read things! But this piece is really to do with journeys — to go backwards, to become a child again, to excavate the lost self. He is, therefore I am.

SG: Do you think, living in Cambridge — which many people would regard as a bastion of privilege if not entitlement — that making art is a form of washing your hands?

IK: Arriving in '89 as a Syrian and an artist, not knowing a word of English — there cannot be worse ingredients for coming to Cambridge. The ground was not paved with gold! But I met a few people who made my life here worth living, and now I see that deficit was my strength. I felt, "I am now here. I can go nowhere else." The only tool I have is my art. I had my first studio behind the Round Church — a fantastic place where I invited people to come to work, and make, and think, and converse. I learned my English from others by ear, not from books.

SG: So your English is spoons made out of bombs!

IK: I was teaching and communicating with people through drawings. And to my astonishment, I actually found a way to stay in this place. I don't feel at all that I belong here. I am not from this geology. It's one of my stations — just happens to be the longest one, but this place is not me. I am interested in collaborating with other disciplines, and with my modest tools, I managed to connect with a few people who nurture creativity.

SG: I suppose it's a question about how we understand that sense that you're not a Syrian artist. Do you think, in your art, Syria is a fantasy? The kind of half-remembered fractured dreams, mixing desire and fantasy, that childhood is for many of us? Because if it is, it makes the politics hard.

IK: Now I am able to see that my work was seeded from the place where I grew up. I used to make my toys from rusty wire, and build sculptures from the volcanic soil. My DNA definitely has been constructed from that mud, but equally it is mixed with muds from other parts of the world. Like us all, I am a palimpsest, and a work in progress. Though it is a privileged place to occupy as an artist, but also a curse. Hearing the stories of Syrian refugees in camps and seeing their reality, such as the paralyzed young woman left with no legs to stand on.... I just felt, "how would I? How could I? How dare I? Who am I to actually work on something as painful as this?" I never had the experience of being a refugee, but I feel what it is like to leave home, to be an alien in a place, to be lonely: it is the only thing that I feel strongly about, and my humble weapon is my art.

SG: You're on a journey, you're between places, you're on a boat, but you can't resist lighting the fire, burning the boat, as you go!

And that's a very interesting moment. But what I don't know is whether your burning is a sense of "I've left the past," or "I'm ashamed of something," or "there's violence in me that I need to express somehow." So what does the burning mean for you?

IK: I will tell you where the burning came from. I did an installation called *Another Day Lost* in five simultaneous locations in London. Every day I used to go to these places and burn one match and add this to the installation as a metaphor of a day lost. Also, I was giving a talk in a church — St. James's, Piccadilly, which happened to be one of the five sites for *Another Day Lost*. At the end of the talk I said that I wanted to honor all people who were forced to flee their homes, and I struck a match, and held it until its light was gone. The time between the birth of the light and its dying, the tension in the whole church was palpable. In this case, the burning is to do with light: light is my tool. But my spent matches could be read as a metaphor of spiritual light and physical light. It also could be read as a form of counting days, in the case of *Another Day Lost*; as a form of burning cities, in the case of *Strike*; as a form of trauma, in the case of *Dark Water Burning World*. A stratum of questions.

SG: I'm not finished with religion. Because I have seen your work often in religious settings. I'm looking at a piece called *Unearthed,* which you chose to exhibit for Kettle's Yard at St. Peter's church — a series of objects made up of mourning ribbons and book covers. Obviously, mourning has a place in church, but this is also a disruption. Can you say a bit more about how you think about ritual and disruption as part of your art?

IK: Disruption, destruction, and transforming established norms and materials are deliberate acts in the creative process. When I was given that space, I immediately responded to the floor because it is made up of gravestones. Yes, my floor piece *Unearthed* is a disruption, because you can no longer reach the overflowing font in the center.

Fig. 20.2. The Dark Side of the "Unknown" Ray. © Issam Kourbaj.

sG: The picture is beautiful. It's about coming up from the earth, it's about mourning, not about burying; about maintaining a sense of doing and saying. It's also about words — again. Words are in your pictures everywhere, and here we have books marked as mourning.

ik: The hardback covers of the books were gathered from what the bookbinders had thrown away. I found that each of them could be a portrait of a person who had never had the chance to be identified. While gravestones are always identified with this glory of carving, there is no carving, there are no names. Instead, I filled the font with water absolutely to the brim.

sG: Could I ask you about one other piece of work? That you've exhibited in Dilston Grove in London, which is called *The Dark Side of the "Unknown" Ray* (fig. 20.2).

"Unknown" is in quotation marks, for reasons that you will have to explain. It's a piece from 2015 and it would be obvious to describe this too as a religious work of art. Because you constructed a beautiful circle and inside you have a clock. You've talked about journeys, you've talked about being "are you here, are you not here?" And here you have a clock that clicks to the moment, and stops and clicks to the moment and stops. So, is this a journey? Is this a failure of identity? Is this the moment at which you say, "is this the temporal version of an inability to speak?"

IK: Beautiful, I really like that. Yes, Dilston Grove (formerly known as Clare College Mission Church) and my work stood for the altar that was absent, but with a twist, so that it was not immediately legible. My son had a clock that had stopped working — out of three arms, the only pulsing one was for seconds. This was something like a heartbeat — still alive, but almost forgotten. It became a silent performance where the unknown ray was the literal translation of the X-ray. I cut the X-ray plates into pieces so when you come close to them you see different body parts. This is why it's called *Dark Side of the "Unknown" Ray:* all the people buried into oblivion in Syria.

SG: Let me ask, then, about the politics of your art. One of your works is this wonderful piece called *Aleppo Soap,* with a mirror, a tap, a basin, and a piece of soap set against a white wall and the slogan "Don't wash your hands" (fig. 20.3). Now this is a very good example of how art and words go together. "Don't wash your hands" is not something you see by a sink, especially today under COVID-19. We are encouraged all the time to wash our hands. Yet you are saying, "please, don't wash your hands." I take it you are making a political statement?

IK: Yes, it is a big ask! It was the last piece you'd see in an exhibition in the Penn Museum called *Cultures in the Crossfire,* where you could see the destruction of the different cultures in Iraq and Syria. I set it against glass from Aleppo that is 3,000 years old. It's a very ordinary object, but the way it was put was the surprise: What I'm asking people to do is not to wash their hands of the destruction of Syria's cultural heritage. Immediately afterwards there was actually a sign where you could take

Fig. 20.3. Aleppo Soap. © Issam Kourbaj.

a piece of paper and ask US Senators to act against what's happening in Syria and to the Syrian people. We all have agency and we ought to use it. I was trying to invite people, after "touring" the past and rich heritage, to revisit the present. Making soap was an ancient tradition in Aleppo. Each family had their own stamp, stamping their name into the soap. You are confronted by a dysfunctional mirror, a dysfunctional tap, a dysfunctional basin, and a piece of soap with its reflection.

SG: This beautifully looks like a very small gravestone. To me — a Jew aware of the Holocaust — the turning of human bodies into soap is a very present and powerful image. To restamp soap with a family name is to say, "You know what? You can't wash this out." You seem to have become more engaged with the world as you've got older, rather than more aesthetic. I mean, moving from your beautiful stage set of *Gilgamesh* to "Don't wash your hands" — that's a journey!

IK: The journey, believe it or not, actually started in Cuba in the mid-1990s. I went there and saw how the Cubans took their furniture and made boats out of it. I came back and I made my *Epic of Gilgamesh*. Again, in 2003, I did a piece about the Baghdad library during the invasion of Iraq, called *Sound Palimpsest*. But when it comes to home, to Syria, it suddenly became very painful. For two years I couldn't do anything. It just felt impossible to bring the news to my studio. I'm always engaged, but how could one articulate the engagement? I found that I always prefer to keep things a little bit hidden, not quite as they appear. Aesthetic versus political is for others to judge; regardless, one needs to spend time with artworks, and be rewarded: attention is the best gift. When I used to have an exhibition in my own studio, somebody coming to spend time with my work was the most beautiful thing. The collectors of my work are given one condition: that I can come and visit and see the way my work has been influencing their life. An artwork is a mobile altar.

SG: So back to migration and religion together — the mobile altar — perfect! So let me ask you about two last works. The first is a piece that I find particularly moving, *My Mother's Note to My Son Sami Kourbaj to Teach Him Arabic Letters and Numbers 2004*. It's a long time since, your son is a lot older, you're a lot older. I want you now to look back at this, sixteen years on, and tell me: Do you now regard this as sentimental? Or do you see this as something crucial and political or religious?

IK: My mother only had one month of schooling, and when I came back to visit Syria, I thought it my duty to teach her to read and write. When I was young, I was always fascinated by the first letter of my name which, in Arabic, means "eye." It does not mean "I," it means "eye." She used to hold my hand as she drew that letter — drawing, not writing — because she was looking at it as a picture. When we arrived at that letter when, later, I was teaching her, I said, "Do you remember that event?" She said, "No, I don't remember, carry on teaching me." She was a keen learner and managed to write the alphabet of my tongue. When my children came to visit years later, she wanted to share her knowledge with them, and teach them the Arabic alphabet and numbers. Not only did she do that, but she also did the powerful thing of trying to convey her feelings. For my two boys she drew two birds, the letters and the numbers. I felt there is so much there that I could learn as an artist from the way she could articulate. If you read Arabic you would see how in her drawing/writing she was trying to express her love to her grandchildren; you would see she was struggling, as she did not have the tools to articulate it with letters. I needed to celebrate the moment of uncertainty, that tension between what one is feeling and what one is articulating.

SG: Let me ask you about the last piece which you are still working on, which is beautiful little lead boats that you've taken from Syria, and turned into little boats with matches, which you set fire to. I find it very moving: that transition into something precarious. Tell me about how you thought about what you were doing with this.

IK: I was looking for an object from Syria, at the Fitzwilliam Museum, a model boat made out of lead carrying three goddesses. In response, I took bicycle mudguards to make my boats and put matchsticks inside. Setting these boats on fire turned into a performance. Spent matches speak about the people in the boats, with burnt parts to reflect the trauma that those women, children, and men carry with them, while water-like resin holds these burnt matches together, just as we all hold and support each other in desperate times. This piece is called *Dark Water, Burning World* — currently travelling in different parts of the world. I'm interested in its simplicity, and its smallness — you can hold it in your hand. Boat is a metaphor, and a metaphor is a boat too, as one is used to transport things and the other to transfer ideas.

SG: One piece I didn't understand perhaps so well, I think, is *Strike*. I wonder whether your destruction of flame, of matches, was the moment at which you were most depressed about the possibility of such metaphor?

IK: The number of days since the Syria uprising has to match the number of matches I burn. The more I burned matches the more they formed a nest. Nest, cities, the burning of the cities — leave to remain. This kind of the nest is being built and burnt at the same time: a tension between two different energies.

SG: Ha — I would have said before what you just articulated that this was the only piece where I didn't see a tension between the desire to say "I am here, Issam" and the burning. This one seemed to be a moment when you were perhaps putting more emphasis on the burning than on the nest?

IK: No this is not about me or about "I am here, Issam." *Strike* is about the barrel bombs that devastated many cities and communities in Syria. A simultaneous performance of construction and destruction.

SG: One last question: I've asked you if you see your work as religious, I've asked you if you see your work as political, I've asked if you write your name on the wall. Issam, where do you see your personal expression in your work?

IK: Let me tell you an interesting story. Once I was in my darkened studio attic in Christ's College, and for the first time I saw a camera obscura — I knew nothing about it then. I immediately thought, there is so much I could play with, so much I could make. I had grants from both the City and the University to produce a feasibility study for building a spire on top of Great St. Mary's in the form of a camera obscura, to celebrate the 800th birthday of the University of Cambridge. Sadly, it didn't happen because of fire regulations. But the concept proposed a place for contemplation: for sitting behind one's eyes to see the world. I am fascinated by science and have a particular interest in light and optics: it has to do with being present in the moment. I transformed my studio at one stage into multiple camerae obscurae. Syria is just what happens to be an inescapable part of my daily landscape. But if I'm given a space where I could really be myself, I would play with light.

SG: So you hide the I — the ego — behind the eye, the first letter of your name, and yet the politics is drawing the eye out. I find it very interesting how art becomes the expression of that.

IK: I wrote a chapter on that — the eye and I — and you can see it online: "Magic and Poetry – 'Eye' and Other Magic Moments" (2011). It was around the time when I was given my first Syrian passport and the passport office confused my name in English. Instead of starting my name with the letter "I," they started it with the letter "E." I was so upset that they had to scratch it out.

SG: You lost an eye/I? And that too on a passport which defines the I/eye!

IK: No, I reclaimed my "I" back! But an "I," like an eye, contains multitudes and a palimpsest-in-progress.

21

"Loving Justice"

Regina M. Schwartz

The United States recently hit a new low in its demonstration of
inhumanity. During relief efforts in the Bahamas, in the wake of
hurricane Dorian, individuals who did not have a visa to the US
were told to leave a rescue ship. It would not take them to Flor-
ida. Even temporary suspension of document requirements was
not in force during the crisis of a deadly, category-five hurricane. The Trump administration is also trying to cut drastically,
again, the number of refuge seekers who may enter the United
States. The supreme court has allowed it to bar most migrants,
particularly from Central America, from seeking asylum in the
US. Migrants cannot apply for asylum unless they have already
tried, and failed, to receive it in one of the countries they passed
through on their way to the US. People from El Salvador, for example, would be returned to Guatemala, hardly a safe place. ICE
agents are forcibly apprehending migrants in the fields, shoppers
in parking lots, students leaving schools. "Immigration detention facilities have been the sites of serious and repeated allegations of abuse, including allegations of sexual assault, violations
of religious freedom, medical neglect, and the punitive use of

solitary confinement."[1] Preventable deaths have been reported. With overcrowding and inadequate food and water, "conditions in ICE custody have been described as 'barbaric' and 'negligent' by Department of Homeland Security experts." The president of Refugees International, Eric Schwartz, reports:

> At a time when the number of refugees is at the highest level in recorded history, the United States has abandoned world leadership in resettling vulnerable people in need of protection. The result is a world that is less compassionate and less able to deal with future humanitarian challenges.[2]

Trump's henchmen cite expense — for processing refugees, for helping them resettle from the war-torn and famine-ridden environments they flee. The irony that America is a country of refugees — marked by their flight from life-threatening persecution and poverty — is no accident. My own grandmother fled pogroms in Latvia, and her sisters, who could not make the arduous journey with their young children, were murdered with their children. I know of no one in America who lacks a traumatic past.

And now the traumas being fled in the present are deepened, sometimes even exceeded, by the outrageous response at hostile destinations. In America, children are forcibly separated from their parents and put in cages, without beds, without even adequate clothing and nourishment, with no guaranteed end in sight for their plight; the nation's pediatricians have published collective petitions about the psychological damage to these children — to unhearing ears. So-called illegal residents are

---

1   American Immigration Lawyers Association, "Featured Issue: Immigration Detention and Alternatives to Detention," AILA Doc. No. 24121300, March 14, 2025, https://www.aila.org/library/featured-issue-immigration-detention-and-alternatives-to-detention.

2   Julie Hirschfeld Davis and Michael D. Shear, "Trump Administration Considers a Drastic Cut in Refugees Allowed to Enter the U.S.," *The Salt Lake Tribune,* September 6, 2019, https://www.sltrib.com/news/nation-world/2019/09/06/trump-administration/.

ripped from their families, jobs, and studies at universities, held as criminals and deported—to places they have never lived, where languages are spoken that they do not understand, to dangerous places. Immigrants have perished crossing rivers, deserts, and oceans; they have been abused, attacked, and, after they have been deported, many have died.

What is going on here? Where is justice? So much thinking about justice relies on economic models: the price of an injury, the price of violating a contract, the distribution of resources according to formulas. When the measures are made, they presuppose scarce resources. Lines are drawn, borders are sealed, to secure those resources for some and deny them to others.

But mark how radically different another idea of justice is, one that is over two millennia old. "The stranger that dwelleth with you *shall be unto you as one born among you,* and thou shalt love him as thyself."[3] That radical language is in Leviticus. Here, justice is not an economic principle that apportions scarce resources; rather, as care or "love" that we owe another, it issues from an unlimited, ever-renewing supply. This remarkable vision, the so-called "love command" in the Bible, joins commands about loving the neighbor (a better translation of *re'a* would be "fellow human"), and loving the stranger, to loving God, with the implication that one cannot love God without loving the stranger. Clearly, if Donald Trump is going to claim, as he has, that he is "the chosen one" he's going to have to change his immigration policy.

In Leviticus, the widow, the orphan, and the poor are especially singled out for this love. Our "fellow human" is described as someone who does not have enough, and so we must feed him, and someone who is away from home, and so we must be hospitable to him. The fellow is also depicted as including someone who can be exploited, lied to, robbed, someone whose wages can be withheld, someone who can be slandered, who can be hated, and someone, moreover, from whom that hatred can be hidden instead of having his offense openly explained

---

3   King James Version, Leviticus 19:34. Emphasis mine.

to him, defining "harm" far more broadly than contemporary liberal rights does. The list also includes someone who cannot speak and someone who cannot see. In short, one's fellow human is not figured here as a fortress of strength, self-sufficiency, or autonomy — the modern imaginary subject whose right to freedom must be protected. No, the fellow human from the poor to the stranger, from one who is speechless to one who is blind, is the very portrait of vulnerability. What then does it mean to love such a fellow human? To respect him, indeed, but far, far more: to help him.

This biblical model is a long way from the mentality of nations, like the US today, that make it illegal for the vulnerable to cross their borders and make it even lawful to dehumanize those who do.

Importantly, this biblical account describes *all* humans as in need, and all humans sharing the obligation to help. The *universality* of the human condition of exile is underscored in the midst of this very command to love the stranger: "the stranger that dwelleth with you shall be unto you as one born among you, and thou shalt love him as thyself; *for ye were strangers* in the land of Egypt" (Leviticus 19:33–35, emphasis mine). This single verse, that the stranger among you shall be as one born among you, for you were strangers, is given wider compass in the biblical story of ancient Israelites exiled in Egypt and exiled again in Babylon. And such exile is not confined to one people.

In the story of the first man and woman, all of humanity is described as separated from their homeland.

Here is John Milton's rendition of this forced exile:

They looking back, all th' Eastern side beheld
Of Paradise, so late thir happie seat,
Wav'd over by that flaming Brand, the Gate
With dreadful Faces throng'd and fierie Armes:
Som natural tears they drop'd, but wip'd them soon;
The World was all before them, where to choose
Thir place of rest, and Providence thir guide:
They hand in hand with wandring steps and slow,

Through Eden took thir solitarie way.[4]

Would that their heirs could choose a place of rest. Instead, refugees are often in flight, never resting. Never home. The injunction to treat the stranger as one born among us — the love command that Christ said was the sum of the law (Matthew 22:36–40) and that Paul endorsed as fully, "Love does no wrong to another; therefore, love *is* the fulfilling of the law" (Romans 13:10) — seems to have been tragically forgotten by so many world leaders and many of their populations. Instead, people have fallen back on the principle of scarcity, and, believing their resources are scarce, they want to hoard them, or are afflicted with fear of difference. And underneath it all, they want, desperately, to live in denial about their own condition of exile. Migrant knowledge is knowledge in denial.

For when we fail to respond humanely to individuals in flight from crises, we are not only in denial about their vulnerability, but also about ours. This includes not facing up to the fleeting nature of life on this planet, the ceaseless movement through time and space that characterizes life itself, with the loss, that inevitably haunts it, of loved ones, of loved places, of cherished moments. We are in denial, too, about the fragility of our homeland. At a time when we know there are no Indigenous peoples, that everyone outside of Africa is a migrant from there, at a time when we know that global warming will increase the numbers who must migrate from tens to hundreds of millions, we would rather not know of our fundamental exilic condition. This denial has devastating consequences, for the victims of that denial are our fellow humans who need our help, now. Chris Abani writes:

> There is something about the way that refugees, more than any other kind of displaced peoples, haunt the assurances of stability that modern statehood aspires to. Perhaps because

---

4 John Milton, *Paradise Lost*, ed. Alistair Fowler (Addison Wesley Longman, 1998), XII.641–649. Emphasis in original.

this body is proof that we have advanced much less in our "humanness," than we would like to believe.[5]

William Shakespeare addresses this poverty of humanness. *Sir Thomas More,* a play penned by many, includes a passage that has survived, remarkably enough, in Shakespeare's own hand. It is a speech given by More in his capacity as Sheriff of London, when he addresses a violent mob, hostile against foreigners, during the Ill May Day riot of 1517.

> Grant them removed, and grant that this your noise
> Hath chid down all the majesty of England;
> Imagine that you see the wretched strangers,
> Their babies at their backs and their poor luggage,
> Plodding to the ports and coasts for transportation,
>
> .   .   .   .   .   .
>
> And you in ruff of your opinions clothed;
> What had you got? I'll tell you: you had taught
> How insolence and strong hand should prevail,
> How order should be quelled; and by this pattern
> Not one of you should live an aged man,
> For other ruffians, as their fancies wrought,
> With self same hand, self reasons, and self right,
> Would shark on you, and men like ravenous fishes
> Would feed on one another.[6]

The haunting image of exiling "wretched strangers, their babies at their backs and their poor luggage, plodding to the ports and coasts," searching for a place to go, is, in our time, realized in photo journalism: images of refugees ever moving. But here, More does not only prophetically conjure the brutal treatment of

---

5   Chris Abani, "The Road," in *The Displaced: Refugee Writers on Refugee Lives,* ed. Viet Thanh Nguyen (Abrams Press, 2019), 15.

6   Henry Chettle et al., Sir *Thomas More, Original Text by Anthony Munday and Henry Chettle, Revised by Henry Chettle, Thomas Dekker, Thomas Heywood and William Shakespeare,* ed. John Jowett (Bloomsbury, 2013), 6.83–98.

"others." He knows that if a code of self-interest prevails — "self same hand, self reasons, and self right" — the victimizers will also be victimized.

> Alas, alas! Say now the king
> Were but to banish you, whither would you go?
> What country, by the nature of your error,
> Should give you harbour? go you to France or Flanders,
> To any German province, to Spain or Portugal,
> Nay, any where that not adheres to England,
> Why, you must needs be strangers: would you be pleased
> To find a nation of such barbarous temper,
> That, breaking out in hideous violence,
> Would not afford you an abode on earth,
> Whet their detested knives against your throats,
> Spurn you like dogs […]
> What would you think
> To be thus used? this is the strangers case;
> And this your mountainish inhumanity.[7]

Ironically itemizing foreign lands that are not English allies, "nay, any where that not adheres to England," More's deeper logic is to break down the very categories of foreigner and native, for we are all potentially displaced, all strangers. He warns the locals, "Why, *you* must needs be strangers" (italics added). We saw that the Bible broke down that stranger/native distinction too: "Treat the stranger as one born among you" (Leviticus 19:34). This command had resonance in the early modern period, not only intoned in the frequent readings of the *Book of Common Prayer,* but dramatized on the early modern stage.

For instance, in his oblivious self-righteousness, King Lear "others" his daughter Cordelia:

> Here I disclaim all my paternal care,
> Propinquity and property of blood,

---

7   Ibid., 6.138–56.

And as a stranger to my heart and me
Hold thee from this for ever.[8]

Then, having estranged her, he heaps on more:

                    The barbarous Sythian
Or he that makes his generation messes
To gorge his appetite, shall to my bosom
Be as well neighbored, pitied, and relieved,

As thou my sometime daughter.[9]

This echoes, but perversely, that biblical injunction to love the stranger, to pity and relieve him. And Lear will not grant this even to his daughter. In this way, the play weaves the command to love the stranger into the core of its plot about a family. Lear must learn to love the stranger or he will never more be Lear. Ultimately, his love of this very child is the only goodness in a world achingly bereft of it. He readies himself for his reunion with her in a poignant scene where, through his experience of being exiled from the homes of his other, self-serving daughters, he becomes aware of the plight of homelessness. No more denial is possible. Lear learns compassion for the vulnerable, and he regrets not addressing their plight:

Poor naked wretches, whereso'er you are,
That bide the pelting of this pitiless storm,
How shall your houseless heads and unfed sides,
Your loop'd and window'd raggedness, defend you
From seasons such as these? O, I have ta'en
Too little care of this![10]

8   William Shakespeare, *King Lear,* ed. René Weis (Longman Annotated Texts, 1993), 1.1.111–14.
9   Ibid., 114–18.
10   Ibid., 3.4.1831–36.

It seems the cure for the rulers who have been unmindful of injustice is for them to suffer themselves:

> Take physic, pomp;
> Expose thyself to feel what wretches feel,
> That thou mayst shake the superflux to them,
> And show the heavens more just.[11]

Is Shakespeare recommending that Trump spend some time in a detention camp to learn his duty? Or worse, have his child put there? My irony only stresses the brutality of imprisoning vulnerable people, an imprisonment that California has just courageously outlawed.

So what about our immigration policy? We need to begin with this baseline obligation to take care of those in need, and go from there, negotiating about the best way to meet those needs. Policy needs to serve justice. Julián Castro made the moral sentiment behind immigration explicit: Humanism must take precedence over nationalism. "When we see families seeking refuge, we don't see criminals, or an invasion, or a threat to national security," Castro writes. "We see kids. We see parents. We see people. We see people first. Because we are people first. And it's time for an immigration policy that puts people first."[12]

I want to conclude with the exquisite biblical metaphor for care, not with a border line that cannot be crossed, but with the enduring image Leviticus gives to us for how to respond to the stranger: "You are neither to strip your vine bare nor to collect the fruit that has fallen in your vineyard. You must leave them for the poor and the stranger" (Leviticus 19:10). In this version of justice, giving is not an option, but an obligation. The stranger needs the fruits of our vineyard; and justice demands that we give them. The only human response to human need is to give. And to replace "mountainish inhumanity" with humanity, we

---

11 Ibid., 1836–39.
12 Julián Castro, "Putting People First," *Medium*, April 1, 2019, https://medium.com/@JulianCastro2020/putting-people-first-e0f765ceeooc.

need to acknowledge our human condition of need, of vulnerability, indeed, of exile.

Bibliography

Abani, Chris. "The Road." In *The Displaced: Refugee Writers on Refugee Lives,* edited by Viet Thanh Nguyen. Abrams Press, 2019.

American Immigration Lawyers Association. "Featured Issue: Immigration Detention and Alternatives to Detention." AILA Doc. No. 24121300, March 14, 2025. https://www.aila. org/library/featured-issue-immigration-detention-and-alternatives-to-detention.

Castro, Julian. "Putting People First." *Medium,* April 1, 2019. https://medium.com/@JulianCastro2020/putting-people-first-e0f765ceeooc.

Chettle, Henry, Thomas Dekker, Thomas Heywood, Anthony Munday, William Shakespeare, et al. *Sir Thomas More, Original Text by Anthony Munday and Henry Chettle, Revised by Henry Chettle, Thomas Dekker, Thomas Heywood and William Shakespeare.* Edited by John Jowett. Bloomsbury, 2013.

Hirschfeld Davis, Julie, and Michael D. Shear. "Trump Administration Considers a Drastic Cut in Refugees Allowed to Enter the U.S." *The Salt Lake Tribune,* September 6, 2019. https://www.sltrib.com/news/nation-world/2019/09/06/trump-administration/.

Milton, John. *Paradise Lost.* Edited by Alistair Fowler. Addison Wesley Longman, 1998.

Shakespeare, William. *King Lear.* Edited by René Weis. Longman Annotated Texts, 1993.

22

Response to Regina M. Schwartz

Rowan Williams

One of the most valuable insights in Regina Schwartz's brief es-say — as in her recent book on Shakespeare[1] — is the linkage of justice with *imagination*. The language we normally use about justice assumes that it is primarily to do with the things that are true of human beings and their claims, independently of any-one's choice or convenience — and that's a valid and significant perspective. But it is, as it stands, a somewhat rootless one. It occludes the need for an imagined structure of relation in which we recognize in one another a shared predicament — a predica-ment which Regina identifies as a common *need*.

I have hesitated to use the fashionable term "empathy" to designate this "imagined structure": empathy as an emotional identification with the situation of others as if it were my own is an ambiguous moral category, despite the ambitious claims made for it by writers and publicists. It can dissolve into forms of cultural and emotional appropriation, strategies for absorb-ing what is disturbingly other into a comforting sameness: "Look, they're so different, yet they feel just what I feel!" The

---

1   Regina M. Schwartz, *Loving Justice, Living Shakespeare* (Oxford University Press 2017).

point is not that there are "really" no differences and that all human beings are fundamentally equipped with a fixed set of claims to justice. Rather, our human condition is one in which we are constantly being challenged to see in the other not a subject possessed of exactly the same set of claims as myself — nor for that matter a potential rival competing with me for limited social goods — but a stranger whose identity I need to contemplate and (so far as humanly possible) welcome if I am to live humanly myself. I am to recognize them as a partner in the work of "humanizing" — humanizing of both us and our social and global milieu. And since recognition is deeply bound up with sharing language, we have to find a means of speaking together in which neither voice is programmed to drown out the other.

The paradoxical thing about this is that we have to learn to imagine ourselves as — in an important sense — beyond our own imagining, or, to put it less teasingly, to imagine ourselves as always lacking, and not knowing what we are lacking. On such a foundation we can begin to think of our relations, socially and individually, as permeated by a willingness to see our identities as always in construction and never under our controlling "panoptic" surveillance. Working for the mutual recognition of shared language is a liberating of both self and other from models of dominance and simple, home-based normativity.

In such a light, justice begins in the *"doing* justice" (as we say) to the particularity of each situation as it arises, each new variety of otherness. Regina is right to make use of the opposition between "humanism" and "nationalism" in one sense, but I'd want to interrogate this a bit further, to avoid the risk of seeing the "essentially" human as rootless or abstract. The "humanism" we seek or try to enact is not best understood as a straightforward universalism, in which local difference is subsumed. Just as with "empathy," there is an ambiguity lurking, to the extent that any universal identity will inevitably be a version of what this or that group regards as normal or standard human identity and human rationality. To argue for a more questioningly interactive journey towards an ethic that is not just local and self-serving is by no means to abandon all aspirations to an unconditional morality, a universal "protocol" of respect and gratitude for human-ity as it is. This is not about a bland cultural relativism incapable of addressing imbalances and patterns of unjust domination in the life of societies we encounter as other. It *is* about attending seriously to what we cannot instantly digest and own, and ac-knowledging our own incompleteness.

Regina notes that there is a sense in which we are all migrants: the human race is nomadic from the first, and the idea that there is a simple "natural" level of territorial belonging is a myth. Put more positively, the truth is that we have all learned over long periods how to live in various local ecologies, and the history of that learning itself becomes part of the ecology inherited by new generations. Inhabiting such a history and geography — without which specifics, as noted earlier, we are not human at all — we may well find, in the typical consciousness of modernity, that where we live — the past we remember or recite, the physically changing landscape we experience — becomes both familiar and foreign. Indeed, if we don't find this to be the case, we col-lapse the entire process of historical learning into an uncritical "presentism," as some call it, the lazy assumption that what we now experience is simply how things "just are," timelessly. And this in turn means losing that sense of contingency and possibil-ity that nurtures a critical engagement with the ecology we live in, the critical engagement which makes possible a fuller "doing justice." Thinking critically and imaginatively about where and who we are shows us how fragile are the constructions of "being at home" that comfort us. Such thinking involves a sort of inner displacement, the recognition of a selfhood or identity that is always in motion, becoming strange to itself and finding new settlements, unsettling itself and arriving at new kinds of con-nectedness. This is why the crude liberal dream of a single global culture, a simple overcoming of local identities, is a dream and a dangerous one: if there is any realization of this fantasy, it is in the malign form of the universal market of advanced capitalism, in which every kind of particularity is exchangeable, capable of being traded for something else. Michael Sandel's discussions both of justice in general and of the culture of pricing every experience explore just this set of dangers.[2]

But the "migrant knowledge" we are concerned about is, as Regina suggests, something that recognizes and works with the basic reality of displacement — the displacing of a protected and agenda-setting ego, the displacing of a single normative culture, the displacing of all kinds of assumptions about social and ideological power. It does not seek to erase difference and turn us all into Esperanto-speakers or the equivalent; it assumes that knowledge is a "migratory" reality, the life of a subject always encountering what it cannot absorb and being challenged by it, enriched by it, simply puzzled by it, but never just coinciding with the boundaries it has inherited. That on its own, however, can sound a bit Panglossian, focusing on the "enrichment" of specific experience by otherness; we are slipping towards the dangerous territory of self-help books on "adventures in empathy." Rather, the migrant knowledge we are seeking to attend to here is the knowledge of real and often violent disruption, the pain of loss: loss of home, language, leverage in society, access to education, hope in a future for yourself or your children, and much more. Simply to recognize and attend to what the migrant knows is to let ourselves (those with the resources and good fortune to be able to organize conferences and create books) be disrupted. Regina quotes King Lear's exhortation to "expose thyself to feel what wretches feel": not as an exercise in imaginatively sharing the frisson of loss from a safe distance, but taking one's own knowing body to where it can sense the other's pain for what it is, not absorbing or aestheticizing it — a warning to us as participants in this project. Ultimately, the doing of justice we are thinking about here is inseparable from a certain sort of bodily encounter, finding a physical place where even if only for the most fleeting moment we (those with the resources, etc.) stand alongside and begin to sense the perspective of loss. Per-

---

2   Michael J. Sandel, *Justice: What's the Right Thing to Do?* (Penguin, 2010), and Michael J. Sandel, *What Money Can't Buy: The Moral Limits of Markets* (Penguin, 2013).

haps in the long run it helps us go back to our conventionally "native" territory to see some of our own losses and displacements more honestly, but what it must entail above all is the willingness *not* to hurry back to that territory, instrumentalizing the loss and displacement of the other. That would be a sure way of keeping the stranger a stranger. We (those with etc.) have the hard task of staying with the very specific strangeness of another's pain and exile, recognizing ourselves in it, recognizing our own flights from this recognition, but also staying with the resistant mysteriousness of the stranger's suffering, "abiding" it, as might once have been said, until some sort of common language is born of this.

Earlier on I wrote of imagining ourselves as beyond our imagining. The Shakespearean world into which Regina invites us with such sensitivity is one where the unimaginable self is displayed in all sorts of ways. Lear's troubles are grounded in the fact that he has never known himself, according to his elder daughters, so that he does not know the difference between being loved and being paid a debt. Macbeth seeks to hide from heaven the suddenly exposed ambition that will drive him to murder. The dying Iago taunts the horrified witnesses to *Othello's* bleak end with the words, "What you know, you know" — as if they are being invited to imagine an evil in themselves beyond imagining yet hideously familiar, invited like Macbeth to own their terrible dreams as theirs, as, like *The Tempest's* Caliban, native to their own imagination. We are not the triumphant proprietors or conquerors of our own inner territory; we do not have ourselves in possession. And as long as we do not or cannot recognize this, we cannot do justice — see clearly, wait on the strangeness of the stranger without hurrying to absorb them, learn the rhythm of response which may shape a new language. Shakespeare, as Regina and others have read him, does indeed prompt us to sit with our imagining so that we imagine the darkness we do not want to name as ours, the urgency with which we try to dispel darkness and powerlessness by "filling the void,"[3] as Simone Weil observes in her notebooks, the resistance to knowing our own need of recognition. If we can learn from this sitting-with, we may find the freedom to sit with the stranger too, and sitting with the stranger will liberate us further for sitting with our unimaginable and elusive personal situatedness, our "self." Out of this comes a justice that is more than distributive fairness: an urgent pressing towards fuller and more self-forgetting attention, and a willingness to let go of whatever attitude, possession, prejudice, or status that would impede this.

---

3   Simone Weil, *The Notebooks of Simone Weil*, vol. 2, trans. Arthur Willis (Routledge and Kegan Paul, 1956), 491.

Bibliography

Sandel, Michael J. *Justice: What's the Right Thing to Do?*
    Penguin, 2010.
———. *What Money Can't Buy: The Moral Limits of Markets.*
    Penguin, 2013.
Schwartz, Regina M. *Loving Justice, Living Shakespeare.* Oxford
    University Press 2017.
Weil, Simone. *The Notebooks of Simone Weil.* Volume 2.
    Translated by Arthur Willis. Routledge and Kegan Paul,
    1956.

V.

Interlude

23

In the Fertile Land[1]

Gabriel Josipovici

We live in a fertile land. Here we have all we want. Beyond the borders, far away, lies the desert, where nothing grows.

Nothing grows there. Nor is there any sound except the wind.

Here, on the other hand, all is growth, abundance. The plants reach enormous heights, and even we ourselves grow and grow, so that there is absolutely no stopping us. And when we speak the words flow out in torrents, another aspect of the general fertility.

Here, the center is everywhere and the circumference nowhere.

Conversely, it could be said — and it is an aspect of the general fertility here that everything that can be said has its converse side — conversely, it could be said that the circumference is everywhere and the center nowhere, that the limits are everywhere, that everywhere there is the presence of the desert.

---

1   This piece was previously published in Gabriel Josipovici, *In The Fertile Land* (Carcanet Press, 1987). It is reprinted with the kind permission of Carcanet Press.

Here, in the fertile land, everyone is so conscious of the desert, so intrigued and baffled by it, that a law has had to be passed forbidding anyone to mention the word.

Even so, it underlies every sentence and every thought, every dream and every gesture.

Some have even gone over into the desert, but as they have not come back it is impossible to say what they found there.

I myself have no desire to go into the desert. I am content with the happy fertility of this land. The desert beyond is not something I think about very much, and if I occasionally dream about it, that contravenes no law. I cannot imagine where the limits of the desert are to be found or what kind of life, if any, exists there. When I hear the wind I try to follow it in my mind across the empty spaces, to see in my mind's eye the ripples it makes in the enormous dunes as it picks up the grains of sand and deposits them in slightly altered patterns a little further along — though near and far have clearly quite different meanings in the desert from the one they have here.

In the desert silence prevails. Here the talk is continuous. Many of us are happy even talking to ourselves. There is never any shortage of subjects about which to talk, nor any lack of words with which to talk. Sometimes, indeed, this abundance becomes a little onerous, the sound of all these voices raised in animated conversation or impassioned monologue grows slightly disturbing. There have even been moments when the very abundance of possible subjects and of available directions in which any subject may be developed has made me long for the silence of the desert, with only the monotonous whistling of the wind for sound. At those times my talk redoubles in both quantity and speed and I cover every subject except the one that obsesses me — for the penalty for any infringement of the law is severe. Even as I talk though, the thought strikes me that perhaps I am actually in the desert already, that I have crossed over and not returned, and that what the desert is really like is this, a place where everyone talks but where no one speaks of what concerns him most.

Such thoughts are typical of the fertility of our land.

VI.

Sound Crossings

24

Sound Crossings: A Poetry Reading

Angela Leighton and A.E. Stallings

ANGELA LEIGHTON: Searching for a title for this reading I plucked one, as you do, out of thin air, and hoped for the best: Sound Crossings.[1] Weeks later, thinking about the phrase again, it began to stir with strange life, in the way words can. For sounds — those straits or inlets of the sea — can be crossed. Or we might sound out crossings, meaning we might listen to their sounds, or fathom their depths. Or to cross might be a sound way to behave, ensuring we hear all sides of a question. Or we might get cross at sensing nothing but sound in a poem or passage of prose. Or sound might always remain at cross-purposes to our formal conventions of rationality, sanity, sense, grammar, in order to confound us — to make what is sound, unsound, by means of... sound. But this might be where madness sets in, or poetry begins.

---

1   "A Poem," from *The Messages* (2012), and "Harbour," from *Sea Level* (2007), are both reproduced by kind permission of Shoestring Press, Nottingham, UK. "Bog Asphodel," from *Spills* (2016); "A Cricket for Pirandello," "Landings," and "By the Bitter African Sea," from *One, Two* (2021); and "Launched" and "Sea Level," from *Something, I Forget* (2023), are all reprinted by kind permission of Carcanet Press, Manchester, UK.

So what is a poem? Perhaps indeed a crossing of sounds: from word to word, phrase to phrase, from mouth to ear, ear to memory — or all of these happening at once. As a child friend once asked me, crossly and curiously: "But what is it for?" Her question was about my pouring olive oil into a jug as she watched, bored and restless, in my kitchen. But it stayed with me, and some years later found its way into this sonnet, simply titled "A Poem":

What is it *for*? the curious child enquired.
Who knows? To handle snugly as a glove,
to fit by chance, to change by word of mouth,
to dream to in a moment's carelessness —

perhaps to hold or hold by, all the world
a cover to discover how a word
might make a listening listened to, not heard,
and nothing come of it but just itself —

or else to pour like oil, an amber slick,
a liquid ingot from its nutty stock,
olivary, expressed from green or black
and solar-golden in the winter light.

It is for *this*, or *this*, a careless blessing:
words, by the way (no message) ... cold pressing.

A poem is a queer multi-dimensional thing: something touched and seen, understood and heard; a still shape on the page that is also constantly on the move; a thing that mixes, mimics, echoes, and deflects what we think we understand. But to consider poetry's crossings, and all the crossed senses and etymologies that lie deep in the language, is perhaps also to recall the crossings that make up the course of human history, and still do. For all languages are live and diasporic. Libraries of exile, to use de Waal's phrase, are at work in the very words we use: like "oil," from the French *huile,* the Latin *oleum,* the Greek *elaion,* with all their viscously liquid vowels — and then who knows which unwrit-ten, sea-crossing languages before these. Here, I too will do a bit of crossing, between my critical self and my poetry-writing self, while also being aware, as we all are, that the privilege of being in this beautiful gallery of finely curated works of art must touch on other crossings, matters of life and death sometimes, that go on elsewhere. The poems I'll read hint at those, but usually in-directly, since my knowledge of such experiences remains in imagination, at several removes. What is also fascinating about this whole project is that it constantly crosses from one form to another — visual, aural, tactile, historical, topographical, even culinary and sartorial — perhaps in order to ask what we mean by knowledge at all, and in what sense it might be "migrant."

I was lucky to have one of those mixed upbringings, as many of us do today, learning my mother's Italian before I learned my father's English — so the sing-song of the Latinate always pulls at my English, sometimes muddling my idioms. I recall an old man up in Yorkshire who, not understanding my BBC English once, muttered an aside in disapproval: "it coomes to summat when we have eyeties teaching English in our universities." Thinking in two languages can be a tongue-tying business — but at some level it's what we all do, as we make those first crossings from thoughts or feelings into words. And then language itself is of mixed heritage, a cross-breed of derivations and a rich preserve, therefore, of historical knowledge that has crossed continents, seas. The next two poems are about something that has always crossed readily from place to place in the company of migrating human beings: plants. The first is about a wild flower, which I first saw in the peat bogs of the Isle of Skye, in Scotland. It's a stunning gold color, but my sense of the indigenous and local was quickly dispelled when I found its name, "Bog Asphodel":

> Once, by Elgol,
> under ikat sunsets, driving affluent rain,
> my two-ply tongue,
> tongue-tied for weeks, word-stuck in kind, recognised:
> bog asphodel.

To a cold conditioning ground, unpastured space,
                    its Delphic heavenly
ring brought sandalled toes, Elysian meadows,
                    Athens, Rome —
gilding the peat bog, winning a pot of gold.

                    Asphodel —
long echo. Here on the bare, bone-breaking heath
                    my tongue's bell,
bi-lingual, local, levies a name from elsewhere,
                    and finds its place.

Asphodel grows wild on the mediterranean maquis. But it also, you remember, carpets the meadows of the classical underworld where its roots were eaten by the shades of the dead — in particular, the dead whose lives were insignificant, un-momentous: "the weak souls among the asphodels," as George Seferis puts it, quoted by Derek Mahon. They were also, by the way, eaten by the hungry poor of Greece and Sicily during the second world war. It's a word with a "long echo," therefore, into history, myth and story, so that finding it, or its near-relation, on a boggy northern heath took me on a little journey of crossings in the language. Names from elsewhere are always, perhaps, how we find our place.

My own "two-ply tongue" is not, however, a natural translator, and crossing from one language to another is something I find difficult. I tend to inhabit either one or the other, as well as the different personalities that go with them. As Iris Origo puts it in her late autobiography: "it began to dawn on me that [...] I myself did not say quite the same things and was not the same person, in Italian as in English." So when I started to translate Italian poetry, it was like trying to put together two halves of my brain which didn't quite match. Alicia and I have both been involved in a project to translate Dante's *Purgatorio* — a maddening enterprise, trying to put that easily rhyming and endlessly inverting Italian into "bog" English. Anyone who translates knows that the task is endless, impossible, yet necessary. It is also closely related to what we do all the time: cross over from thought to word, memory to writing, from stories long ago to this here and now. Translating "Visita," a poem by Luigi Pirandello who is generally better known for his short stories, novels, and plays, turned out to be a reminder of the point where translation will not work. This was the impossibility of translating his phrase: "Nascere grilli è pure qualche cosa"—literally, the birth of crickets is also something. But "grilli" are also fancies, whimsy, a creature that hops off the top of one's head. The poem took off from there. On the way it recalls the story of another wild flower: namely, Oxford ragwort. This plant was brought to Oxford's botanical gardens in the eighteenth century from the slopes of Etna in Sicily. But it hopped over the walls, as plants do, and with the development of the Great Western Railway it began to seed happily along the cinder tracks, from there spreading to most of Britain. Flowers, like languages, are natural migrants. But translating, too, is a hopping over walls and barriers: from one language to another, one context or world-view (often contained in a single word) to another. Pirandello, by the way, asked to be buried in a rock in the garden of his childhood home where his ashes are to be found. This poem is dedicated to the French scholar and translator, Roger Pearson, "A Cricket for Pirandello":

> Our trade's translation, whether poems or prose—
>   and here in Rome
> struggling to render Pirandello's "crickets"
> I must lose the creature or else the dream,
> meaning's gravity or else the grace.
> *Nascere grilli,* he writes, to signify
> fancies, daydreams, born on the hop...
> but no insect makes a leap that's fit
> for Englishing that device of wit.
>
> So here's a leap-poem, Roger. It goes
>   channel-hopping
> from me to you, scrambling the frontiers—

since we who traffic from tongue to tongue,
mother to other, native to strange,
must make thought's impulse dance to the tune
that words call, by whims of their own:
idiom or pun, some self-stranging homonym,
the distant phones that ring in a phoneme.

Now skip: think ragwort, that hardy immigrant,
    taking root
in Oxford's first botanical garden,
later, on Isambard's cinder-tracks
riding westwards, seeding the dry ways —
but remembering still in the rails' sapped clinker
how once it rode the charcoal flows
of Etna's pyroclastic scree —
one hop ahead, gold-gracing earth's gravity.

So *Nascere grilli…* On a Sicilian plain
    small jumping jacks,
blue and orange in the hot afternoons,
would gleam beside his rockfast tomb —
flashes of insight, lost as seen.
We'll dream — so words go jumping free
from page to eye, from mouth to ear,
to hatch wild fancies in translation —
cricket-strangers on the ground's foundation.

All his life Pirandello returned to the place of his childhood on the south coast of Sicily, by "the bitter African sea," as he called it — bitter even then. Alicia and I share a fascination with the classical seas of story and history, as well as with their languages — Greek in her case, Italian in mine. The seas of Magna Graecia extend to Sicily and all round the south of Italy, up to Naples. They carried some of the first trade routes of the Mediterranean, the first routes of story and myth, as well as routes of human exodus, migration, and war. Sicily, which lies at the heart of these sea passages, has been in its time Phoenician, Greek, Arabic,

Norman, and Spanish, and its extraordinary cosmopolitan history is recorded in some of the street names of Palermo, written in Arabic, Hebrew, and Italian. I've been returning to Sicily for many years now, fascinated by its layer on layer of history and story, of archaeological evidence and mythic memory, as well as its modern problems of migration and emigration.

So I'll now turn to a series of poems about the sea — that element which recalls our evolutionary beginnings, which marks boundaries and breaks them down, which challenges our national, rooted natures, affects our balance, tunes our sense-perceptions, but drowns us too. There are thin lines everywhere on the sea, and crossing it means risk and knowledge, danger and new-found lands. These two poems, one quite early, the other more recent, I suppose hint at an ongoing obsession. Putting them side by side, I realize that the first contains the story of the second in embryo. It is called "Harbour":

> From creel-pots' crochet, dumped networks of nets,
> staggered crates, a trailer, bales of twine,
> bit and knots and art and old sea stench
> under the nightly floodlight's yellow halo,
>
> saints' wrack, livings, rot, planking, buoys,
> rounding guts of rope, oarlock, airlock,
> with aquapac and VHF, and luck,
> light, weather, balance, ebb, flow,
>
> something draws us out beyond the jetty's
> throw, its sea-sliced steps and stop, its checked
> halt, systoles of dulse, litter, scum,
> to falls of sea-room falling wide as we come.

The second is called "Launched." It is set, like "Harbour," on the edge of land, and carries the same outward impetus of daring and desire, risk and failure:

A wish as Odyssean, as old as time,
drives this child's one toy of a thousand ships:

a rickety craft of sticks in binder-twine,
a white-rag sail to twitch in the onshore wind.

From a stubby pin of cane, a mast aspires.
The knotted joins are frayed, the flat hull gapes.

Millennia before the wheel a log was launched
when some mute human mounted a dream to leave —

just so this primitive mock-up bobs and turns,
bounced on the waves' small hobbles, rocked and trialled

like a saint's coracle trusted to weather and luck
yet carried by some momentum the spirit craves.

It rides one level slack, then rafts a rhythm
that will play catch-up, but now only taps … taps

as the ocean's covert incalculable pulse upholds
this tacky throwaway, a ropey panpipe of twigs.

Then one wave risen out of sync just swivels the thing
and it surfs, backed up by the roll, to an easy landing.

A slake of mudflats shines in the noonday sun.
Wet sand, raked by a tide, displays what must come.

But the child, driven by hope, and passion, and faith,
wades deeper in to speed her wish, test-launch

her self's way out from safe and steadying ground
to a space (at heart) as wide and free as the world.

Perhaps the sea, that infinite, polylingual tongue, reminds us of our evolutionary, watery beginnings, while remaining at once an inviting singer and a dangerous siren. I've always, till recently, lived near the sea, and when far from it I miss its deep resources of sound. Poems seem rather like islands in a sea — they snag noises from the welter of rumors that lie around us. But if sea marks our origins, and can become a place of playtime and holiday, it can also kill. As Joseph Conrad puts it: "The most amazing wonder of the deep is its unfathomable cruelty."[2] Any sea shore, perhaps like any shore of a poem, is therefore haunted by what the tides might wash up.

As in this next poem. There's an afterword, I should explain, which refers to the *Quinta del Sordo* — that is, the house of the deaf man, on whose walls Goya painted his late, terrible paintings, one of them of a dog drowning in a quicksand. This is another poem about watching a child at play, burying herself in the sand, but it's also about something else. It's called "Landings":

Tucked to the chin in the sand's worn grain,
cradled fast in its stony crumble —
waves, her ancient lully, birth-wail,
earth, her bedding, mineral domain —
these take her in, unaccustomed comforters,
and she, a settler in their sandy wastes,
smiles and plays. I dust the last
yellow granules on her flat-out hand —
a hard packing, ticklish embrace.

Yet fearful, too, having watched that child
scoop hillocks of sand over herself
to make a mummy-mound (Anubis, embalmer,
dog of the dead), but leave exposed
one talking head — old joker to the end —
smiling, smiling, across the tumulus

2   Joseph Conrad, *The Mirror of the Sea* (Doubleday, Doran & Company, 1928), 137.

of her new hot bed? Look, she cries,
outwitting her own disappearing trick:
I'm drowned, buried. No kidding. I'm alive.

And I see (see still) a beach of small mounds,
the dumped refuse of a wrecked cargo —
each body barrelled to a rounded vault,
wrapped, absolved, in its hummocky pad;
and children's faces smiling, smiling,
like lively headstones sharing a joke.
It might be a dream's wild animation:
the sand's soft-fall, light as a plaything,
now heavy as a stone slab to lock them in.

Afterthought:

Could Goya hear — in his painting's dark wit
on the white walls of the Quinta del Sordo —
that listening-drowning dog, ear cocked
to catch some voice (from a lord gone deaf)
to halt or explain the unending desert,
the ochre void of an engulfing quicksand?
To drown, landing, is a curse to the sky.
She breathes, and sand-falls trickle either side.
Whose home-ground waits to take so many in?

I'll draw to a close with a few last thoughts on sound and cross-ings. The way that poetry goes from page to eye, from eye to brain, from brain to ear, involves a kind of perpetual migration of sense, through tactile, visual, intellectual, aural, sensible — and back again. It also goes from then, when it was written, to now, when it's read, from poet to reader, reader to other readers, ac-cumulating meaning from each new context as it goes. It thus puts knowledge, if that's the right word, in process, since knowl-edge of a poem is never arrived at, never complete. It is a sea journey without an end. But maybe that's why we want the arts in our lives — to have our wisdom confounded, our knowledge nonplussed, and so have to start again, making sense of what plays noises against meaning, soundings against narrative, as if seas were always lying behind the articulate separations of our languages. This next, more recent poem, is called "Sea Level":

Exhausted — in sleep so deep it trawls
a depth of still, to feel for the sea's

push and leave, hush and slither,
the slack of a thing inching to take

sticks, stones, shell, weed,
and braille the sand beneath each wave

like the last touch of a blind man's hand
reading a page of the earth's lost ground.

*

For here's the fault-line of an old contention:
sea draws, withdraws, a creature steeped

in itself, no hurry, and heaves like breathing —
then spills, and leaves its secrets torn

to pieces, cut-work bridalling the rocks,
and falls, collapses, stiffening to froth

as the drag sings and circles, winning
its dream of us, returned to beginning.

Migrant knowledge; sound crossings … I'm very aware that having time and place in which to compose and then publish poems is a lucky privilege, and that outside any one poem's comfortable boundaries lies the world we inhabit. In that world the ground we stand on, the passports we hold, the freedoms we claim, might come at a cost, both to ourselves and to others. And this

373

ought to tell us, also, when to shut up — when, for instance, the world might press too much on the limits of what can be said.

So I'll end by returning to Pirandello, and his "il mare aspro africano." It is still bitter today, and its killing powers have underlain the story of many recent migrations, as well as many of history's sea stories. This last poem, and last word, was written close to Pirandello's birthplace, and its repeated end-stopped rhymes express something of that necessary speech and silence, the crying out and the shutting up of poetry, in the face of life's real disasters. Points of silence are as important in any poem as its sound-crossing words. So I'll end with "By the Bitter African Sea":

> Limestone. Flatlands. A deserted beach.
> Aleppo pines tormenting the skyline.
> This is not a poem I can write, or refute.
>
> A big sea heaves, too bitter to swim.
> The keel of a boat draws a line in the sand.
> My tongue's in trouble at its very root.
>
> For the long night crossings, too many to count.
> Sigh of a keel. Dead children. Landings.
> My tongue's unskilled to speak, or confute.
>
> Sea, a strong drink. Sand, soft touch.
> What was washed up has been covered, removed.
> This is not a poem to sound, or mute.

A.E. STALLINGS: I love Angela's title for this reading — "sound crossings" — for many of the reasons she has already elucidated. "Sound" is the medium of poets, of course, and crossings are the essence of translation, which means, after all, to carry across: trafficking meaning over the borders of language. "Sound" is itself such a strange word in English, many different definitions coming via different routes and languages into the same deep, round syllable: As a noun, the music we hear is sound (from the Latin sonus), but a sound is also (from the Germanic side) a swimmable or seemingly swimmable stretch of water. As a verb, it might mean "resound," or it might mean to plumb the watery depths. As an adjective, it means safe, whole, or complete — safe and sound is a watertight formula. To sleep soundly is to sleep deeply. Sound is also handy for the rhymer in English — it rhymes with "round" and "found" and "bound," but also "frowned" and "pound," "ground" and "drowned." One of Homer's favorite epithets for the sea — the Aegean Sea — is *polyphloisboio:* the loud-roaring sea, a sea full of sound. The stretch of water between Turkey and Greece — the background to so much of the Iliad — is a crossing, it turns out, that even at its narrowest is not swimmable, nor easily measurable, nor safe.

I have been spending a lot of time thinking about poetry and language and that sea — a sea that is ultimately linked to Pirandello's "bitter African sea" not only as part of the greater Mediterranean, but as a modern border, a historical place of cultural exchange, and one of the most lethal routes of migration.

As a poet, a translator, a mother, and a Classicist living in Greece, I little thought that the refugee crisis, which reached its nadir in 2015–2016, would come to radically alter my relationship to classical literature, translation, and poetry. These seemingly separate aspects of my life, though, all ended up being touched by the crisis washing up on Greek shores, and in Piraeus and Athens itself. 2016 began with a spate of drownings on eastern Aegean shores, often of children (Alan Kurdi, the boy in the famous photograph, was one of scores), many of these reported in the local news — I should note that my husband is a journalist — but barely reaching the awareness of international media. One morning I realized, after dropping my own children off for their school bus, that forty-five people — at least seventeen of them children — had drowned that same morning in two separate shipwrecks: a classroom full.

January 2016 alone claimed the lives of 250 people on that particular sea crossing. The rector of the University of the Aegean (based in Mytilene), Stephanos Gritzalis, distressed at the tragedies unfurling almost daily in the nearby waters, quoted

Aeschylus's *Agamemnon,* hoping that (in Greek) "we would cease to see 'the Aegean blossoming with bodies.'" But he was also quoting Seferis, who himself borrows that line for his famous poem of exile, "In the Manner of G.S." — a poem that contains the line "Wherever I go Greece wounds me." I began to see several things at once: that children the age of my own children were drowning in the same waters we swam in for recreation; that this migration was part of a continuous history of Aegean migration, war, violence, and exile that stretched back farther than the *Iliad;* and that poetry had long been its witness. Could I read the *Iliad* the same way again, realizing that the violent backstory to the wrath of Achilles had to do with the raiding of towns on Lesbos and on the shore just across, in modern Turkey, this same stretch of water?

But then a second issue arose: How do you write about such things — assuming you are moved to address them in poetry — without exploiting the stories of others? How do you achieve the necessary distance and perspective while confronting what were current events? As news stories from local Facebook volunteer groups about drowned children infiltrated my subconscious, seeping into my dreams, I also began thinking about the word "empathy" — a word coined in English in 1909 on the model of the German term *Einfühlung,* but which in modern Greek still carries a negative sense — to feel passionately *towards* or *against* someone. This poem tried to position my family's own luck with respect to the plight of families we were reading about, or, in the case of my husband, reporting on:

Empathy

My love, I'm grateful tonight
Our listing bed isn't a raft
Precariously adrift
As we dodge the coast-guard light,

And clasp hold of a girl and a boy.
I'm glad that we didn't wake

Our kids in the thin hours, to take
Not a thing, not a favorite toy,

And we didn't hand over our cash
To one of the smuggling rackets,
That we didn't buy cheap lifejackets
No better than bright orange trash

And less buoyant. I'm glad that the dark
Above us, is not deeply twinned
Beneath us, and moiled with wind,
And we don't scan the sky for a mark,

Any mark, that demarcates a shore
As the dinghy starts taking on water.
I'm glad that our six-year-old daughter,
Who can't swim, is a foot off the floor

In the bottom bunk, and our son
With his broken arm's high and dry,
That the ceiling is not seeping sky,
With our journey but hardly begun.

Empathy isn't generous,
It's selfish. It's not being nice
To say I would pay any price
Not to be those who'd die to be us.

Another way of achieving some distance was form itself: the "as-bestos gloves" Adrienne Rich speaks of in picking up materials that cannot be touched "bare handed." The drowned often end-ed up in unmarked graves, and I began to think that the form for dealing with the almost daily shock and horror of learning of new deaths was that ancient form from the *Greek Anthology*: the epitaph and the epigram. The *Greek Anthology* was itself full of epitaphs for the drowned, for instance for a maiden, Lysidice, from Cyme, a city on the coast of Asia Minor, washed up on a beach after a shipwreck, or a fisherman, swamped in a storm, whose body washes ashore with his hand eaten away by fish. These events were not only the stuff of history or legend, but, as so much of the literature of the Aegean, things that were simply still happening.

Epigrams also often had a wry twist to them, as the fisherman nibbled by fish: A grim irony often struck me as the only way to deal with the bureaucratic absurdities that led to such senseless loss of life. I began writing these every few days, a way of noting down and processing and marking these events. The best of these I eventually compiled into a single "poem," using the *Agamemnon* quotation as an epigraph, and ending on a parody of Simonides:

Aegean Epigrams[3]

"We beheld the Aegean blossoming with bodies." — Aeschylus, *Agamemnon*

Upon an unseaworthy wooden vessel

Call it a tub, call it a casket,
(And all their eggs tucked in this basket.)

The woman from Leros

The woman from Leros said:
"Small bodies wash ashore,
Sea-chewed, a few days dead.
I don't eat fish anymore."

---

3   A.E. Stallings, "Aegean Epigrams," Section 3 of "Refugee Fugue," in *Like* (Farrar, Straus and Giroux, 2018). The translation of Aeschylus is my own.

378

From an autopsy report of an unknown drowning victim, Ikaria:[4]

Female. Nine years old. Found wearing a blouse,
And a pair of sweatpants patched with Minnie Mouse.

Duties

Which one seems more chilling:
Copenhagen willing
To confiscate cash and bauble
From Mosul, Homs, and Kabul;
Or smugglers making a killing
Palming Charon's obol?

Fathomless

A fathom deep, the body lies, beyond all helps and harms,
Unfathomable, unfathomable, the news repeats, like charms,
Forgetting that "to fathom" is to hold within your arms.

Word problem

The 21-foot-long dinghy can hold up to 30 people, max.
If you squeeze on 64, wave a 9 millimeter at their backs,
In 6 Beaufort, 2 nautical miles out into international waters,
Which do you not save first — infants, sons, mothers, fathers, daughters?

Paradox

Of the ones that happened to die, the little ones and the old,

---

4 I should note that the doctor who performed this autopsy, John Tripoulas, is himself a poet and has written his own poem on this, "Faces Are Silent Words," in *Polytropos: Poems* (Dos Madres Press, 2024).

By hypothermia, or drowning, all died of cold.

Nothing to declare

As if in a sea of red tape
The faulty life-jackets tossed:
There is no custom house, no guards,
At the border these have crossed.

Proposed epitaph for drowned refugee children

Go tell the bureaucrats, passerby, that all is shipshape, fine.
The stuff that trickles from your eye is only a little brine.

Another form that suggested itself to me, that also works by
a wry, ironic twist, was the literary blues form. Perhaps I had
been thinking of it because of Auden's "Refugee Blues," although
Auden's poem does not really strictly adhere to the American
form. But it was also the blue of the Aegean itself — those gor-
geous, wine-bright, intense blues, where my children would
splash, and make and destroy sandcastles (whenever I would
watch them doing this, I would also think of that striking simile
in Book 15 of the *Iliad,* where Apollo casts down walls like a
child kicking over a sandcastle), that same water that ribboned
round the limbs of drowned refugee children. "Aegean Blues"
came out of these thoughts, and was even set to music, by musician and poet Andrew Shields of the Human Shields:

Aegean Blues

The sea is for holidaymakers, summer on the beach,
Surely there is space enough to spread a towel for each;
Dry land isn't something you should pray to reach.

Look, how glad our kids are, making their sandy town,

And how they build the battlements the laughing waves tear
down.
But it's the self-same water, where some swim, and others
drown.

The sea is full of dangers, the shallows and the deep.
The sea is full of treasures, down there five fathoms deep,
The sea is full of salt: there are no more tears to weep.

The ferryman says we cross tonight; and everyone pays cash.
Charon don't take Mastercard, you have to pay him cash.
The water seems so calm tonight, you hardly hear the splash.

There was a boy named Icarus; old Daedalus's son,
Turned into a waxwing, black against the sun.
He drowned because he tried to fly. (He's not the only one.)

Why would a kid lie in the sand, and not take off his shoes?
Why would he lie there face down, the color of a bruise?
The sea can make you carefree, nothing left to lose.

There's indigo and turquoise, there's cobalt, sapphire, navy,
And there's a dark like wine, my love, out where things get
wavy.
Listen, that's the worry note, reminds me of my baby.

As I became involved in volunteer work with refugees in Athens, and I became more personally involved with people and their stories, I was often struck by the place names, often part of the wider Greek world of Cavafy's Levant. I sometimes felt that we had all become characters in Cavafy poems, as when I spoke with a Syrian sculptor living in squalid conditions in one of the refugee "squats" in central Athens. I found myself putting his story into the form of a Cavafy poem, dividing the lines as Cavafy does in some poems that are about divisions and broken lives:

Days of 2016

He'd been a sculptor   on a small scale
In a town south of Damascus.   He'd worked in stone.
His masterpiece, he said   was a mother and child
no bigger than this   and showed his fingernail.

The tools he needed   were like the tools used
by opticians, tiny screwdrivers   little files;
rubble, stone he could find   even here in Athens,
in this shabby neighborhood.   Sometimes he mused

in front of the figures,   marble and white-eyed,
on days when the museum was free   statues larger than men
but broken-limbed youths   magnified with Time
older by aeons   than many who have died.

His children, his wife were safe: praise be to God!
But so much had been destroyed   his life's work lost.
The Lion consumed all!   Lion, he said.
That's what it means, in   Arabic: Assad.

On another occasion, I was speaking to a young Syrian man, whose graduate studies in English literature had been interrupted by the war, at the same squat, and he exclaimed, in English, exactly this: "I want to go to another land!" How could I not hear it as the opening of Cavafy's "The City," in Evangelos Sachperoglou's translation. Cavafy's poem, about how life and youth leaks away in waiting, had come for me to embody the despair of the young refugees in their twenties, their lives stalled right at the point they should be blossoming. I ended up versifying this conversation (perhaps not very successfully) as a kind of adaptation of Cavafy's poem, beginning, "I want to go to another land. I want to cross the border."

In some ways I think the form that most defined this era for me in the refugee crisis and in volunteer work was the list — one of the most ancient forms of poetry there is, if we grace it with the Homeric "catalogue," as his list of ships that crossed the sea on the expedition to Troy. Lists might include what ships were coming into Piraeus from the islands, what times, how many refugees were aboard, and from what countries.

Lists also became needs lists. When the border with Europe shut on March 20, 2016, Piraeus suddenly became a tent city. And needs changed as the weather changed, and as people stayed longer: first sleeping bags and tents and food, then laundry soap and lice shampoo and medicine, then diapers and milk for newborns, short-sleeved shirts, sunscreen, flip-flops. As a poet, it was hard not to read the lists as poems, and in the end I ended up borrowing one almost wholesale as a found poem, "APPENDIX A: USEFUL PHRASES IN ARABIC, FARSI/DARI AND GREEK, from the Guide to Volunteering in Athens, as updated for March 17, 2016." "Welcome to Greece!" it begins, and after a litany of many needs and potentially useful phrases, concludes:

What country is your family from?
pharmacy
medicine
hospital
doctor
tent
sorry, it has run out
we do not have it now
new shoes only if yours are broken
wait here, please
I will return soon
Follow me / come with me
Come back in...
5 / 15 / 45 minutes
one hour
quarter / half hour / half day
today / tomorrow / yesterday
How many people?
Sorry

Stay calm
One line, please

Next person

The Aegean crossing remains among the most dangerous refugee routes in the world, and a terror that nearly ever asylum-seeker in Greece has undergone. At the squat where I volunteered, very young children would sometimes draw harrowing pictures of the sea crossing, sometimes with brown, lifeless figures face down in the water, or with a Turkish coastguard boat trying to sink them with a fire hose. Or a girl drew female figures in the water struggling to swim, pulled down by their long robes and veils. Women at the poetry workshop I was running at Melissa often returned to the subject of the perilous sea voyage.

One news item in particular got my attention in 2017 — a Turkish music student, Baris Yazgi, had drowned in the crossing, his body washed ashore with his violin.

Unusually, this was a case where the name and something of the life of the drowning victim was known. The poet in me knew there was a poem there, but it was not an epigram, or a list. In the end, I started thinking of the myth of another musician, Arion, who, being trafficked by pirates, was thrown overboard, only to be saved by dolphins who had heard his beautiful singing. It had been a while since I had researched this myth, but I was immediately struck by the fact that he was "Arion of Lesbos."

Baris Yazgi was not saved by dolphins of course, but part of the magic spell of poetry is holding ajar the door to a universe where, contrary to fact, such a miracle could have happened.

I hope it is not just the myth at work here, but the vocabulary of instrumental music that has so much resonance with the crossing of water — "sound" here doing its double duty, as well as scales, vessel, pitch, and bridge, and even, at least on the page, "bow."

This poem appeared, under a slightly different title, in the *New York Review of Books,* and was shared over Twitter. As a result, it caught the eye of some exiled Turkish journalists who, in turn, translated the poem into Turkish and shared it online again. As the poem crossed over from English to Turkish, with its cargo of music and myth (inevitably shedding the multivalence of the English puns), my hope was that perhaps someday it might travel to the young man's family, letting them know that his death was noted, he was not another nameless among the numbers.

For a Young Turkish Violinist, Drowned on the Aegean Crossing (4 May, 2017)
(i.m. Baris Yazgi)

Reports said you were found
Clutching the case
Containing your instrument as well
As music of your own composition.

You knew what it was to place
Faith in a hollow wooden vessel,
Carried on waves, lilting in harmonic motion,
Scales like water running through your fingers.

I think of Arion of Lesbos, and his harp,
Saved by a dolphin in the legend;
Of accidentals, flat and sharp,

Of pitch, and yaw. I think of the deep sound,
Of the bow rolling across arpeggios,
No bridge but the violin's bridge.

Bibliography

Conrad, Joseph. *The Mirror of the Sea*. Doubleday, Doran & Company, 1928.

Stallings, A.E. *Like*. Farrar, Straus and Giroux, 2018.

Tripoulas, John. *Polytropos: Poems*. Dos Madres Press, 2024.

25

Oltre Mare
(after Baxendall and St Clair)

Rachel Spence

Where does an image begin? A poem end?

Suppose I were to begin by saying you will never know me. Will you listen anyway?

He painted me in Venice,
                    city of crossings.

Before Constantinople's fall in 1453, the only Venetian architects to go further east than Byzantium were the boatbuilders aboard the galleys. Some scholars believe one of these men used his knowledge of shipbuilding to transcribe the pointed arches he saw everywhere about him in the Arab world.

   I remember   windows.

he was a little on the dark side ... since Jews tend to be dark and she was a Jewess.

He knew this. Whitened me anyway.

Listen to my shawl, the whisper of its warp and weft.

Blue new world.
Whole blue world.
Brave blue world.

Hues were not equal, were not perceived as equal.

Nothing is equal.

There are three levels of adoration: latria *is the ultimate worship due only to the Trinity;* dulia *is what we owe the Saints, Angels, and Fathers;* hyperdulia i*s a more intense form of this due to the Virgin alone.*

Only ultramarine would do.

Most of it came from a single source — the Sar-e-sang mines. Tucked in the mountainous folds of Afghanistan. The Venetian explorer Marco Polo, who visited in 1271, wrote of a *high mountain out of which the best and finest blue is mined.*

Sometimes I'd throw my mind out of the studio
onto the *fondamenta* that bordered the lagoon.
The Dolomites like smoke or ash.

Beyond the sea.

Wrong sea. Wrong mountains. Wrong blue. But still,
a whiff of elsewhere. Cooling as iced water in August
when Venice curdles.

The Silk Road, which runs through the mountains of the Hindu Kush, was used by the caravans that shuttled goods between East

*and West. Ultramarine was first bumped along the Silk Road by
donkey and camel in the forms of lumps of lapis lazuli.*

Almost everyone comes from somewhere else. Erasures like
a palimpsest. One forgetting layered on another. Absence
becoming its own foundation. The ground beneath your feet
a disappearing act. Your life a work of levitation. Unwritten.
Unmapped.

*When these reached the Mediterranean coast in Syria they were
loaded onto ships bound for Venice.*

Syria.

For those few hours, there was not even a sea
between us.

Bibliography

Baxandall, Michael. *Painting and Experience in Fifteenth Century Italy: A Primer in the Social History of Pictorial Style*. Oxford University Press, 1972.

St. Clair, Kassia. *The Secret Lives of Color*. John Murray, 2016.

26

After an Unspeaking[1]

Anthony Vahni Capildeo

This is the circus for dead horses only
We are in a tent but there is no outside
                              no breathable outside
There is mud and stars but no ticket-seller
                              and no in-between atmosphere
Somebody uncertainly approaching certainly could not stand up
The mud would suck him down
The stars would suck her up
This is the circus of exclusions, not approximations
The dead horses canter at a soft pace
                              satin around their hooves
The dead horses jump from buckets, landing softly
                              taffeta over the sawdust
This is the trick of assertions without any ground
                              no overlap with anywhere
Your city exists and is unaffected by the circus
                              don't be mean about the ribbons

---

1   This poem was previously published in Vahni Capildeo, *Like A Tree Walk-ing* (Carcanet Press, 2021). It is reprinted by kind permission of Carcanet Press.

If they mean nothing to you, they should mean nothing to you
What if the ribbons are in this temporary atmosphere
                              in the only atmosphere
The symbol of grace
But I am breathing sawdust and I cannot see sawdust
                              and my pockets are full of receipts
But twigs are clinging to my clothes and the tent-pole is not a
tree
                              leaves are on my shoulders like
                              expired tickets
And I am fond of horses, even these ones grinning without
                                        stopping…
How did you get here? You did very well to get in
We have to muffle their hooves. They might have to cross a frozen
                                        river
Hooves muffled as if with eastern basketwork, yes eastern
                              enclosed horses
                              far-distant horses

I was in an airport and a man said it was all about him
He was the colour of a number of ladies' perfume boxes
                              duty-free, rosy with broken veins
He was lyrical, it was only him and the girl behind the counter
His instant love went into a box and into another box and into
                              would you guess it

A third box
But by the final couplet he was alone again
His solitude took up all the lounging space in the airport
                              paid and free
And none of the security cameras, only the girl's insecurity
                                        non-cameras

Occupied themselves with him
Throughout the numerous terminals
Ignorable special gift displays, his timeless well-stacked gift
                                        replay

And one thing I surely can tell you
This is what romance looks like and you had better review it
in print
For throughout the numerous terminals
he was innumerably unpolitical
He was a poet and worked as a poet and this is how poetry works:
the girl answered him blushingly
perplexed in all the right ways
I don't have her training, I don't know what she said
I don't take your word for her lines or that I no longer resemble
My passport photograph

potentially unpoetic
actually a serious problem
By now he's in a magazine as well as being in a faster queue
pearling along without price
almost but not quite beyond purchase
Would you ransom him perfect-bound
does she have his digits
You would be right to call me bitter but I don't care
That the female security guard is feeling up my tights
Electric blue and black stripes, my foot on a stool like a little
bucket
So long as there's a café on the other side
I don't care
My I.D. is uncertain but like a certain kind of poet I want caffeine
nothing has killed my want of
caffeine
Bring me a horse as well, why not, I am ancestrally out for stars

What was wonderful was to find war could involve neither
death nor waiting
Because everyone was long dead and in translation
Still I dare not inform the prophetess that she is no more
A series of epithets, no more than a series of epithets
with her burning hair
she eats time like air
And never looked forward to being in a poem

So long dead, so often in translation
                                        as not to be political
I suppose she did look forward to being history
Which is not the same, cantering at a soft pace
Which is not the same, reaching down for the stars in a sky-
facing bucket
                        tented over
                        void-filled to the rim
I wanted at least a blanket to give her in this cold and quilted
                                                                circus
But she already was holding out the purple veil she kept for
                                                                spare
And I had given away my sword, a real-life event
                        best left without record
For so long its curvature had been my security though now I
                                                                hold
                to other things
And couldn't prove what was gone, having no proof in my
                                                                possession
No proof of the bird-head hilt and sharp curve as ever in my
                                                                possession
                        and it was the wrong kind of sword
The trick of disappearing was neither hers nor mine
                        only words
For to point out what isn't there in a gently textiled circus
                is political if ever under review
A good review at minimum three days' work, how beautiful
                without pay

This is why please do not mention the ocean except as bluegreen
Whaleroad swanroad path of exile only for domesday-booked
                                                living bone
                        excise such crossing times as might be political
You must see it without the wrong ships in mind because
The ocean in a poem must not become political
                        and further
                        bluepurple

It is unfortunate your friend's book was political before it was born
Because of where he was born
        some places are political
Also his body thunders politics, let it remain dark in text
        some bodies are political
From their conception
        let them not imaginatively conceive
Though you know nobody brighter in love
In the camp as in the city, across the sea and across the desert
        no prizes for loving
We feel his love launched as if the political were personal
But haven't your missiles already landed?
How is your personal not political?
        free and spacious
        fine and small
Your poetry has the biggest free trade deal the world has ever
                 known
        unilateral and non-reciprocal
I am tuned in and hearing you musically the while you refuse
                 to know

When Fay Weldon's team came up with the slogan
'Go to work on an egg', did the Holy Spirit move them?
When some underling did the drapery for the luxury photograph
And leftover children at the hairdresser glimpsed infinity in the
                 purple waves
Who dare say the Holy Spirit did not move them?
Why are you bringing the Holy Spirit into this?
I didn't and if I did, I didn't understand you
I understand you didn't mean me to do this after you
        didn't bring, didn't dare bring…
As most people reading wouldn't
        wouldn't believe
Far less advertise the Holy Spirit
        like Duane Dove's fine flavour chocolate
        or a bar of Dove soap
And the signpainter who ought to have died but persists

In embarrassing and luckily undocumented environments
Shakes involuntarily in every part of his body except his brush-
                                                    hand
And the typographer who is much too young and persists
In collecting the signpainter's art for never-to-be-
                                        commercialized fonts
Is too close to the edge of the forest and too far into the city
To be a true artist. This is not true
Art. Make no mistake. True art
                    is otherwise
And on the curriculum and not without citation
And has a studio without needing a studio
                        nor dreams of demanding a studio
And the curriculum from which this poet learnt is cancelled
By time passing
                    and now not without citation
Don't touch me
this is no kind of office
Even if I walk to the lighthouse I only walk to the lighthouse
You have a card that opens the way to the river
The way to the river is closed
                    I don't have a card
Some movements are truer and more co-operative than others
Just look how
                    I've lost form

27

A Swelling Is Time

Yousif M. Qasmiyeh

The past, out of all times, is what can be seen in eyes long gone.

To see the past as a happening in its shade, my mother would carefully sieve our UN-gifted seeds... The dry for us and the hovering bits for the birds that never were.

What we ate was what she planted in secret under her pillow: remains of nothing in the shape of distant prayers.

> *I was not alone.*
> *My mother, with a cane and her poor eyesight, was to my right*
> *[Nothing to our left]*
> *Now I hold her by the hand like a drifting sound*
> *heart to heart, throat to throat*
> *to walk together as incomplete selves*
> *Bodies hung by thin air*
> *The sweat of old age and time*
> *Suspended returns to the eyes that once saw.*

You say to the clock hung adjacent to all religious things in the only room: my time is a swelling, my mother's yeast for the aged bread left aside as proof for time.

Nothingness, hide not in imagination. Nor ascend the psalms of night. What is left, for you and me, is the suspicion in suspicion.

When the sky is just a crow, with air raids as infinite as their ruins, the body's task is to ponder its body: here, in this place, people ascend to normality on crutches.

Only a body feasts on the body.

I shall imagine my tongue drowning in languages that are not mine so I would speak in water.

Seeing is the thing's substitute. What is deferred in seeing is the thing for its only time.

To pretend not to see what is amassing in your hands while what you carry is just a heart barely attached to your body. To pretend that all is well for once while they prod you from the back to remind you that it was time to look.

I ask — a question for me: What it is in writing that has no such thing as a present but is written — solely written — for a future subject to many pasts?

They would normally write their names in graphite so they would rub them out and write them again as names for suspected names.

I begged her to take me with her. Then, I could see what she could do to her eyes in wakes: tears in the aftermath of tears, her veil slowly unravelling, two edges caressing the dead's face.

What the eyes could see was not all. There were many. Some carrying what they could in haste: sponge mattresses, plastic bags stuffed with memories, kids on backs and in slings…It was in the dead of night when almighty shrieks were heard. As recounted by my mother, it was my father who first ran to find out. When he returned, sweat pouring down his face and elapsed body, he uttered no words. Instead, he pulled the bed sheet over his face to sob alone.

Whose eyes are forever stones? In Arabic, tombstones are also witnesses.

Tears are gifts to the blind.

The bird that lost its way into the camp was chased by screaming children until it died.

The same bird was not announced dead. For it to become permissible to eat, it is to be slain in the future.

To this day, in the camp the word "origin" is used as a tense. In those distant and near origins, time pronounces its face in the absence of a body.

It is the camp that makes Palestine near. When we say the camp, we say what it is that is not a camp.

To become a camp is to come and become simultaneously.

In poetry, the wound is continuously postponed.

28

Poem for the One Who Has Just Arrived

Bhanu Kapil

Write a sentence on a windowsill
with your fingertip,
articulating dust.

Is it raining in a book
you haven't written yet?

Write a sentence
on the glass,
in January, when the heat
in the room
combines with your breath
to make steam.

Are you waiting
for someone?

With your back
to the camera,

CROSSINGS

write a sentence in pencil
on the table,
so lightly
it doesn't leave a mark.

There's no book.
Now it's June.

Write a sentence
on the stem
of the lime-pink reed
poking up
from the fountain.

Who is this writing
for?

A light blue line
in an exercise book
belonging to a child
resembles a vein,
stabilizes script.

Keep writing.
Stop.

Write a sentence
on your arm, your leg,
your torso,
the sole of your foot
with a borrowed pen.

Then hold the page up
to the light.

As if the sun
has a memory
of you.

And not the other way around.

29

Mishearing: A Traversal

Amit Chaudhuri in conversation with Subha Mukherji

SUBHA MUKHERJI: Amit, as I've thought of "sound crossings" in the context of migrant forms, your "Misheard Tunes" have repeatedly come to my mind and reverberated. Tell me: what's the idea behind this project?

AMIT CHAUDHURI: The project on "mishearing" comes out of a series of fitful reroutings in my musical life, turns which I would never have predicted. It also comes out of growing up in metropolitan Mumbai in the 1960s and '70s, and, of course, travelling to England, which made me aware again of so many things without me being aware that I was becoming aware, including the English language itself.

SM: Would you say that your musical and linguistic or literary turns are parts of the same imaginative movement?

AC: Yes! I've written about this in my novel *Odysseus Abroad* (2014), where the main character, a young Bengali student, looks at Shakespeare's "Shall I compare thee to a summer's day?" again when he is in London, especially the words "summer" and "fair," which had no meaning for him earlier, any more than the justice of "temperate" did. Alongside language, I began to think about musical reroutings too. My mother was a great singer of the modern Bengali art song — songs by Tagore, Atulprasad, and Nazrul. I had heard her ever since I was a child, but I had no interest in Indian music then. However, I was drawn to the songs of a film called *Sangam* when I was three. By the time I was six or seven, we acquired a hi-fi and a couple of LPs which included *The Best of The Who*, through which I got into pop and rock music. That consumed me. Ma tried to teach me Tagore songs: I would sit and learn, and then run away.

In the '70s I developed an interest in American folk music, and in the singer-songwriter as a model: not so much Bob Dylan as Neil Young, Joni Mitchell, and James Taylor. Around the age of sixteen, I began to compose songs on the guitar and broadcast these on the radio as well. At that time, however, I also became interested in Hindustani classical music. So when I had just got into Junior College, my mother began to be taught *bhajans* and *ghazals* by a new teacher, Govind Prasad Jaipurwale. Listening to him, I was very struck by the way he could modulate his voice to do various things. He could — in what we call improvisation — add and change a phrase. The same phrase would be sung, but the next time he sang it in a slightly different kind of way. Around the same time, I also began to listen to *raag*-based songs (or "raga," the term used in the West), making discoveries. I continued to play the guitar, compose, and sing, on my quest to be a Canadian singer-songwriter! But this other thing was taking over, and with it an almost religious vision of Hindustani classical music as somehow being connected to my universe in a way that Neil Young, say, wasn't. This was accentuated by my discovery of Indian music's peculiar relationship to the universe in the sense that raags are sung at particular times of day and during particular seasons. That made me think of this music and its relation to the sounds and the times of day that I had experienced as a child, and later, as a young man, in the twenty-fifth-story flat in Maker Towers in Mumbai.

I rethought and rearticulated these experiences in a different way in the light of my discovery of the *raag*. And I began to gradually give up the guitar. At Junior College, I planned, instead, to do A-levels in order to go to England and develop my career in poetry. In fact, I gave most of my time to Hindustani classical music *riyaaz* (practice) and stopped socializing. My only friends were the family that taught me music, who played the tabla and the harmonium, and my parents — till 1983 when I went off to England.

By then, I had begun to shed my records — selling some of my rock collection. When I arrived in London, the rock phase was over in the world, or seemed to be, as was the singer-songwriter phase. A new kind of music had come into being in the 1980s, one that I felt no connection with; the same with disco. Instead, I got deeper and deeper into Hindustani classical music. From 1983 to almost 1999 when we officially came back to India, I didn't listen to Western music at all. My daughter Radha, born in '99, was about six months old when I decided to investigate my old record collection, because by this time I had lost that earlier zeal of the convert. Another thing I did was buy a cassette of Jimi Hendrix's posthumously released blues collection. I remember sitting and listening to this cassette and realizing something obvious which I had never realized before: that the blues is a five-note or pentatonic scale which is identical to certain well-known raags. The other thing is that the blues guitarist employs "bent" notes: instead of going from one string to the other down the fret, which is what classical guitar is all about, the rock or blues guitarist sometimes pulls the string sideways to create that *meend* (or glide).

sm: Can you tell me more about these "bent" notes?

ac: So you can produce a kind of slightly anodyne version of the glissando by going up the fret. But a far more expressive way of moving from one note to another — a neighboring note — is by creating a bent note and pulling the string. Sitar players have developed the technique after Vilayat Khan, who was pulling the string to an incredible degree of complexity to produce the embellishments of the voice on the instrument, stretching one note into other notes. The bent notes produced by Hendrix cannot do what the sitar has achieved in Indian classical music, in keeping the example of the human voice. The guitar is not equipped for that. However, it produces some bent notes, and those bent notes reminded me of the meend. As I was listening to that, I began to hear one thing in another. A week or two later, I was singing this raag which I sang right now, and some of the notes I was singing reminded me of the riff to "Layla" by Derek and the Dominoes, Eric Clapton's 1970 band; I heard the overlap because I'd been listening in that new way. And I must have been listening in that new way because I'd had such distance from that music which I'd once grown up with.

SM: That's the distance where metaphor is born. And without that distance, there can't be a crossing, right? Can you tell me a bit about sound crossings in your music — the music you hear and the music you make? What knowledges and memories play into it? And what *forms* are forged in this interspace?

AC: A particular space in which two different musical sounds and musical systems come together unexpectedly: that spatial continuum is what I find generative. A kind of simultaneity that exists in a present moment, a specific temporality, but one which also involves a sense of the spatial. An encounter rather than a recollection; an act of coming upon — like the old man in Ingmar Bergman's *Wild Strawberries,* stumbling upon his past self. A space and a moment where I began to see similarities and possibilities which could not be researched or looked for through an act of the will.

SM: Would you say this music is more found than made?

AC: Yes, it is found, which is why I call my second CD *Found Music.* So many things happened when I moved back to Calcutta in '99. I'd had enough of Margaret Thatcher's and Tony Blair's England. And I thought: there is nothing for me here, I want to go back to somewhere where, even if it's a backwater, there are some discoveries for me to make. Then I also felt the huge constraint of being a novelist, and being known as a novelist. This is an extremely artificial paradigm created by the market, where one declares oneself a novelist by producing novels periodically, and I wanted to break out of that. I began to write short stories and essays. On some level I must have opened myself to the idea of formal experimentation, of being released from the very professionalized constraints that had been imposed on artists. The free market seemed to want to weed out the untidiness of creativity, the unpredictability of it, the way it is often governed by chance.

SM: That's another question I wanted to ask: what role is played by chance in these mishearings? There seems to be a quality of unplanned happening about them. When you first became aware of this as a concept — as you say — while not being aware of it, did it strike you as something you could control in some way? Or do you just stay open and let it happen to you?

AC: As I began to create the repertoire, I became aware of the potential for rediscovering and reusing found material (though I was blissfully unaware of the term "found object"). Around 2004 I began to meet with musicians in Calcutta to put together something, and I began to explain to them what I had in mind. Of course, what I had in mind at the beginning was hearing Eric Clapton's "Layla" riff in the raag "Todi," and how that became the basis of a composition. But then the second mishearing happened in the foyer of the then new ITC Sonar Bangla. Emerging into the lobby where the *santoor* (a Kashmiri musical instrument) was playing as it often does in hotel lobbies, it seemed to me suddenly that the santoor had begun to play "Auld Lang Syne." Now that happened because the santoor was playing a folk major pentatonic, found in raags "Bhopali" and "Pahari"; and "Auld Lang Syne" is based on the same structure.

SM: Are these heard affinities about discovering a pattern which already existed, or about accident?

AC: Accident and chance and found material became very important to me, beginning with "Layla" and "Auld Lang Syne." "Summertime" came into existence because I could hear raag "Malkauns" in it and I told my accompanying musicians that this is how I wanted to structure it. Then one day I was walking on Park Street and I began to hear the theme to All India Radio but played in a different raag in my head. And I thought, I would like this to be heard in a jazz context where I can improvise on this theme tune....

SM: You became aware of this possibility, but you were also aware that all you can do is be receptive: it had to come to you. You can't do a misheard song by commission, can you? But did it induce a different attention or attunement, did it change you as an artist or in the way you hear things? Is there a conceptual connection between your musical migrations and the way your imagination works as a writer?

AC: It brought out things in me as an artist which were latent. One of them is that creativity and thinking are not two different things: the imagination and the critical faculty are the same thing in many different ways.

SM: Do we mishear in the same way as we misread? Is there something specific, or maybe somatic, about mishearing that sets it apart? We all read with an intertextual awareness, but somehow we don't necessarily do that with music. Do you think that there's a kind of influence one way or the other? Because you've just said that the two are not separate things and yet there seems to be something quite specific and minute about the act of mishearing which seems new in a way that making connections between writers doesn't.

AC: I realized that receptivity was always important to me, as was listening. I'm a writer of non-narrative fiction, which is a paradox, and I look to a form of receptivity which allows one to find excitement in the unnoticed. That creates an energy unavailable in narrative. For me narrative is dead, it's a synonym for a static construct. And it's only what is on the edge of narrative that, for me, is exciting. Listening is similar, and in India we're listening all the time...which means that our worlds are only very partially visible. The ear is registering what is invisible and its ongoing transactions all the time. I realized this especially, again, after being in a closed space in England where the lifting up of the window was a letting in of something else. Coming to India after living in that kind of space, I found that to be conscious is also to be distracted.

SM: So it's partly about capturing the poetic life of distraction! But also about the role of an amphibian life — living in, or between, two places — in this kind of receptivity. Would you say that having lived and worked in the UK as well as in India, across different phases of your life, is also a vital crossing that enables the attunement you need to mishear creatively?

AC: I doubt that the "moment of mishearing" would have occurred had I not spent all those years in England during which I deliberately proscribed the music of my childhood and early teens (rock, pop, and American folk), dwelling only in the music I discovered from when I was sixteen years old (Hindustani classical, Tagore songs sung by my mother and Subinoy Roy, S.D. Burman's early recordings of Bengali *raagpradhan* or raag-dominant compositions, and Hindi film songs from the 1950s to the 1970s). There are many answers to your question, but this is the simplest one.

SM: I was asking you earlier about the relation between your literary reading and writing, and your musical mishearing. Do we mishear in the same way we misread?

AC: What I'm increasingly aware of is my interest in the blurring of the boundary between life and its representation — I discuss this in my seventh novel, *Friend of My Youth* (2017). This has always been of interest to me both in writing and in art, and especially in music. The *khayal,* in that it's not *about* a time of day (like morning or evening) or *about* a season (like spring), but *of* the day and *of* a season, dismantles whatever it is that separates an artifact from day-to-day existing. Our day and year and their specific periods (and, therefore, by extension, our life) is part of the raag's text rather than being exterior to it; that is, the time of day is not an *object* of representation as far as the raag is concerned. My inability to distinguish between "East" and "West," musical and non-musical sounds (I misheard the tune of a Vengaboys song in the tonal registers of a homeless person selling a newspaper in Berlin, resulting in the song "Motz"), means that, for me, the distinction between art and life is constantly becoming irrelevant. When you have narrative, you have a clearer sense of formal demarcation between what's represented and the representation itself. This is what I realize I have all along been questioning. Music from the Hindustani tradition taught me that music need not be mimetic, and that writing is not about life but a form of living.

sm: With the blurring of this distinction, does mishearing offer an alternative episteme? In our project, we've been thinking of the migrancy of knowledge, migrant knowledge, and the knowledge that migrants bring. Migrancy seems to us to be at the heart of the perceptual, creative act that constitutes your project too. Do you think that this makes musical knowledge different from the way we normally think about knowing? Not structured, generic, or representational…? There are knowledges in our heads — about contexts, traditions, and grammar — which are suddenly coming together and clicking into place in a particular relationship. As though one hadn't thought about it before, but suddenly one hears them speaking to each other, sees them within the same frame. A kind of Shakespearean double-seeing. You knew all the rock music and then you got into Hindustani music, and you resist narrative, but there *is* a narrative in that story, which is essentially an odyssey — a journey, a return, and a discovery and recognition — in a kind of cognitive event that you call a "moment of mishearing." What kinds of knowledge transactions are going on here? If you didn't, for instance, have the knowledge of Hindustani classical music the way you did — because you've studied it deeply — would you have heard the pentatonic affinities? Can *any*body "mishear"?

AC: In those moments where things open up, one begins to reassess one's thinking at a certain point of time. Hindustani classical music is not so much a form of knowledge to me as a form of reassessment. When I encountered it and began to learn it, there were certain questions which came to me. The first had to do with the lack of the composer as a central figure and the other had to do with the nonrepresentational quality of the raag. And yet it's embedded in, and related to, our everyday life. So in what way was it related if it was not in the single way that we had been told things are to be related through art, which is through representation? Even then I had to begin to rethink, without thinking I was rethinking, the concepts and knowledges that had been handed down to me by the European Renaissance's ideas of representation, and to an extent the Enlightenment's.

SM: Do you mean the mimetic theories of the period?

AC: Mimetic theories, and also what the images in Renaissance paintings were doing.

SM: I was thinking about images, because when we were talking about distraction I was thinking about all the little animals, the dogs and cats and also the servants and loaves of bread that you see in the margins of Renaissance classics — momentous Christian events like the Last Supper. They completely decenter the painting and scatter your attention, and you see differently.

AC: I suppose this long relearning through Indian classical music — becoming aware of fissures in the so-called Western tradition itself, and registering my primordial recoil against the Renaissance and its legacy — does have to do with centrality. The idea that this is the main figure in the painting, the rest is the background or in the margins. And with expression — faces expressing emotion. All this had to be thrown out. Even as I was writing my first two novels, I was giving much more time to the background than to the foreground, and I would have been aware of the prejudice all around me against privileging objects above writing about the emotional life of the human being.

Fusion comes out of ideas which have exactly this history. For example, Western music can have background and foreground. The chords can provide the harmonic setting for the melody in the foreground, and form part of "modal harmony" — an usually linear progression of chords, like clothes hung on a clothesline. Now we've already entered the domain which one is trying to break out of — a humanist domain where we're giving centrality to something and making assumptions about its integrity.

SM: So is non-fusion the resistance of integrity?

AC: It's resistance to various things of which this is one instance. Generally something has to be in the foreground and we identify it as the central thread or thing. Western classical music is governed by one particular standard, the natural C on the piano. Against it, you measure all the other notes and scales and compositions, whether it's an F sharp or C minor. There's no such thing in Hindustani classical music. The tonic is very important but it could be in any scale. Singing a raag is based on your awareness of the tonic and the interval and all the other notes, which form a constellation. You're also aware of everything you're hearing as you sing and how it connects to those notes, whether it disturbs them or not. A phone ringing could be ringing at *gandhaar* (the third) and an air-conditioner could be humming at *tivra ma* (the sharp fourth) or *ma* sharp, and if there is a *teevra ma* in the raag, then its fine, but if there's none, then it is a disturbance.

SM: This reminds me of your track on the Berlin U-Bahn!

AC: Yes — and it is already there in Hindustani classical music. Bharata (in the *Nāṭyaśāstra*) tells us about all the animal sounds — the peacock's cry, the elephant's trumpeting, the mooing of the cow — that have led to the seven notes, and so everything is alive and everything is text. That distinction between world and representation breaks down again! This is key to the mishearing project. Everything is music, and it goes back to the "found" object. If your mind has begun to listen to the world in that way, it is not surprising that you would hear the lower tonic to the upper tonic as the U-Bahn is moving into the station, and the sound that the doors make before they are closing — *ma* and *pa,* the fourth and the fifth notes.

SM: In the current political situation of the world, not just India, is there a particular potential and power in tuning ourselves into these mishearings, given how the project is rooted in the plural legacy of our musical tradition?

AC: I would, rather, like people to become more aware of the value of beauty. Of the traditions in modernity including Bangla, and the ones in Europe, including French and German, which accommodated the search for the beautiful and tested our capacities for enjoying it. At a certain point in time, a hostility to beauty came into existence. I used to notice this in the '80s: a kind of derision towards beauty, and a pointed glorification of the grotesque, a marginalization of the finer ways of listening and experiencing. This has now gone on for years, till we have almost forgotten how to listen, to read. And that leaves a great moral vacuum, I think.

SM: And a discursive embarrassment?

AC: An embarrassment that has led to an impoverishment of human experience. A vacuum in which there is no experience of delight.

sm: We have been thinking about physical crossings as a traumatic happening in the world. But your music taps into the play and joy in crossings inherent to certain art forms.

ac: I think the twentieth century (or maybe even from the Romantics onwards), despite all its traumas, really celebrates the delightful. Modernism itself is about delight. Once you shake it free from the narrative of its mimetic obligation to represent the traumas of the twentieth century, especially in Europe, you realize how much of its formal disjunctions have to do with play and liberation and joy. We have subsumed the narrative of modernism and its experimentations under the narrative of angst and abjection: this is not correct.

sm: So does a crossing over from the mimetic to the nonrepresentational find an embodiment in "mishearing" then? Thank you for the provocation, and the reminder that such a rerouting of the imagination leads to freedom and beauty, so that art's traversal becomes a principle of delight!

30

A Lot of Dirt

T.M. Krishna in conversation with Subha Mukherji

SUBHA MUKHERJI: I have a confession. I had never actually heard your music until the summer of 2019, as I was co-organizing the event Migrant Knowledge, bringing together artists, activists, and scholars to think about the condition of migrancy and its relation to forms of imagination and ways of knowing. It was like a miracle. Your music pierced me and spoke uncannily to the issues I was trying to think through. It was also, for me, a way of going back, of coming home. I wanted to begin the event by playing your rendering of "Dhano dhanya pushpe bhora." But most of the assembly didn't know Bengali or Tamil, so I hesitated. Then I thought: that is exactly the kind of crossing we need now, in the world we are living in. You were singing a patriotic Bengali song, familiar to us and dear to our hearts, in a style all of your own and in a language that was not your mother tongue, gloriously unconcerned with regionally specific musical *gayaki* (style). That defiant anti-grammar really spoke to me, because we Bengalis can be very parochial about our culture. Hearing you sing this song in the aftermath of India's revocation of Article 370 (which had, by constitution, granted Jammu and Kashmir special status and autonomy for some seven decades), it felt as though this was music finding its secular voice amidst the cacophony of Hindu nationalism. The way you claimed the song — it was an assertion of the intrinsic, inextricable braid which is our aesthetic legacy, a braid that our Hindu-supremacist government is trying to separate into strands artificially. But there was no arrogance about the act of claiming. Rather, there was a kind of love, a sweetness that seemed to come from the very act of crossing boundaries of state, politics, language, and religion: a sweetness that is in real danger of turning to gall in Narendra Modi's India. If there's a question here, it's about music and democracy. You have written about how your music breaks away from entrenched casteism and social hierarchies. Are these other "crossings" also part of the activism of your art, or is the art a more affective happening?

T.M. KRISHNA: I don't see any difference between art and activism, actually. The problem is in perception. To me, art and activism are about responding to that which is within and that which is outside, in a non-passive fashion.

SM: So it's an active response to the world?

TMK: That's all it is. Art is a human act, not something found in nature. We call some sounds music, but nature never categorizes. So music, or movement, or color, are an interesting recognition by the human species. In that recognition lies the possibility of change, of movement through deep feeling. It can be defiance, it can be a question, it can be a cajoling, it can be a nuance, it can be reinterpretation. The core is that it does something to our inner self; the beauty of art is its ability to induce a possibility of non-selfishness.

SM: The possibility of being "out of the self"?

TMK: Exactly! And I use "self" not just in the sense of the individual but also in a societal context, because the self is created by society. So, somehow a musical phrase or passage provides us the possibility of release from parochialism. Democracy also seeks to move us away from a reiteration of individual identity.

sm: Are writing, singing, and speaking different facets of the same act for you?

tmk: They are. But music is my tune, my window to life.

sm: But you have to tune in and listen, right?

tmk: I completely agree. I *think* musically in a fundamental fashion. Sometimes it's beneficial and sometimes it's a hindrance, because one of the problems of thinking musically is always remaining in the abstract. At times I am not tactile enough when writing, so I have to read it and acknowledge that it's not going to make sense or reach the reader in a comprehensible way — because I'm trying to make sense of it intellectually. Most of these understandings come only ex post facto. Democracy is at the base of all this for me — whether we are talking about caste, or religion, or transference. It took me time to recognize it as a conversation about democracy.

sm: Tell me a bit more about what you mean by "democracy"?

tmk: When I started singing in styles that were questioned, or with content that was questioned, or when I was asking questions about the world and the identities I inhabit, these were all acts of democracy. For long I struggled with the fact that most aesthetic conversations remain segregated from political dialogue. We very rarely recognize that the notion of ugliness, for example, comes from a very undemocratic impulse, and it slips through the conversations on equality. Maybe because I'm a musician I found that muddling the world of aesthetics was very important.

sm: And muddying it? Messing it up?

TMK: "Aesthetics" is a word that is rarely challenged, and that creates a hierarchy of aspiration which we never examine as being discriminatory and undemocratic in itself.

SM: Exactly, and the assumptions of superiority and refinement and vulgarity! I have, for instance, heard the term in Kolkata, doing wedding trousseau, "oh that's a crude green, a Muslim green." It's just a particular shade, but you're giving it an affiliation.

TMK: Yes, one of the problems is that so many things are taken to be sacrosanct and self-evidently sophisticated. For me the challenge is first to question the notion that there is something intrinsically special about anything we do: the world of Carnatic, or Hindustani, music, or whatever. We also need to find a way to hear from voices not normally heard. It's very easy for me now to step outside this world but I feel that it's very important that I remain in it. At the same time, being able to have conversations which are beyond this world will also empower other voices and enable many other aesthetics and sound worlds to emerge.

SM: That absolutely goes to the heart of it. The politics of it was, for me, the more expected bit. Given the timing of the particular performance of yours which we started with, of course it felt like a deeply political moment. What took me by surprise was the rawness of the emotion. It felt — and this may sound strange — almost like an act of faith in a world structured by rationalist hierarchy. As I played it, I choked up at one point. I wondered where that was coming from. My first feeling was embarrassment: "Oh my goodness, there are all these people in this room, and I'm choking up, *shit*." Then it did something electric, because it proved contagious. Suddenly it brought everyone together because it gave the audience permission to feel together. There's a discursive embarrassment about emotions, certainly in academia. I said to my friend Gil Harris who was in the room, and is in the little room of this book, "I messed up." And he said, "No, don't worry about it, because it actually broke down some barriers." And he added that he had, just a few days before, broken down giving a talk because he was — we all were — affected by Article 370, by what was happening in and to India. That moment was precious for me. That sense of community, and the way it grants permission to feel, resonated with what we had just observed: a kind of knowingness in your relation with your accompanists. In the video I saw and showed, the camera focused on the faces of the mrdangam-, violin-, and tanpura-players — who just stopped when you choked up and paused, looked at your face, took the cue from your expression and kept the bassline going as you were recomposing yourself. The distance between the soloist and the collective craft of music dissolved at that moment. To what extent is your music a communal practice and to what extent is it solitary? Who owns your music?

TMK: Ownership is very difficult to pin down. Any kind of single ownership is what I have tried to challenge. In any Carnatic concert there are four co-musicians. I changed the seating pattern first. We used to sit with the main performer — me, a vocalist — sitting right in the center; the violinist towards the left, mrdangam artist towards my right, both not facing the audience, instead facing me. The other instrumentalists were usually behind me. I decided one day to question how we sit on stage. I started arranging us much like a jazz quartet, in a "C" formation. It instantly moved me out of the center and I discovered how difficult that was for me. I had been so used to being at the center — its visual impact, its control, its power! The moment you twist, turn, and trouble power, something magical happens. And to question power is to question performance itself. The realization in such specific moments opens up to questions as huge as India, or Article 370.

SM: And this takes me to a question that came up for me — about vulnerability. The vulnerability I felt when I choked up was responding to yours — that moment in the concert which took away your power and opened you up.

421

TMK: I was going to use that word myself — "vulnerable." Until we become vulnerable, we don't do serious work, we only perform. Many great performers will tell you that art is an epiphany, but they are still in control. It's a paradoxical statement — fraudulent, even. The possibility of something profound happening opens only when you give up control, a fundamental condition for having a real conversation.

SM: Because conversation is about letting the other in....

TMK: That's where the meaning of a song lies, because that's where magic happens.

SM: The word "happen" is interesting: it's almost a passive thing. When you were caught in the raw in the middle of singing, that *happened* to you, unscripted. Are you in fact saying that the artist needs to surrender disbelief for magic to happen, that art is a form of dispossession, not possession?

TMK: Exactly.

SM: For me, listening to that song was a very embodied reality. I was moved by the way you move your hands, for instance. I felt that there was something in those gestures that was turning an act of resistance into a caress, as if you were gently pushing the music over and across a cultural border and letting it spill over an artificial dam. That made me wonder about the different boundaries that are crossed when art becomes a visceral experience. Working on drama, I'm very aware of the fourth wall — theater's broken when that wall isn't. How does the ecology of the musical event work for you? Do you traverse the fourth wall more easily than a professionalized singer? It struck me that so much of it was about presence, about being together, watching, and somebody engaging with their whole body. It's like the way Jacqueline du Pré used to play the cello. She threw her whole body into the playing, and it was such a generous act.

It also makes me wonder how you found the migration to online performance in the strange years of COVID-19?

TMK: The position that I write from in my book *A Southern Music* (2013) may be relevant here. There, I ask about the role of text in music; I discuss art music, how important semantics is, the meaning of the words, and meaning beyond semantics.

SM: What do you mean by "art music"?

TMK: For example, it's what I would call jazz, Carnatic, or Hindustani music. It's an old term and has been used in musicology for ages. The idea is that every form of art has intentionality. The intentionality is related to a cultural context, but it's also about form, structure, history, and aesthetics. I'll give you an example. If you look at Qawwali, Gospel music, and Hindu religious music, they all have the same intentionality: to make you feel divinity in a collective trance. The aesthetic structuring of these forms is similar, with repetition of certain lines, words, and tunes for congregational singing, and a lot of the "calling of the Lord." Now, how do you categorize Western classical music or Carnatic music? These forms do not have this kind of intentionality. Can we abstract literal human experience, beyond the literality of the event? Like a Pablo Picasso painting, say? The event may have inspired the context of the painting, but the painting takes you beyond the event, so art music will fall into that category. The difficulty in understanding or accepting this vis-à-vis Carnatic music especially is the fact that texts in nearly all our compositions are religious in nature. We forget that the texts also have an inbuilt syllabo-melodic aesthetic function. In India, post-1857, a lot of nationalistic conflations collapsed aesthetics into semantics. I argue in *A Southern Music* that the semantic meaning is irrelevant to art music. I can show you different examples of the same words sung in different tunes and different registers and ask you whether it's the same experience. It isn't, even if you know the meaning of the word. The question is "why do you have a different experience then?"

Although I still broadly stand by this view, I realized that there are some functional and structural issues that the argument didn't address — which boils down to the fact that the only way we understand the world is through the semantic. How do you get a person to move from word meaning to sonic, or abstract, meaning? That's when I started changing the lyrical content in Carnatic music. Suppose "Rama" gives you a profound experience, can we complicate that by making you respond with similar depth to things that you don't normally feel profound with or about? Then you create the possibility of profundity emerging from something else. That's when I started singing Islamic texts, Christian texts, and atheistic texts.

SM: Didn't some temple in Maryland cancel an event when you claimed Christian hymns as your own?

TMK: Oh yes, they cancelled my concert. I had security for that whole tour of the US, because there was a fear that I would be attacked.

SM: And you responded by saying you'd release a song on Jesus and on Allah every month! Did you?

TMK: Yes, I did it for eight months. It wasn't just a religious conversation; it was also about the hierarchy in dialect. For the first time in the history of Indian classical music, we sang a song that used the contemporary dialect of the common person. I had started working with writers to create content in dialects that are not usually part of this uppity world. It was a journey into multiplicity and diversity.

SM: Even the way you were turning a particular word when you were singing a familiar Bengali song — the very pronunciation, the rolling of a word slowly on your tongue, created an affective estrangement which opened up a whole new world. When you use that to dislocate music from its class and caste context, that's even more radical.

TMK: That's the most important part for me — that meaning is embedded in utterance. We unlock that every day; the way we say "ok" can mean a hundred things. Now imagine an aesthetic body through which you can celebrate that possibility. It starts moving, and in any direction, and I can almost taste sound on my tongue. The moment you allow for everything to *move* ... that is grammar.

SM: And isn't it lovely that the etymological Latin root of moving — as in "emotionally moving" — is *movere*, which is to actually cause movement?

TMK: Yes, I think grammar gives you everything possible to feel, but we never think of grammar that way.

SM: We think of it as a collection of rules, but you are saying that it's an affective tool?

TMK: Of course: when you're astounded by a passage, it is profound grammar. Anything we have experienced in seriousness, like a conversation, is so profoundly filled with form. For form is all grammar is. We make the same mistake in grammar and music as we do in literature — thinking of it as a dry toolkit. We have partitioned grammar and imagination into binaries. But it doesn't work that way. People ask me, "Are you traditional or radical as a musician?" I say I'm extremely traditional as a musician. Because I use "tradition" in its most profound sense, to mean connectivity. Besides, art need not always be pleasurable....

SM: Apropos, I wanted to come back to the matter of *mess* and disturbance and not just beauty. Remember that incident with the Carnatic singer who was barred entry into temples in Kerala because he had sung a hymn to Jesus? But Christian and Muslim participation in Carnatic music goes way back. I remember him saying he could have gone in if he were an insect — a housefly, for instance. I wonder, can music be an insect now, or even art more generally? Might a space be opening up for different forms of art to cross the thresholds between them and speak to each other, and to the inherent migrancy of forms? When we cross borders physically a great deal can be stripped from us. Not only our possessions but our language, our clothes, our baggage. What remains? What is ours that is inalienable? Imagination, stories, bodies perhaps; can this be collected and brought together to shore against our ruins in some ways?

TMK: I don't think we have a choice right now, do we? We have to find a way. And we need to resist the impulse that directs us towards immediate reward and prepare for a marathon which aims at longer-term, intangible rewards.

SM: We have never mined that potential, have we?

TMK: We have never respected the migrancy of people. We accepted it but we didn't respect it, and I think that is one of the big gaps that has allowed this right-wing, absolute, violent noise to emanate and almost establish itself as the identity of India. This is an important moment for shedding a lot of those accretions.

SM: And I think you'll find the migrancy of form meeting the migrancy of people, because there is something inherently mobile about certain forms. Think of ballads, or songs, or stories: they slip across borders no matter how rigorously you police them.

TMK: Absolutely. Carnatic music itself is completely migrant. But the question is: Am I going to acknowledge and respect its migrant nature? Am I going to actively work with it? The latter is crucial. And within that conversation lies those words that we use: vulnerability and surrender, disparity and dialogue. For instance, we have a project with the Jogappas — a small, transgender community living between the Karnataka–Maharashtra border, hugely marginalized and discriminated against. We are collaborating with them on a performance which taps into their ancient mythology and their goddess Yellamma. This migrancy, this vulnerability, has to be preserved and translated in the way we're engaging with the sounds the colors, the words, and the movements. In the long-term idea of a democratic India, this is the only way we can actually create a serious, aesthetic, social, political conversation.

SM: In the bleakest moments of this year, when you sang "Hum Dekhenge" — the song which had become the theme of the protest against the Citizenship Amendment Act and the National Register of Citizens — in four languages in Shaheen Bagh, where there was a vast but peaceful sit-in protest, mostly by working-class Muslim women, it was electrifying and contagious. It made me go to a protest march outside India House in London, and everyone burst into this song.

I noticed, when I saw the video of you at Shaheen Bagh, that you paused at one point and spoke to the audience: the wall broke and it became participatory. Given what you have done with the event of musical performance, can you ever go back to the proscenium stage, or do you need to reconfigure it?

TMK: What I do is try and find as many spaces as possible, all kinds of spaces — whether it's a bus, or a beach, or indeed the proscenium stage — and then let one seep into the other. Then the proscenium becomes easier to break down. When a person enters an opera house, the experience is already given, pre-known. Now suppose you mess up the fundamental notion of what should be experienced: everybody is lost and that's probably the best place to start.

SM: You want to get lost together! Now, I wanted to ask you a question about your book *Sebastian and Sons,* where you have written about the history of the mrdangam — made by Dalit ("untouchable") artisans. You've opened our eyes to how it originates in a field of violence. An animal is killed and its skin is flayed and cleaned to make the instrument. The association of music and its pleasure with violence and pain, of course, goes all the way back to ancient Greek mythology, hauntingly depicted in the Renaissance by Titian in his famous painting, *The Flaying of Marsyas.* Marsyas was a satyr — half-man, half-goat — who challenged the god Apollo and his skills at the lyre, boasting of the superiority of his rustic musical instrument, the AULOS, a kind of reed pipe or flute. Apollo won the musical duel and punished Marsyas for his hubris by flaying his skin from his body. Titian's painting shows a figure who is either Orpheus or Apollo — we're not sure — playing the lyre, creating beauty as Marsyas is being skinned. Marsyas's expression is strangely serene and detached. In Ovid's *Metamorphoses* (VI), he actually asks the question "why do you peel me out of myself?" He is the chosen one, in a sense, as well as the kill. This mythical moment has been interpreted variously as savage, transcendental, or a victory of the clarity of form over chaos, or of art over craft, *or* as a purification ritual which expunges the ego. But as the novelist Iris Murdoch is known to have said in many conversations, interviews and indeed, directly or indirectly in her novels, it is about anything *but* purity, it is about the hopelessly mixed condition of human life. Now this is one of the forms that the peculiar migrancy of music or indeed art takes. The way it travels between the slaughterhouse and the concert hall, the artisanal and the aesthetic, the material and the ethereal; the way it does not shy away from discomfort and messiness. Art abjures sanitization. Do you feel this impinging on the way you practice?

TMK: The realization of art is the realization of ugliness. It is not something outworldly, but grounded in the dust and the dirt of reality.

SM: You once said in an interview (in 2014) that there's "a lot of dirt" in Carnatic music.

TMK: Not just Carnatic music. There's dirt everywhere. I think *Sebastian and Sons,* apart from obviously engaging with the craft and the work, also engages with the impurity of life as its essential purity. To be able to grapple with the fact that you can't reconcile this, and yet you still seek a way of engaging with it with humanity and empathy.

SM: I have a personal childhood memory with a very literal association of dirt and music. Very near where I grew up in Kolkata there's a little shop called Hemen & Co. It's a tiny shop on a corner. I remember always seeing — I don't know what the technical term is — the swollen part of the sitar, of the tanpura resting on the dirt outside, at one stage in the making.

TMK: Oh I know the company, they make lovely tanpuras.

SM: They are still there. They have made thousands of instruments for famous musicians, and also for less famous singers like my mother! We always used to take our harmonium to Hemen & Co. It just makes me wonder at how ubiquitous the odd mixture of dust in Indian musical traditions is, and the contrast between the verticality of musical performances and the radical horizontality of the process of its making.

TMK: That's the great struggle, isn't it? Not just performance but the notion of the great artistic tradition itself is so vertical. When you look at the fundamental creations, they're all horizontal. There is something interesting that happens with instruments that are made of skin. As you come down the caste ladder, the difference between the maker and player keeps reducing. All Dalit percussionists make their own instruments ... who will make it for them? They have to be the performers and the makers.

SM: That's fascinating. To slightly shift the focus, have you consciously thought about translation as an act of reclaiming and sharing? So much of the beauty that you brought into the grit, the mud, the sweat, the congestion, the physical tribulation of that gathering at Shaheen Bagh lay in the fact that you were opening it up into these "impure" spaces. And in the way you

said "now I'll sing in Malayalam." The audience were just rap-
turous.

TMK: I think translation is an act of defiance, it's an act of recreation, it's an act of selflessness. It challenges power, it challenges
ownership, it challenges time, it challenges space....

SM: It challenges history....

TMK: It challenges everything. That day as I landed in Delhi
I suddenly thought, "there have been translations of the song
'Hum dekhenge'.... Why don't I just sing each verse in different
languages?" I quickly rallied and got them all together and, in a
way, it became a song by itself. So it was not just tied to a single location — translation widened its ambit and made it about
every person, irrespective of where you were, what language you
spoke. It was impossible to tell whose form it was.

SM: Ha — so translation evacuates authority out of the text and
almost forces it to be generous? That act of being able to give up
ownership, of being able to say, "OK, now it belongs to the world,
you do what you want with it."

TMK: This is very important when discussing democracy and
politics today, because we have lost this giving. We are still
talking about the original now, in this country and around the
world — whether it is about immigration, or about Hindu identity, or whatever. But there is no such thing.

SM: It's also tied up with that spurious notion of the *pure,* isn't
it? Since COVID-19 the word "migrant" has taken on resonances
in India that were previously unknown. The image of migrant
laborers walking hundreds of miles, thirsty, hungry, dropping
dead, trying to cross borders between states to get home, will
haunt our sleep forever. Now in the face of the humanitarian
tragedy triggered by all these theatrical, unplanned and yet at
the same time culpably late lockdowns, how can art take on the

right kind of migrancy to meet this reality, to give it form, to speak for it? What artforms are created by the phenomenon of migration, by our encounters with it, and in what forms do displaced people themselves find a voice? Crisis can energize aesthetic imagination, but how do we avoid parasitism and ensure synergy?

TMK: We don't realize that 98% of artists are not very different from daily-wagers or from agricultural laborers. They live on the margins and off that day's little performance. So their lives are usually culturally limited to certain geographical contexts, but they still have to travel to various villages to perform. Everything got shut down from March 2020. Migrant workers were stuck in their place of work, unable to go home, and moving artists were stuck in their homes, unable to move for work. This inversion was astounding, because we were listening to both voices. One of the things this has also shown us is that none of us have recognized every human being as a cultural being. Have we talked about migrant workers' cultural inhabitation? Have we talked about their cultural expressions? Have we cleared a context within their workplace for them to celebrate their being, their language, their sound? We've done nothing. They have just remained tools that we use. The migrant workers as a collective are merely instruments. This has to be broken.

I'm really interested in artforms that are coming out of a recognition of the inalienable hybridity of our lives of labor and art. This has been wonderful, thank you.

VII.

Gazing Across Borders

31

The Lost Country

Dragana Jurišić

"Once upon a time, in a faraway part of Europe, behind seven
mountains and seven rivers, there was a beautiful country
called Yugoslavia."
— Slavenka Drakulić, *They Would Never Hurt a Fly*[1]

On September 15, 1991, I went for a walk with two of my closest
friends down by the banks of the river Sava that flows through
my hometown of Slavonski Brod. It was Sunday; we were bored
after a three-month-long summer holiday and very excited
about going back to school the next day. We were sixteen years
old. The usually busy river promenade was eerily empty of people that day. However, we did meet a group of mustached men.
It was immediately clear to us that they were army officers. It's
strange how you can always recognize policemen and military
even when disguised in their Sunday best. They told us to go
home immediately, and stay there. Under my breath, I muttered
where they could go. As we ran off giggling back to our own
homes for lunch, one of my friends, I forgot which one, shouted

---

1   Slavenka Drakulić, *They Would Never Hurt a Fly: War Criminals on Trial
    in The Hague* (Viking, 2004), 1.

back towards me, "It's soooo boring, I wish something exciting would happen."

My family's apartment was on the eighth floor of a building positioned right on the town's main square. The windows of the apartment looked at the large Yugoslav National Army (JNA) garrison. I remember my mother cooking Sunday lunch and then the doorbell rang. Outside our front door was a group of Croatian soldiers. They told us to put all of our valuables into the hallway and go down to the basement. And then it started. They attacked the JNA compound.

I remember thinking it all must be some sort of a joke.

I remember being excited and scared at the same time.

I remember how I put all my LPs into the hallway so they wouldn't get damaged by the crossfire.

I remember that my father and my brother were out that afternoon.

I remember bullets spraying the front door of our building.

I remember hearing what sounded like someone trying to get in.

I remember my mother screaming "it's them" and running towards the door.

I remember grabbing onto her until all my nails broke.

I remember meeting my neighbors for the first time in the basement of our building.

I remember thinking "pity I've met them only now when we are all about to die."

I remember the building burning above us.

I remember being sad about all those books my parents bought through the syndicate and never read . . . only consumed by me and the fire.

I remember being pissed off that I would die a virgin.

I remember when they came to pull us out.

I remember how I learned to zigzag run in order to escape snipers' bullets.

I remember taking shelter in the local supermarket.

I remember falling asleep on bags of washing powder, next to a boy I had a secret crush on (he was our local basketball star).

Fig. 31.1. Belgrade, Serbia. Photo by the author.

I remember him waking me up at 3 a.m. and whispering: "What can I get you, Madam?"

I remember asking for ice cream and champagne.

I remember captured Yugoslav army soldiers sitting, scared shitless, opposite us.

I remember Croatian soldiers handing them boxes of sweets.

I remember walking into our burned down apartment the following morning.

I remember feeling relief that all the mess was gone and I would not need to clean up my room.

I remember that everything melted except for a big orange gas bottle, lying in red crackling "coals," waiting to go off like some post-apocalyptic witch's cauldron.

Fig. 31.2. Starigrad, Croatia. Photo by the author.

I remember the soles of my red converse shoes melting.
I remember walking out.

The story of me as a photographer starts on the day when our family apartment got burned down together with thousands of prints and negatives my father, an ardent amateur photographer, had accumulated. On that day I became one of those "refugees" with no photographs, with no past. Indeed, my memories of the events and people I encountered before that Sunday in September 1991 are either nonexistent or very vague. I learned then the power photography has over memory. The day after the fire was the last time my father took a photograph, a perfunctory snapshot to record the damage for the insurance company. Where he

Fig. 31.3. Split, Croatia. Photo by the author.

stopped, I started. The act of photographing, of looking at the world through the camera lens, helped provide a semblance of control over an otherwise unpredictable world.

Rebecca West wrote, "Violence was, indeed, all I knew of the Balkans: all I knew of the South Slavs."[2] Yugoslavia was a short-lived country in both of her reincarnations.[3] The name Yugoslavia was first used in 1929, then abolished fourteen years later, reestablished in 1945 as a Socialist Federation, and disintegrated once more in 1991.

---

2   Rebecca West, *Black Lamb and Grey Falcon: A Journey Through Yugoslavia* (Canongate, 1993), 21.
3   In the Serbo-Croatian language, the word "Yugoslavia" is of female gender.

Fig. 31.4. New Belgrade, Serbia. Photo by the author.

Josip Broz Tito's Yugoslavia enjoyed its golden age between the early 1960s and the early 1980s. It had a relatively high standard of living, a fast national growth rate, low unemployment, equal pay for women, free medical care and education, subsidized public transport and property rents, etc. Tito famously described himself as the leader of one country with two alphabets, three languages, four religions, five nationalities, six republics, surrounded by seven neighbors, a country in which live eight ethnic minorities. Yugoslavia, a socialist federation composed of six republics (Slovenia, Croatia, Bosnia and Herzegovina, Serbia, Montenegro, and Macedonia) and two autonomous provinces (Vojvodina and Kosovo), started falling apart at the seams after his death in 1980.

Fig. 31.5. Govedarov Kamen, North Macedonia. Photo by the author.

Tito's death coincided with another destabilizing factor: the collapse of communism and the awakening of nationalism in Eastern Europe. Emerging political parties and their leaders used nationalism and the accompanying rhetoric in order to develop a culture of fear and mistrust between different ethnic groups in Yugoslavia. Misha Glenny, possibly the best-known writer on Yugoslavia, filed a report in February 1991 to the BBC, in which he wrote that the leaders of Yugoslavia "were stirring a cauldron of blood that would soon boil over." He was reprimanded by his supervisors at the BBC for being an alarmist and told that "this is the end of the 20th century, not the beginning

[...] there would be no war in the Balkans."[4] Unfortunately they were wrong. As well as creating a culture of fear and mistrust, the obliteration of the Yugoslav identity, common to all ethnic groups, started in earnest on all sides. Describing how this process worked in Croatia, Dubravka Ugrešić wrote that it took only five years of repressive measures "to create the first precondition for the final idiotization of the nation." That precondition, she said, was a collective amnesia which caused its citizens to forget both their personal history and history in general.[5]

The Yugoslav conflicts started in 1991 when Slovenia decided to leave the Yugoslav federation. This provoked a ten-day military intervention by the JNA. Due to its short duration, the number of casualties was relatively low. The Slovenes came out of this fight victorious. Considering that the JNA was one of the largest European armies at that time, Slovenia's victory can be attributed to their geographic position (it bordered three EU countries: Italy, Austria, and Hungary) and the fact that Croatia, the much larger republic holding the majority of the Yugoslav coastal waters, declared independence on the same day as Slovenia.

Unfortunately, Croatia was not to be as "lucky" as Slovenia. Frightened by the new and extremely nationalist Croatian government, the large Serb minority in Croatia, supported by the JNA, rebelled against the new Croatian state and took control of over a third of Croatia's territory. This independent Serbian territory within Croatia's borders was named Srbska Krajina. The campaign of ethnic cleansing started in the occupied parts of the country, and the JNA, supported by the Serbian paramilitary forces, also began a campaign of the systematic shelling and destruction of cities such as Vukovar and the ancient, UNESCO-protected city of Dubrovnik. In 1995, tables turned — in two major military offensives called "Storm" and "Flash," the Croatian army reclaimed most of its lost territory. This triggered an exo-

4   Misha Glenny, *The Balkans, 1804–1999: Nationalism, War and the Great Powers* (Granta, 1999), 634.

5   Dubravka Ugrešić, *The Culture of Lies: Antipolitical Essays,* trans. Celia Hawkesworth (Phoenix, 1999), 210.

dus of ethnic Serbs, as well as a series of war crimes committed by the Croatian army against Serbian civilians.

Bosnia and Herzegovina, the most ethnically diverse republic in former Yugoslavia, was almost completely devastated in the war. Both Serbia and Croatia had strategic interest in Bosnian territory and, as it is now known, Croatian president Franjo Tudjman and Serbian president Slobodan Milošević met secretly in 1991 and carved up the country between them. The Bosnian government unfortunately placed their faith in the international community, as they believed that the international community would not allow a United Nations (UN) member state to be wiped off the map. The population of Bosnia learned over time that peaceful negotiations with their Serb and Croat counterparts had brought them only defeat. So they started to fight back. War then turned into a vicious three-sided battle. The Bosnian government pleaded with the UN Security Council to lift the arms embargo so they could defend themselves. This was refused with the argument that this would only cause more lives being lost. More honest reason was provided by James Baker, the Secretary of State under US President George Bush, when he said: "We don't have a dog in that fight."[6] As a consequence of not lifting the arms embargo, Bosnian Muslims were exposed to a merciless ethnic cleansing from both the Serbian and the Croatian side.

It is difficult to estimate the exact number of people who were killed in the Bosnian war. What we do know is that half of the population, approximately two million people, either fled, were killed, or were expelled. Thousands of women were raped; concentration camps were resurrected and mass murder on a scale not seen in Europe since the Second World War took place in the town of Srebrenica in July 1995. More than 8,000 Bosnian Muslim boys and men were executed by Serb forces under the command of General Ratko Mladić within a space of just a few days. Srebrenica, declared a safe area by the UN and under

---

6   Cited in Laura Silber and Allan Little, *Yugoslavia: Death of a Nation* (Penguin, 1997), 29–30.

the guard of Dutch peacekeeping forces, was "cleansed" of Muslims in less than a week, while the UN peace forces powerlessly looked on.

While the international community tried to decide on how they should act, the Bosnians were thrown into turmoil. The feeling of helplessness amongst Bosnian Muslims was especially vast, and echoed very well in Slavenka Drakulić's book *Balkan Express: Fragments From the Other Side of War* (1993) when she described her reaction to the first air raids. Even though Drakulić describes air raids in Zagreb, the capital of Croatia, the experience is recognizable to the majority of the people who find themselves under attack:

> At that point, I understood exactly the meaning of destiny. It is when you know that this is it: there is no choice any more, no solution, no escape, and you are not even horrified, not even tempted to resist, but just ready to take whatever the next moment brings. Even if it brings death.[7]

When reading this, it is hard not to think of video footage that resurfaced in 2005, which showed Muslim boys who were executed a decade earlier, by their Serbian captors in Potočari. In this video footage we see a beautiful sunny day, we see Serbian soldiers chatting to each other in a field of tall grass and wildflowers about what they are going to do that night, whether they are going out for a drink or off to meet their girlfriends. The teenage Muslim boys are being brought one by one into the field, where these same "benevolent" soldiers gun them down, as a comma perhaps to their conversation. The Muslim boys don't plead for their life, they do not protest, they are not crying. They step calmly in front of their executors and their young lives are taken away from them in an instant. Death is silent.

The Srebrenica massacre changed NATO's policy of non-involvement. Soon after the events in July 1995, a major airstrike

---

7   Slavenka Drakulić, *Balkan Express: Fragments from the Other Side of War* (Hutchinson, 1993), 24.

Fig. 31.6. Govedarov Kamen II, North Macedonia. Photo by the author.

offensive started against the Bosnian Serbs and together with a joint Bosnian and Croatian offensive, Bosnian Serbs were pushed back from a third of the territory they occupied. Subsequently, more than 60,000 NATO troops were deployed in the area.

Still, this was not the end. In 1999 the war moved to the Serbian province of Kosovo, where the Albanian population sought independence from Serbia. The Serbs attacked Albanian towns and villages, targeting predominantly the civilian population and forcing them to flee. After peace talks failed, NATO went on a seventy-eight-day airstrike offensive against Serbs both in Kosovo and in Serbia. According to the International Criminal

Tribunal for the former Yugoslavia (ICTY), an estimated 750,000 Albanian refugees returned home, while around 100,000 Serbs fled Kosovo in fear of retribution. Twenty years on, the situation today is still very tense and unresolved.

Montenegro — which was part of the State Union of Serbia and Montenegro until 2006 — was considered to be partly responsible for all the events mentioned above, especially Kosovo.

North Macedonia — or as it is formerly known, "the former Yugoslav Republic of Macedonia" (FYROM), due to its name dispute with Greece — still manages to avoid conflicts, although the tension between Macedonians and Macedonian Albanians is a tinder box waiting to go off. If this happens, the war might spread outside of the borders of former Yugoslavia, and pull in Albania, Bulgaria, and Greece.

The term "balkanize" (meaning to fragment and revert back to "primitive" and "hostile" states) became firmly associated with Yugoslavia around this time. The media coverage of the Yugoslav wars was based on generalizations about the people and their history. The clichés about the Balkans, which became outmoded long ago when reporting from non-Western areas, were circulating freely in the majority of the news reports on the conflicts. As Glenny commented, "the Balkans apparently enjoy a special exemption from the rules against stereotyping."[8] The West saw the Yugoslav conflicts as unfathomable, and its people motivated by mysterious ancient hatred and congenital bloodthirstiness, something that Glenny argued "is always invoked when the great powers seek to deny their responsibility for the economic and political difficulties that the region has suffered as a consequence of external interference."[9] The Balkans were constructed as the other within Europe. In the words of Slavoj Žižek:

In former Yugoslavia we are lost not because of our primitive dreams and myths preventing us from speaking the en-

---

8   Glenny, *The Balkans, 1804–1999*, xxi.
9   Ibid., 661.

Fig. 31.7. Kosovska Mitrovica, Kosovo. Photo by the author.

lightened language of Europe, but because we pay in flesh the price for being the stuff the Other's dreams are made of [...]. Far from being the Other of Europe, former Yugoslavia was rather Europe itself in its Otherness, the screen onto which Europe projected its own repressed reverse.[10]

At least 1,500,000 Yugoslavs vanished together with their country. They disappeared, like Atlantis, into the realm of imaginary places. Ugrešić called this the biggest atrocity in modern day Europe, yet not many have gone looking for these lost people.

---

10 Cited in John Taylor, *Into the Heart of European Poetry* (Transaction Publishers, 2008), 132.

Fig. 31.8. Skopje, North Macedonia. Photo by the author.

Today, in countries that came into being after Yugoslavia's dis-integration, there is a total marginalization and denial of the Yugoslav identity.

The project *YU: The Lost Country* was originally conceived as a recreation of a homeland that was lost. Following Roland Bar-thes's assertion that photography is more akin to magic than to art, I was on a journey in which I would somehow draw a magi-cal circle around the country that was once mine and resurrect it, where I would reconnect with "my" people, a place where I would be understood. Instead, it became a journey of rejection, displacement, and exile that was stronger back "home" than in the foreign place where I chose to live. The realization that the whole world is a foreign land became pervasive for me.

Fig. 31.9. Kosovska Mitrovica II, Kosovo. Photo by the author.

When in exile it is imperative to hold onto your memory the fragments of the place you have left, as these fragments house the self, and without this imaginary home one's very identity is in jeopardy. What happened in the area that was once Yugoslavia is the repeated exile and exodus of its people throughout history. What I personally learned from the war is that once the country is no more, the streets that you grew up on are renamed, the borders you knew are redrawn, and the history books you learned from are rewritten. As Peter Osborne says, your existence,

has become a non-possibility, for all points in which memory is anchored, through which the lines of life's narrative are

449

threaded, have vanished. Not only have the exile's claims on a place in reality been denied, their access to the processes in which human identity is made has been blocked. To be deprived of one's space is to be deprived of the right of memory and thus the right to selfhood.[11]

There are a significant number of well-known artists who are exiles and émigrés. Once a person loses their original world, they realize how fragile all the other worlds are. The fragmentation that occurs as a result, in return, provides a wealth of material to be explored through artistic means. Photography, in particular, contains elements such as fleetingness, which allow it to capture that sense of rootlessness and dislocation with relative ease. Both exile and photography intensify our perception of the world. In both, the memory is its core. Both are characterized by melancholy. As Salman Rushdie said, exiles live "more comfortably in images, in ideas, than in places."[12]

11 Peter D. Osborne, *Traveling Light: Photography, Travel and Visual Culture* (Manchester University Press, 2002), 125.
12 Salman Rushdie, *Imaginary Homelands: Essays and Criticism, 1981–1991* (Granta, 1992), 184.

Bibliography

Drakulić, Slavena. *Balkan Express: Fragments From the Another Side of War.* Hutchinson, 1993.

———. *They Would Never Hurt a Fly: War Criminals on Trial in The Hague.* Viking, 2004.

Glenny, Misha. *The Balkans, 1804–1999: Nationalism, War and the Great Powers.* Granta, 1999.

Osborne, Peter D. *Traveling Light: Photography, Travel and Visual Culture.* Manchester University Press, 2000.

Rushdie, Salman. *Imaginary Homelands: Essays and Criticism, 1981–1991.* Granta, 1992.

Silber, Laura, and Allan Little. *Yugoslavia: Death of a Nation.* Penguin Books, 1997.

Ugrešić, Dubravka. *The Culture of Lies: Antipolitical Essays.* Translated by Celia Hawkesworth. Phoenix, 1999.

Taylor, John. *Into the Heart of European Poetry.* Transaction Publishers, 2008.

West, Rebecca. *Black Lamb and Grey Falcon: A Journey through Yugoslavia.* Canongate, 1993.

32

Trade Winds

Susan Stockwell, with a response from Carla Suthren

SUSAN: *Trade Winds* is a sculptural installation made up of many small boats crafted from international paper currency, maps, and travel tickets that float on top of a mass of copper coins. The flotilla of boats, as if on a journey to elsewhere, weaves its way across the coins, that resemble both a sea and a continent. Are the boats contained or free? Is the money enabling or restricting?

Concerned with issues of migration and borders, trade, colonial and social history, geo-politics, ecology, mapping, and material culture, this artwork asks pertinent and open-ended questions that are especially relevant to our current and future world.

The work provides a quiet space for reflection in which to enjoy the playful, tactile objects while also provoking questions about our relationship to money and how it shapes our fragile world ecology. In the context of this beautiful, tiny chapel, *Trade Winds* acquired a reverential, intimate feeling with added meanings provided by the Norman origins of St. Peter's Church at Kettle's Yard and his status as the patron saint of fishermen.

Fig. 32.1. Trade Winds © Susan Stockwell, 2019. Photo by Paula Bee-telstone.

As part of the Migrant Knowledge event this artwork added a different voice. Visual art can have a rich multiplicity of meanings and readings, which are often difficult to articulate and are best seen and felt. Perhaps this piece acted as a mirror for the viewer's own experiences and stories. People were protective towards the small, fragile paper boats, reading meanings into the combinations of currency, text, and maps and asking what shape or continent the coins formed. The irony of money as artistic material placed within the context of a church invites many questions: for instance, do we worship money as we worship art? What is our relationship with money? Are we ruled by the power of money and is this destroying us?

Fig. 32.2. Trade Winds © Susan Stockwell, 2019. Photo by Subha Mukherji.

Global warming, too, is largely a result of colonial trade and colonial behaviors. The future of migration and the inevitable displacement of peoples are, in turn, bound to be inflected by climate change. We are all citizens of the world and yet we divide it up and claim areas as our own — colonizing. It is these places of irony and interrogation from which the ideas for my work come. Being involved in the Migrant Knowledge event brought this into sharper focus and has inspired new ideas and work.

CARLA: Carved into the heart of the tiny, picturesque church of St. Peter's in Cambridge is a tale of migration. The building has been altered and reduced and reconstructed over the centuries, but the oldest element that remains is the distinctive square font, decorated with a series of stone mermen, each holding the tails of his neighbors in either hand. This dates back to the mid-twelfth century: era of crusades, cathedrals, and the rise of the Plantagenets. As the guidebook to St. Peter's observes, "Mermen and mermaids grasping one end of divided tails are a fairly common motif in French Romanesque churches but rare in this country."[1] This striking and unusual feature hints at the movement of people, ideas, and skills in the Anglo-Norman world.

As a setting for *Trade Winds,* it could hardly have been more evocative. Copper coins were spread and heaped like a dragon's hoard across the stone floor, trailing up to the doorway and past the altar, and lapping fortuitously around the font. The tiny boats nestled in dips and troughs, or perched precariously on the crests of coppery waves. Driven by imagined winds, some shoaled together, while others crisscrossed one another's paths or ventured off alone. The tonal variation among the coins, from those crusted over with age to the shiniest new pennies, transposed the infinite variety of the sea into a strange new palette. And yet, change your perspective, and the massed coins become the continent, shaped by an invisible sea. Skirting around the edges of the church, treading carefully, you could walk all the way around the installation, experiencing it from every angle. Being able to reposition yourself spatially in relation to this multifaceted artwork offered embodied ways of re-knowing.

This physical engagement extended further still. As visitors flowed in, they began to add their own coins to the work spontaneously, some tossing them in as if it were a wishing well, others carefully shoring up coastlines or building little promontories. Adults as well as children added their contributions with consideration and delight. Some instinctively wanted to repair "damage" caused by coins being displaced by a careless foot here and there. One small girl very solemnly and carefully picked up the tiniest boat which had been knocked over, and nestled it back into a bed of coins. Meaning was continually created through this collaborative curatorial enterprise by strangers, just as it was created through the interaction between the work and the space of St. Peter's Church, and recreated through the

---

1   Lawrence Butler, *Church of St Peter off Castle Street,* Cambridge, https://cdn.visitchurches.org.uk/uploads/images/Churches/Cambridge-St-Peters-Church/Cambridge-St-Peters-Church-Guidebook.pdf.

personal histories and perspectives of each person who encountered it. Transforming the paraphernalia of the everyday into an imaginative provocation, *Trade Winds* shaped alternative and mutable forms of knowing, across space and time.

VIII.

Refuge and Refugees,
Human and Other

33

Kudzu in the Patchy Anthropocene

Yota Batsaki

Invasive plants are a scandalous case of migrant knowledge. Often introduced into their new habitats by the deliberate or accidental agency of humans, they occasionally escape containment and proliferate wildly, displacing native species and disturbing local ecological relationships that evolved over thousands of years. Their success is an unwelcome reminder of our partial or misplaced knowledge of living organisms and ecosystems. Having eluded our control, invasives are branded "noxious weeds": regulated, criminalized, ripe for extermination. Yet our desire to eradicate them is predicated on the erasure of other kinds of knowledge about them and their travels — perhaps even on willful forgetfulness. Kudzu, known in the United States as "the vine that ate the south," is one of the most notorious and recognizable. Although its name reveals its foreignness, kudzu has become emblematic of a certain kind of Southern landscape.

Kudzu's conquest of its adopted territory is rendered iconic by the art of William Christenberry (1936–2016), a pioneer of color photography whose works are in the collections of the Getty, the Museum of Modern Art (MoMA), and the Smithsonian American Art Museum. Christenberry's family hailed from Hale County, Alabama, the heart of cotton (and later

Fig. 33.1. High Kudzu, near Akron, Alabama, 1978. © William Christenberry. Source: Adamson Gallery / Editions

kudzu) country, and he spent his childhood summers there.
Although he eventually settled in Washington, DC, he returned
to the south every year to record its gradually overgrown landscapes and decaying structures. Christenberry's saturated palette of greens, reds, and browns captured the verdant luxuriance
of kudzu, a vine famously capable of growing a foot per day;
he found it "rather beautiful in the way it envelops things [...]
and forms these very fascinating topiaries."[1] Yet the photographs
also hint at a more sinister creep, an uncanny sense of menace
underlying the roadside canopies of unrelenting greenery (fig.
33.1). Kudzu's present harm is well-known. As it climbs, envelops, and covers, it crowds out native plants, smothers mature
trees, and is a nuisance to ecologists, farmers, loggers, and utility

---

1   William Christenberry, interviewed by Jarrett Gregory for the exhibition
    After Nature, New Museum, July 17, 2008–October 5, 2008, https://archive.
    newmuseum.org/sounds/7278.

companies alike. Yet, while rooted in the local, Christenberry's seemingly modest photos of kudzu open up a broader window into the Anthropocene: the period defined by the impact of human activities — including plantation monoculture and the burning of fossil fuels — on the planet's life systems.

Kudzu (*Pueraria lobata*) is native to China, Korea, and Japan. Now considered a pest in the United States, it enjoyed a more dignified debut. Its first appearance was in the Japanese Pavilion during the 1876 Philadelphia Centennial International Exhibition, a stage for the competitive display of technological ingenuity, natural resources, and cultural capital. Originally prized as an ornamental exotic, kudzu was subsequently grown in the US South as fodder, and later adopted by Franklin Delano Roosevelt's administration as a remedy for soil erosion. The early-twentieth-century environmental crisis brought about by settler colonialism and maladapted agricultural practices is better known through images of the Dust Bowl in the Midwest. However, the South was also experiencing massive soil loss in this period as a result of land exhaustion brought about by the plantation system and the sharecropping practices that followed it. In the 1930s, erosion came to be considered a national menace and an environmental disaster of global proportions.[2] Kudzu was grown in nurseries and widely and deliberately planted by the Soil Conservation Service to hold together the ravaged soil. The vine proved more successful than its promoters had ever imagined and over the decades began to carpet the fields and smother the abandoned structures of the South.

Like so many migrants, kudzu did not arrive on a previously pure and untouched land.[3] When the first Europeans arrived in what is now Alabama in the early sixteenth century, they found a region of thick forests and central prairies inhabited by the

---

2 David R. Montgomery, *Dirt: The Erosion of Civilizations* (University of California Press, 2007).

3 On the similarities between the rhetoric of biological invasions and xenophobic tropes deployed by nativist ideologies, see Banu Subramaniam, "The Aliens Have Landed! Reflections on the Rhetoric of Biological Invasions," *Meridians* 2, no. 1 (2001): 26–40.

Choctaw and Chickasaw. The arrival of the Spanish was followed by French and English colonists. The latter prevailed in
the early 1700s. In 1802 the first cotton gin was constructed in
Alabama; white settlers began pouring in, ignoring treaties and
displacing Indigenous peoples. The Great Removal of 1838 initiated the mass deportation of Indigenous populations to Okla-
homa, opening the way for cotton cultivation. By the middle
of the nineteenth century, Alabama was the center of the Cotton Belt. By then, many of the original white settlers were also
driven out by moneymen with large plantations supported by
the toil of Black enslaved people. Their coerced labor had, by
the 1850s, made the planters some of the richest in America, but
they were brought low by the Civil War and Confederate defeat,
followed by the ravages of soil erosion and the invasion of the
boll weevil, a pest that decimated the South's cotton economy.
The plantation owners turned to poor whites to supplement the
flight of formerly enslaved labor, leading to new forms of exploitation of both Black and white workers through sharecropping
and tenant farming practices. By the early twentieth century,
cotton cultivation in the South was becoming less and less competitive; the final blow to the region's rural workers was dealt by
the introduction of mechanization in the 1950s.[4]

Invasive weeds have accompanied the different waves of
migration to the American continent for centuries. The earliest European settlers brought with them plants that often overtook them and surged ahead of their advance and biological
attack — often to the point of extermination — on native organisms, including the continent's Indigenous human communities.
Weeds thrive on human disturbance: deforestation, overgraz-
ing, the abandonment of traditional forms of agriculture, and
the rapacious folly of monoculture. Alfred Crosby has argued
that migrant weeds played an important role in protecting the
soil laid bare by settler colonialism, shielding it from water and

---

4   Dale Maharidge and Michael Williamson, *And Their Children after Them:
    The Legacy of* Let Us Now Praise Famous Men, *James Agee, Walker Evans,
    and the Rise and Fall of Cotton in the South* (Pantheon, 1989).

wind erosion and from baking in the sun: like "skin transplants placed over [...] abraded and burned flesh [they] aided in healing the wounds that the invaders tore in the earth."[5]

But while many of those earlier human introductions of foreign plants were accidental, the deliberate planting of kudzu in the South was driven by scientific thinking and supported by technical expertise. The chief proponent of soil conservation in America, Hugh Bennett, was confident that the plantings were "based on the best information in the possession of scientific agriculturists: agronomist, forester, range specialist, soil specialist, erosion specialist, agricultural engineer, economist, extension specialist, game specialist and geographer."[6] In the prevailing climate of scientific confidence, environmental disaster, and national emergency, early warnings about kudzu's potential threat were dismissed. A 1939 pamphlet by the Department of Agriculture acknowledged the "rather prevalent belief that kudzu is likely to become a serious pest" but concluded that "belief is unfounded."[7] The vine was practically coaxed into becoming an invasive plant in the American South.

This failure to appreciate kudzu's growth potential exposes our tendency to simplify plants by ignoring their relationships to other species and to their environments. Since the beginning of modern botany and its gradual divorce from medicine in the early modern period, Western knowledge of plants has relied on the study of the singular specimen, preserved in the herbarium or depicted in a scientific illustration. Colonial botany favored this approach because it rendered foreign plants stable, transportable, and exchangeable: modular things that could be experimented upon in the botanical garden and scaled up in nurseries or plantations. Both our scientific study of and our technological mastery over plants have long required that we

---

5   Alfred Crosby, *Ecological Imperialism: The Biological Expansion of Europe, 900–1900* (Cambridge University Press, 2004), 170.

6   Hugh H. Bennett, "Soil Erosion — A National Menace," *The Scientific Monthly* 39, no. 5 (1934): 385–404.

7   R.Y. Bailey, "Kudzu for Erosion Control in the Southeast," *Farmers' Bulletin* no. 1840 (US Department of Agriculture, 1939), 31.

treat them as discrete units amenable to transplantation, following their extraction from the web of multispecies relationships, land management practices, and particularities of climate and soil that make up their ecosystems. This concept of the plant as a unit that can be managed is key to the maximizing imperative of monoculture and capitalist production. The same logic of plantation monoculture that ravaged the land and people of the American South was applied to the remedy. Ironically, kudzu scaled beyond its promoters' wildest expectations, eliding the bounded and controlled deployment of its growth potential. Kudzu's legendary pace of growth debunks the notion of the plant as a passive resource. Kudzu is uncontainable, the speed with which it grows akin to a predatory animality: "You keep still enough, watch close enough," Southerners will tell you, "and damn if you can't see it move."[8]

Migration reminds us of the inevitably contextual and precarious nature of knowledge and its transmission. What is often lost in the translation of the plant into a new context is its rich and multidimensional being. Kudzu has been, for millennia, a valued plant in the East. A nineteenth-century Japanese treatise on kudzu, *Seikatsu Roku* (Account of processing kudzu starch), records the manifold characteristics of the plant and its ecological, economic, and cultural importance. Written by the agricultural innovator Ōkura Nagatsune (1768–1860) and illustrated by a student of the famed printmaker and painter Hokusai (fig. 33.2), it celebrates kudzu as a "useful thing [...] in useless places," a hardy and resilient ally against famine that can grow in depleted soils and steep mountainsides.[9] While fulfilling basic needs of ecosystems and humans, kudzu is also part of a culture of refinement that has included, through the centuries, the production of paper, fine textiles, and delicate food concoctions. Ōkura's work falls within the genre of agricultural improvement and deploys techniques of meticulous description, artful illus-

8   Michael Pollan, *Second Nature: A Gardener's Education* (Atlantic Monthly Press, 1991), 104–5.

9   Ōkura Nagatsune, *Seikatsu Roku* (Bunshodo Fujii Uhei, 1828).

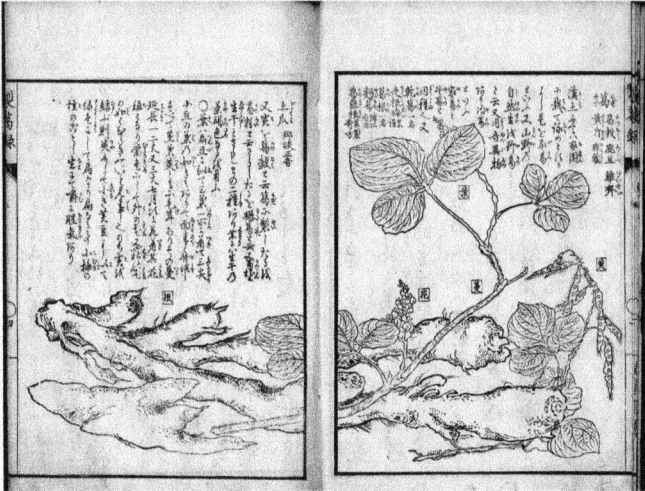

Fig. 33.2. Ōkura Nagatsune and Arisaka Hokuba, *Seikatsu Roku* (Kyoto: Bunshodo Fujii Uhei, 1828). The first illustration of kudzu in *Seikatsu Roku* labels each anatomical component of the plant from root to leaf, including flower, stem, and pod, and summarizes its nutritional, medicinal, or ornamental functions. Photo by Joe Mills.

tration, and mechanical reproduction to disseminate information for growing and processing kudzu. The treatise also refers to kudzu's medical properties through the tradition of Chinese *materia medica* (materials used in medicine), a reminder of the perennially migratory nature of knowledge that recasts the vine's putative origin, Japan, as just one more stop along the itinerary of transmission and adaptation.

In *Vibrant Matter* Jane Bennett teases out the recalcitrance of things that refuse "to dissolve completely into the milieu of human knowledge"[10] and identifies them across a continuum that may extend from the living organism to minerals, landfills, or electrical currents. She borrows Bruno Latour's concept of the "actant" to describe a form of agency devoid of what we would

---

10   Jane Bennett, *Vibrant Matter: A Political Ecology of Things* (Duke University Press, 2010), 3.

recognize as intention or will, yet capable of producing real and palpable effects. Christenberry's photographs of kudzu confront us with our precarious control and inadequate knowledge, the unexpected triumph of a thing that appears indifferent to intention, sinister in excessive proliferation, and relentlessly resilient. Bennett argues for an attitude of methodological naivete in our encounter with the non-human other, a moment of epistemological humility and ontological uncertainty held long enough to "render manifest a subsistent world of nonhuman vitality."[11] Without personifying and ascribing agency to that other thing that "thwarts our desire for conceptual and practical mastery,"[12] such naivete may nevertheless open us up to a more inclusive ecological ethic.

In its extraordinary success coupled with its noxious effects on other life forms, kudzu reenacts the dominant model of human activity in the Anthropocene. Invasives have been defined as the plants that elicit the most anthropomorphic description: They are aggressive and opportunistic, ecological imperialists second only to humans.[13] Among kudzu's strategies for survival is reproductive ingenuity. The extraordinarily beautiful and fragrant flower only matures on a climbing vine, but the plant can eschew sexual reproduction in favor of putting out roots and cloning itself when forced to lie low. Kudzu husbands its resources, using other plants as climbing structures and therefore eschewing creation of a woody mass in favor of energy production through its leaves. Human-induced climate change appears to favor kudzu. The vine thrives on increased levels of carbon dioxide and the warmer temperatures brought about by our fossil-burning activities. One of the frequent charges brought against invasive species is that they lack the mutualistic relationships with native species — other plants, pollinators, animals, human communities, etc. — that support and enrich local ecosystems. Kudzu's lack of reciprocity and perceived inability to coexist

---

11 Ibid., 17.
12 Ibid., 15.
13 Crosby, *Ecological Imperialism*, 150.

harmoniously with other life forms in its new habitat holds up a mirror to imperialist, capitalist, and extractive attitudes towards the earth's ecosystems.

We need to recognize the rich personalities of plants, the ways in which they resist the categories in which we seek to contain them. Yet Christenberry's fascination with kudzu throughout his career stemmed from the sense that the vine's dominance distilled and clarified something important about the landscapes of his childhood: "I think that everything I've been about for a number of years has been simplification, simplification. Getting down to the essence of something."[14] Peeling back the layers of landscape and cultural history concealed beneath the kudzu patch reveals what Anna Tsing has called the "patchy Anthropocene." With this concept, she connects the ecological simplification of plantation monoculture and the feral proliferation of pests or invasives as two sides of the same coin. Tsing gives the example of coffee rust, to which coffee plants are fairly indifferent in their natural habitat, but which has become an epidemic in far-flung plantations.[15] Whereas plantations are the prime example of "modular simplification," the pests or invasives that proliferate in monoculture's aftermath are "feral proliferations." Their intersection is the space where kudzu thrives and migrant knowledge falters, for "Anthropocene patches emerge in the relationship between simplifications and proliferations."[16]

The patchy Anthropocene is intimately linked to the legacy of the plantation and the trauma of monoculture: "the slave plantation system was the model and motor for the carbon-greedy machine-based factory system that is often cited as an

14 Lynda Roscoe Hartigan, "William Christenberry (1936–2016)," *American Art* 31, no. 3 (2017): 112.

15 Anna Lowenhaupt Tsing, Andrew S. Mathews, and Nils Bubandt, "Patchy Anthropocene: Landscape Structure, Multispecies History, and the Retooling of Anthropology: An Introduction to Supplement 20," *Current Anthropology* 60, no. S20 (2019): S186.

16 Ibid., S187.

inflection point for the Anthropocene."[17] The plantation is designed to maximize the yield of both plant and human labor through coercion and the preponderance of one organism at the exclusion of others in the pursuit of an economic product. To exist, the plantation displaces Indigenous communities and native species while generating forced migrations of plants and people. In turn, this modular simplification creates the radical disturbance that erases natural diversity and previous land management practices, and renders a landscape ripe for feral proliferation. Invasives and pests then ripple through a landscape prepared by the ravages of ecological simplification. While colonial and capitalist interests and planning create the conditions for the emergence of these landscapes, however, they "do not fully determine the results."[18] Invasives may thus disrupt both capitalist productivity and the economistic understanding of biodiversity as the provision of "ecosystem services" within a market of more-than-human entities.

William Christenberry's photographs of kudzu exemplify this Anthropocene landscape, emerging from colonial and capitalist-driven ecological simplification, imbued with the past horrors and contemporary after-effects of slavery and exploitative labor, and giving rise to feral proliferation. The images capture the uncanniness of the Anthropocene: the ecological and human trauma concealed under the kudzu patch. This uncanniness is rendered more haunting by the absence of people: the human communities that have abandoned or been driven out of the ravaged land following successive waves of forced migrations and displacements. Ultimately, what may be most unsettling about the kudzu patch is the way it mocks our rhetoric of resilience, which can perpetuate problematic structures of exploitation and extraction under the guise of crisis management.[19] Kudzu landscapes, despite attempts to render them pro-

17   Donna Haraway, "Anthropocene, Capitalocene, Plantationocene, Chthulucene: Making Kin," *Environmental Humanities* 6, no. 1 (2015): 162.
18   Tsing, Mathews, and Bubandt, "Patchy Anthropocene," S190.
19   Mark Vardy and Mick Smith, "Resilience," *Environmental Humanities* 9, no. 1 (2017): 175–79.

ductive, resist the enframing of nature as inexhaustibly available to human consumption and the potentially totalizing discourse of sustainability that risks subsuming differences (social, political, economic, ecological) under the appearance of consensus — that nature must be brought, one way or another, to serve human ends. Ultimately, kudzu's runaway success confronts us with the unwelcome possibility that a resilient nature may, rather, be indifferent to our needs and oblivious to our absence.

Bibliography:

Bailey, R.Y. "Kudzu for Erosion Control in the Southeast."
     Farmers' Bulletin no. 1840. US Department of Agriculture,
     1939.
Bennett, Hugh H. "Soil Erosion — A National Menace." *The
     Scientific Monthly* 39, no. 5 (1934): 385–404. https://www.
     jstor.org/stable/15812.
Bennett, Jane. *Vibrant Matter: A Political Ecology of Things.*
     Duke University Press, 2010.
Christenberry, William. Untitled interview by Jarrett
     Gregory. New Museum. https://archive.newmuseum.org/
     sounds/7278.
Crosby, Alfred. *Ecological Imperialism: The Biological
     Expansion of Europe 900–1900.* Cambridge University Press,
     2004.
Haraway, Donna. "Anthropocene, Capitalocene,
     Plantationocene, Chthulucene: Making Kin." *Environmental
     Humanities* 6, no. 1 (2015): 159–65. DOI: 10.1215/22011919-
     3615934.
Hartigan, Lynda Roscoe. "William Christenberry (1936–2016)."
     American Art 31, no. 3 (2017): 110–15. DOI: 10.1086/696117.
Maharidge, Dale, and Michael Williamson. *And Their Children
     after Them: The Legacy of* Let us Now Praise Famous Men,
     *James Agee, Walker Evans, and the Rise and Fall of Cotton in
     the South.* Pantheon, 1989.
Montgomery, David R. *Dirt: The Erosion of Civilizations.*
     University of California Press, 2007.
Ōkura Nagatsune. *Seikatsu Roku* [Account of processing kudzu
     starch]. Illustrated by Arisaka Hokuba. Bunshodo Fujii
     Uhei, 1828.
Pollan, Michael. *Second Nature: A Gardener's Education.*
     Atlantic Monthly Press, 1991.
Subramaniam, Banu. "The Aliens Have Landed! Reflections
     on the Rhetoric of Biological Invasions." *Meridians* 2, no. 1
     (2001): 26–40. https://www.jstor.org/stable/40338794.

Tsing, Anna Lowenhaupt, Andrew S. Mathews, and
   Nils Bubandt. "Patchy Anthropocene: Landscape
   Structure, Multispecies History, and the Retooling of
   Anthropology: An Introduction to Supplement 20." *Current
   Anthropology* 60, no. S20 (2019): S186–S197. https://www.
   jstor.org/stable/26854768.
Vardy, Mark, and Mick Smith. "Resilience." *Environmental
   Humanities* 9, no. 1 (2017): 175–79. DOI: 10.1215/22011919-
   3829199.

34

Small Things, Strange Shores: Poems

Mina Gorji

Psittacula

Flash of green! — up in the silver birch —
neon, squawking
almost gawdy green —
against the dappled quiet
of suburbia, its lawnmowers
and distant radio.
They say that captive parakeets
can learn to speak —
what might they tell us
of ancestral green,
bright days wild
in Himalayan trees?

Waiting for Snow

we feel instead
the emptiness of rain.
Inside the house it's cold.
We have been waiting
for the world to be forgiven
(for a moment) into white.
The pavement glitters
crystalline with ice.

Grandmother had never felt
the snow before;
she knew the touch
of monsoon rain,
humidity so thick
the body slowed,
before the shock
of Edinburgh rain,
soaking her saree
with its cold and grey.

Reeds

Listening to a reed-flute, the Persian poet Rumi heard a lament. Cut from its bed, the reed sings of longing, of the pain of separation, of being distanced from our roots. In so many ways we are distancing ourselves — from the natural world, from our home. Losing our sense of place. The reed's song is a lament.

Wicken Fen. Listen to the sound of the wind in the reeds. The reedbeds here are full of life, much of it beyond the frequency of human ears. We cannot hear the sound of wainscot moths emerging from the hollow reeds — the sound of their wings against the night. What other sounds are beyond our hearing?

So many moths are calling, flying, landing, feeding, pairing, dying, in these reeds. Their names have a music of their own: *Muscosella, Willow Tortix, Bordered Sallow, Silver Barred, Scallop Shell, Small Seraphim, Brown-tail, Reed Dagger, Flame wainscot. Webb's wainscot* moth is resting on a reed stem. Its larvae are nocturnal, feeding on the reeds at night, hiding, by day, inside its hollow stem. This moth can be found in reedbeds all across the East of England, and also in Iran, hiding at night inside the hollow stems. Listening.

The Wasp

who makes no honey gave us ink.
In early spring oak galls appear:
darkening in autumn
they gestate.

Emerging into English light,
this tiny emigrant
was smuggled in Aleppo oak —
an alien acorn.

IX.

Migrant Food

35

Exile and Food

Claudia Roden in conversation with Subha Mukherji

SUBHA MUKHERJI: Your account of your childhood in Cairo is so wonderfully redolent. Can you tell me about what food meant to you then, and whether you knew what it meant to you? Did migrating to Britain change or develop your relationship to Mediterranean food and its culture? For me, food means so much more when you are leaving a place or realize that you have left it, physically at least.

CLAUDIA RODEN: I grew up in a very extended family on both sides, the Doueks and the Sassoons, with three grandparents from Syria and my maternal grandmother an Alphandary from Istanbul. My Syrian grandparents came to Cairo and went to live in a new area called Sakakini that had just been built on drained marshland. A lot of people from Syria, especially Jewish merchants, settled in this quarter which is still known as the Syrian quarter. There, my relatives continued life as it was in Aleppo, and that included cooking all the things they remembered from their life there. My parents moved to a little residential island called Zamalek when I was small. As we had a very large extended family, our life was very much about visiting each other, and visiting always meant food. And so food was something that I associated with people and hospitality.

SM: Reading the introduction to your book, I got a vivid sense of Egypt's cosmopolitanism. It sounds as though there were two parts to it, the older Arabic part and the Parisian cosmopolitan Cairo which kind of reminds me of what I've heard of Beirut. Did food cross this divide freely, or were there two worlds of scents and tastes and flavors?

CR: We were indeed like Beirut, and French was the lingua franca of the country. If you went to the cinema, you got your ticket in French, and if you went to the big stores, you spoke French, not Arabic. You did speak Arabic if you went to the butcher, and Greek if you went to the grocer — our cheeses like feta and halloumi were mostly Greek — and my mother spoke Arabic to Awad, our cook. I went to The English School Cairo, and on the first day the names were read out in class and we had to shout out what religion we were. "Muslim!," "Copt!," "Jewish!," "Greek Orthodox!," "Christian!" Teachers kept telling us "only English, only English" because we all spoke many languages with each other. You'd say some things in French, then you'd speak in English, then sometimes in Arabic or Italian. In my family, at home we spoke French. Growing up, we ate mainly French and Syrian food and some Judaeo-Spanish food. Our nanny, Maria, cooked for us her Slovene/Italian dishes when we were small. Many of the recipes in my book are from my family and other people who were leaving Egypt, expelled after the Suez Crisis in 1956. They were in a state of trauma, heading for different countries, thinking they would never see each other again. Exchanging recipes was a way to remember each other by.

SM: When everything else is stripped from you, the memory of food becomes a way of holding on, doesn't it? You say they were exchanging recipes. What form did this exchange take? Were the recipes remembered or written down?

CR: There wasn't a single cookbook in Egypt, not one. And there weren't printed recipes. Some people had little handwritten notebooks, but most didn't — they kept their recipes in their head. They were passed on from mother to daughter down the generations and taught to cooks who came from villages.

SM: Which means, does it, that each family has their way of cooking the same dish?

CR: Our community was a mix of Jews from all over the old Ottoman lands and around the Mediterranean. Many had come to Egypt at the turn of the century when the Suez Canal had opened and Egypt had become the trading hub of the region. When I started collecting recipes in my early twenties, women who gave me recipes — they were always women of my mother's age — said "it's from Aleppo!," "this is from Izmir," "it's my grandmother's from Salonika," "from Tunisia and Livorno!" It made me realize how very diverse we were.

When I was fifteen, I went to Paris for three years. I was a weekly boarder in a French lycée. I got to know French cuisine and also enjoyed eating all kinds of foods with the families of girls I met at school from places like Algeria, Morocco, and Vietnam. There was one cousin from Egypt who had been arrested as a communist in Egypt and then became a journalist in Paris. I would have lunch with him and his wife every Sunday. He made something that was a "poor dish" in Egypt, *ful medames,* out of tins of dried broad beans. He dressed them with olive oil, lemon juice, and garlic, and accompanied them with hard boiled eggs and salad. This meal embodied our nostalgia for Egypt. Then I came to England to study art. I spent two years at St. Martin's in Soho in the '50s. The food in cafeterias, self-service eateries, and affordable restaurants in London was horrible then. I lived in a flat with my two brothers and I cooked all the time for them and for the friends we invited. I made things like stuffed vine leaves and vegetables and filo pies. When we ate at our friends', we got spaghetti bolognaise or mushroom omelet.

sm: The friends who came over when you cooked — were they mostly British?

cr: They were British. I also discovered Indian food because one of our neighbors was an Indian painter called Avinash Chandra. I met him and his wife Prem on the night bus. They invited us to dinner often. The house where we rented a flat was owned by an elderly Jewish couple. The wife — everyone called her auntie Janey — treated us like her children. When we came home there was always something she'd leave on our kitchen table — like chicken soup or a cheesecake. That is how I got to know Ashkenazi Jewish food.

sm: Your story about cooking as a student reminds me of my father's story of when he was in Oxford in the late '50s. He had never cooked at home, because Indian men never cooked in those days. But when he was in Oxford, he learned to cook. He rented a room in a Polish woman's house. She was a bit like the kind of woman you were talking about, because she would occasionally cook something and put it on the table. There my father had enough space to cook for four people and he would make a chicken curry or something vaguely Indian and people loved it!

cr: In those days there were no Lebanese restaurants, no Turkish restaurants, nothing. You couldn't buy filo, you couldn't buy bulgur, chickpeas, couscous, anything. It seems funny now to think that some years after my first book came out supermarkets began asking me what they should stock and gave my recipes to their producers to use. In the first edition of my book I wrote "a courgette is a baby marrow"! To buy aubergines you had to go to a market in Camden. It was a total desert here in the way of food.

sm: Even the change since I first came to Oxford as an undergraduate in 1988–1990 has been stunning. We had a Chinese restaurant, a chippie, a Jamaican restaurant — which was the "coolest" — and an Indian restaurant in our neighborhood, but nothing remotely as cosmopolitan as now; so I can just imagine what it was like in the '50s.

CR: People weren't talking about food because it was seen as frivolous. And it was not considered polite. I remember Caroline Waldegrave (who ran Prue Leith's Cookery School) telling me that when she got married her mother told her, "When you get invited to dinner you must write a letter of thanks — but don't ever mention the food!"

SM: Because mentioning food was vulgar?

CR: Yes. I would ask everybody what they cooked and what they ate when they travelled because I was researching recipes. They were embarrassed. I started collecting recipes when people left Egypt in the expulsion of 1956–1957 in the last stages of the Suez crisis. For several years I was completely immersed in the world of Jewish refugees from Egypt — they were Arab Jews (now called Mizrahi) and those whose families originated from Spain and Portugal and had migrated through the Mediterranean and Ottoman worlds. I got the recipe for the Orange Cake which went viral and became famous all over the world from "Madame Galante" from Aleppo. I was intrigued because no one else from Aleppo had the recipe for the cake. It turned out that the recipe had originated in Spain and migrated with a few families through Portugal and Livorno. As I took down all these recipes, I realized that everybody — from Iran, Iraq, Greece, Syria, Turkey — was claiming the same dish as their own: "this is our *Baklava!*," "our stuffed vine leaves!" So I really wanted to find out where it was all from originally. When I went to the British Library looking for Arab cookbooks, there wasn't a single contemporary one. I asked the librarian and he gave me a list of items relating to medieval Arab cookery, including three thirteenth-century medieval culinary manuscripts, an English translation and commentaries about one from Baghdad, a Spanish translation of an Al Andalusi/Maghrebi one, and a sociological study by a French Marxist Orientalist called Maxime Rodinson of one found in Damascus. I was enthralled to see that you could find out what happened in a place through food.

sm: One of the things that struck me while we were talking is that we think about food as a kind of home. Even if you are not politically in forced exile, you can feel uprooted — exile is a state of mind. And because memory is so sensory, remembering food is a powerful trigger: remembering smell can bring a whole world back. Is food both home and un-home? Do we carry home or exile when we carry our food in our memories and our senses across borders? Is food the ultimate migrant object, inherently mobile? Or would you say that the migrations of food are more specific to the history of particular communities, their roots and their uprootings?

cr: For all immigrants and exiles, food is the one thing from their homeland that they can hold onto which gives comfort and joy. What we call "Jewish food" is really the food of countries where the Jews once had stable communities and adapted local foods to fit their dietary laws. Because Jews moved, their food is often a hybrid from two or more homelands. The various Jewish foods of India, for instance, have influences from Iraq, Syria, and Portugal with the flavors of India.

sm: A couple of winters ago I did a tour of old Kolkata, and visited the Synagogue, which is exquisitely preserved. But there are very few Jews left in the city — you could count them on your hands. The man who takes care of the Synagogue is Muslim and has a deep understanding of Jewish architecture and culture. I wondered whether food has served as a kind of bridge between not just cultures and societies but also religions? Because Jewish and Islamic cultures in India are traditionally thought to be opposed.

cr: Throughout history Muslims and Jews have mostly been in an interdependent relationship. For instance, in Spain where the Muslims conquered the Iberian Peninsula, it was the Jews who had been persecuted by the Visigoths who helped them in and opened the doors. Muslim Spain was for the Jews a golden age.

SM: I completely felt that in Córdoba. I remember sitting in the Jewish quarter and I could smell cinnamon, I could smell cumin, I could smell Islamic as well as Indian spices, and I had just come from the *Mezquita* —

CR: Toledo is known as the city of three cultures because Christians, Muslims, and Jews coexisted there for centuries. The nuns who sell pastries in churches and convents say their almond specialities are both Arab and Jewish. At the time of the Inquisition, when the Jews were banished from Spain in 1492, a great number of mainly rich families chose to stay and convert to Christianity. Some who had unmarried daughters sent them to convents as was true also for old Christians. The nuns came with their little maids whose families were usually Moriscos (former Muslims) and these young girls cooked and made pastries. Spanish cuisine has Jewish and most obviously Arab influences, yet a lot of Spaniards are still in denial about the influence of the Jewish and Arab culture.

SM: I have seen that myself in Spain. To pick up on the theme of trade and merchant cultures, something I discovered recently is a kind of weird generic mobility about recipes in the Indian tradition. There is a paradox about the genre there. Although the earliest cookbooks go back to 1831, in day-to-day life it was largely an aural tradition passed down the family line, usually through women. I wanted to show you the only cookbook that I bought with me from India. It is in tatters and there are practically no pictures. It was written by a wonderful writer of children's books called Leela Majumdar and another woman called Kamala Chatterjee. This was the only cookbook I had seen when I left for the UK to do my undergraduate degree. The following year I got married and received it as a wedding present.

CR: What year did it come out?

SM: 1979. It went through seven reprints because it became so popular. The first Bengali cookbook, which is also India's first printed cookbook — the one from 1831 — is *Pakrajeshwar*. There's another one, *Byanjanratnakar,* that is also from the early nineteenth century. But the first proto-recipes book or proto-cookbook was buried in a thirteenth-century book of folk poetry in Bengal. It is called the *Mangalkavyas,* which is a book of poems of benediction which, in the middle of singing praises to Indigenous Hindu/Bengali deities, embeds poems and songs of praise for the food cooked by the women of that region and of that time. We get a vivid glimpse of the differences in the cuisine of the east and west of Bengal, which of course became much more pronounced and political after the Partition of Bengal. But we also get vignettes of the differences between culinary traditions of the farmers, the hunter-gatherers, and the rich merchants for whom hospitality and its style were among the intangibles of class. Have you come across such generic mixing or grafting in the Mediterranean cultures of cuisine? And is there a tradition of the poetry or music of food?

CR: These thirteenth-century Arab recipes were written by people who were part of the courts — the cooks could not write! In the caliphates of Baghdad and Córdoba, where there had been a big explosion of interest in gastronomy, courtiers and princes wrote songs and poems about food. Much of the refined culinary culture of Baghdad was adopted from ancient Persia — that is, Iran — as you can tell from the names and tags of the recipes. You find echoes from there in Sicily, which was occupied by Arabs, in countries like Morocco and Tunisia, and all the way to Barcelona. A hybrid Hispano-Arabic cuisine that developed in Spain caused a revolution in North Africa with the arrival of Muslims banished from Spain. An example of the mixing and sharing of cultures is the pigeon pie called *bstila,* said to be Andalusian in Morocco and Moorish in Spain.

sm: Ah yes — the *bstila!* I kind of assumed it was Spanish-Islamic. So it's such a shared heritage that it is difficult now to tell the direction of influence of migrancy if you like!

cr: There's also the cuisine that developed in Constantinople — now Istanbul — when it was the capital of the Ottoman Empire, from all the different occupied territories and the steppes of Central Asia where the nomadic Turks came from, which went on to spread throughout the empire over most of the Middle East, the Balkans, part of North Africa, and beyond. That is why you get pilafs, rice pudding, baklava, and *kadaifi* in most countries that were Ottoman. The British Empire didn't spread its cuisine in the same way all over the world.

sm: But in Calcutta we do have these colonial clubs like they have in Cairo, I believe. And they have some British recipes, Indianized, of course. So you get dishes like mulligatawny soup. And the really recherché thing hardly anyone makes so well these days as the Indian clubs is prawn cocktail: a genre by itself. And for me, the most exquisite cucumber sandwiches are to be found in Calcutta rather than Britain.

cr: Go to Claridge's — they still have them, along with specialities that people from all over the world go to for a taste of something essentially "English." I went to an English club in Bombay for tea. And of course we had English clubs in Cairo — sporting clubs. But when the English were there, they didn't allow the locals to become members unless they were hugely wealthy or important.

sm: When I was growing up it was just the same, these restrictions. But it wasn't just about being rich, it was about social clout. For instance, my parents are members of a couple of clubs and they're not rich. But they are from a distinguished academic family, and that was their passport. Women couldn't become members but could only enter as daughters or wives. So of course I shunned that whole world. But now I'm interested in it as a sociological phenomenon. Talking of food and class and "taste" in a sense that straddles the two, and how migration plays into this tangle, let me tell you about my experience as a child. My mother was a very gregarious person, who married into a sedate, scholarly family, so she felt very deprived. Her family were refugees from what was East Bengal and is now Bangladesh. They moved to West Bengal during the Partition of Bengal and, like other refugees, they brought with them East Bengali cuisine which was, at least in those times, significantly different from West Bengali cuisine. My father's family was solidly West Bengali — she felt that not only were they scholarly and sedentary, but their daily food was subtle to the point of being dull and soul-killing. My mother, who was more like a friend than a parent when I was growing up, told me that the food of her marital home — where she lived with her husband and his parents and brother — felt symbolic of a change in the texture of her life when she arrived after a 90% arranged marriage. Apparently, lunchtime was a time of tragic epiphanies when she would often lock herself in the bathroom and have a cry: The fish were so bland and insipid in their stew that it was as if "they stared at you." She came from a large family where she was one of eleven children and where the food was plentiful, spicy, and robust in a way that West Bengalis would call unrefined and vulgar. Eventually she decided to take things in hand and give my father a touch of a raucous excess. And then there was a sea change in the cooking of our house, and I witnessed it. But the cultural registers of culinary difference that were a legacy of the political Partition of Bengal remained, largely as a matter of humor. Did you see anything like this in your childhood?

CR: Yes, in most countries you find upper class food does not have very strong flavors. In Turkey, the classic food of Istanbul is very delicately spiced, and has little garlic and no chili. At a conference dinner there several years ago, when local academics had been asked to greet us foreign gastronomes and food writers, I was sitting next to a sophisticated Turkish woman. When we were served food from Gaziantep (near the Syrian border and Aleppo) she was very embarrassed. It was very hot and spicy, full of chili and garlic. She said, "We never eat this!" She saw it as vulgar. And now UNESCO has chosen Gaziantep as a City of Creativity for its gastronomy! Migrants are terribly important in bringing new foods to countries. They're usually cheap foods that can be made without significant capital or material resources and can be sold in the street. And then, in a weird way, they become "national dishes" sometimes in their new habitat.

SM: A whole world, then, of the paradoxes of migrant life and the politics of food, contained in a dish and served on our tables.

36

A Journey in Taste

Faraj Alnasser in conversation with Subha Mukherji

SUBHA MUKHERJI: I wanted to start by asking you an obvious question: Did migrating to Britain change or develop your relationship to Mediterranean food and its culture?

FARAJ ALNASSER: The Palestinian poet Mahmoud Darwish writes that "the further we move away" from our past, our home or our homeland, "the closer we come..." ("The Hoopoe"). I was Syrian when I left Syria. Leaving made me want to learn more about my roots. Being away from home made me miss so much, like my family gathering at the table, the farm, the type of food, the vegetation, the weather. The beautiful thing about food, though, is that it goes beyond borders. For example, hummus is made in Syria but they also make it in Lebanon, in Egypt, in Palestine.

SM: What I'm hearing is that there's an entire way of life that food has come to stand for: the farm, the seasons, the cycles of life. Would you say that food stands for all of that much more perceptibly once you have left?

FA: I find I'm in a more romantic friendship with food. When I make a dish from home it's not just a dish, but a healing, a remedy.

SM: You mentioned hummus. I notice that, yes, my Lebanese friends say, "We make the real hummus" and when I went to Israel, people said, "It was born in this place, in this shop in Jerusalem." And then I had *your* hummus and thought, "Wow, this is the best hummus." When you have become a citizen of the world in some ways, does that intensify your sense of ownership of a particular food, or does it make you more relaxed about it?

FA: Sometimes I feel that things should be made in a particular way. At the same time, I also think that, like us, food crosses borders. For example, tomatoes were introduced to Syria in 1750 and became part of our cuisine. Now lots of our dishes, like *shakshuka,* have tomato in them.

SM: Once you start thinking about the history of ingredients, you realize that there's a paradox about food. We identify food with what home means to us, but it has always already brought the world home to us. No?

FA: Yes — food is like a free bird. It travels all over the world and you cannot control its migrations.

SM: Lovely thought! Yes! On to your own history: Whenever you've talked about your childhood in Aleppo, it's been so vivid, so evocative. Can you tell us a bit about what food meant to you then and perhaps more importantly, did you *know* what it meant to you?

FA: My grandmother had a farm and grew her own vegetables. She had her own pistachio trees, fig trees, pomegranate trees, and olive trees. I couldn't wait for late summer each year to climb the fig tree and eat them. I would go to the market with my mother and grandmother and aunts. I used to love sneaking between them and hearing them gossip and seeing what they were doing. It was only after I left that I started to realize how important food is to us. I called my grandmother in Aleppo last week and asked what she was up to, and she said, "Well, I have fifty kilos of tomatoes, I have to peel them, squeeze them by hand, and dry them to make paste. Your aunt brought me fifty kilos of red pepper and I have to clean and dry them to make chili flakes." It made me wish I were with her. When I came to the UK, cooking helped me to express my sorrow, my homesickness —

SM: Your longing.… What was the first thing that you cooked and when — do you remember?

FA: Yesterday was my sixth anniversary in the UK. I was writing about it, and going through photos that I captured in the journey. I captured the first dish I cooked when I arrived in the UK, it was *mujaddhara,* salad, and chips. That was the first dish I made in two-and-a-half years for myself, after being homeless. It felt to me like time to start again.

SM: Did you have a kitchen where you were staying?

FA: When I came to the UK to seek asylum six years ago, I was under the protection of the government. I was sent to stay in temporary accommodation in Huddersfield which had a kitchen, and I lived there for a few months before I got my refugee status.

SM: And you were able to create again — cooking is about self-expression too, isn't it?

FA: Exactly.

SM: I'm curious about the form in which recipes travel. Where I grew up, in West Bengal, the earliest cookbooks go back to 1831, but there are very few of them. In day-to-day life it's largely an oral tradition, not recorded in writing so much as passed down through the family line. What was it like in the Aleppo of your childhood, and in what form did you bring recipes over when you left?

FA: My grandmother from my mum's side is a great cook, but she cannot read or write. When my mum got married, she needed to learn how to cook. So my grandma recorded all her recipes on a tape. And she would say, "If it's too salty, it's fine, if it's over-spiced, it's fine, if you're afraid of something, go ahead and face it." She gave it to my mother and my mum started to follow these recipes and later became a better cook than her mother. Because my mum came from a poor family, she didn't want to see her children have the same experience. She wanted us to go to college and be educated, and she wouldn't let me help her in the kitchen. But when she went out, I used to sneak into the kitchen and do some cooking. Sometimes the food would get too salty and burn, but one time it worked: she tasted it and said, "That's delicious, Faraj! Ok, you can help me in the kitchen." I learned a lot from her.

SM: The way your grandmother framed cooking as trial and error makes me think of how you and I cook. We don't cook with precise measurements. But of course, if you want to write a cookbook then you need to put in measurements. Have you thought of writing a cookbook? Being such an intuitive creator, how would you go about it?

FA: I struggled when I worked in a kitchen and they gave me recipes to follow. When I cook, things taste different each time. So I think writing a cookbook would be a big challenge for me. I also think that people who want to cook need to be less afraid of recipes. As my grandmother said to my mum, if you make a mistake, it's fine.

SM: You recognize that food needs to have a kind of grammar to be written down and transmitted but we need to find a grammar that is not constricting, a grammar that allows space for error, experiment, improvisation. I find that when I tell people how I've cooked, say, a particular Bengali dish, I always say, "Look, grasp the basic concept. You flavor with seeds, you sauté...." If you've got the ideas, then the details are a moveable feast.

FA: Yes, you need the foundation, you need to understand certain things, and then you do what you like to do. You play.

SM: Every time you've cooked for me you've told me stories about the item you've cooked. It seems to me that there is an inherent migrancy about stories. Stories slip through borders; nobody can keep them in. Perhaps there's also a migrancy about food: food is the ultimate migrant object, as you're presenting it. What role have food stories played in your own journey from Syria to the UK?

FA: It's not just that my body left Syria to come to the UK, it's that Syria itself moved with me. Aleppo is inside of me. The souk's inside of me, my mother's kitchen is inside of me, the farm, the summer days, the spices, the water, the air, the memories, and the stories. The other day I saw these damask rose petals, and it reminded me of the April and May time when we'd go to the market and see it full of damask rose for making rose water or rose jam. My grandma used to make that jam for us. I called my grandma and she told me how to make it. I made the jam, and I gave some to my neighbor and she said "Faraj, how beautiful it is to imagine these petals which are in Cambridge but used in a recipe that travelled miles across the ocean from Aleppo towards Europe to England." She started to ask me about the story of the jam and how it's made. Each dish has its own story. For example, each Friday we'd go to *hummusji,* the shop that sells hummus. Some of these shops are 200 years old, and they are inherited by generations of the same family. We'd never make hummus because we only ever bought it from them. When I eat that, I remember the gathering and my mum making things in the kitchen and someone buying fresh bread and bringing things together.

SM: The way you're describing it, it's like a scene from a play, it's theater. It's brought alive by stories. That seems to be your way of linking your past with your present, of telling people what your life was like. And that eyewitness evocation, that vividness, relates to some of the work Natalya and I do on the rhetoric of the Renaissance. It's almost as if food not only comes with narrative, but demands and provokes it. It is itself an impulse to tell, an impulse to recreate, an impulse to stage.

FA: I still remember what my neighbor said: "Faraj, I haven't been to Syria, but I feel like I have now." Similarly, I haven't been to India, but I feel like I've been through the beautiful dishes you make for me.

SM: It's like a spot of time when you inhabit another world, another land, in your senses.

FA: Especially smell. You smell things and you go miles away.

SM: You mention that your mother didn't want you in the kitchen. What was the relationship between gender and cooking in your childhood? If you had stayed, do you think your class and gender position would have meant that you would not have done what you do now?

FA: In Syrian restaurants the chefs are mainly men, but culturally, men don't cook at home. I'm not sure if I'd be a chef if I were in Syria. And if I were, I wouldn't be respected in the way I'm respected now. My hummus wouldn't mean what it means here. If I were there and tried to tell them about their rose jam ... I mean, every mother in Syria makes rose jam!

SM: Ha — so the migrant nature of food allows it to become an art, as it were! As you say, if you cook hummus or rose jam in Aleppo, what story would you tell? Now, I came to the UK much earlier than you did and I have witnessed the transition of migrant food from the strange to the trendy. Does this transition map onto the trajectory from exile to cosmopolitanism that someone like you, who came as an exile but then ended up being a chef at Honey & Co., experienced?

FA: It does sound like it has changed a lot from what it was like in the '60s and '70s, or even the '80s. When I came to Cambridge, the first thing I worried about was whether or not I'd be able to find Middle Eastern shops and the ingredients I use in my kitchen, but when I came and walked around on Mill Road and saw Pakistani, Turkish, Indian, and Chinese shops which sell everything, I felt I was at home.

SM: The culture has become more hospitable, perhaps. Is there any sense in which it also poses a bit of a challenge because Mediterranean Arab cooking is now all the rage in London, if not the whole of the UK? Does it put you under extra pressure to bring something new to the scene that is distinctive, that is all yours? What are you going to bring to it that is all yours?

FA: My philosophy in the kitchen is to bring alternatives to meat dishes. When people think of Middle Eastern food, they think kebabs. But what about making it vegetarian and more sustainable? We have a lot of dishes called *bi zeit,* which are cooked with olive oil instead of meat. For example, you cook spinach with spices and mushrooms and olive oil. You cook the green beans with red sauce, and chopped tomato with garlic and coriander and olive oil. This is what the working class usually eat because they often can't afford meat. These dishes are delicious and nourishing and have interesting stories, but you don't often find them in Middle Eastern restaurants.

SM: So it's not only about opening up the diversity and range of the cuisine, but also about tapping into the culinary culture of a particular place vertically, across classes. We've talked about how food travels. Food is also one of the most synesthetic experiences. How much of the *total* experience can migration carry across, and are there elements that are irreducibly local and located, and which cannot be translated?

FA: One issue is vegetation. For example, growing figs in this country is not the same as growing figs in Syria. You might get a few good figs but it's not the same as the ones that I have at my grandmother's farm. The tree is smart enough to understand that this is not the same soil, not the same water, not the same sun. Maybe we cannot hear trees, but they have much to tell us and to teach us, especially with global warming.

SM: It's interesting that you relate it to the climate crisis. What role might food have to play in our futures?

FA: Will we be able to have the same things because of drought? What will we lose? Will we have the same trees or same flour or same wheat as we had before in, say, fifty years' time? This is the reason I'm thinking about vegetarian alternatives and what we can use instead. It's related to the climate crisis on the one hand, but on the other also how people lived before, in the ancient time.

SM: Perhaps food has undiscovered, untapped resources that'll help us adapt to the challenges and shape our future in a way that might be better for the world.... Teach us more sustainable ways of living.... It can be a bridge in so many senses — from our past to our future, as you hint. I wonder if it can also do social bridging, especially when it is immigrant cooking. In every country there's a high and a low culinary culture. Does migrant food help to bring the two together in its adopted country?

FA: When I talked to my mother the other day and told her that my friends came over and that I made *mujaddhara* and hummus and salad, she said, "Faraj, aren't you ashamed of yourself?" Her understanding is that to be hospitable and generous one has to make a great dish with meat. But here it's different: refugees brought the food of different classes together on one table.

SM: Perhaps in a migrant context, those class barriers, and ideas of register, break down more easily. I remember the first time Rowan Williams, coeditor of this volume, came to lunch or dinner. My mother asked what I was cooking and I said, "I'm making daal and rice." And my mother said, "Is this how we brought you up?! You are feeding a guest, and not just any guest but the ex-Archbishop of Canterbury, *daal* and *bhat*?!" I revised the whole menu! I had thought nothing of it but for my mother, I was violating the first principles of hospitality and getting the register of food wrong in making such a modest meal. Claudia Roden, who is also interviewed in this book, described Middle Eastern cuisine as "rich in variations and poor in precision." Is freedom from culinary grammar a luxury we cannot afford in immigrant situations, or should we be assertive of it?

FA: Food writing is often not very precise. For example, I have got an Arabic cookbook from ninth-century Baghdad. There are many ingredients they did not have at that time: no tomato, no potato. The recipes describe just what is inside of the dish, they do not say how much. They just say, "a bit of that, a bit of that." When the dish travelled, everyone started to make it the way they heard of it.

SM: Interesting — so imprecision becomes a way of preserving a space for diversity, particularity, variety! You mention that in the ninth-century that they didn't have potatoes and tomatoes. Can you tell us a little bit about the trade routes?

FA: The interesting thing about that Arabic book, written during the Abbasid caliphate, is that some of our contemporary dishes already existed then — baklava, *mujaddhara, freekeh,* lamb stew with quince and pomegranate molasses, etc. They used lots of dates, olives, and olive oil. Lots of recipes came via the Silk Road at that time. But some went back to more surprising places too; the other day an Aleppo chef was talking about a recipe that goes back to Korea, and had travelled via the Silk Road to Aleppo. We've slightly changed it and now use orange blossom so it's more Middle Eastern. It's fascinating....

SM: We have talked about how food unites. But migrant food can also divide. A long time ago, I had weevils in the kitchen of my college flat, the kind that come out of flour. A college official came to inspect, opened my cupboards, and said, "Oh it smells, it's full of strange spices." Quite apart from the fact that that's how racism operates, it made me feel that there are boundaries created by the senses, by smell especially. Do you have any perception of how food defines otherness rather than belonging and blending?

FA: Sometimes people are afraid of things that are new to them....

SM: I can understand the unfamiliarity but the notion of strangeness can tip over easily either into wonder and fascination or into repulsion.

FA: Some people might find foreign food difficult. We need to understand this mentality. I think about myself: I came from a culture in Syria where the food is only Syrian food. You'd never, ever see a foreign food shop in Syria. So the first time I tried Indian was when I came to the UK, the first time I tried Italian was when I came to the UK. And it blew my mind.

SM: Yes, there's a sense in which differences are resolved. But is there a danger in thinking that way about food, in that people do tend to homogenize migrants? This brings me to a memory. My friend Nadina, who's also in the book, cofounded the Melissa Network for Migrant and Refugee Women in Greece. I attended a cooking workshop organized by the network in a restaurant in Athens which had opened its doors to Nadina's group of migrant women from Afghanistan, Iran, Iraq, and Syria for the day. What struck me there is that they had a very playful, joyous, mischievous attitude towards difference. But there were some American food historians who were hierarchical and categorizing and completely out of tune, saying to the Iranians, for instance, "Learn how to make dolmades from the Afghans, this is the right way of doing it, not that." Because they make their dolmades in a very delicate, thin way. And there was this Iranian woman who was really strong and funny; she just winked at the other women and said, "Let's show them how to make fat dolmades!" It's this prescriptive thing, whereby dolmades became a symbol of Middle Easternness, while all of these women were having fun with their understanding of Middle Easternness: Yes, there is something, but it's not one thing, it's made of lots of strands and it's fun to compare and have differences. It was a really interesting event where I felt that there were two very different approaches to internal difference and discrimination.

FA: Yes, to preserve it and enjoy it. When I cook with my Turkish friends or Lebanese friends, we also make vine leaves and I say, "Everyone makes it in his own way, this is how I grew up with it and I stick with it and love it. But you make it in your own way, and we'll see how it looks."

SM: How do you think Brexit will affect the migration of food and recipes?

FA: It's affecting finding ingredients, to be honest. Now when I go shopping, there are lots of brands I can't find. That's because things used to come from, say, Turkey and go through Europe and then come here. And everything's doubled in price. It means I have to think about alternatives.

SM: Perhaps this will open up a space where we can all begin to think of food a little differently; not in terms of mechanically putting together ingredients, but in terms of principles?

FA: A friend of mine was born in Venezuela but his grandparents migrated from Syria to the US, the US to Venezuela. And he grew up with Aleppo food there at that time. But they didn't have any

Middle Eastern ingredients there: say, pomegranate molasses, or bulgur wheat. Just rice and lentils. He said his grandmother struggled a lot at first but then she started to be creative — if she could not find a specific thing, she would find the closest thing and tweak the recipe. In the face of climate change, now, will we be able to find things from the same sources, the same places, in the future? Can we make food resilient and adapt to a new diet? Think back to ancient Egypt — how they used to cool their food, how they stored their food for years and years....

SM: There is something communal or group-based about cooking. Is that quality possible to preserve during migration, or does it change into a solitary act of remembrance?

FA: Cooking is something that makes me feel connected to others. But even when I am on my own, I love to cook for myself. When I make a dish, I feel that I never left home, like I never experienced exile.

X.

Moving Things

Fig. 37.1. Photo by Faraj Alnasser.

Faraj Alnasser

I left home as a refugee searching for new land, as I have no land. I locked doors with padlocks as I locked my heart, scared of the unknown future. I contemplated the engravings that my uncle had drawn elaborately while he was sculpting the keys, with tales etched into their corners. Long nights were spent telling stories. Maybe the keys are older than me. How strange it is that they carry more secrets than me, and perhaps hold more hope than I can hold within myself, so they do not change with circumstances, but remain steadfast. When we returned from a long journey, we took out the keys with glee, filled with joy at our return! Returning from school every day, I pulled out the key to the house. "He who loses the key loses the house," my grandmother used to say. When you lose your house key, you lose the possibility of return, you lose your bed, your library, your kitchen, your mother, your dinner table, your safety, your family's place, and your birthplace (for I wasn't born in the hospital). I hold on to my keys. I cannot afford to lose them.

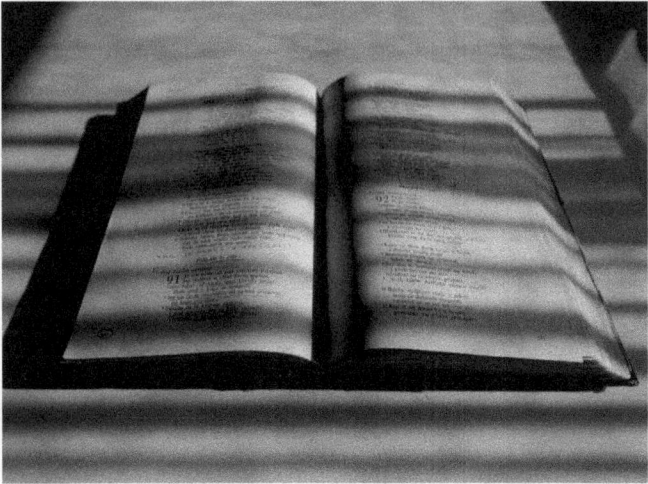

Fig. 38.1. Photo by Dragana Jurišić.

Dragana Jurišić

When Croatian snipers came into our apartment on September 15, 1991, and gave us two minutes to gather a handful of belongings to bring to the shelter, I acted automatically without much thought and threw a pair of large scissors, army boots, and an oversized leather-bound Bible into my red rucksack. The army boots and large scissors, which were a useful tool and a weapon, made sense, but for years I wondered about the Bible. In my memory, sixteen-year-old me had no interest in God. Why would I pack a large heavy book to weigh me down while I fled, trying to escape the Yugoslav army's sniper's bullets, is still unclear to me. Did I bring it with me as some kind of a lucky charm or perhaps to bargain with the Almighty, promising that if I was spared, I would do my best to become a better person? I really do not know.

I left Croatia in 1999 with no memories of interacting much with the book in the years preceding my exile. When I came back home in the Summer of 2021 and opened the Bible, I was surprised to see that I underlined a number of passages. I must have made the marks during the period when we ended up homeless, refugees in our own country, being shuffled between different emergency accommodations. I was an avid reader and this was the only book I had in my possession during the period of homelessness. When I opened the Bible on the bookmarked page, I could see in my teenage handwriting, above Psalm 91 which I underlined, written in capital letters, "WHEN IN DANGER," and recalled reading the psalm over and over again like a mantra during endless bombings and airstrikes:

> He will cover you with his feathers, and under his wings you will find refuge; his faithfulness will be your shield and rampart. You will not fear the terror of the night, nor the arrow that flies by day, nor the pestilence that stalks in the darkness, nor the plague that destroys at midday. A thousand may fall at your side, ten thousand at your right hand, but it will not come near you.[1]

---

1   Psalm 91:4–7, New International Version.

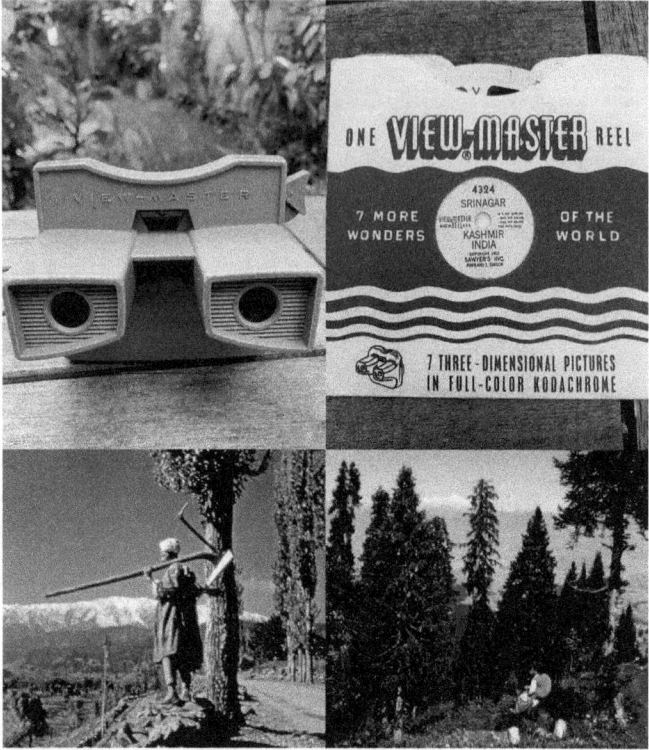

Fig. 39.1. Source: Subha Mukherji.

Subha Mukherji

This drab, beige View Master (Model J), on the left, made in Belgium in the 1970s, was the "coolest" thing I grew up with in a middle-class Kolkata household — a special-format stereoscope invented in 1939. Its twin (second from left) was a cardboard reel, with seven full-color 3D slides of "Kashmir, India" — a "wonder of the world." To my child's mind, it was an object of pure magic that brought the world home: Belgium, only known to us through *Tintin,* and Kashmir, paradise on earth, a place proximate yet other-worldly, which I had seen in Bollywood films, dreamt of going to through many nights when I lay unsleeping, and eventually, one day, did visit. Its muddy exterior only intensified the miraculous iridescence of the world it gave me access to. I left this wonder of ingenuity behind when I came to the UK as a student, but I brought it with me in 2000 as it was dawning on me that I had perhaps become a settled, if accidental, immigrant and a citizen of the globe. It opened up a secret world of mystery and beauty which now brought home to the world. But in that age of innocence, neither I nor the view-finder knew what a palimpsest it was to become. Now, Kashmir is no longer a habitable fantasy; I am unlikely to be able to return, ever, in my life-time. Here in Cambridge, as I gaze at those images — snow-capped hills, the farmer looking across the peaceful valley, and the rider riding into the deep woods — the landscape shimmers into what Louis MacNeice would call "green improbable fields," where unhome momentarily becomes home again, where an idea of India, fading into the fogs of communalism and state violence, shimmers in outmoded Kodachrome and yearns for a local habitation and a name.

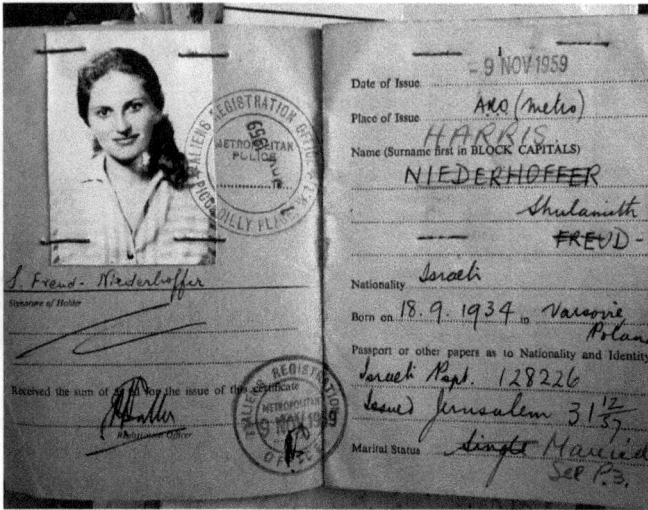

Fig. 40.1. Photo by Jonathan Gil Harris.

Jonathan Gil Harris

In early 2020, just before COVID-19 left most borders bolted and padlocked, I found my mother's British alien registration card — folded alongside other official papers from another life, another hemisphere, another universe — at the bottom of her Chinese tea chest in New Zealand. I brought it back home with me to India. Its makeshift emendations showed how my mother had been repeatedly named and renamed, through the multiple self-reinventions forced on her by war, deportation, death of her parents, adoption by her uncle, migration, and marriage. "Hebrew" derives from an ancient Egyptian word that refers, not to a nation, an ethnicity, or a language, but to a condition of perpetual unrootedness. Despite the modern state of Israel's efforts to root "Hebrews," my mother was a "Hebrew" in that archaic sense, for better as well as for worse. Forged through too many traumatic dislocations, her multiple identities nonetheless display unexpected deliverances, transgressive connections, small resistances to the ways in which states capture and control their subjects. The project of identifying citizens with finality is always doomed to failure: I love that my mother's multiply rewritten card, which was meant to root her, ended up doing the complete opposite.

Fig. 41.1. Photo by E. Fiddan-Qasmiyeh and Y.M. Qasmiyeh, 2021.

Yousif M. Qasmiyeh

Out of a tin box full of needles, of different sizes and shapes, with wonky and straight eyes, alongside loose and rolled-up threads of subdued colors, I picked it up. Without even looking in her hardly open eyes to seek consent, I snatched it, to see it at close range and in the company of my tears: a photograph of my mother's face wandering alone in her ever-shrinking pastures. I first put it in my pocket, then moved it to my wallet alongside my ID for Palestinian refugees and the draft of a love letter I once wrote for my brother to his lover in graphite and traces of ink to give the impression of age. The letter reached the lover but my ID and my mother's picture are still in the company of one another.

An eye for an eye so both my mother and I could see in each other's eye what it is to be seen: dissipating edges; black and white losing their blackness and whiteness for the sake of a third tinge of a color; speckled surfaces; eyes looking at the camera and seeing themselves as serenity for the constantly unsettled in their present. I so want to imagine that it was just fine for her, then, to come from the camp to the city, carrying her dialect on her back and knowing that, as a refugee, being photographed can be done beyond the question of aid, for the sole reason of being photographed—a fresh topography for a photograph which would leave Baddawi camp in my wallet secretly so as to be archived alongside my moments with my mother, as the son who has always feared her absence to the extent that I, as a child, would hide within the folds of her dresses, to accompany her from one camp to another, always in our time and through a no-place which never belonged to us.

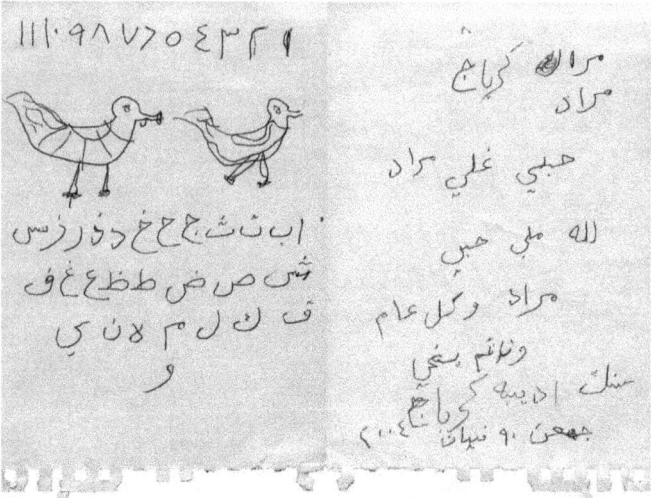

Fig. 42.1. Front: A handwritten note by my mother to my son Mourad; back: "Arabic" numbers (1–11), Arabic letters, and drawing of two birds. Source: Issam Kourbaj.

Issam Kourbaj

As a child, I was a keen learner. I started to go to school when I was five, but had so many difficulties learning to write the alphabet of my tongue, particularly the first letter of my name, I. The sound of the initial of my first name, both in Arabic and in English, had mystical echoes; "I" is pronounced /aI/ and it means "eye" in English. In Arabic, ع is pronounced /aIn/ and that means an eye too. My mother, then well into her forties, had hardly any schooling, but set out to help me forming the first letter of my name. She asked me to show her my ع and I did. She held my hand in her hand and together we "drew" that letter. She asked me to do it again. She was very generous, made me understand that this was not just a letter, part of a word, a fragment of a whole language, but a picture. It took me many attempts, with and without her hands, and then I drew it, not very well, but I did; ever since, I started to learn how to form my "eye."

Many moons later, my mother was living alone, my father having died. We had all left home. I thought I must teach her how to read and write. I started to teach her. Of course, she had many difficulties learning to write the twenty-eight letters of our alphabet. When we arrived at forming the eighteenth letter, the

"ع," I held her hand and reminded her of the way she held my hand when I was little, and together we "drew" it. She couldn't remember; she was so keen to carry on learning the remaining ten.

An affectionate handwritten note from my mother to her grandsons

My mother tried her hand at writing simple broken letters, in phrases that reflect the struggle to communicate through written language. It reads with difficulties:

> To my precious darling Mourad, God be with you and Happy New Year

> Your grandmother
> Friday 9 April 2004

Fig. 43.1. Photo by Natalya Din-Kariuki.

Natalya Din-Kariuki

This glass belonged to my late aunt Yasmin. It was part of a collection of crystalware that she acquired while living abroad in Northern Ireland in the 1970s, and which she carried with her when she migrated to the United States before bringing it home to Kenya, where my grandfather had migrated from India some decades earlier. As a child, I often had sleepovers at her house in Nairobi, where she and my uncle would drink red wine with their dinner. I, too, would get a sip, served in this glass, the perfect size for my tiny hands. Something about the experience was thrilling. It felt like a pact, like a secret, like being part, even if only for a moment, of the glamour of adult life. When I travelled with the glass to the UK, where I live now, I feared that it would break. I marveled at how my aunt had managed to cross several continents with such a delicate thing while keeping it intact. Looking at it, I am transported temporarily to another time and place, and reminded not only of the love that she and I shared, but of the way that this strange combination of fragility and resilience shaped her migrant experience, and my own.

Fig. 44.1. Still from an animation of a tale from "The Huntsman and the King's Son."

Dine Diallo

Those who make the crossing of the Mediterranean from Africa have nothing material left. But they bring us their knowledge, memories, and imagination. Dine Diallo was told many stories by his grandfather. This one comes from a cycle of tales, "The Huntsman and the King's Son," which explores ideas of justice:

> Once upon a time there was a woman who had a baby and a cat. Sometimes the cat was left to mind the baby. One day, a huge serpent entered the house—but the cat seized it and bit it in two, and dragged the pieces outside. When the mother came back and saw blood everywhere and all over the baby, she thought the cat had killed her baby. And she took a stick and killed the cat.
>
> Soon after, the baby woke up. Then, outside the house, the mother found the head and the body of the huge snake, and she understood that the cat had saved her baby.

Afterword

Rowan Williams

1.

As the process of putting together this collection has advanced, against a background of political developments that make its subject matter all the more urgent, we have become more sharply aware of how our own terminology might be interrogated. Subha's Introduction notes that the vocabulary we use to speak of variously "displaced" communities of experience is not innocent: as it is with the familiar and recurring tropes of "deserving" and "undeserving" poor, so in this connection also. The "refugee" is granted a measure of moral legitimacy as someone whose presence away from their home territory is not a matter of choice. So in the current UK climate, Ukrainians are imaginatively accorded full legitimacy in a way that, say, Afghans are not — even though the actual nuts and bolts of receiving even Ukrainians have not been exactly a model of compassion or efficiency. The "asylum seeker" has a more ambivalent status; they are agents to the degree that they are "seeking" something from us, and so the legitimacy of their claim is open to testing. To designate someone simply and without qualification as a "migrant" tends to load on them the full weight of having chosen to leave where they belong and intrude into the territory of another, and this "choice" is seen as a potentially threatening self-assertion that necessarily poses a problem for and limits the choices of a host society. In the light of this, the language of migrancy can increasingly act as a catchall designation for the displaced, in a way that sanctions suspicion. Both the truthfulness and the judgment of displaced individuals is seen as requiring challenge and interrogation. "Migrancy" comes to have uncomfortable resonance with a traditional rhetoric about the dangers we face from rootless wanderers who will never be assimilable in our particular place and who will compromise our collective racial and cultural identity — a familiar trope of anti-Semitism, modern and premodern. If we in this book utilize "migrant" as covering the widest possible range of what I've called "displaced" experience, we need to acknowledge the shadows around the word and the ways in which it can be used to encode and reinforce the power of identitarian, "insider" definitions. We need to be clear about using the word strictly as an adjective for what and who it is that is in motion, in transit, for whatever reason — enforced exile, flight from imminent danger, the choice of more secure opportunities, or whatever it may be. And, as many of our contributors here spell out and illuminate so vividly, thinking about migrant knowing and imagining in the immediate, concrete context of displaced persons and communities can make us see more clearly the "migrant" character of a huge range of human habits of thought.

2.

We come to know what we know quite literally because of where we are; we know what we know as the *bodies* we are — which is why we have had to learn in recent decades so much more about how the male, white, heterosexual, cisgender body has developed and deployed the power to define a world in which other bodies have in some degree to deny what they know *as the bodies they are,* in order to "make sense" in a world where the definitions and protocols come from another (another's) place. At the same time, growing into a better awareness of this more and more shows us the contingent and hybrid nature of so much of what passes for "standard" forms of knowing. Normative positions, too, have stories; they have adjusted to what were initially strange environments. The bare fact of physical growth and decline, the long history of the brain's evolution, the interplay of nerves, glands, hormones, and the like with what we are capable of thinking, all this implies that what we call knowing is irreducibly a "migrant" reality — the engagement with an environment that does not sit still and allow itself to be immobilized in a canonical and unchanging scheme. Current panics about how new perspectives on gender threaten to turn their back on "biology" underrate the mobile and cross-woven character of bodily knowing. To say that there is a "migrant" element in our sexuality and our gender identification is in no way to minimize the fact, even the "givenness," of our embodiment; quite the contrary, if anything — so long as we do not identify "bodily" with "static." We are always material systems looking for more sustainable equilibrium with, and enhanced possibilities of movement within, the material systems around us with which we are already enmeshed. And on top of this, as a couple of our contributors emphasize, the migrant dimension in the organic reality of non-human life, including plant life, and the critical damage done by our illiteracy about this, need to be remembered. The collapse of pollination systems, the effects of a forced (and thus highly political) introduction of non-indigenous flora and fauna in certain parts of the world to solve local problems around production — these developments are showing us how some of the violence and short-termism that characterize our attitudes to human migration play out in the wider organic world.

We could say that no one's knowledge is ever simply what it was, because no one is simply where they were. Because our language and imagining exist in time as well as place, and because time changes how place is understood or negotiated, some sort of displacement is built into our thinking. But this can't be said in a way which sidesteps the distinctive nature of a knowing that arises from the *forced* displacement of individuals and communities. We can talk about "migrancy" as a dimension of all knowledge, and learn something significant from this about the embodied and local character of learning processes. And we can examine the kind of voluntary migration that takes place with the goal of augmenting the knowledge and control I/we have — the voyage of "discovery" or conquest, what has been called the great European "migration" of the colonial project, from the sixteenth century onwards. But this is a displacement which we can manage to our own advantage without being dispossessed of what we already know. And this self-focused displacement is typical of the individual scholar or observer as much as of the collective culture of colonization. To put it graphically, the "migrant knowledge" of the conquistador and that of the violently enslaved and transported African are not comparable. Understanding more of what the latter knows means reckoning with dispossession as well as displacement, with the violent assault on the agency of the displaced that underlies the experiences of so many, including many whose voices are recorded here. And the focus of this book is not only on what is known in these experiences of dispossession but also on what *forms* of material, verbal, and visual culture emerge to embody and communicate the reality of dispossession.

3.

The old Latin tag from Horace about how, when we travel, we may "change the sky under which we live but not the mind within" is true in one sense — change of place can't be relied on to resolve or release the problems we take with us which are bound up in our history and identity — but in another sense does less than justice to what happens in displacement and dispossession. Some of the most searching pages of this book present the reader with instances of what is done with objects, songs, and recipes that travel with those who have been displaced, whether by circumstance or by open force. What makes a displaced person pick up this rather than that as they leave their home is a vastly rich and diverse world of motivation. People report their own surprise at what they decide will travel with them; I have a vivid recollection of a woman at a refugee center in Romania describing her decision to take a rather cumbersome traditional ethnic musical instrument from her home in eastern Ukraine when Russian troops advanced on her home town. Objects are so often brought not simply to carry a passive meaning that will assist nostalgic recollections but because they are seen or sensed as resources for *active* coping with the strange environment ahead. They will become tools in a new world of reference and interpretation, modifying and being modified. These objects too, we could say, have been "dispossessed" of their semantic homes, and must re-establish a context for themselves. "Migrant form" could be defined in this connection as the product of that imaginative bridge between what is lost and what is conserved which grounds the displaced person or community sufficiently strongly to allow them to speak into a strange environment, both to communicate or share and to reinforce and rework what is to be said about their own identity. Historically speaking, we might look at the rituals that are part of Santeria in Brazil or the spirituals of the African American South; at the cultures of the Jewish shtetl of Eastern Europe and its metamorphosis in the reverse process of Eastern European migration into Israel in the last seventy or so years; at the cultural, political, and religious transformations of the Iranian diaspora of recent decades; at how Palestinian, Somali, or Sudanese identities have been paradoxically consolidated and deepened by traumatic levels of displacement; or indeed at the surprising history of Anglo-Indian cuisine. In these and other phenomena, it is not that a lost cultural world is being reinstated, which would not literally be possible, or even that it is being wistfully evoked as absent. What is happening is that communities "reinvest" in aspects of that lost world as vehicles for connecting more effectively with where they now are. One of the most serious traumas of displacement is the kind of suffering which surfaces in the inability to activate or reinvest, because the violence involved in displacement has so undermined confidence in any future agency. "How can we sing the Lord's song in a strange land?" is the question of the Jewish exiles in Babylon in Psalm 137; the deep and angry passion of this lyric is all about not forgetting what is lost. Yet the very existence of the lyric is testimony that a "migrant form" has been created *in* the fact of lamenting — and eloquently lamenting — the apparent impossibility of managing loss on such a scale. The depth of the lament expresses the once-experienced confidence in what has been lost, and so the lament's force recovers something of that confidence within the context of a strange landscape.

4.

"Migrant form" in words and artifacts thus becomes a statement of capacity within a setting where everything seems to conspire to create lack of capacity, lack of initiative. Degrees of trauma will vary, depending on what exactly creates the situation where migration comes to seem the best or only option. Without diminishing the acute grief of forced displacement, even here — as this volume shows — the displaced person can use what they have brought with them as raw material for shaping new meanings in negotiation with the new environment. Traditions of song and storytelling are at least as important as the ways in which material objects are used and reimagined, and several of our contributors provide vivid illustration of this. Much could be said about how music in particular produces complex experiences of recognition in alien circumstances and alienation in familiar circumstances. Once again, a personal recollection: The transformation of some English hymn tunes into the basis for a liturgical Mass setting of texts in a Southern African language group, a musical setting very widely accepted within these groups as common currency for Anglican worship after a century or more of usage. Migrant form, as displayed in these ways, is a dramatic embodying of how to live out of a tradition while learning one's way around a nontraditional landscape. It may carry with it all sorts of ironies in the ways it uses what is received both from background culture and from host society;

it may sometimes be parodic and transgressive in this respect, and thus difficult for both background and host environments. Most obviously, it challenges the crude binary of ghettoization or assimilation: It expresses the perspective of a genuine subject, an "author," who has been formed by tradition and experience to such a level of awareness that they can actively respond both to what they have inherited and to what they have been forced to reckon with in their displaced setting.

From one point of view, this collection is a celebration of that awareness, and of the remarkable individuals who produce these forms in so many diverse media. From another, it is a question to the assumptions we make about the nature of culture. "Multi-culturalism" is one of those words used by polemicists to make both positive and negative points — and the confusion has a lot to do with an unwillingness to pause and ask what is being taken for granted about "culture." Very often, a set of behaviors, beliefs, or attitudes is identified and labeled from outside, by a dominant group who will define the space that may be occupied by subaltern communities; those communities are encouraged to "know their place" by a socially powerful authority, which will decisively tell them what that place is. A "culture" is (nominally) validated by being accepted as a picturesque or simply opaque corner of the social map, as a domesticated and acceptably labeled form of otherness. A "multiculturalism" which works with any such model (and the working may often be well-meaning and even unconscious) will fail to reckon with what "migrant knowledge" knows and "migrant form" embodies — the fact of the imaginative freedom the migrant may discover to reinvent both inherited and unfamiliar cultural processes in creating a new and more "polyphonic" identity. Identities like this can be unsettling for those who have not yet grasped that cultures are innately mobile, hybrid, and adaptive — "cross-woven," as with all kinds of embodied knowledge. There will always be those for whom "hybridity" is an eccentric and undesirable weakening of what should be a clear identity. Think of the anxieties around linguistic "contamination" and the systematic marginalizing or demeaning of "creole" or "pidgin" languages. As so often, one of the focal problems here is the ingrained reluctance to remember how any group or individual actually *comes to know,* in time and in unpredictable encounter.

5.

Humans do not simply speak; they translate. They carry over (the literal meaning of "translation") the things they know and can articulate in one setting into another where those things are changed, and where they also change the new environment. Cultures are built and rebuilt around moments of "carrying over": the recognition of the self in what is strange, the negotiating with what is strange in order to go on being oneself. The migrant experience casts light on this basic process of discovering and constructing meaning. It may sound over-ambitious to put it like this, but there is something "metaphysical" in what this experience uncovers for us. Identities, patterns of continuous and intelligible action, are not fixed and timeless, but neither are they just made up arbitrarily: They emerge in the processes by which those underlying patterns grapple with fresh stimuli and produce fresh forms; they emerge as such patterns of energy are reconstructed in the discovery that they can cope with, incorporate, or converge with what seemed alien. Once again, we are reminded that, in thinking about cultural plurality, we are not stuck with the alternatives of assimilation — in which an original identity is negated or deeply buried — and the essentializing conservation of some kind of officially permitted foreignness.

But it is crucial not to make this simply a bland reduction of migrant experience to a source of edification and education. Back to where we began: the map of migrancy in the world of today is a map of the gross inequalities of power. It is true enough to say that, in the broadest sense, migrant reality casts light on something deeply bound up with the historical and linguistic transactions that make us human. But we have to bear in mind that the capacity of forcibly displaced humans to retain and display their humanity in the ways this book records and explores is something won in circumstances of systemic inhumanity — circumstances which will humiliate, silence, and often kill those whose strength is fatally undermined by being at the receiving end of this inhumanity. There are children traumatized by loss and terror in civil wars, bombardment, epidemic, violent separation from families (a separation regularly reinforced by the panic and moral laziness of politicians). There are women whose exposure to trafficking and sustained abuse of all sorts intensifies the vulnerability they may already have known in their own societies and will face afresh in host societies. There are all those made old, drained, and hopeless by the frustrations of bureaucracy as well as the threats of armed terror or state repression. There are those whose sexual orientation or gender identification puts their lives exhaustingly and daily at risk in a way hard to imagine for many in the contemporary West. Not everyone finds a voice. Not everyone survives the passage. "Good chance" does not come to all.

So a collection like this cannot be a consoling celebration of the "strong" which allows us to forget about those who have been or are being silenced in one way or another. To be thankful, to express gratitude and admiration for those who continue to make meaningful, articulate, challenging patterns out of the violence they have endured, is important. Just as important is to keep alive the questions of why we tolerate systems or policies that demand such exceptional levels of resourcefulness; why we continually fail to sustain useable systems of support, redress, and encouragement; and why we still recycle the corrupt language of blame and stigma which is so ready to treat the "migrant" as someone who has made a choice whose unyielding legal and political consequences they have to live with. "You knew the risks" is a chilly response to the already desperate.

6.

In so much of the public debates around "migration," there is a noticeable absence of voices from those most directly concerned, and a tendency to slip into generalized narratives about geopolitics. The resurgence of exclusivist and often highly mythologized nationalism treats migration as an abnormal phenomenon which threatens the integrity of nation states; uncontrolled inward migration must be resisted for everyone's sake, "unwelcoming environments" must be created which will be deliberately slow in offering benefits, integration, and citizenship, even for those with established asylum claims. The least unthinking and hardline versions of this may appeal to the risks of stripping countries of origin of their own citizens, especially those with socially significant qualifications. In reaction, there are some who believe that the response to forced displacement should be a universal abandoning of boundaries, a dissolution of the entire apparatus of the nation state as it has emerged in modernity.

Both attitudes suffer from the failure to ask what migrants have to say about their experience. The violence that leads to displacement may not always be overt and legally sanctioned, and the tools by which claims are assessed are notoriously inadequate, so that many who are genuinely at risk in an environment where the more obvious forms of public disorder or discrimination are not instantly evident are readily assimilated to those who are thought of as choosing to seek new opportunities. The odd language of "economic migrancy" conceals the reality of people who may not be persecuted but are faced with unsustainable futures for themselves and their families in a collapsing economy. They are seldom simply choosing a more advantageous economic future from a set of viable options. The only way to get a clearer picture of what choices are really available is to attend, again and again, to the particularity of the stories told and the statistics available.

But equally the messianic picture of a world without boundaries does not map on to the experience of many migrants with any exactitude. As our contributors make plain, it is not that "migrant knowledge" leaves behind the reality of belonging, nor that the migrant does not want some sort of integration in a host society. And the opportunistic opening of boundaries which maintains an insecure global market of mobile labor is not exactly an ideal situation for the vulnerable worker: Migrant *labor* in its commonest forms cannot be ignored as a high-risk, high-cost mode of survival, and it features significantly in some of the contributions to this volume. Once again, if migrants are actually invited to speak about what they know, what they want, what they fear, some kinds of generalization become a lot less plausible.

7.

This closing reflection is deliberately more theoretical than most of what the book contains, but I hope it illustrates how attention to what migrant experience discovers and creates can generate an interpretative perspective that helps us think critically about both the whole process of our knowing and making, and about the more immediate moral challenge of how the distribution of power in our world intensifies the threat of violent displacement. And I include in this — remembering again the impact of mishandled and misunderstood "migrancy" in the non-human world — the accelerating "violence" of climate catastrophe as it makes various areas of the globe increasingly uninhabitable or uncultivable. The migrant knowledge we listen to and celebrate in this collection shows how power can be and is reclaimed in all sorts of reworkings of story and legacy, as well as all sorts of "formal" strategy. If this celebration highlights both the creative dignity of the human-as-migrant and the abiding structural injustice that menaces or destroys the exercise of that dignity for unprecedented numbers in our world, it will have brought into focus the nature of "migrant form" in the way the editors would hope.

Contributors

Faraj Alnasser was born in Aleppo where he grew up in a large family. He survived a gruelling journey through Europe before finding a home in the UK. Arriving at the age of nineteen with no education, no English skills, and no relatives, Faraj persevered and overcame three years of homelessness. In 2016 he was matched with a Jewish family who not only hosted him, but supported him and sent him to school to learn English. He found his second home, and peace, with them. His longing for his hometown, family, and grandmother led him to discover the healing power of food and its connection to memories and aroma. Faraj's passion for cooking led him to win a scholarship at a prestigious cookery school in London and train at Ottolenghi. Today, he owns a small business called Faraj's Kitchen, delivering vegan and vegetarian home-cooked Syrian food.

Aditi Anand is Artistic Director of the Migration Museum, and is a creative producer and curator working within the arts and nonprofit sectors. Previously, she produced and managed a multimedia education project in India that is currently being implemented in over a thousand schools, and was communications lead for India's largest media for social change initiative. She has also worked in New York with the Museum of the Moving Image and with the interactive design firm, Local Projects.

Clelia Bartoli is Professor of Sociology of Law, Politics of Migration and Human Rights at the University of Palermo. Her studies focus on human rights, migration, critical theory of the State, institutional racism, epistemic violence, subalternity, social inclusion, and experimental pedagogy. She established "Polipolis," a wide experimental educational program for unaccompanied minors, and on that occasion she began collaborating with "Stories in Transit," a program led by Marina Warner. She co-founded Giocherenda, a collective of young migrants who invent and animate cooperative games. Her English publications include *Legal Clinics in Europe: For a Commitment of Higher Education in Social Justice* (Diritto & Questioni Pubbliche, 2016) and *Chile Revolts: From the Uprisings toward the Constitutional Process* (Accademia University Press, 2022).

Anupam Basu is Assistant Professor of English at Washington University in St. Louis. An early modernist working on print culture and drama, his work has increasingly succumbed to the seductions of scale as he develops techniques to make the entire Early English Books Online Text Creation Partners (EEBO-TCP) corpus tractable for search and analysis as part of the ACLS- and Mellon-funded EarlyPrint project. He is currently working on a monograph on form and scale that asks how we might rethink literary forms through computational analysis. He has also published on the representation of poverty, vagrancy, and criminality in popular literature.

Yota Batsaki is the Executive Director of Dumbarton Oaks, a Harvard research institute, museum, and historic garden in Washington, DC, where she also directs the Plant Humanities Initiative, a collaborative endeavor to research and communicate how plants have shaped human cultures. Her recent work has appeared in *Environmental Humanities, Environmental History,* and *Critical Inquiry.*

Gillian Beer was formerly King Edward VII Professor of English Literature at the University of Cambridge. She commissioned domestic pots from Edmund de Waal when he was an undergraduate and has followed his work ever since.

Annabel Brett is Professor of Political Thought and History at the University of Cambridge, specializing in the political thought of the late medieval and early modern periods. She is the translator of *Marsilius of Padua: The Defender of the Peace* (Cambridge University Press, 2005), and the author of *Changes of State: Nature and the Limits of the City in Early Modern Natural Law* (Oxford University Press, 2011).

Anthony Vahni Capildeo, Fellow of the Royal Society of Literature, is Professor at the University of York and an Honorary Student of Christ Church, Oxford. A Trinidadian Scottish writer of poetry and non-fiction, Capildeo's interests include traditional masquerade, silence, plurilingualism, and place. Their nine books and eight pamphlets have been recognized with awards including the Windham-Campbell Prize for Poetry, the OCM Bocas Prize for Poetry, the Cholmondeley Award, and the Forward Prize. Capildeo has served as a guest editor of a special ecopoetics issue of *Stand* magazine, and as a contributing editor at *PN Review* and the *Caribbean Review of Books*.

Valentina Castagna is Associate Professor of English Literature at the University of Palermo. She is a member of the Unipa Research Centre "Migrare" (Migration), CIR. Since 2015 she has worked with Marina Warner on the international project Stories in Transit in the UK and Italy. She has published books and articles in the field of Women's Studies and contemporary fiction and on medieval works such as *The Book of Margery Kempe,* focusing on contemporary rewriting of myths and popular culture, and on life writing.

Amit Chaudhuri is the author of eight novels, the latest of which is *Sojourn* (New York Review Books, 2022). His first major work of non-fiction, *Calcutta: Two Years in the City*, was published by Knopf in 2013. His second work of non-fiction, *Finding the Raga* (New York Review Books, 2021), a critical meditation on North Indian classical music and his discovery of, and relationship with, this tradition won the James Tait Black Prize for Biography in 2022.

Supriya Chaudhuri is Professor Emerita in the Department of English, Jadavpur University. She has written and published in the fields of Renaissance studies, Indian cultural and literary history, modernism, urban studies, travel writing, sport, and cinema. Recent publications include the edited books *Religion and the City in India* (Routledge, 2022) and *Commodities and Culture in the Colonial World* (Routledge, 2018, with Josephine McDonagh, Brian Murray, and Rajeswari Rajan), as well as articles in *Spenser Studies, Bioscope, Études Épistémè, Thesis 11, Postcolonial Studies, Literature Compass,* and *Revue des Femmes Philosophes*.

Nadina Christopoulou is cofounder and Director of Melissa Network in Greece. Her research work focuses on diaspora narratives, migration, and childhood, as well as migrant women's solidarity networks. On the basis of that research, together with migrant women leaders in Greece, she co-founded Melissa Network in 2014, an award-winning organization with women members from over forty-five countries. She has also been working on the creation of a visual and narrative archive of the migration spiral that Greece has experienced in the past century, hoping one day to turn it into a museum of movements.

Brian Cummings teaches English at the University of York and is the author of *Mortal Thoughts: Religion, Secularity, & Identity in Shakespeare and Early Modern Culture* (Oxford University Press, 2013) and *Bibliophobia: The End and the Beginning of the Book* (Oxford University Press, 2023). He is Fellow of the British Academy and of the Society of Antiquaries, and recipient of a grant from the Leverhulme Trust (2020–2023) to write on Erasmus.

Rosita D'Amora is Associate Professor of Turkish Language and Literature at the University of Salento (Lecce, Italy). Her research interests range from Ottoman social history to contemporary Turkish literature, addressing issues related to different forms of representation and auto-representation of Ottoman and Turkish society.

Edmund de Waal is an internationally acclaimed artist and writer, best known for his large-scale installations of porcelain vessels, often created in response to collections and archives or the history of a particular place. His interventions have been made for diverse spaces and museums worldwide, including The British Museum, London; The Frick Collection, New York; Ateneo Veneto, Venice; Schindler House, Los Angeles; Kunsthistorisches Museum, Vienna; and V&A Museum, London. De Waal has published *The Hare with Amber Eyes* (Picador, 2010), *The White Road: Journey into an Obsession* (Picador, 2015), and *Letters to Camondo* (Picador, 2021). He was awarded the Windham-Campbell Prize for non-fiction by Yale University in 2015. In 2021 he was awarded a CBE for his services to art.

Olga Demetriou is a social anthropologist and Associate Professor at the Durham Global Security Institute, Durham University. She has written on displacement and borders, and the exclusions created in places mired by legacies of conflict. She is currently working on European refugee regimes and how they produce marginal orders of protection through law (complementary protection), politics (access to citizenship), and space (locations of first reception).

Saifoudiny (Dine) Diallo was born in Guinea and lives in Palermo, Italy, where he founded the association for social promotion Giocherenda with other young people from different countries. He is a HIP ambassador for Philip Zimbardo's Heroic

Imagination Project and, as president of Giocherenda, he collaborates with Marina Warner for the Stories in Transit project. He is co-protagonist of Gabriele Gravagna's documentary film *Io sono qui* (2017).

Natalya Din-Kariuki is Associate Professor in the Department of English and Comparative Literary Studies at the University of Warwick, where she works on the literary and intellectual history of the sixteenth and seventeenth centuries, with a particular focus on travel writing, transnational and transcultural encounters, and rhetoric and poetics. Her work has appeared in journals including the *Review of English Studies, Huntington Library Quarterly,* and *Textual Practice.*

Valerie Forman is Associate Professor at the Gallatin School at New York University. She works on theories and practices of labor, trade, migration, slavery, and capitalism in, through, and around early modern literature and history in the transatlantic world. Her first book is *Tragicomic Redemptions: Global Economics and the Early Modern English Stage* (University of Pennsylvania Press, 2008). Since 2019, she has advocated for and participated in mutual aid projects with migrant people in NYC, at the border in Tijuana, and in immigration detention centers throughout the United States. She is also a co-facilitator of the Abolition Lab at NYU.

John Gallagher is Associate Professor of Early Modern History at the University of Leeds, and the author of *Learning Languages in Early Modern England* (Oxford University Press, 2019). He is a historian of language, migration, and education, focused on the history of Britain and Ireland in early modern Europe. His articles and essays have appeared in *Renaissance Quarterly, Huntington Library Quarterly, Renaissance Studies, The Italianist,* and elsewhere. He is the co-editor of the *Historical Journal.* His current research explores migration and multilingualism in early modern London, and the history of multilingual cities more broadly. John is a BBC/Arts & Humanities Research Council

New Generation Thinker and writes regularly for the *London Review of Books*. In 2023, he won a Philip Leverhulme Prize for History.

Simon Goldhill is Professor of Greek at the University of Cambridge and Foreign Secretary and Vice-President of the British Academy. His most recent books are *The Christian Invention of Time: Temporality and the Literature of Late Antiquity* (Cambridge University Press, 2022) and *What Is a Jewish Classicist? Essays on the Personal Voice and Disciplinary Politics* (Bloomsbury Academic, 2022). He has worked closely with the Council for At-Risk Academics (CARA), and with the charity Refugees at Home.

Mina Gorji is Associate Professor of English at the University of Cambridge and fellow of Pembroke College. She has written about the poetics of place in John Clare's poetry, and her first poetry collection, *Art of Escape* (Carcanet Press, 2020), explores migration at different scales. In her collection *Scale* (Carcanet Press, 2022), adapting to the cold of a new continent opens a chromatic investigation of feeling across time and space.

Jonathan Gil Harris is Professor of English and Founding Dean at Ashoka University and the author of *The First Firangis* (Aleph Books, 2015) and *Masala Shakespeare* (Aleph Books, 2018), as well as many books on early modern culture, ideas of the foreign, and globalization, including *Foreign Bodies and the Body Politic: Discourses of Social Pathology in Early Modern England* (Cambridge University Press, 1998); *Sick Economies: Drama, Mercantilism and Disease in Shakespeare's England* (University of Pennsylvania Press, 2004); *Untimely Matter in the Time of Shakespeare* (University of Pennsylvania Press, 2008); and *Marvellous Repossessions: Globalisation, The Tempest, and the Waking Dream of Paradise* (Ronsdale, 2012).

Akid Hassan is a construction worker, painter and decorator, and artist. He has been a Cypriot citizen since 2020. He was born in al-Hasakah, Syria, and, as a Kurd, has been stateless under Syrian legislation. He moved to Cyprus in the mid-2000s and has lived there since, under different precarious statuses, despite being married to a Cypriot national for part of that time and the parent of a second Cypriot national. Having been refused Cypriot nationality along with his siblings and parents, he staged a hunger strike in 2017 which lasted for sixty-seven days and received attention and support by local human rights organizations and the UNHCR. He was granted citizenship in February 2020.

Gabriel Josipovici is the author of over twenty novels and books of short stories and ten critical books, including *The World and the Book: A Study of Modern Fiction* (Stanford University Press, 1971), *The Book of God: A Response to the Bible* (Yale University Press, 1986), and *What Ever Happened to Modernism?* (Yale University Press, 2011). His plays for stage and radio have been widely performed.

Dragana Jurišić is a Yugoslav artist and Assistant Professor of Communications at the Dublin City University. Working primarily with image, text, and video, and looking at the effects of exile and displacement on memory and identity, Jurišić has shown her work extensively and won many awards, including the Golden Fleece Special Recognition Award, IMMA 1000 Residency Award, and numerous Bursaries and Project Awards. Her work is in a collection of the National Gallery of Ireland, Arts Council Collection, and the Irish State Art Collection.

Bhanu Kapil, Fellow of the Royal Society of Literature, is a Fellow of Churchill College. She is the author of six full-length collections, including *How To Wash A Heart* (Pavilion Poetry, 2020), winner of the TS Eliot Prize, and *Incubation: a space for monsters* (Kelsey Street Press, 2023). Kapil is the recipient of a Cholmondeley Award from the Society of Authors and a Windham Campbell Prize from Yale University, both for her body of work.

Issam Kourbaj comes from a background of fine art, architecture, and theater design. He was born in Syria and trained at the Institute of Fine Arts in Damascus, at the Repin Institute of Fine Arts & Architecture in St Petersburg, and at the Wimbledon School of Art. He has lived in Cambridge, UK, since 1990, where he has been artist-in-residence, bye-fellow, and lector in art, at Christ's College. His works have been featured at museums around the world, including Fitzwilliam Museum, Museum of Classical Archaeology, and Kettle's Yard House and Gallery; Penn Museum; British Museum and Victoria & Albert Museum; Brooklyn Museum; Tropenmuseum; and the Venice Biennale.

T.M. Krishna is one of the preeminent vocalists in the rigorous Karnatic tradition of India's classical music. As a public intellectual, Krishna speaks and writes about issues affecting the human condition and about cultural matters. His book *Sebastian and Sons* (Context, 2020) received the Tata Lit Live Award for the Best Non-Fiction book. His musical productions and collaborations include the Chennai Poromboke Paadal with environmentalist Nityanand Jayaraman; performances with the Jogappas, transgender musicians; and co-conceptualizing and performing Karnatik Kattaikuttu. In 2016 Krishna received the prestigious Ramon Magsaysay Award in recognition of "his forceful commitment as artist and advocate to art's power to heal India's deep social divisions." In 2017 he received the Indira Gandhi Award for National Integration, and in 2019 he received the Swathi Sangeetha Puraskaram, the highest honor for musicians, instituted by the Kerala State Government.

Angela Leighton is senior research fellow at Trinity College, Cambridge. She has written widely on nineteenth to twenty-first century literature, most recently *Hearing Things: The Work of Sound in Literature* (Belknap Press of Harvard University Press, 2018) and the edited collection *Walter de la Mare: Critical Appraisals* (Liverpool University Press, 2022, with Yui Kajita and A.J. Nickerson). Her poetry has appeared in many magazines, including *The New Yorker, Times Literary Supplement, The Guardian, The Dark Horse, PN Review,* and *London Magazine.* She has published six volumes of poetry, among them *Spills* (2016) and, most recently, *Something, I Forget* (2023), both with Carcanet.

Sue McAlpine has found herself in museums for most of her working life, starting at the Museum of London in education when it first moved to the city in 1976. She set up an education service at Gunnersbury Park Museum, worked as an oral historian and community curator in Notting Hill, and then worked as exhibitions curator at Hackney Museum, connecting closely with the community. Her most favorite place has been the Migration Museum, collaborating with people from all over the world, making exhibitions from personal testimonies, highlighting the stories of migration to and from the UK. Sue's latest project has been supporting art students from the Ukraine, proving that art and performance are more resilient than war and violence.

Subha Mukherji is Professor of Early Modern Literature and Culture at the University of Cambridge. Her research interests and publications range across Renaissance English literature, early modern law and drama, form and faith, literary epistemologies, migration, and contemporary Indian art.

Joe Murphy and **Joe Robertson**, both British playwrights, are the founders of Good Chance, which builds temporary theaters of hope promoting freedom of expression, creativity, and dignity for everyone. Their debut play, *The Jungle,* came from their seven months running a theater in the Calais refugee and migrant camp. It premiered at the Young Vic in 2017, then transferred to London's West End (2018), St. Ann's Warehouse (New York, 2018–2019) and The Curran (San Francisco, 2019). The play received universal acclaim, the South Bank Sky Arts Award for Theatre, and an Obie Award. In 2021, Good Chance embarked upon *The Walk,* an 8,000-kilometer moving festival of welcome across Europe with Little Amal, inspired by the character from *The Jungle*.

Yousif M. Qasmiyeh is a scholar, poet, and translator. He is the Joint-Lead of the Baddawi Camp Lab, as part of the Imagining Futures GCRF-Network+ project, and was Writer-in-Residence for the AHRC-funded Refugee Hosts project. His essays, poetry, and translations have appeared in *Modern Poetry in Translation, Critical Quarterly, GeoHumanities, Cambridge Literary Review, PN Review, Stand, New England Review,* and *Poetry London.* His collection, *Writing the Camp* (Broken Sleep Books, 2021), was a 2021 Poetry Book Society Recommendation and was selected as one of the Best Poetry Books of 2021 by the *Telegraph* and *The Irish Times*, highly commended by the 2021 Forward Prizes for Poetry, and shortlisted for the 2022 Royal Society of Literature Ondaatje Prize. His latest books are *Eating the Archive* (Broken Sleep Books, 2023) and *The Southern Eye: Co-Seeing Displacements* (Broken Sleep Books, 2024).

Claudia Roden was born in Cairo. She came to London to study art and stayed on when her family had to leave Egypt after the Suez crisis in 1956. Drawn to the subject of food through a desire to evoke a lost heritage, she continued to write cookbooks with a special interest in the social, cultural, and historical background of food. She has written about the cooking of the Middle East, North Africa, the Mediterranean, Italy, and Spain, and about Jewish food. In 2022 she was awarded a CBE for her services to culinary culture. In 2023 she was awarded an honorary doctorate from the University of London.

Mohamed Sarrar is a Sudanese musician and actor based in the UK. As part of the Good Chance Ensemble, Mohamed co-wrote and recorded a world music album *Sounds of Refuge* with John Falsetto and Ammar Haj Ahmad. Mohamed's theater experience includes *The Jungle* (Young Vic, West End, St Ann's Warehouse, Curran), *Rain Rain* (Bamboozle UK Tour), *The Welcome*

Party (Theatre Rites, Manchester International Festival), *Border-line* (UK Tour: London; Brighton Fringe Festival, Manchester; International Tour: Berlin, Kerala, and Copenhagen), *Encampment* (Good Chance at Southbank Centre), and *The Hope Show* (Good Chance, Calais).

Efi Savvides is an artist based in Nicosia and the founder of Artstudio Laboratories, an educational center for contemporary art and design. Her research explores conditions of exclusion established by government institutions, especially in relation to migrants and refugees in Cyprus. Savvides produces records of excluded life stories that stand as chapters within "minor histories." This peculiar archiving of actions, events, and facts remains her main artistic goal, while its political awareness works critically in indirect ways.

Regina M. Schwartz is Professor of Early Modern Literature, Religious Thought, and Law at Northwestern University. She is the author of *Remembering and Repeating: On Milton's Theology and Poetics* (University of Chicago Press 1993), *The Curse of Cain: the Violent Legacy of Monotheism* (University of Chicago Press, 1997), *Sacramental Poetics at the Dawn of Secularism: When God Left the World* (Stanford University Press, 2008), and *Loving Justice, Living Shakespeare* (Oxford University Press, 2017). She has also edited *Transcendence: Philosophy, Literature, and Theology Approach the Beyond* (Routledge, 2004) and *Toward a Sacramental Poetics* (University of Notre Dame Press, 2021, with Patrick J. McGrath).

Rachel Spence is a poet and arts writer based in the United Kingdom and Italy. Her most recent poetry collection is *Daughter of the Sun* (The Emma Press, 2025). In 2023, she published *Venice Unclocked* (Ivorypress, 2022), a literary meditation on time in Venice in collaboration with the Venetian photographer Giacomo Cosua. Her nonfiction book *Battle for the Museum* (Hurst, 2024), which explores the relationship between art, power, and money, was a *Financial Times* Book of the Year.

A.E. Stallings is a US-born poet, translator, and critic who lives in Athens. Her most recent poetry volume is a selection of poems, *This Afterlife: Selected Poems* (Carcanet Press, 2022). Her most recent book of verse translation is an illustrated version of the pseudo-Homeric *The Battle Between the Frogs and the Mice* (Paul Dry Books, 2019). She is the recipient of numerous grants, fellowships, and prizes, including a Guggenheim and a MacArthur fellowship. Since 2015, she has been running a poetry workshop with refugee women at the Melissa Network for Migrant Women in Athens. She was elected the forty-seventh Oxford Professor of Poetry in 2023.

Susan Stockwell is an established international artist working across sculpture, installation, and film. Her practice is concerned with examining social and colonial histories and engaging with questions of social justice, trade, cultural mapping, and feminism. Susan is best known for her site-specific installations and dress sculptures that have been exhibited widely, including: Tropenmuseum, Amsterdam (2022); Museum of London (2021); Royal Shakespeare Company (2015); TATE Modern (2013); the Katonah Museum of Art, New York (2012); and the Victoria and Albert Museum (V&A) London (2010, 2005, 2001). Her work is held in international collections including The House of European History, Brussels; Tropenmuseum, Amsterdam; Black Rock Investments, Yale Centre for British Art, USA; and the University of Bedfordshire and V&A Museum London.

Carla Suthren is a postdoctoral researcher at the University of Verona, working with Silvia Bigliazzi on her PRIN-funded project on classical reception in early modern English drama. She has published articles on various aspects of the reception of Greek tragedy in Renaissance literature, including Jane Lumley's *Iphigeneia* and Gascoigne and Kinwelmersh's *Jocasta*.

Marina Warner writes fiction, criticism, and cultural history. Her award-winning books explore myths, symbols, and fairy tales, including *From the Beast to the Blonde: On Fairy Tales and*

Their Tellers (Farrar Straus & Giroux, 1994) and *Stranger Magic: Charmed States & the Arabian Nights* (Chatto & Windus, 2011). She has published five novels and three collections of short stories, and her essays on literature and art have been collected in *Signs & Wonders: Essays on Literature and Culture* (Chatto & Windus, 2003) and *Forms of Enchantment: Writings on Art and Artists* (Thames & Hudson, 2018). Recent publications include *Temporale* (Sylph Editions, 2023) and *Sanctuary: Ways of Telling, Ways of Dwelling* (HarperCollins, 2025). She contributes regularly to the *New York Review of Books* and the *London Review of Books*. She is Professor of English and Creative Writing at Birkbeck College, a Distinguished Fellow of All Souls College, University of Oxford, and a Fellow of the British Academy. In 2015, she was awarded the Holberg Prize in the Arts and Humanities.

Clair Wills is King Edward VII Professor of English Literature at the University of Cambridge. She has written on Irish migration to post-war Britain in *The Best Are Leaving: Emigration and Post-War Irish Culture* (Cambridge University Press, 2015), and on post-colonial and European migration in the wake of the Second World War in *Lovers and Strangers: An Immigrant History of Post-War Britain* (Allen Lane, 2017).

Pip Williams is a writer, theater maker, and performer from London. He is the co-artistic director of critically acclaimed theater company We Talk Of Horses, and has made work in collaboration with the Southwark Playhouse, Vaults, Camden People's Theatre, and The North Wall. He has performed with Boundless, Somna Theatre, and MoCo Theatre, and is an associate artist with Swings And Roundabouts Theatre.

Rowan Williams taught Theology in Oxford, Cambridge, Bristol, and Yale. From 2002 to 2012 he was Archbishop of Canterbury, and from 2012 to 2020 Master of Magdalene College, Cambridge. He has published widely on religion, literature, and politics, and was Chair of the development charity Christian Aid for eight years. He now lives in Wales, and is Chair of the

Peace Academy/Academi Heddwch. Recent books include *Justice and Love: A Philosophical Dialogue* (Bloomsbury Academic, 2020, with Mary Zournazi) and *Collected Poems* (Carcanet Press, 2021).

www.ingramcontent.com/pod-product-compliance
Lightning Source LLC
Chambersburg PA
CBHW050327270326
41926CB00016B/3350